MW00365428

THE ILLUSTRATED ENCYCLOPEDIA OF WORLD SAILING

David Pelly

NEW YORK

PENTAX
ASAHI PENTAX

Foreword

When I clubbed together with some friends in 1963 to build a small cruising yacht that we named *Suhaili*, I had no idea what I was letting myself in for. What I could never have foreseen is the extraordinary variety of yachts and events that I have become involved with during the past 25 years. It is this tremendous scope that makes sailing so interesting and writing an all-embracing book about it so difficult.

Between the Olympic aspirant who trains for years in the hope that one day he will stand on the winner's rostrum to the cruising yachtsman whose main aim is to just quietly slip away and forget the pressures of civilization for a few days, there is a world of difference. Who could imagine that the windsurfing enthusiast with his jazzy, high-tech board and designer wet-suit could be interested in the same kind of thing as the couple who have sunk all their savings in a cruising yacht with the aim of spending, say, five years sailing gently around the world?

Yet fundamentally they are linked by their love of the sea and their dependence on the elements. *The Illustrated Encyclopedia of World Sailing* reflects this breadth of interest by touching on every aspect of the sport.

We British are well aware of our rich maritime history but many sailors from many nations find a place in the long history of sailing. Yachts themselves are quite remarkable in their variety. There are plenty of very specific books about yachts but few which cover the whole field from Optimist to maxi ocean-racer in the way that this one does.

In any sport, certain key events create an impetus which then percolates down to every level. In sailing, one can point to the America's Cup, the Admiral's Cup and the Observer Single-handed Transatlantic Race as events that quite literally shape the yachts we sail, while more recently the two great round the world races, the Whitbread and the BOC Challenge, have had an enormous influence on the way yachts are designed, built and equipped. Not only these but all the really important races that shape the sport are described in this book.

The author first started writing about yachts at about the same time as I started sailing them, so you could say that we have grown up under the same influences. This is certainly the most comprehensive sailing book so far attempted and one of the most informative and entertaining. Like *Suhaili*, I am certain that it will go far and stand the test of time.

Robin Knox-Johnston CBE, RD

Robin Knox-Johnston CBE came to fame as the first man to sail single-handed, non-stop around the world. Since then he has been a competitor in almost every type of yachting event, specializing in long-distance ocean racing.

House Editor: Donna Wood
Editor: Margaret Daykin
Art Editor: Gordon Robertson
Designer: Glynis Edwards
Production: Craig Chubb
Picture Research: Moira McIlroy

This edition published in the USA 1989
by Exeter Books
Distributed by Bookthrift
Exeter is a trademark of Bookthrift Marketing, Inc.
Bookthrift is a registered trademark of Bookthrift Marketing, Inc.
New York, New York

ISBN 0 671 10146 3

Typeset in 10/11 pt Times by Quadraset Limited
Printed and bound in Hong Kong

Contents

The start of a race in the Admiral's Cup, the no-expense-spared international team event that is regarded as the world championship of ocean racing.

K
4
5

The History of Sailing

The history of sailing is long, and peopled by some remarkable characters and extraordinary yachts. Kings, princes and noblemen were the first yachtsmen and it was not until the present century that sailing came within the reach of ordinary people. Smaller, cheaper boats using modern materials have led to the very rapid expansion of sailing in recent years. Today, it is genuinely a sport within the reach of anyone.

Left: *Yachts of the 'Big Class' racing in the Solent during the 1930s — a painting by Steven Dews. From left to right,* Candida, Westward, Cambria.

It is important not to try to make history too neat. The affairs of men are seldom orderly and to say that 'yachting' officially began on the restoration to the throne of England of Charles II is far too tidy an explanation. The history of pleasure vessels is very much older than that.

What is certain is that the word 'yacht' comes from the Dutch or German 'jaght' or 'jacht', meaning a hunt or chase. From this comes the idea of a hunting ship — a fast warship — and hence a ship built for speed. The word does not express the idea of a vessel built for pleasure but it was used for the small and relatively speedy sailing boats which well-to-do-Dutchmen of the 17th century used for sailing around their coastal waters.

ORIGINS

Vessels built for pleasure or display by kings, princes and nobles are far older. Cleopatra (68–30 BC) cruised down the Nile in her barge and Venetian princes were rowed along the canals of Venice in the grandest of vessels, richly carved, gilded and caprisoned. It is safe to assume that the monarchs of most coastal nations had some form of regal craft to carry them on state occasions.

The Latin poet Horace (65–8 BC) mentions sailing for pleasure and, according to the Roman historian and antiquary Suetonius (AD c70–c160), Caligula was fond of sailing and owned a yacht. Making a leap forward to the 16th century, we know that a small craft named *Rat of Wight* was built for Queen Elizabeth I of England, 'for national entertainment', and that in 1604 King James I ordered a miniature warship for his eldest son, Prince Henry. Named *Distain* she was about 25ft (7.62m) long and was to enable the young Prince to 'disport himself in, about London Bridge.'

That yachting was not a new idea in England at the time of the Restoration is shown by the household accounts for Hurstmonceux Castle, in Sussex, for the years 1643/4. These contain several references to 'my Lord's yaught', which was apparently kept at nearby Pevensey.

We must certainly give the Dutch a lot of the credit for developing the idea of sailing purely for pleasure. Water was always the main highway of the collection of city-states that now forms The Netherlands and practically all trade was dependent on water transport. So it is not surprising that a class of vessel gradually developed for visiting, entertaining or just for showing off the owner's prosperity and taste. Some pictures of the period suggest that races were held from time to time as well.

During his exile, Charles II got to know and admire the Dutch way of life and when, in May 1660, the news arrived that he had been proclaimed King of England, the first thing to be arranged was a grand cruise from Breda to Delft, during which a great feast was prepared and eaten on board and a good deal of wine drunk — a tradition that has been maintained by cruising yachtsmen ever since.

Thanks to the wealth of Dutch marine paintings of the period, we know that these 'jaghts' were like little warships, complete

Right: *A Dutch traditional barge yacht. Although built in modern materials, the lines and rigs of these traditional yachts are remarkably similar to those used in Holland towards the end of the 17th century.*

with small cannon. They had high poop-decks with elaborately carved and painted transoms and flew huge ensigns showing where they came from. The smaller yachts, being designed for shallow waters, were based on sailing-barge hulls and commonly had lee-boards in place of a keel. They were generally sloop-rigged (one masted fore-and-aft-rigged) with a sprit mainsail. By the 1630s, the sprit had given away to a gaff, sometimes with a square topsail above, and this was called a *bezaanjacht*. Such is the enthusiasm which present-day Dutch yachtsmen have for traditional craft, that one can see yachts with almost exactly the same rig sailing today, three centuries later.

In the same year that Charles II returned to England, the City of Amsterdam presented

Above: The first of many yachts owned by Charles II, Mary *was presented to him on his accession by the City of Amsterdam. This lively painting by Van de Velde shows* Mary *punching along on a close reach with the topsail partly lowered. The foredeck crew look as if they are getting extremely wet.*

him with a yacht, *Mary.* She was a little ship of about 100 ton (capacity, not weight) and seems to have been about 60ft (18.28m) long on deck. She was rigged as a topsail gaff cutter, had eight small guns and, as usual, lots of decoration. She was, in effect, a larger and smarter *bezaanjacht*.

However, what makes Charles II so important in the history of yachting was not that he owned a yacht but that he was a real sailing enthusiast. Within a year of receiving *Mary* he had ordered another, English-built yacht *Catherine*, while the Duke of York had *Anne* built and these two were raced against each other and *Mary.*

Charles had a scientific outlook (he founded the Royal Society) and was always seeking to improve things, including his yachts. During his reign, he seems to have had about 20 different yachts, most of which were designed by Phineas Pett, the constructor of the Royal Navy. Most also had endearingly informal names: the smallest was the 27-ton *Jamie*, which tradition says the King designed himself, and the largest of them all was the 180-ton *Saudadoes.*

It was while sailing on another of his yachts, *Fubbs* — named after his chubby friend, the Duchess of Portsmouth — that the King was seen helping to handle the sails 'like a common seaman' when the yacht was caught in a squall. He was one of those lucky people who never felt seasick and used to find it very funny when nobles and courtiers whom he invited on board went scurrying to the lee rail with green faces.

There was some resentment that the King spent so much time and public money on his yachts but his motives were not solely hedonistic because each one was built to demonstrate some improvement of hull or rig. His great influence on the sport of yachting was that he made it respectable and encouraged other enthusiasts to build their own pleasure vessels.

One of his most important acts of patronage was to commission Captain Greenvile Collins to produce a book of charts of the British coastline. Before this, mariners had had to rely on very inaccurate charts of Dutch origin. To make the work possible, Charles lent two of his yachts, *Merlin* and *Monmouth* to Collins who spent seven years compiling *Great Britain's Coasting Pilot*. The charts that he produced for this vitally-important publication were to guide ships around British waters for the next century.

The first yacht clubs

As far as is presently known, the first club to be devoted to pleasure sailing was the Water Club of the Harbour of Cork, founded in

1720. The present Royal Cork Yacht Club is a direct descendant, making it the world's senior yacht club by a considerable margin.

Early records do not suggest that racing played any part in the club's activities, which seem to have been mainly social. The highlight of the club's season appears to have been sailing in formation. An 'Admiral' was elected annually and on special days the club yachts would form up in line astern and sail past while the Admiral took the salute. Interestingly, there is a very old tradition of 'Admiral Zeilen' in Holland which is continued to this day on special occasions. The headquarters of the Water Club was on Haulbowline Island in Cork Harbour, just across the water from Cobh and down-river from the City of Cork. This is now part of Cork docks, so the modern Royal Cork YC is at Crosshaven, on the miraculously unspoilt Owenboy River.

The oldest club to retain its original name, and still have its clubhouse in more-or-less the original spot, is the Starcross Yacht Club. This was founded in 1772, on the middle reaches of the beautiful River Exe in Devon. Lord Courtenay of nearby Powderham Castle was the moving spirit but it was a genuine club with a number of members, rather than just a boat-house for the castle.

It was another royal patron, Henry Frederick, Duke of Cumberland, brother of King George III, who gave yacht racing its initial boost in England. In 1775, he presented a silver cup for a race from Westminster Bridge to Putney Bridge and back and in the same year The Cumberland Fleet, ancestor of the present Royal Thames Yacht Club, was formed. The members were noblemen and gentry and unlike Charles II they did not handle the sails 'like common seamen'; they had professionals to do it for them.

The other side of the coin was the emergence of a number of local 'regattas', held annually at seaside towns where the local fishermen would compete in sailing or rowing races, tugs of war, mud-wrestling and other such sports. Quite a number of clubs grew from these regattas, which were essentially organized by and for men who earned their livelihood on the water.

The Dabchick Sailing Club of Brightlingsea, in Essex, is one example. For many years membership was restricted to those who earned their living on the water, as it was felt that in this way they could enjoy an occasional race free from the presence of the gentry. In later years, many of the best professional yacht skippers and hands were recruited from the ranks of Essex fishermen and bargemen.

Many people enjoyed sailing without belonging to any kind of formal association and when The Yacht Club, later to change its name to the Royal Yacht Squadron, was formed in 1815 it is clear that the members were people who had already owned yachts for some time and were in the habit of sailing, and perhaps even racing, at Cowes in the Isle of Wight.

As far back as the 1770s, races were recorded as taking place at Cowes and in 1788 there was a race around the Isle of Wight for a purse of 30 guineas. The Napoleonic wars held back the development of the sport, so the formation of The Yacht Club probably satisfied a pre-existing need.

To begin with, clubs such as the Cumberland Fleet did not have premises; members met at Smith's Tea Gardens, in London. It was not until 1860 that they acquired their first club-house. Similarly, The Yacht Club was formed in a London coffee-house and occasional meetings and dinners were held at a hotel in East Cowes until they purchased a house in West Cowes, in 1825.

We can see that the original yachtsmen were royalty, noblemen or wealthy gentry, for the very simple reason that owning a private vessel was a very expensive business. The royal precedent meant that most people's idea of a yacht was a substantial vessel, comfortably and even decoratively fitted out and, in almost every case, manned by a crew of professional sailors. Many years were to pass before we find yachtsmen able to manage and maintain their own boats unaided.

This is why sailing came to be regarded as an exclusive, even snobbish sport. In the period up to the beginning of the First World War, working people had neither the leisure nor the means to undertake any but the most basic of recreations and yachting was certainly not one of them.

By the beginning of the 19th century, royal yachts had little connection with sport any longer. The heads of most maritime nations maintained yachts but they were vessels of state, small ships fitted out for entertainment on a grand scale. That is not to say that some men and women of high estate did not also enjoy sailing for its own sake.

The age of industrialization put wealth into many more hands and with it the ability to enjoy pastimes. When the New York Yacht Club was formed in 1844, there were only a handful of clubs in the world but just two years later, 16 clubs had been granted the style 'Royal' by the British crown. From this point on, growth was rapid, with hundreds of clubs being formed in all the developed countries of the world.

Sweden was quick to follow the example being set in England and the Royal Swedish Yacht Club was founded in 1832. In France, the Société des Régates du Havre was founded as early as 1840 and the Circle de la Voile de Paris in 1858.

Towards the end of the 19th century, yachting acquired its fashionable image. The major yachting regattas at venues such as Cowes, Kiel and New York were high-spots in the social calendar to which people of quality and rank repaired, whether or not they were interested in sailing. Those with enough money could maintain a steam-yacht, a delightful floating home in which to entertain and perhaps visit other fashionable spots such as the south coast of France.

Incidentally, a quaint survival of the social season is provided by the fact that, to this day, the dates of Cowes Week are fixed so that they fit in between the conclusion of racing at Goodwood and the opening of grouse-shooting on the 'Glorious twelfth of August'.

So, like it or not, yachting became associated with money, power and fashion, an image that was to dog it for many years. Perhaps surprisingly, this was also the case in America. The first yacht recorded in American history was a 100ft (30.5m) monster named *Cleopatra's Barge*. Millionaire merchant George Crowninshield spent $50,000 on this luxurious craft, an immense sum in those days, that is, in 1815.

The Eastern Yacht Club of Boston predated the New York Yacht Club by a couple of years but neither of them remained in the same place for very long. The Southern Yacht Club of New Orleans, founded in 1849, still stands on the original site so, in some ways, it rates as the most senior of the US Clubs.

Not surprisingly, canoeing soon became a popular pastime in America but, for reasons lost in history, these enthusiasts never got together with the sailors. By the 1890s, not only were there many active canoe clubs in the USA, they had developed the sliding seat sailing canoe and a British-America Cup was donated. In the 1930s, Uffa Fox and Roger de Quincey managed to win this trophy and later to combine the British and American rules, so creating the International 10 sq metre canoe. Even so, these vessels were regarded as canoes, not yachts.

Americans have never been so keen as Europeans on centralization and the bureaucracy that usually goes with it. They were happy to let individual clubs each run their own show long after Europeans were busy trying to create unified rules. Senior US Clubs such as Seawanhaka Corinthian YC made their own rating rules *and* set up important international events.

Arrival of the amateur

There must always have been some amateur yachtsmen but in the early days they were

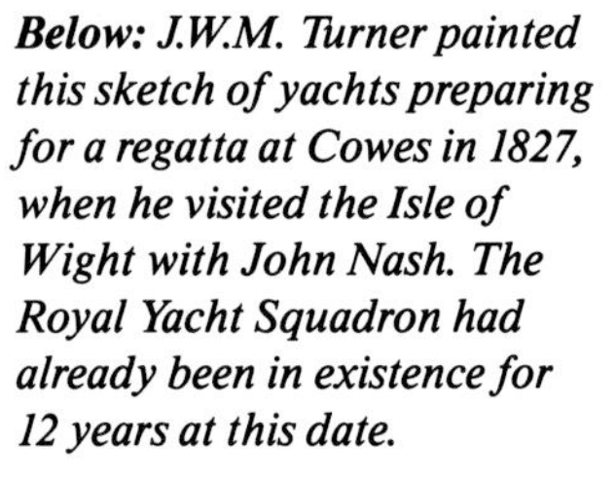

Below: *J.W.M. Turner painted this sketch of yachts preparing for a regatta at Cowes in 1827, when he visited the Isle of Wight with John Nash. The Royal Yacht Squadron had already been in existence for 12 years at this date.*

likely to be the more retiring types — what we would think of today as cruising yachtsmen. And they had neither reason nor urge to get into the history books.

However, the founding members of the senior yacht clubs were certainly enthusiasts; being the first of their kind they could not be merely followers of fashion — they had to set it. For example, Lord Yarborough (first commodore of the Royal Yacht Squadron) was a great seaman who made many long and intrepid cruises. He was convinced that the club could further 'National Utility', by helping to improve the design of small naval ships. In fact, Yarborough's most famous yacht, *Falcon*, was built as a small warship, complete with guns. But after he sold her, she became an opium smuggler in the service of Jardine, Matheison and Co.

The first man to sail a private yacht around the world was Lord Brassey, who completed a circumnavigation in his 565-ton schooner *Sunbeam* in 1877. Due to the size of the yacht, virtually a small ship, he was able to make the voyage in relative comfort. Even so, it should be recorded that he was also the first yachtsman to hold a Master's Certificate and he acted as both captain and navigator of *Sunbeam* for this historic voyage. There is a delightful story of how on one occasion he sent the men aloft in bad weather to furl the stuns'ls.

'I wish the old ______ was up here himself,' grumbled a seaman.

'The old ______ *is* up here himself,' came the gruff reply as Brassey appeared alongside him on the wildly-swinging yardarm.

An example of the other side of the coin, during the same period, is provided by Edward Fitzgerald, scholar and translator of *The Ruba'iyat of Omar Khayyam*. Fitzgerald lived in Suffolk and loved the peace and solitude of the East Coast. He owned a small schooner, whimsically named *Scandal* because, he said, it was the fastest thing out of Woodbridge. Fitzgerald gave part-time employment to a fisherman to look after *Scandal* and share in all ship-board jobs when they went sailing. They never went very far afield but made many short cruises up and down the East Coast, usually with one or two of Fitzgerald's friends aboard.

There must have been many more enthusiasts of his type, but because they were

Below: *Uffa Fox at the helm of his International 14ft Dinghy* Daring (K201), *planing through to weather of* Pintail (K200), *sailed by another distinguished designer, Tom Thornycroft. Fox's first International 14* Avenger *was first in 52 out of 57 races in her first season.*

neither famous nor attempting to do anything out of the ordinary there is no record of their sailing activities. Yet the real growth of amateur sailing came from people such as this, whose motive in taking up this sport was a simple love of being afloat.

Amateurs in racing

There has never been a requirement for racing yachts to be steered by amateurs; on the contrary, it was long felt too dangerous for them to be let loose on anything other than the smallest classes of racing yacht. So, amateurs had to work their way up the scale and, from the turn of the century onwards, there was a variety of small keelboats such as One-Raters and Half-Raters which could be raced by an amateur with one or two paid hands to do the heavy work.

The creation of the modern Olympics, with its strong emphasis on amateurism, gave a powerful boost to this concept. Yachting became a part of the Olympic Games in 1900 and, from this point on, the idea of the owner being a mere passenger aboard his own yacht gradually faded as more and more men and women acquired the necessary skills.

It was the development of dinghy-racing in the inter-war period that finally gave the amateur complete control of his own vessel. Classes such as the International 14ft Dinghy provided racing at relatively low cost and also called for new levels of fitness in addition to sailing skill. The result was a very rapid expansion of 'Corinthian' (amateur) sailing and many new clubs came into being to cater exclusively for the needs of people who raced their own boats.

Ocean racing did not come into existence in a regular sense until the 1920s and was always the province of the amateur skipper, although many of the larger boats carried paid hands. In recent years, however, there has been a reversal of the process; yachts competing in the top international events such as the Admiral's Cup are frequently sailed by professionals. Regrettably, this has happened in an insidious rather than open way because many of the competitors do not wish to acknowledge their status as professionals.

The reason that professionalism has returned to racing is that the pressure of modern events and the increasing sophistication of the boats entered makes it impossible to compete except on a full-time basis. The true amateur has therefore been excluded from these top-class events.

Rise of the shamateur

Success in yacht racing depends to an extent greater than nearly any other sport on having the best possible equipment and complete mastery of it, i.e. in having a better boat, sails, equipment and technique than the others. This places power — and temptation — into

the hands of the people who design and make the various components. In one way, it has always been both desirable and beneficial to have tradesmen involved in the sport because if, for instance, sailmakers did not sail, how else would they gain the practical experience necessary in order to judge and improve their products? On the other hand, the competitor who is able to supply himself with new equipment 'off the shelf' whenever he wants it has a clear advantage.

Recent years have seen the increasing domination of racing by helmsmen who have some kind of professional connection with the yachting industry. In some cases, they are people who have become involved in the business because of their love of the sport but, having done so, then use the sport as a means by which to advertise their wares. Even this seems quite reasonable when the sailor involved can only spend a certain number of hours per week on the water because he needs the remainder to run his business, but when firms become big enough to employ 'salesmen' who are in effect 'sailsmen', the case is less easy to defend.

Owners of racing yachts have sped up this process of professionalism rather than fought against it. For some time, it has been the case that the owner of, say, an Admiral's Cup trialist, will approach a designer or sailmaker and offer to place a substantial amount of business in that firm's hands in return for the services of one of the talented sailors who just happen to work for the firm. The sailor will then expect to have his, or her, expenses covered by the owner — who has in effect indirectly procured the services of a professional yachtsman.

Yachting 'super-stars'

One of the more recent developments in yachting has been the emergence of free-lance 'super-stars' who make no pretence of amateurism and who will sail for whoever cares to pay their fee. The emergence

Left: *A modern International 10 Square Metre Canoe showing how the helmsman sits on the end of a long sliding seat which gives enormous power to a very narrow hull. It is this that makes the canoe one of the fastest of all single-hulled small boats.*

Left: Falcon, *seen here in a Far Eastern setting, was built for the first commodore of the Royal Yacht Squadron, Lord Yarborough. She was built like a small warship, including guns, as Yarborough felt he could be 'of national utility' by helping to improve the design of small naval craft.*

Right: How to give yachts of different sizes and designs a fair rating so that they can race against each other has always been one of the trickiest problems facing yachtsmen. One solution is to create restricted classes within which yachts can race without handicap even though they are not exactly the same. This is Velsheda, *built to J-Class of the Universal Rule.*

Below: Philippe Jeantot, twice winner of the BOC Challenge race, is typical of the tough, competent professional yachtsmen who today dominate the field of long-distance and short-handed ocean racing.

of sponsored yachting events, which have brought sufficient money into the sport to make it worthwhile paying people to win them, is largely responsible for creating this class of sailor. This is particularly true in France, where the sponsorship of yachting has gone further than in any other country. In areas such as the offshore multihull circuit, helmsmen who achieve a reputation for success are then able to command quite high fees for competing in future events.

A further development is that of the 'super-star' acting as a contractor to a commercial sponsor. The sailor proposes to undertake the design, building and campaigning of a boat in return for exclusive advertising rights. Or he may have possession of an existing yacht which can be sold to a sponsor for a particular event or series. Thus we find yachts, particularly multihulls, which change their names with frequent and confusing regularity — depending on who currently has them under contract.

A variation of this situation can be seen in very major and expensive events such as the Whitbread Round the World Race. Here, star skippers act in an entrepreneurial role by lining up a number of sponsors, usually one principal backer plus a number of subsidiary ones, in order to be able to go ahead with the building of a yacht. In this, they are often in the chicken-or-egg dilemma of needing sponsorship before they can build a boat and needing a boat before they can hope to find the necessary sponsorship.

DEVELOPMENT OF YACHT RACING

The diarist John Evelyn gives a stirring description of a race between Charles II's yacht, *Catherine*, and the Duke of York's *Anne*. They raced from Greenwich to Gravesend and back and, in Evelyn's words, 'The King lost it going, the wind being contrary, but saved stakes in returning.' Awaiting them at the finish was the King's purpose-built kitchen-boat ready to serve a hearty meal to the participants.

Inevitably, as the flagon was passed around the cabin, the talk would have been of the race and, with only a little imagination, one can guess that the Duke of York would have pointed out that *Catherine* was longer on the waterline and jolly well ought to be faster downwind. The King would have replied that *Anne* had more sail area on a shorter hull and should, therefore, be faster on a beat to windward. And there in a nutshell we find the problem that has been exercising the minds of yachtsmen and designers ever since: how to run a fair race between two boats of different size and type.

Where you have two or more boats built exactly the same, what yachtsmen call a 'one-design class', there is no problem — the first boat home wins. As soon as there is any difference, however, some kind of handicap is called for, and this is where the trouble begins. This might seem a rather technical issue to raise in a history of yacht racing but the way in which ships and yachts are measured has a very big influence on the way in which they are designed, so the history makes little sense without some understanding of such important influences.

Tonnage

In order to give a yacht a handicap for a particular race, it is first necessary to give her a 'rating', that is, to place on her some figure which expresses her *potential* performance. Whether or not the yacht comes up to expectations depends on the skill of the crew in getting the best out of her. Early attempts at rating were generally based on tonnage and right up to the early challenges for the America's Cup there are references to 'Custom-house measure' as a basis for fixing the rating.

The trouble with tonnage is that it is a measure mainly of capacity — originally of the number of 'tuns' of wine that a vessel could load — and that its proper purpose was in valuing a ship for harbour dues. Thus, length multiplied by breadth multiplied by depth of hold was the original formula ($L \times B \times D$) and this tended to result in squarish ships which could carry the maximum cargo for a given tonnage.

VELSHEDA

When yachts began racing in England, a modified form of tonnage was introduced, known as 'Thames Tonnage'. The formula for this is $(L-B \times B \times \frac{1}{2}B) \div 94$. Length was measured between stem and rudder-post and there is no control of depth or sail area. In the United States 'Custom House Tonnage' continued to be used until the first Seawanhaka formula was introduced during the 1870s.

'Custom House Tonnage' gives only an approximate indication of size and tells very little about potential performance, especially as there is no measurement of either sail area, the basic driving force of any sailing vessel, or of displacement. The Yacht Club (Royal Yacht Squadron) discovered its inadequacy as a basis for handicapping as early as 1827 when, in an effort to make more equitable the racing that had already being going on for several years on a no-holds-barred basis, it offered cups for yachts not exceeding 75 ton and not exceeding 45 ton. This was not popular with owners such as Joseph Weld and Thomas Assheton Smith who had already realized that it was easily possible to make a yacht longer and slimmer without changing the tonnage.

Next, the Club decided to try a series of classes which allowed a certain range of tonnage within the class up to a fixed maximum, and at the same time began to dictate what equipment must be carried, the type of sails used, and so on. This worked reasonably well for a year or two, until they found how easily conditions couched in such phraseology as 'Only normal sails to be carried' could be circumvented.

In 1841, the first attempt was made to give a time allowance according to tonnage. All the yachts in a race started at the same time but an allowance of one second per mile of distance sailed was applied for every ton difference between the yachts competing. Today, this is known as 'Time-on-distance' handicapping. Its fatal flaw is that it depends entirely upon whether the race is a fast or a slow one, for in light winds a small yacht can sail just as fast as a large one which has to give her time.

A member of the RYS, G.H. Ackers, invented the 'Ackers Graduated Scale' which awarded time allowance on a combination of tonnage and the distance to be sailed, but still gave no consideration to the length of time taken. So it went on, with the RYS members, just as enthusiasts in other countries, gradually feeling their way around these tricky problems.

When *America* made her historic visit to Cowes in 1851, one thing that Commodore

Below: *When the schooner-yacht* America *arrived at Cowes in 1851, she caused a sensation because she was so different from the English racing cutters of the period.* America*'s machine-woven cotton duck sails were a decisive factor in her success.*

Stevens was adamant about was that he was not going to take part in a handicap race — as far as he was concerned it was no-holds-barred or nothing. This was sensible of him for *America* would have ended up owing time to the big but narrow cutters such as *Alarm*. *America* was a refinement of a very wholesome type of working boat and, for a time, did influence British designers who adopted the schooner rig. But they were never keen on the beamy hulls favoured by American designers and the two schools of thought continued to grow apart.

In the early stages, yachts had been like refined versions of fishing boats or small naval vessels but as racing began to be taken seriously, owners demanded more radical designs from builders and a new breed of real racing yachts emerged. However, due to the inadequacy of the tonnage system of rating, what emerged became increasingly strange. By the 1850s, the science of naval architecture was finding its feet and there was no argument about the fact that the length of a vessel was the basic speed-producing factor while depth and beam were the things that slowed it down.

In an effort to get a grip on what was becoming an increasingly chaotic situation, in 1875 the Yacht Racing Association was formed in England. Its aims were to produce an effective handicap rule and to clarify and regulate the racing rules. Both were worthy objects but easier said than done and the YRA's first effort at a 'tonnage rule' was a disaster because, thanks to the straightforward mathematical relationship between L, B and D, it was possible to increase length and decrease beam without changing the tonnage and, as a result, racing yachts in Europe became excessively narrow in relation to their length.

Uffa Fox has an illuminating and quite hilarious description of sailing a replica of an 1880 3-tonner named *La Mascotte* from Brightlingsea to Cowes. This 'Plank-on-edge cutter' was 28ft (8.53m) on the waterline with a mere 5ft (1.52m) beam; if you stood in the cabin with hands on hips your elbows touched the sides. Uffa was surprised how fast she sailed (average 8 knots for 200 miles) but appalled by the discomfort of a yacht that sailed at such an acute angle of heel that the keel was clearly visible. She was as wet as a half-tide rock and totally impractical.

In 1858, the Royal Yacht Squadron attempted to bring a measurement of sail area into their rating system, using a method proposed by the New York Yacht Club but, after a short time, dropped it again. This was perhaps the first of a whole series of missed opportunities of unifying European and American rating systems.

So, the British racing cutter of the 1870s and 80s was strange to look at but quite fast and efficient. American yachts of the period could scarcely have been more different, because designers there had always favoured beamy, shallow hulls with retractable centreboards to make up for the lack of depth. The great advantage of this kind of hull is that it can be powerful without being heavy and its drawback is that once heeled too far it can lose stability and capsize. This actually happened in the case of the notorious *Mohawk*, an extreme 'skimming dish' type built in 1875 for the vice-commodore of the New York Yacht Club. Measuring 141ft (42.97m) long by 30ft (9.14m) beam she had a staggering 32,000 sq ft (2,976 sq m) of sail but drew only about 6ft (1.83m) with her immense centreboard raised. She capsized at anchor, while her sails were being hoisted, drowning the owner, his wife and three others.

This brought an understandable reaction in America where, for a time, there was even enthusiastic support for the plank-on-edge cutter. A yacht of this type, designed by

Above: *The American schooner* Sappho *sailed over to England in 1870 and was bested in a series of races by Mr James Ashbury's* Cambria. *This inspired Ashbury to make the first of two challenges for the America's Cup.*

***Right:** King George V at the helm of* Britannia. *This was probably a posed photograph as the king did not normally take the helm during racing, even though sailing was one of his greatest pleasures. The yacht was scuttled at sea when he died.*

G.L. Watson and named *Madge*, was shipped over to New York in 1881 and won seven out of eight races against top local yachts. A faction whose members called themselves the 'cutter cranks' was created, but this dispersed after two classic narrow cutters, *Genesta* and *Galatea*, failed to impress with their performance in the America's Cup.

In England, the scientist William Froude carried out experiments to show how wave drag and skin friction were produced and this led designers to try to reduce the wetted area of their hulls. One of the first to grasp the principal was the English agricultural engineer and amateur yachtsman Harvey Bentall, whose design for *Jullanar* had what was called a cut-away forefoot. He removed unnecessary areas of the hull underwater, which at the same time reduced wetted area and made the keel more of a fin rather than part of the body. *Jullanar* was a most successful, trend-setting design and continued to win races for many years.

One of the reassuring things about yacht design is that the sea imposes its own sense of order and freakish designs nearly always die out of their own accord eventually. Accidents such as the capsize of *Mohawk* in America were matched by cases of plank-on-edge cutters being sailed under in European waters. In a notorious accident during the 1880s, the plank-on-edge cutter *Oona* sank with all hands in the Irish Sea and, rather like the sinking of the *Titanic*, this compelled people to consider the vexed question of seaworthiness. The designer Dixon Kemp proposed a new rating, in which waterline length was multiplied by sail area and divided by 6,000 to obtain the rating; beam did not come into the formula at all.

The Dixon Kemp rule was an enormous improvement and remained in force from 1886 to 1895. It immediately resulted in much beamier, more seaworthy yachts which not only performed well but had plenty of room inside their hulls. Thus, a combined cruising and racing yacht became a practical proposition. It was a delightfully simple rule that gave designers almost complete freedom and resulted in some of the finest, best-looking yachts ever built. Unfortunately, as before, designers eventually began to take advantage of the freedom to produce freakish 'rule-cheaters' and yet another rule was called for.

Because Dixon Kemp's rule measured length on the waterline rather than overall, it was immediately worthwhile to have extended ends or 'overhangs'. This resulted in what we now regard as the classic appearance of yachts such as *Britannia*, designed by G.L. Watson for the Prince of Wales. This beautiful yacht, which was certainly Watson's masterpiece, showed that yacht design had truly come of age because she was as successful a racing machine as she was a work of art. She sailed through two reigns, during which time she was re-rigged and refitted to conform with the emergent 'J' class. This

revamp was a surprising success and, as Uffa Fox pointed out, her lines were remarkably similar to those of the 1930 America's Cup defender *Enterprise*. She was finally scuttled on the death of her second royal owner, George V.

What prompted 'Bertie' (the Prince of Wales, later King Edward VII) to order *Britannia*, was the fact that his nephew — Kaiser William II of Germany — had taken up yacht racing. William bought the former America's Cup challenger *Thistle*, and renaming her *Meteor*, raced her at Cowes in 1892. Not to be outshone in his own country, the Prince of Wales had to have at least as fine a yacht. At the same time, other owners ordered *Valkyrie II*, *Satanita* and *Calluna*, and in 1893 the American yacht *Navahoe* sailed across the Atlantic specifically to do battle with them.

These giant vessels formed 'the big class' and created a kind of travelling circus which sailed around the English coast from regatta to regatta. They were professionally manned, of course, and the races were run as a public spectacle. Efforts to make yacht racing viewable have generally been a failure until television came along but, in this case, the yachts were so big that they looked impressive even from several miles away and the courses were laid in order to make them come as close to the shore as was safe. The circus began at Harwich on the East Coast and gradually worked its way around to the Clyde, via such fashionable watering-places as Southend-on-Sea, Ramsgate, Ryde, Cowes, Weymouth and Dartmouth. These visits very often coincided with the local town regatta featuring rowing and running races, tugs-o'-war and the like to attract large crowds and must have been very festive occasions.

The first week of August saw them all gather at Cowes, where the owners themselves would come aboard and might even take the helm. An exception was Lord Cardigan who, on being asked whether he would care to take the helm aboard his schooner *Enchantress*, replied, 'No thank you. I never take anything between meals.'

The last quarter of the 19th century was certainly the golden age of yachting and Cowes was its jewel. There, for one week in the year, the crowned heads of Europe rubbed shoulders with the noble, the rich and the fashionable and all were entertained by the sight of these huge and graceful yachts with their towering pyramids of canvas and scurrying crews of uniformed sailors.

Even so, rule tinkering continued and, in 1896, the YRA brought in the Linear Rating Rule where waterline length, girth and half of the sail area were multiplied together and divided by two to give rating in feet. This was not the most successful rule and, among other things, had the unfortunate effect of outclassing the Prince of Wales' *Britannia* which, for the time being, was consequently obliged to retire from racing.

But things were now beginning to stir in several countries. In the United States, the great designer Nathanael Herreshof, having 'poached' the America's Cup with such success, was persuaded to turn gamekeeper by providing a measurement rating rule that really worked. This was named the Universal Rule of Measurement and provided for a series of classes, identified by letters of the alphabet. It was this rule that was used for the interwar challenges for the America's Cup when the competing yachts rated to 'J' Class of the Universal Rule.

In England, Brooke Heckstall-Smith, secretary of the Yacht Racing Association, realized that the French, German and English rating rules were all coming up for renewal at about the same time and, in 1906, he arranged a conference in London of sixteen nations. This was effectively the origin of the International Yacht Racing Union and its first act was to appoint a technical commission to design a new rule. Johan Anker of Norway, Alfred Benzon of Denmark and R.E. Froude, son of William Froude, were among its members in those early days.

Above: *George Watson designed the clipper-bowed* Thistle *for the 1887 America's Cup challenge. Due to an error on Watson's part, she turned out to be longer on the waterline than declared and this led to a tremendous fuss which nearly ended with the match being cancelled.*

Opposite: *The royal racing yacht* Britannia *under her original rig, and flying the Prince of Wales' racing burgee. A product of the Dixon Kemp rule of 1886, she came to be regarded as an ideal type of large racing yacht and was certainly one of the most graceful ever built.*

Opposite, top: Sheila, Duchess of Westminster looking very relaxed at the helm of her 8-metre Saskia, *in which she won a bronze medal at the 1908 Olympics. This charming painting by Charles Murray Padday shows the duchess smartly-dressed in Edwardian motoring gear including straw hat held down with a scarf. The man behind her is her tactician Philip Hunloke, who later became sailing-master of the royal cutter* Britannia.

Opposite, below: Mr and Mrs Harold Vanderbilt, arriving at Southampton in June 1939, with the intent of racing their new yacht Vim.

The method adopted was to postulate what they considered an ideal type of yacht and then devise a rule that imposed heavy penalties for straying away from the model. They also used a much more sophisticated measurement system that could detect whether a hull was heavy or light, beamy or narrow, average or excessive in overhangs. This they called the International Rule, carefully ignoring the work that had already been done by Herreshof who achieved remarkably similar results by a slightly different method. A most important new feature was that all yachts built to the International Rule had to be built under Lloyd's Register survey and conform with construction rules laid down for each class. The importance of this point is that the Lloyd's survey ensures that the yachts are well and substantially built.

It was the lack of such a 'scantlings rule' in America that made it possible for Herreshof to design America's Cup defenders that were scandalously light and built of an incompatible mixture of metals such as steel, bronze and aluminium that caused rapid and destructive corrosion. In contrast, yachts built under Lloyd's survey to the International Rule were strong and lasted for many years.

Like the yachts it covered, the International Rule was built to last — indeed, it is still in use today. Like the American rule, it provided for a series of classes — except that they were defined by the product in metres of the rating formula. Any number of classes are possible but the ones that are familiar today are the 6, 8, and 12-metre classes which still race regularly; the 12-metre was used for the America's Cup from 1958 to 1987.

Some much larger yachts were built to the International Rule in the period leading up to the First World War, the 23-metre class being the largest, but the real flowering of the International Rule was in the interwar period.

Below: Racing in the International 6-metre Class at the 1936 Olympic regatta, which was held at Kiel on the Baltic. The inter-war years were the hey-day of the international keelboat classes.

THE OLYMPICS

Yachting made its first appearance in the Olympics in 1900, when there was racing on the Seine and at Le Havre. The rules called for yachts to be steered by amateurs. It was the first time this had been a requirement for a yacht race. This was before the creation of the International Yacht Racing Union and the International Rule, so the old tonnage classes had to be used. Yachts raced without time allowance in six different tonnage classes and there was one further 'open' class run on time allowance. Thanks to this curious arrangement, the British helmsman Lorne Currie won two gold medals, one for the ½ – 1 ton class and another for the 'open' class.

This must have been pretty confusing for all concerned and, indeed, there has long been the suspicion that the Olympic authorities never quite understood what the yachtsmen were up to and therefore let them get on with it without much interference. Yachting is like skiing in that it is virtually never held in the same place as the main games although it *is* held at the same time. The Los Angeles Olympics were a rare example of yachting being relatively close to the main stadium, at nearby Long Beach.

There was no yachting at the 1904 Olympics in the USA but when London was the host, in 1908, there was racing on the Solent for the 6, 7 and 8-metre Classes and on the Clyde for the 12-metre Class. This was the first regatta controlled by the newly formed International Yacht Racing Union (IYRU). The host country won all four gold medals and Sheila, Duchess of Westminster, became the only woman helmsman to win an Olympic medal for yachting (the bronze, in the 8-metre class) prior to 1988 when a women's event was added.

The entry of yachting into the Olympics brought much more pressure on the Racing Rules which, at that time, were still fairly basic. It became an important part of the work of the IYRU to refine and protect the Rules, and this is just as true today. Because the union foolishly ignored the Universal Rule at their 1906 conference, the North American Yacht Racing Union went their own way and continued to maintain their own rules until Harold Vanderbilt re-wrote and combined the two sets of rules in the 1930s.

The International keelboat classes continued to be used throughout the interwar years but in an inconsistent and irregular way. The most chaotic regatta took place in 1920, when the International Rule was undergoing a revision and because of this it was possible to enter for both 'old' and 'new' versions of the 6, 6.5, 7, 8-metre classes, plus the 10 and 12-metre classes. In addition, there were classes for the 30-sq metre and 40-sq metre, measured by an entirely different rule; and 12ft and 18ft dinghies. Thus there were 14

sets of medals on offer but many of the classes had only a single entry and were walk-overs.

As a result of this shambles, the IYRU received a severe rap over the knuckles from the Olympic Commission and the 1924 regatta went to the opposite extreme by having only three classes: 8-metre, 6-metre and single-handed dinghy. Perhaps the saving grace of the 1920 event had been the introduction of the 12ft and 18ft dinghies, bringing small boats into the competitive field for the first time. The 18ft dinghy had not worked out too well as one person was expected to handle this big and heavy craft, including setting a spinnaker!

The International one-man dinghy, a heavy, 12ft clinker clunker with a gunter lug rig was not exactly exciting but did create an event that, in character, has become the most Olympic of the yachting classes: one man (or woman) facing the sea and his (or her) competitors alone in a simple boat of standardized design. By contrast an event in which arcane questions of design or rule interpretation can be crucial seem quite foreign to Olympic ideals.

For the 1936 regatta, there was a specially-designed Olympic Monotype for the one-man class. However, the organizers made the foolish mistake of permitting two entries per nation and this meant that the German No 2

Above: The Star two-man keelboat has been in the Olympics, with a short break, since 1936. The class is particularly strong in America, where racing is exceptionally competitive. The large sail area makes it a tricky boat to sail well.

was detailed off to ram his colleague's main rivals — never mind that he himself would be disqualified. Fortunately, this dastardly ploy failed and D. Kagchelland of the Netherlands just beat W. Krogman of Germany to take the gold medal. In any case, it was the last occasion on which more than one representative per nation was allowed.

The most significant event in 1932 was the introduction of the Star keelboat to the Olympics. William Gardner had designed this remarkable two-man keelboat as early as 1911, as a modification of a smaller boat named 'The Bug'. It was intended to be as cheap as possible and was built like a box with a flat bottom and sides that met at a sharp angle. The keel consisted of a flat metal plate with a lump of iron bolted on to the lower end. The surprise was that it sailed really well and after a change of rig in 1929 (the first of several), the Star was ready to shine at the Olympics. And shine she did.

The Star remained an Olympic Class from 1932 to 1972, when it was replaced by the Tempest but after a single olympiad in the wilderness, the Star regained its Olympic status and shows little sign of losing it again. As well as being a tricky, demanding boat to sail, the Star Class has taught the sailing world a lot about organization. It has a strong owners' association which organizes club, area, regional and world championships, in addition to keeping a tight control on the class rules. In fact, the Star Class has built up such a strong organization over the years that there is some doubt whether it is administered by the IYRU or *vice versa*.

The 12-metre made its last appearance at the Olympics in 1920 — in those days it was regarded as an average-to-small racing yacht. But, in retrospect, it seems incredible that the yacht used for the America's Cup until 1987 was thought suitable. Nevertheless, the pressure was on to make the Olympics as accessible as possible and that clearly meant replacing big, expensive yachts with smaller, cheaper ones. In the post-war austerity era, only one of the International Rule classes was left, initially the 6-metre and then, up to 1968, the 5.5-metre.

Britain was the host of the first post-war Olympic Games, in 1948, and had to scratch around a bit to find suitable boats as few had survived the long gap of 12 years since the 'Hitler Games' of 1936. The Dragon, a popular Norwegian-designed 29ft keelboat was a fairly obvious choice in addition to the International 6-metre and Star classes but there was a shortage of suitable small boats. Certainly, there was no realistic opportunity of building sufficient Olympic Monotypes and, in any case, it had not been a particularly successful design. Instead, the British organizers offered to *lend* competitors a 12ft Firefly dinghy for use as the one-man boat.

This was the first time that the equipment was provided by the host nation, a precedent which some have regretted as it greatly increases the cost of running the event but, at the same time, it succeeds in the objective of making the Olympics accessible to as many nations as possible. For a number of years it was open to competitors to decide whether they preferred to bring their own one-man dinghy or borrow one from the organizers but nowadays it is regarded as an important principle that all of the one-man boats should be provided as this is the best way of ensuring that they are strictly equal.

It has often been suggested that *all* of the boats participating in the Olympics should be provided but in the case of complicated and highly-refined classes, such as the Flying Dutchman, this is not really practical as it takes many months to work one up to peak efficiency.

The year 1948 also saw the beginning of a sharp increase in the standard of Olympic sailing, mainly due to one man, Paul Elvström of Denmark. Prior to this, countries had simply picked for the Olympics the sailors who seemed to be doing best at the time but Elström undertook a proper Olympic campaign with an extensive physical training programme. Yachtsmen had not thought of themselves as athletes before, but Elvström, who was only 18 in 1948, showed how much fitness counted when he capsized in a heavy squall, righted the boat, baled out, got going again and won the race.

Elvström won gold medals in four successive Olympics, the only man to achieve this in any sport. Furthermore, he was still an Olympic competitor in 1984, when he sailed a Tornado catamaran with his daughter Trine as crew, just failing to win a bronze medal by one place!

The Firefly had been a stop-gap solution and was not designed to be a one-man boat but, by 1952, the Finn dinghy designed by Rikard Sarby had been adopted for this role. It has the unusual feature of a single sail set on a bendy, unstayed mast which makes the rig look a little like a drawn bow. It is a heavy, tiring boat to sail and calls for great strength and fitness in addition to the usual sailing skills. The helmsman has to get his bodyweight as far as possible outside the boat and in so doing is not allowed any kind of body harness but must rely on toe-straps to stop him falling over the side.

At his home near Copenhagen, Elvström constructed a sitting-out bench which was the same height and profile as the side-deck of his Finn and would spend hours on this strengthening his leg and stomach muscles. As a result, he was able to sit out further and for longer than anyone else. Moreover, when the wind was strong he would wear many layers of old sweaters and could increase his bodyweight dramatically simply by dipping these in the water.

So began the era in which Olympic competition became the pinnacle of achievement, particularly in small-boat sailing. It takes complete dedication over a period of years to reach the standard required. Sailing is one sport in which it is possible to be a competitor at almost any age from 7 to 70 and therefore, Olympic medallists can contribute enormously by continuing to compete long after their days of glory are over. This gives a sense of continuity — and raises the general standard.

In the early 1950s, the IYRU saw that it must help to modernize the Olympics by introducing new, up-to-date classes to replace the old faithfuls and particularly to reflect the growing popularity of dinghy sailing. During 1952, trials were held to find a new International two-man dinghy class — and the fast and exciting 20ft (6.09m) Flying Dutchman was chosen. It was first given a place in the Olympics in 1960 and has remained there to this day.

Emboldened by this success, the IYRU embarked on a rolling programme of replacing one class in each Olympics (from 1948 onwards, there had been five classes). But this did not work out as well as hoped. The first class to be discontinued was the Dragon, which was felt to be rather old-fashioned and expensive. After trials, the Norwegian-designed Soling was chosen as the Dragon's replacement. This was a great success, as the Soling was designed for GRP construction

Below: *Paul Elvström of Denmark is by far the most successful Olympic yachtsman, with four gold medals in successive games from 1948 onwards. In 1984, he represented Denmark once more, this time in the Tornado catamaran class with his daughter as crew, and missed the bronze medal by one place.*

T
G-196
T
Z·83
T
Z·67
T
K·94
69

and, although not tremendously popular, has proved a good Olympic class.

Attempts to replace the Finn and Star, however, both backfired. Extensive trials to find a suitable one-man dinghy produced the Australian-designed Contender, a boat of totally different character, being lightweight, fast and very tippy. This called for too much vision on the part of national delegates to the IYRU — mostly men in late middle age who would have difficulty imagining themselves sailing a super-fast, one-man trapeze dinghy such as the Contender. So, although the Contender was granted International status, it never gained sufficient votes to dislodge the Finn from the Olympic spot.

In the case of the two-man keelboat, with a view to replacing the Star, trials were held which produced an interesting two-man planing keelboat, the Tempest. Designed by Ian Proctor of Britain, it was a good boat and everyone felt it must be given its chance so, in 1972, it became an Olympic class and the venerable Star was ousted. But the Star had many powerful friends who never ceased to lobby on its behalf and such was the pressure they brought to bear that in 1980 the incredible happened — the Tempest was dropped and the Star reinstated.

Luckily, not all the Union's efforts at modernization were so frustrating. In 1976, two new classes which have both proved successful were brought in. The French-designed 470 — 15ft 5in (4.70m) in length — was brought in as a low-cost, smaller, two-man dinghy. Series-produced in GRP it is a type of boat which the average club sailor can afford and has widened the base of the Olympic pyramid.

The Tornado catamaran, designed by Rodney March of Britain, is one of the fastest and most exciting of all small boats. Even so, it was an act of considerable faith on the part of the IYRU to make it an Olympic Class. Happily, that faith has been justified. Although specialized and rather expensive, it has proved to be a very challenging boat and a worthy member of the Olympic family.

Left: *The Tempest two-man keelboat had the misfortune to be accepted as an Olympic class and then removed again after only two Olympiads. It was an exciting and demanding class but failed to gain sufficient popularity to warrant its continued use in the Olympics.*

Below: *The Tornado catamaran is easily the fastest of the Olympic classes and one of the fastest small boats of any category. One drawback of this high performance is that a special course needs to be provided for it, which adds to the difficulty and expense of running the Olympic regatta.*

Below: Cathy Foster and Peter Newlands, who represented Great Britain in the 470 Class at the 1984 Olympics. Other than the Duchess of Westminster in 1908, Cathy Foster was the only woman to have steered a yacht in the Olympics prior to 1988 and the only one to have won a race, although she failed to gain a medal.

Where the IYRU really got into trouble was with the Olympic sailboard class. In the early 1980s it became obvious that thousands of young people were taking up this new form of sailing and that it should be represented in the Olympics. The trouble was that the American Hoyle Schweitzer (see page 40), claimed exclusive patent rights over the Windsurfer design and he held a stranglehold on the production of them, especially in the United States. The IYRU, however, will only choose as an Olympic class one for which it holds the design rights, so that it can licence builders in various parts of the world. The Union therefore chose the German Windglider sailboard, whose manufacturer was prepared to sell his design rights. This put them into head-on conflict with Schweitzer.

Eventually, after a great deal of rather undignified horse-dealing, the Windglider was used as the first Olympic sailboard at the Los Angeles games. But by then fashions had changed; the Windglider had become virtually unsaleable and the builder went out of business.

After this embarrassment, the IYRU resolved that for 1988 the sailboard would be chosen well in advance and then built and provided by the host city. But once again they ran into a veritable minefield of technical and business difficulties.

Women in the Olympics

The most recent development in Olympic sailing concerns the place of women. The Olympic Programme Commission thinks in

terms of 'disciplines' rather than classes. In other words, to them the Soling is not the Soling — it is the 'Three-man keelboat'. Furthermore, they think of all events as being either for men or for women and the concept of a sport such as yachting or riding which has always been open equally to men or women is difficult for them to grasp.

Notwithstanding the Duchess of Westminster, relatively few women have reached Olympic level in yachting and the only woman in the post-war Olympics to skipper a boat in the Olympic regatta has been Cathy Foster, who represented Britain in the 470 class (two-person dinghy) at Los Angeles, where she won one race but not a medal.

When the IYRU asked for another class for 1988, they were told they could have one — if it was a woman's class. So, after a lot of soul-searching, the 470 Class has been split into 470 (men) and 470 (women). Interestingly, Cathy Foster strongly opposed this move because she much preferred to compete in an open class. The other classes are still open to either sex.

The Olympic course

Traditionally, yachts raced around existing navigation marks that happened to be in roughly the right place but, thanks to the Olympics, the concept grew of a special, standardized course. It was soon found that the only way to give every yacht in a fleet the same chance at the start was to make them set off to windward, that is, with the start line drawn at right-angles to the wind direction. This makes the first leg a beat (sailing to windward) and to try the yachts on a variety of headings, the next two legs are reaches (sailing with the wind from the side).

After these two reaches, the yachts have completed a triangle and returned to the point of departure. They next repeat the first beat but then run straight downwind to the starting point before beginning a third and final beat to the finish. Several variations are possible but the basic 'triangle and sausage' pattern is always adhered to and this Olympic course layout is also used for the majority of other major yacht-racing events.

Its drawback is that it calls for a big, unobstructed space so it cannot take place on rivers or small lakes. If the wind changes during an Olympic course race, the committee is supposed to rapidly move the buoys so that the course's orientation to the wind direction is preserved and this calls for skilled management and a good deal of man- and boat-power. Thus, running Olympic-course racing involves a club in considerable logistic problems which do not exist when fixed marks are used.

THE OLYMPIC COURSE

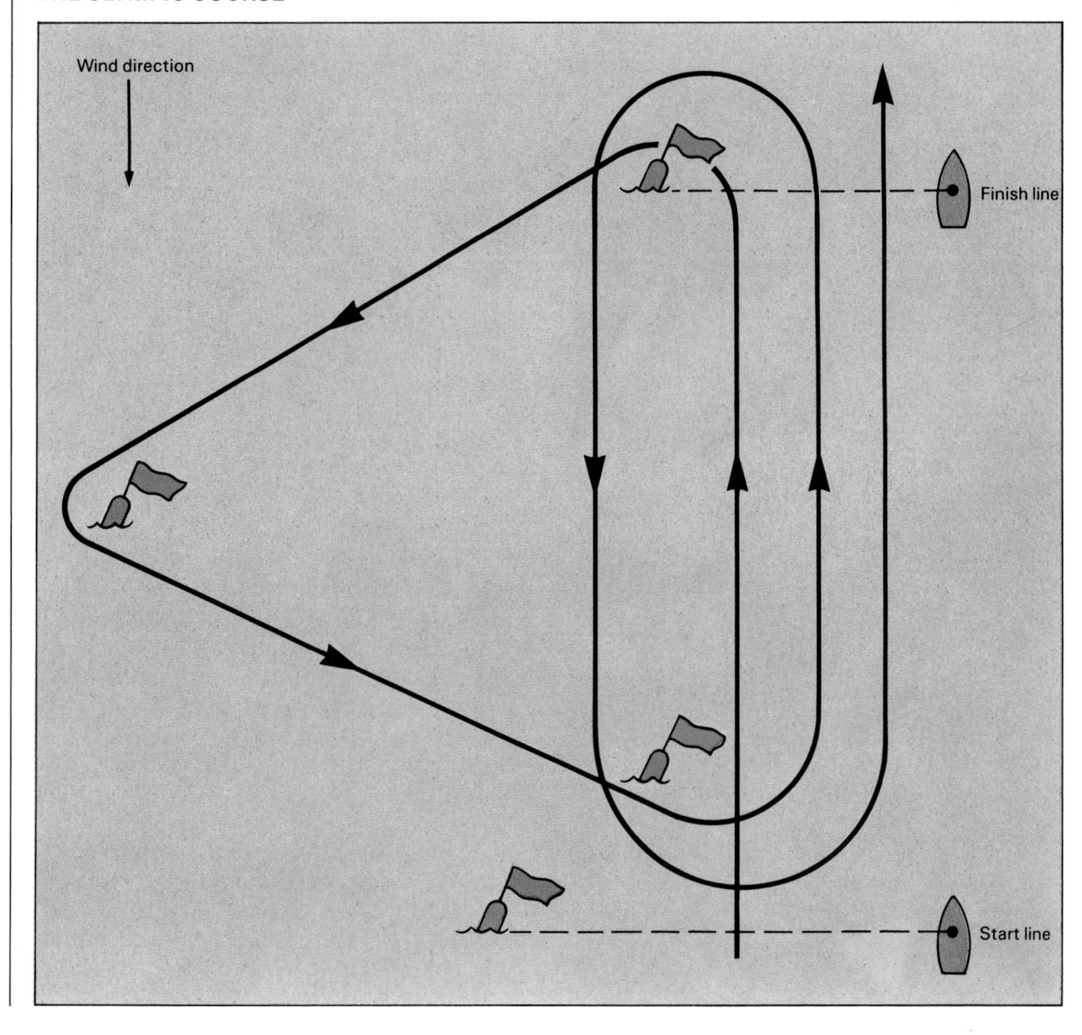

THE YACHT RACING RULES

These are the responsibility of the IYRU and have really grown in parallel with the Olympics. In the 19th century yachts followed the Merchant Shipping rules, which were very basic and not in any way designed to cope with the cut and thrust of racing. So cut and thrust was exactly what occurred, and there were several recorded instances of a yacht's crew attacking a rival's rigging with cutlasses.

As late as 1829 there was a regrettable incident during the King's Cup race at Cowes. Lord Belfast's *Louisa* collided violently with Mr Joseph Weld's *Lulworth*, whereupon the crews engaged in battle, each trying to disable the other's rigging. This drew the justly-famous judgement by the Royal Yacht Squadron Committee that 'the use of axes in the cutting away of rigging was unjustifiable'.

When James Ashbury made the first challenge for the America's Cup, in 1870, he found that American skippers had no concept of a right of way rule and simply crossed ahead of *Cambria* if they thought they could get away with it. It was obvious that the sport was not going to get anywhere until proper right-of-way rules could be developed. It was all very well for rugged characters like Lord Belfast to declare — as he did in 1829 — that if anyone tried to cross ahead of *Louisa* he would do his utmost to cut their yacht in two, but it was clear to those with cooler heads that it was no basis for a sport.

The right of way rules grew up slowly because, like English law, they are based on case histories. Once it had been established that the use of axes was 'unjustifiable' then, in future any yachtsmen using one could be disqualified, and so on. Various clubs had their own rules and it was not until 1906 that the whole of Europe agreed to standardize. The twin principles of the rules were established as being 1) to prevent collision and 2) to ensure fair competition.

The American yachting authorities had been invited to the 1906 conference but did not attend, so the North American Yacht Racing Union continued to maintain its own racing rules. As already mentioned, it was left to Harold Vanderbilt to bang some heads together, and in 1930 he personally undertook the drafting of a joint set of rules. At this point, the United States finally joined the International Yacht Racing Union which, as a result, became the true world governing body.

The post-war era has been one of co-operation with eminent authorities such as Gerald Sambrooke Sturgess in England and Devereux Barker in America gradually honing and refining the rules to remove lingering inconsistencies.

Surprisingly, the Yacht Racing Rules — to give them their proper title — have recently come under renewed heavy pressure because of the commercialization of the sport. The old Rule 26, which banned all forms of advertising in yachting, has come under fire because it hinders the development of sponsorship. If, for example, you want the Snibbo Group to sponsor your challenge for the America's Cup they may well say, 'Yes, but we want the yacht to be called *Snibbo Warrior*.' This, you have to tell them, is not allowed under Rule 26. However, the power of Rule 26 has gradually been eroded and from 1988 onwards, *Snibbo Warrior* and others like her will be seen taking part in mainstream yachting events in addition to the fringe ones which have been 'open' for some time.

The IYRU has also decided to embrace professionalism in yachting in future, although for the time being the intention is to make a distinction between open and amateur events.

In the early days of yacht racing, if there was a dispute over a race, the organizing club would set up a 'Protest Committee' which would take evidence from the parties, consider the facts and disqualify one or other of the parties. In major events such as the America's Cup, it was painfully obvious that the New York Yacht Club was acting as judge and jury in its own case and that independent protest committees would be preferable. But it was the Olympics that established the system of international juries, which is now followed for all major international events. A club running such an event has to set up a panel of disinterested experts from several countries, and these people have to be approved by the National Sailing Authority. Nowadays, juries are given a lot more power and they can overrule the organizing committee on most points.

***Right:** The unmistakable 'branding' of the yacht* Biscuits Lu, *a competitor in the 1986 BOC Challenge, single-handed round the world race, is just the kind of thing that Rule 26 was framed to prevent. In recent years, however, it has become easier to obtain exemption from this rule and this has been one of the factors in the increasing commercialization of yachting.*

Olympic points

Most major yachting events consist of a series rather than a single race. For instance, a dinghy championship normally takes a week and consists of six races, the best five results to count. In the simplest points system, the winner scores 1, the second 2 and so on; but this often results in a tie, so it is better to reward the winner by awarding him three-quarters of a point and the others 2, 3, 4 and so on, as before. This nice, simple system is still used by many clubs.

For the Olympics, however, it was decided to use a 7-race series and a points system which is roughly logarithmic for the first six places (1=0, 2=3, 3=5.7, 4=8, 5=10, 6=11.7, 7 and thereafter=place+6). This system hardly ever results in a tie but it is rather difficult to work out in your head while beating to windward in a Force 6 and wondering which of several boats you must cover in order to win the regatta . . .

RISE OF SMALL-BOAT SAILING

The 1920s saw the beginning of what was gradually to become a complete revolution in yachting — the rise of small-boat sailing and the vast increase in the sport that went with it. Sailing was at last coming within the grasp of the middle classes and in response to their demand, smaller and cheaper boats were designed.

In England, many of the leading clubs already had their own one-design racing classes — quite a number of them such as the Royal Burnham and Royal Corinthian One-designs and the ever popular X One-design still exist. These were small keelboats to be sailed by two or three people, and the idea was that the club itself would sponsor a design and ensure that all the boats were identical.

Left: The 'X' One-design Class was introduced in 1908, and is still one of the most popular small day-racing keelboats on the South Coast of England. Once the backbone of club sailing, keelboats such as the XOD suffered a decline in the post-war period but are now making a considerable comeback.

Above: *Many rule-changes have made the modern National 12ft Dinghy a very different boat from the clinker-planked 'Uffa King' of 1936, but the class still fulfils the original aim of providing good racing at a reasonable cost.*

This makes the racing fair, removes the need for handicap, and keeps down the cost.

The next step was to create 'National' classes — which could be sailed at any club in the country. Britain took the lead in this because it was a practical development in a small, compact country. The vast distances between sailing centres in the USA made it much harder to encourage inter-club racing. And in European countries, sailing tended to be based on particular areas rather than on a national basis.

In 1922, the Yacht Racing Association — forerunner of today's Royal Yachting Association — brought together the rules of the West of England, Norfolk and Small Boat Association dinghies to create the National 14ft Dinghy (later International 14ft Dinghy). This was not a one-design but a set of rules within which 14ft dinghies of various designs could be built — what is known as a 'Restricted Development Class'. It was immediately popular and was followed by the National 12ft Dinghy.

A whole new generation of keen, young people were attracted to these boats. Their annual championships, the Prince of Wales Cup and the Burton Trophy, became two of the most important events in the yachting calendar and brought freshness, enthusiasm and rapid growth to the sport.

In parallel with this opening up of the yacht racing scene, cruising was also beginning to become a popular activity. In the interwar-years, however, there was still no such thing as a mass-produced boat and even the most modest 5-tonner was individually designed and built to the owner's requirements. Furthermore, there were no such things as sailing schools. Tyros were expected simply to pick up sailing skills either from their parents or by sailing as crew for an experienced yachtsman. This is why the tradition of the paid hand continued for so long. The typical amateur yachtsman did not actually know how to reef, splice, steer, row or scrape down varnish any more than he knew how to cook or to iron a shirt. So just as a typical middle-class family of the 1920s had a maid and a cook at home, so they found it quite natural to have a hand to look after the yacht.

But learn they did, and through the inter-war years, the image of the 'Corinthian' yachtsman fully capable of any task aboard, gradually emerged, starting from the smallest yachts and gradually extending upwards.

After the Second World War, yet another new class of people found themselves enjoying the prospect of extra leisure time and many looked towards water-sports but were frustrated by shortages and the high cost of any kind of boat built by traditional, labour-intensive methods. The 'Do-it-yourself' boom came to their aid, however, and in several countries yachting magazines published designs for small boats which could be built at home.

Soon, living-rooms, garages and school workshops were echoing to the sound of saw and hammer as thousands of dinghies and even small cruising boats began to take shape. What made this possible was the development of marine plywood and waterproof glue so that the average handyman could build a tolerable hard-chine dinghy without the need for the traditional boat-building skills of lofting, steaming, bending and shaping.

The 1950s and 1960s saw an enormous boom in small boat sailing throughout Europe, although this interest was not so pronounced in the United States, where there had not been the same complete shut-down of sport during the war years. With the influx of new enthusiasts came new clubs, many on inland waters near cities and the members of these did not necessarily wear ties and blazers or speak with expensive accents. These new recruits wanted to learn in a hurry and so sailing schools came into existence. France led the way, not only with club-based training programmes but also with seamanship schools, such as the one based at Les Isles de Glenans, where people could spend a fortnight's holiday and come out at the end of it with a thorough grounding in sailing, navigation, seamanship and general self-confidence in their ability to cope.

British yachtsmen were remarkably slow to see that the growing skill and confidence of yachtsmen from Continental Europe resulted from sound training methods and consequently lagged behind in this vital area. Finally, in the late 1970s, the Royal Yachting Association began to take training seriously and was almost overwhelmed by the demand for space on the 'Yachtmaster' scheme, when it got under way. Today, virtually every maritime nation has self-education schemes for yachtsmen, in some cases backed by law. In France and Germany, for instance, skipper's licences are required for various levels of competence and in this way the sport has become more like flying, in which no-one would dream of taking off on their own without the appropriate qualification.

Below: *The Yachting World Heron was designed by Jack Holt for amateur construction in the 1950s, when very few people could afford a professionally-built boat. The arrival of glass fibre construction removed some of the appeal of home-building in plywood but the class is still popular and can be built in either material.*

In the United States, where things were left to operate on a more local level, the leading clubs all had their own 'Junior Programme', in which youngsters spent their vacations learning to sail. But commercial sailing schools also came into being to cater for adult education. Organizations such as the US Power Squadrons play a leading role in the self-education of American yachtsmen, while the US Coastguard has the role of ensuring that yachts are seaworthy and carry the proper safety aids.

Mass production

The key to really wide ownership of boats lay in mass-production and, not surprisingly, it was the United States — the largest boat market in the world — that led the way with the introduction of factory produced boats in the 1950s. For some people, the appearance of glass-reinforced plastics (GRP or glass fibre for short), reduced boat-building to the same status as making refrigerators but, from the buyer's point of view, it meant a very substantial reduction in the cost of getting afloat. Early GRP boats were pretty dreadful because it takes time for any new technology to mature but this form of construction gradually became the norm.

The key to factory production is that although the design and pattern-making processes require just as much skill, or even more, than traditional boat-building, production can be carried on by semi-skilled workers. Furthermore, the rate of production can be greatly increased. Glass fibre brought with it many advantages other than cheapness: it does not rot and is not eaten by marine organisms. It does not require to be painted nor does it lose its finish to sun or salt. In short, it meant that there was very much less need for maintenance with such a boat.

Boat-building had always traditionally taken place in a draughty shed on the banks of a river but plastics construction calls for even temperature and humidity levels, so this is better carried on in a purpose-built factory well away from the water. The early trouble with this was due to the fact that many of the new breed of factory boat-builders had absolutely no idea of the demands of the sea and so many early production boats looked like automobiles that had somehow taken a wrong turning and driven into the water.

But competition pretty soon eliminates the weaklings and the huge popularization of sailing could never have taken place without modern construction methods.

***Below:** Modern yacht construction, showing a 'chopper-gun' being used on a deck moulding. The gun cuts and shoots out a stream of short pieces of glass fibre which is mixed with resin and catalyst as it leaves the gun.*

Composite construction

Straightforward glass-reinforced polyester is all right for a stock cruising boat, but the material is rather bendy and heavy so racing sailors were soon demanding higher specification materials. The first improvement was to stiffen the skin by forming it from two layers of GRP separated by a layer of foam — what is called 'foam sandwich'. Some very large and successful one-off yachts have been built by this method, including the 77ft (23.47m) *Great Britain II* which has sailed around the world more times than any other yacht.

Foamed plastics or end-grain balsa can be used as a core material but, in recent years, lighter, stiffer cores made from resinated paper honeycomb or other very low-density materials have become available. Normal GRP construction uses glass fibres either in the form of a woven cloth or random chopped-strand mat. Both of these involve crimping of the fibres where they cross each other and this introduces a source of flexibility to the laminate, so bands of unidirectional fibres are used in areas that are subject to high stress.

The glass itself is often replaced nowadays by higher strength reinforcing materials such as Kevlar, Dupont's aramid fibre, or carbon fibre, and the matrix is often epoxy rather

than polyester resin. This kind of 'high-tech' construction offers enormous gains in strength-to-weight ratio and structural stiffness but carries the penalty of very sharply increased costs. As an example, when the fleet for the 1985 Whitbread Round the World Race was being built, £1m was the typical cost for the hull alone of an 80-footer. At least half as much again was needed to cover the expense of fitting out the boat.

The big boom in the 1950s and 1960s was in dinghies and other small day-sailing boats. In the 1970s and 1980s, the focus moved to cruising yachts. With the steady rise in disposable incomes, people feel the need to get away and have a change of scene at the weekend. This could mean coastal cruising or offshore racing or, at the simplest level, just staying on board a boat for a couple of days and making a short venture downriver.

Above: Great Britain II, *which is thought to hold the record for sailing round the world more times than any other yacht, was an early example of sandwich construction, using a foam core in between two skins of glass fibre.*

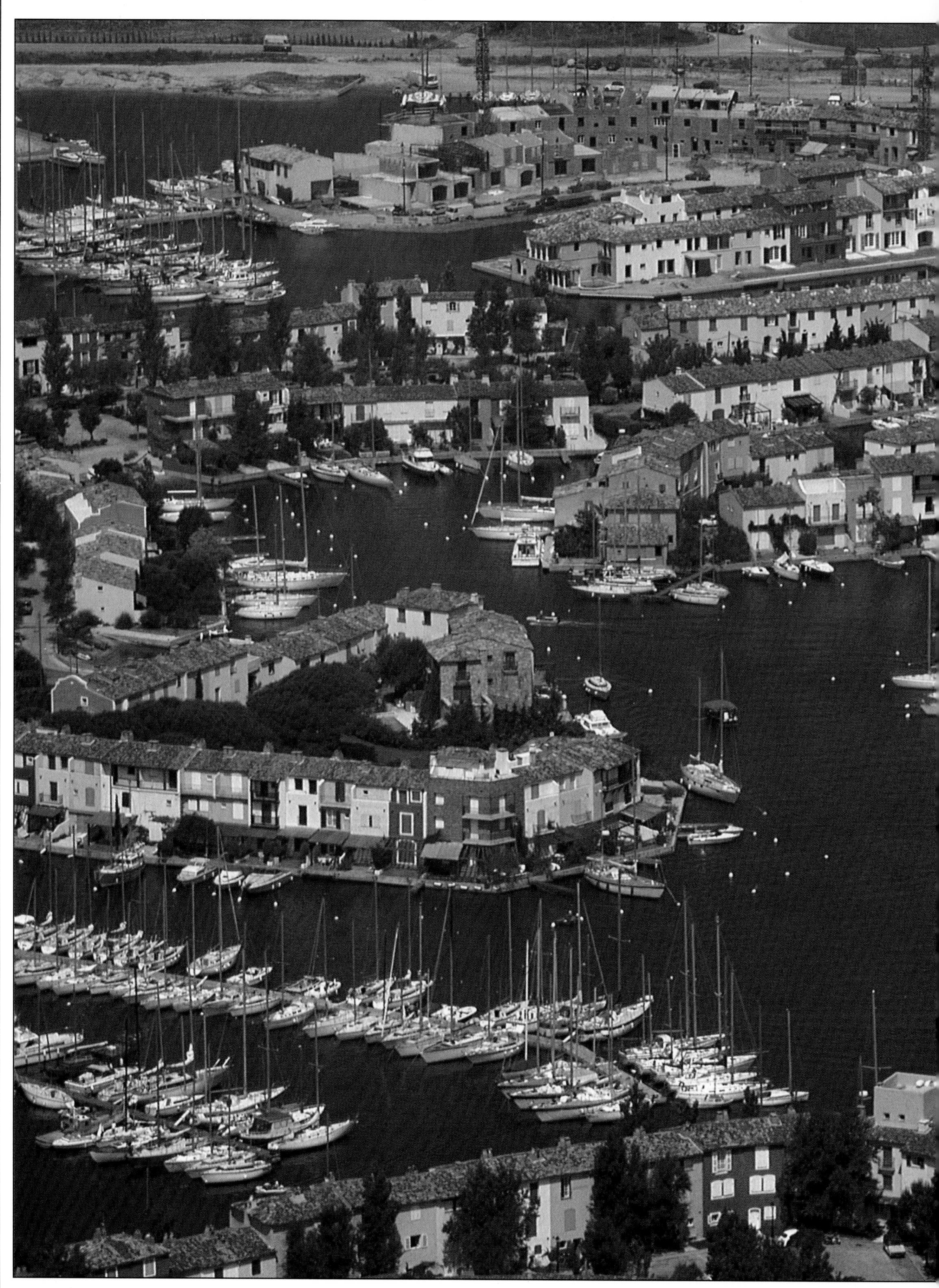

Marinas

This pattern of activities depends very much on having somewhere suitable to keep this larger boat. Traditionally, big boats were kept on moorings but it does not take long for every river and creek to become full up. Therefore, a purpose-designed yacht harbour in which yachts lie alongside floating pontoons becomes desirable. The trouble with this kind of development is that it is expensive, and the people who put their money into construction want to maximize the return by including other profitable enterprises such as shops, restaurants or housing units.

This type of marina was first developed in the USA, where people were less inhibited about changing the coastal landscape. One of the most celebrated examples is Marina Del Rey, in Los Angeles, where several square miles of marshland was dredged to form an enormous harbour. Today, thousands of people live there as well as using it to harbour their yachts.

In the early post-war years, Europeans were very wary of this type of development but more recently have taken to it with enthusiasm. The French, in particular, have shown how a partnership of public and private investment can be used to open up new areas of coastline. The area to the west of Marseilles, for instance, was a mosquito-infested hinterland until a big surge of development, along with government-sponsored *demoustication* during the 1970s turned it into the new resort area known as the *Côte Emeraude*.

Now, virtually no coastal town in France is without a yacht harbour — and if properly designed these are generally felt to enhance rather than spoil the scenery. This is because the French are basically in favour of what they call *animation* or activity, whereas in Britain people are educated to believe that the landscape is sacred, however dull. In France, the design of marinas has taken two diametrically opposite directions. On the one hand, there is the type of development typified by the fake village of Port Grimaud, near San Tropez, where instant antiquity was the aim of the architect. Quite nearby, one can find marina developments of aggressive modernism in which pantile and whitewash are exchanged for concrete and steel. Which you prefer, is a matter of taste.

Sailboards

In the late 1960s, a group of friends in Los Angeles — particularly Hoyle Schweitzer and Jim Drake — began playing around with the idea of putting a sail on to a surfboard. Actually, they were not the first because, in 1965, *Popular Mechanics* magazine had published an article by a man named Newman Darby, in which he described a kind of plank-like craft on which he proposed to stand holding a square sail. But Darby's craft never came to anything while Drake and Schweitzer gradually succeeded in making theirs work. The

Left: The 'vernacular' approach to marina design is exemplified by Port Grimaud in the Gulf of St Tropez. Although not to everyone's taste, it is a great deal easier on the eye than the type which is no more than a marine parking lot.

Above: *Hoyle Schweitzer sitting among a pile of brand-new Windsurfers being prepared for a championship. Although his claim to have invented the sailboard is disputed, he was certainly the man who commercialized the idea.*

two breakthroughs were firstly to attach the rig to the board with a universal joint so that it could be moved in any direction and, secondly, to extend the sail with a curved, double-sided boom or wishbone.

These were the essential features of what the two men called the Windsurfer, and after a great deal of falling in the water they found it was possible to stand up and control the thing. There was no need for a rudder because the board could be steered by moving the rig around while a simple dagger-board stopped it from drifting off sideways. Moreover, once they had mastered the technique of sailing the primitive Windsurfer, they discovered that it was enormous fun and very good exercise.

Realizing that they had hit on something saleable, Schweitzer and Drake took out a patent on their Windsurfer and began to manufacture it in 1969. Drake was a research scientist and did not want to get into commerce so he sold out to Schweitzer, who put all his savings into building a small factory. Strangely enough, it did not go too well as, in California — the land of crazy pastimes — it was just one more funny idea. But one or two were brought back to Europe by travellers and there the idea really caught people's attention.

A Dutch textile firm, named Ten Cate, heard about the Windsurfer and, in 1970, sent a salesman to Los Angeles with the idea of selling sailcloth to Schweitzer but ended up by buying 100 Windsurfers instead. Back in Holland, these sold like hot cakes so the firm immediately ordered another 1,000. Schweitzer's small factory could not produce so many in a short time so Ten Cate bought a licence to manufacture the Windsurfer in Europe.

There then followed a heady period during which windsurfing became the fastest-growing sport in Europe and Ten Cate struggled to keep pace with ever-growing demand. Pretty soon, other manufacturers started to bring out their own versions and Schweitzer sent lawyers knocking on their doors with writs for patent infringement. But although his patent held sway in Holland, Germany and Great Britain, it did not apply in France and factories there began turning out sailboards at an ever-increasing rate.

Eventually, the patent failed in most European countries or licence agreements took care of it and during most of the 1970s the new sport of windsurfing took off at a tremendous rate. Not only was it a new form

of sailing but it brought with it a new form of freedom, for the sailboard is so simple and portable compared to the most basic boat that there is no longer any need for yacht clubs, moorings, slipways and all the other paraphernalia. Just strap the board and rig on the roof-rack and off we go!

Of course, there were many problems in the early stages. Board-sailors trespassed on the foreshore, ran into swimmers, got tired and needed to be rescued and found a hundred and one other ways of making themselves a nuisance but, in spite of tut-tutting by the authorities and the established yachting fraternity, the sport itself was so attractive that its progress was unstoppable.

Schweitzer conceived the idea of holding world championships at attractive beach resorts, with all the equipment being available for rental. Thus, all the competitor needed to do was pack a swimsuit and jump on a plane. In the early stages, everyone thought that you needed to be super-strong to win a race on a Windsurfer but at the fourth such championships, at Nassau in the Bahamas, an unusually small, 14-year-old boy from Hawaii named Robbie Naish proved them wrong. He could not only sail faster than anyone else, he could make a Windsurfer dance. He could sail backwards, or from the wrong side of the sail or with the board balanced on edge. He made sailing look like playing around on a skateboard.

In short, Robbie Naish became the first of a new generation of sailboard super-stars who acquired such skills that what they did bordered on an art-form. They soon broke away from straightforward racing and developed new activities and new styles of board to go with them. Wave-jumping, speed-racing, slalom, freestyle, long-distance racing and other such activities have broadened the appeal of board-sailing and produced a new breed of professional sailor. Nowadays there is a professional sailboard circuit in which a number of events form a championship — rather as in motor racing.

This is the top end of the sport. The bottom end is the cheap and ill-designed sailboard that some Mediterranean hotels keep lying around to justify the brochure claim that 'windsurfing' is one of the many

***Below:** These original Windsurfers with their teak booms and baggy sails look somewhat dated now but all the basic features of the sailboard are present and have not changed in any fundamental way since.*

sports on offer. Between the two extremes lie the many thousands of private owners of sailboards who have no intention of competing, because the sheer pleasure of sailing around and making nice carve-gybes is sufficient. In this respect, the sport has become very like skiing — in which the vast majority of participants are recreational skiers who can only gaze in wonder at the antics of the small number of super-stars. The other parallel is that the majority of newcomers to boardsailing take lessons. A skilled instructor can save you from taking an awful lot of falls.

A sailboard is now the fastest sailing craft of any kind. In 1986, the Frenchman, Pascal Maka recorded a speed of 38.86 knots over a distance of 500 metres. And the Atlantic Ocean has been crossed on a sailboard.

Below: *Pascal Maka of France, seen here carving a gybe on his sailboard, became the fastest man in the world under sail when he was timed at over 38 knots in 1986.*

OCEAN RACING

Today one of the biggest, most active and competitive branches of sailing, ocean or offshore racing had very shaky beginnings which left the public with the impression that racing on the ocean was a highly dangerous business.

In the depth of winter in 1866, as a result of a wager of $90,000 between three wealthy American yachtsmen, their schooners set off from New York to race to the Isle of Wight. *Henrietta*, *Vesta* and *Fleetwing* were big yachts of over 100ft (30.5m) in length but, even so, the misgivings of many were proved correct when six men were lost overboard from *Fleetwing*. All three yachts finished within hours of each other on Christmas Day. The winner was *Henrietta*, owned by 25-year-old James Gordon Bennett who, incidentally, was the only one of the three intrepid yachtsmen who actually went along on the race.

A few years later, in 1870, when the British yacht *Cambria* was named as the initial challenger for the America's Cup, she first raced across the Atlantic in competition with the American yacht *Dauntless*. The winner was *Cambria*, which took 23 days to sail from Daunt Rock (Ireland) to Sandy Hook, the entrance to New York. With an average speed of 128 miles per day, this was a fair performance for a yacht of 108ft (32.9m) overall and the records suggest that the crew did not press her unduly.

There was another transatlantic race in 1887, and then a really famous one in 1905, from Sandy Hook to the Lizard, for the Kaiser's Cup. It was won by the enormous, three-masted schooner *Atlantic*, in the astonishing time of 12 days, four hours, one minute, 19 seconds, and this record stood for 70 years. *Atlantic*, designed by William Gardner had impressive dimensions: 187ft (57m) LOA, 137ft (41.76m) LWL, 29ft (8.85m) beam, 15ft (4.57m) draught and 18,514 sq ft (1,720 sq m) sail area. Owned by Wilson Marshall, she was a lovely and very modern yacht with an external ballast keel but her secret weapon was her firebrand of a captain, Charlie Barr, who was later to have such an impact on the America's Cup. In spite of all entreaties from the terrified owner and guests, Barr resolutely refused to reduce sail and drove *Atlantic* recklessly down the path of a series of deep depressions. Her best day's run was 341 miles and her average 248 miles or 10.3 knots.

This was spectacular stuff in which enormous vessels, virtually small ships, were sailed by full professional crews but, almost unnoticed, a more significant race took place in 1904 — when a small fleet of yachts *sailed by amateurs* raced from Brooklyn to Marblehead. The winner was *Little Rhody*, skippered by Charles Tillinghast. There were nine entries for this 330-mile race and six finished. The moving spirit behind it had been Thomas Fleming Day, founder and editor of *Rudder* magazine, who was almost alone at first in putting forward the idea of long races specifically planned for small yachts with amateur crews.

After another relatively short race the following year, Day proposed a race from Brooklyn to Bermuda, in 1906. Only three yachts competed and Day himself was skipper of the winner, the 38ft (11.58m) yawl, *Tamerlane*. Thus, the Bermuda Race became the first regular, long-distance race for amateur yachtsmen. Entries remained small and in an effort to stimulate them Day dropped the requirement for amateur skippers and for yachts to be under 40ft (12.19m). Nevertheless, the race died out after five years. Incidentally, the final winner of this early series was the lovely Herreshof schooner, *Vagrant*, which had been given to Harold Vanderbilt as a graduation present by his parents.

***Above:** The lovely Herreshof schooner* Vagrant *was given to Harold Vanderbilt when he graduated from college. He promptly entered for the 1910 Bermuda Race and won.* Vagrant *was recently rediscovered and completely restored by British yachtsman Peter de Savary.*

DS 2

Left: Jolie Brise, *which won the first Fastnet Race in 1925, was a working boat rather than a yacht but the arrival of the American yacht* Dorade *in 1931 signalled the change to a pure racing type.*

The first regular long race appears to have been the Chicago-Mackinac Race, which has been held annually since 1898. One cannot call this an *ocean* race as it is held on fresh water but the Great Lakes are a lot bigger than the English Channel and the Mackinac can be very tough indeed.

Day was ahead of his time but, in 1923, another magazine, *Yachting*, revived the idea and promoted a new race to Bermuda, with the support of the newly-founded Cruising Club of America. This time the idea stuck and the race to Bermuda became a regular fixture. The CCA developed a measurement-based rating rule to enable yachts to compete on handicap.

Things began stirring in Europe after the yachting writer Weston Martyr wrote a report about the Bermuda race and gave the opinion that a similar event should be promoted in Britain, lest the Americans get ahead in the development of a new sport. He also suggested the course: from Cowes, around the Fastnet Rock off the south coast of Ireland, and back to the finish at Plymouth. He ran into immediate opposition from the yachting establishment. The entry of small yachts with amateur crews in such an 'extremely dangerous' race would be 'sheer lunacy' wrote one yachtsman. But Martyr knew that was all nonsense and formed a small committee with Lt-Cmdr George Martin and Malden Heckstall-Smith, who was then the editor of *Yachting Monthly*.

Fastnet Race

In August 1925, seven yachts started from Ryde in the inaugural Fastnet Race. The winner was the Le Havre pilot cutter *Jolie Brise*, owned by George Martin. At the party after the race, the (Royal) Ocean Racing Club was formed — with Martin as the founding Commodore. Like the CCA in America, one of the first acts of the RORC was to produce a rating rule and once again the opportunity was missed to organize a unified 'Atlantic Rule'. This had to wait for more than 40 years when the two rules were combined in the International Offshore Rule (IOR).

From 1928, races across the Atlantic became a regular occurrence. They were mostly one-way races, from America to Europe, this being much the easier direction to sail in the North Atlantic. The races enabled American yachts to come over for the main events of the European summer season and then cruise home in the sunshine via the trade-wind route. This took them conveniently home to Florida where, from 1930 onwards, a race was held in early spring from St Petersburg, Florida to Havana, Cuba.

This was the beginning of what became the 'Southern Circuit' of races around Florida, run very early in the season when it was agreeable to get away from the icy eastern United States.

From 1931, the Fastnet and Bermuda races were held on alternate years, to allow yachts from either country to cross the Atlantic to compete. This was the beginning of a sensible international co-operation which would no doubt have flowered earlier, but for the Second World War.

Offshore racing developed rapidly in the post-war years but initially on a regional basis. In America, races were run and yachts designed for CCA racing. In Europe the RORC rule was adopted by most countries. As a result, racing in the Channel and North Sea soon took on an international flavour and the major events such as the Fastnet Race always had a healthy number of French, Dutch, Scandinavian and Mediterranean entries, in addition to the occasional visitor from the USA.

Admiral's Cup

In 1957, in an effort to encourage more American visitors to Cowes Week and the Fastnet Race, five senior members of the RORC presented the Admiral's Cup. This was to be an event for teams of three yachts per nation which were to race in a series of four races, culminating in the Fastnet Race. This brilliant concept met with an enthusiastic response and it soon became the most important international event for sea-going yachts.

Below: *The Admiral's Cup. Given to encourage American yachts to race in Cowes Week, it developed into the most important ocean racing series in the world and has been widely copied.*

All the same, it was obvious that there could never be true international competition until everyone was using the same rating rules. This was finally achieved in 1970, when a joint committee chaired by Olin Stephens created the International Offshore Rule. This was rapidly adopted by all of the offshore racing clubs of the world and, from 1971 onwards, was used for the Admiral's Cup.

It was created by and for ocean racing enthusiasts and the International Yacht Racing Union, then going through one of its feeblest periods, took no part. As a result, a new world governing body, the Offshore Racing Council, was created and this still maintains its independence from the IYRU. The link between them is that the Yacht Racing Rules are used by all types of yachtsmen and in recent years there has been an effort to stop the two main branches of the sport from drifting apart.

IOR has been a victim of its own success to some extent, because racing to this formula has recently become so sophisticated and expensive that many amateur owners have been put off from competing. To cope with the demand for a simpler rating system and a less dedicated form of race, the Channel Handicap system was devised in England and the Scandicap in the Baltic. These divisions have shown a very fast growth and in 1987, there were more yachts taking part in CHS racing than IOR.

Sponsored Spectaculars

During the last 20 years, some great ocean-crossing 'spectaculars' have been created, the first of which was the Observer Single-handed Transatlantic Race. Some of these, such as the Whitbread Round the World Race are great and important sporting events and some are fairly disreputable advertising ventures. All have grown up outside the world of conventional ocean racing and are generally organized on an *ad hoc* basis rather than as part of some coherent sporting theme. For instance, other than some of the people taking part, there is almost nothing in common between, say, the BOC Challenge (single-handed around the world) and the TAG Europe Race (short, linked races in fully-crewed, big multihulls). The important events are dealt with fully in the chapter entitled *The Great Races*.

Multihulls offshore

Like offshore racing in the early days, racing offshore in multihulls was at first thought to be quite crazy when it began in England and California in the 1960s. When one of the competitors (Bill Howell's *Golden Cockerel*) capsized during the inaugural Crystal Trophy Race for multihulls in 1967 there were plenty to say 'I told you so'.

One problem was the extreme difficulty of finding a sensible rating system for multihulls. Weight is so critical to an unballasted craft that only a system in which whole boats

are physically weighed before every race could be considered effective, and this is not really practical. The French cut through this problem by organizing races without limitation; it seemed an odd idea but resulted in the class of giant catamarans and trimarans up to 80ft (24.38m) in length which compete on the open circuit.

Multihulls got their real chance in 'open' races such as the Observer Single-handed Transatlantic Race and the Round Britain, in which there was no limitation on design. They proved that two, or three hulls are better than one (or at least, faster). Multi-hulls came to dominate all of the ocean events open to them and it was French initiative such as that of Michel Etevenon which led to the creation of events specially for big multihulls.

Cats and trimarans of up to 80ft (24.38m) soon became prohibitively expensive so, in 1986, the idea of a cheaper, restricted formula was created. 'Formula 40' is for multihulls up to 40ft (12.19m) in overall length, with a maximum sail area and minimum weight. Although not really an offshore boat, the prototype did spectacularly well in the 1986 Round Britain Race. Since then, a professional circuit has been created for these very exciting boats and this could develop into a very vigorous branch of the sport.

Above: *The foil-stabilized trimaran* Paul Ricard *in which Eric Tabarly and Marc Pajot fought a prolonged battle for victory in the first Transat en Double Race with* VSD, *the eventual victor, sailed by Eugene Riguidel and Gilles Gahinet.*

FD
F-245

Yachts of the World

Big yachts, small yachts, racing yachts, cruising yachts — they all have their place in the vast fleet of world-wide yachting.
In this chapter, we take a brief look at each of the types, to see how they are designed and built and how they serve their purpose.

***Left:** The start of a race for the Olympic Flying Dutchman class. These big, fast dinghies have very sophisticated construction and equipment and it takes a long time, a great deal of money and effort to reach the top levels of the class. However, it is just this kind of all-round challenge that many sailors regard as its greatest strength.*

YACHTS OF THE WORLD

Most people begin their sailing in dinghies because these are comparatively cheap and do not require a lot of expertise. If you go to a sailing school, you will certainly begin in this type of vessel. Here we review the main ones.

Dinghies

Dinghies were originally tenders to yachts rather than a type of sailing boat in their own right but there was always a demand for a small boat in which beginners could learn to row and sail. Initially, these were sturdy clinker-built boats with a simple rig — very often a single lugsail of some kind. This type of rig was chosen because the short spars could be stowed inside the dinghy when it was being towed or carried on deck.

Dinghies that were built by one yard or were well known in a particular area gradually formed competitive classes and as this type of sailing became popular in the years following the First World War, the better dinghies found favour over a wider area. A good example of the way in which this happened is provided by the International 14ft Dinghy. In 1922, the Yacht Racing Association amalgamated the rules of three popular classes, the West of England, Norfolk and Small Boat Association dinghies, to form the National 14ft Dinghy Class. This prospered and was adopted as a class for international competition in 1927. It is still keenly raced today.

Dinghies of this kind were given rules rather like those applying to larger racing yachts, allowing the designer freedom to experiment within a certain framework. In the case of the International 14ft Class, for instance, maximum length, maximum sail area, minimum weight and minimum rise of floor were specified but the designer had freedom over the shape of the hull. Thanks to this kind of 'Development rule', racing boats soon emerged from the working-boat ancestry.

These were craftsmen-built dinghies and fairly expensive as a result. The American William Crosby, the editor of *Rudder* magazine, seems to have been the first to suggest the idea of amateur construction. In 1931, he designed the Snipe dinghy and, to prove that an amateur could cope, had the prototype built by a 14-year-old boy. The plans were then published in *Rudder*, giving readers the chance to begin hitting their thumbs with hammers and cutting themselves with chisels.

The Snipe was very heavy by today's standard, especially as it came before the era of plywood, but it introduced the idea of a

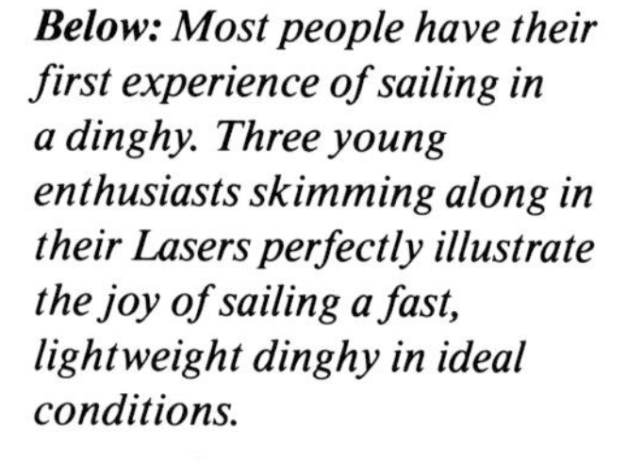

***Below:** Most people have their first experience of sailing in a dinghy. Three young enthusiasts skimming along in their Lasers perfectly illustrate the joy of sailing a fast, lightweight dinghy in ideal conditions.*

'hard chine' shape made from basically flat panels meeting at an angle. The design was a great success and many thousands of Snipes were built by amateurs. Though outdated now, the Snipe is still raced — but built in glass fibre.

The great boom in dinghy-building came after the Second World War, when the availability of marine plywood and waterproof glue made it far easier for the amateur to build a small boat. In England, the leading designer of DIY dinghies was the Putney boat-builder Jack Holt, who worked with Teddy Haylock, Editor of *Yachting World*, to produce a whole catalogue of easy-to-build small boats. The best known today are the International Cadet, Heron, GP14, Hornet and Solo.

Another major boost for the home-builder came with the development of the 'stitch and tape' method of building, as used for the Mirror Dinghy and many others. The home-builder is supplied with plywood panels already cut out or accurately marked to shape, ready to be 'sewn' together, using twists of copper wire. Next, glass tape and resin is applied to one side of the joint and, after it has hardened, the twists of wire are cut off flush and glass fibre is applied to the other side. The great appeal of this system is that the hull finds its own shape correctly, like a ready-to-sew dress pattern, so the level of skill required is not very great.

The boom in home building died away when dinghies became widely available in glass fibre, though there are still plenty of enthusiasts who build their own boats. Glass fibre construction fits in particularly well with the idea of 'one-design' classes, in which all boats are as similar as possible. This kind of class is cheaper and gives closer racing but stifles development, so most classes that are theoretically strict one-designs have to undertake modernization from time to time. A good example would be a changeover from wooden to aluminium masts or from plywood to glass fibre construction.

Even the strictest of one-design classes do change. For instance, the Laser — a class for which uniformity is an article of faith — has been fitted with completely new spars and sail during its life.

The modern racing dinghy can be an extremely sophisticated craft, thanks to the intense development pressure that keen racing brings. In recent years, great effort has been put into improving the stiffness of hulls and providing very exact control of the rig. A serious racing dinghy such as a 5-0-5, International 14 or Flying Dutchman costs about as much as a small car.

In the 1950s and 1960s, the boom period for dinghies, literally dozens of new designs appeared every year but, fortunately, there has been a good deal of rationalization since then. Even so, yachtsmen are sturdy individualists and remain intensely loyal to designs that they like or which have a local following. Eventually, some of the older designs acquire a nostalgic appeal and are maintained as nautical antiques. An example might be the 12 Square Metre Sharpie, a pre-war design of German origin which is a complete anachronism yet still keenly raced in a few clubs.

The first really major step forward in design was the development of the planing dinghy by Uffa Fox and others during the late 1920s. Having been an apprentice to S.E. Saunders, a builder of racing powerboats and seaplanes, Fox understood the shapes needed to make a hull rise up and plane along the surface of the water rather than ploughing through it. He knew that it would not work with the very rounded and 'rockered' (banana-shaped) hulls then typical for dinghies. But a flat-bottomed 'speedboat' hull would sail appallingly badly because of its very high resistance at low speed. Therefore, the shape needed was one with a V-shaped forebody and a substantially straight run aft while still retaining the basic shape of a sailing dinghy.

***Above:** The Snipe was the first dinghy to be designed for amateur construction and promoted by a magazine, when* Rudder *published the plans in 1931. Though rather heavy and undercanvassed by today's standards, the Snipe is still raced in a number of countries.*

Above: The International 14 was one of the first high-performance racing dinghies and is still one of the most exciting. Recent rule changes permitting a much lower weight and twin trapezes have given the class a new lease of life. Here, James Hartley and Ian Tillett have got their boat in perfect balance on a shy spinnaker reach.

When Fox's planing International 14 *Avenger* came out in 1928, she won 52 first places in 57 races! From this moment on, dinghy sailors could look forward to the thrill of zooming away like a speedboat whenever the wind was strong enough.

As well as having a suitable shape, a planing boat needs to be lightweight and have a high power-to-weight ratio. The former came gradually with improvements in building techniques but the latter is a more complex problem. Power can be increased by piling on more sail area but cannot be harnessed without stability — a sailing boat without stability just falls over on its side when the wind hits it. Yachts get their stability from the shape of the hull and from the ballast keel, which resists heeling.

Dinghy sailors used to think that ballast in the form of a heavy metal centreboard was essential but it gradually dawned on them that when the boat is being sailed upright — as it should be — ballast has no useful function. On the contrary, it slows the boat down by adding to its displacement. A more useful form of ballast would be the crew, who have to be there anyway, and are allowed to move around; they represent 'live' rather than 'dead' ballast.

The first and most obvious action is to sit on the windward side of the dinghy to balance the wind's pressure. Immediately it became clear that the further out the crew sit, the faster the boat goes and therefore toe-straps were fitted inside the boat to enable the crew to get their body-weight right over the side with only their legs remaining inside the hull. Many racing dinghies are still sailed this way, with the crew vigorously hanging over the side. It calls for strength and endurance and this is what makes a dinghy like the Olympic Finn such a hard boat to sail well. The Finn sailor has to make fast, accurate tactical decisions and carry out a very finely-developed sailing technique at the same time as enduring extreme physical exertion.

Those dinghy sailors with a less masochistic outlook and an inventive turn of mind naturally sought for ways of using crew weight more effectively and less painfully. In the early 1930s, the leading small-boat sailor Beecher Moore hit on the idea of having the crew of his Thames Rater *Vagabond* stand on the gunwhale of the boat, holding on to a rope from the mast. This idea was taken up and developed by Peter Scott, who added the idea of attaching the rope to a stout leather belt worn by the crew. Used briefly in the International 14ft Class, this 'trapeze' system was very effective but was banned as being a rule infringement.

Other classes soon rushed in where the International 14 feared to tread and many high-performance dinghies are now fitted with trapezes for one or both of the crew (including, nowadays, the International 14). The modern trapeze artist wears a harness which is like a pair of reinforced shorts with a metal hook at waist level which engages a ring on the end of a wire from the mast. A well-designed one is perfectly comfortable and enables the crew to get his weight right outside the dinghy without the sustained discomfort of 'sitting out'.

As an alternative to the trapeze, the crew can sit on a plank or frame extending out from the side of the boat. The best known example of the plank system is that used on the International 10 Square Metre Canoe, which has a plank that slides out to one side of the boat or the other, to suit either tack. This plank is so long that the sailor climbs out completely beyond the side of the boat.

In a dinghy where the trapeze or sliding seat is not permitted, another approach to maximizing stability is to widen the boat as much as the rules allow. Thus, a dinghy such as the National 12ft is nowadays built with very flared topsides in order to get the crew weight well out from the centre-line. Another variation of this is seen on the International Moth, where a framework made of tubular metal extends out from the sides of what is a basically narrow hull.

Rigs of dinghies

Wood was the normal construction for dinghy spars until the 1950s, when the demand for good-quality spruce outstripped supply and tubular aluminium spars were introduced. At first these were just metal versions of wooden masts which had been designed to stand as straight as possible but, in England, the designer and mast-maker Ian Proctor began to see the advantage of having deliberately bendy masts as a way of adjusting the sail shape for different wind strengths. The basic idea was to start with a straight mast and a fairly full sail that would be suitable for light-to-medium conditions. As the wind increased, the mast could be bent backwards like a bow to flatten the sail and free the leech, allowing the wind to escape without producing so much heeling-force.

Bendy metal spars brought a big all-round improvement in the performance of dinghies and worked particularly well with the early synthetic sailcloth materials, such as Terylene in England and Dacron in the USA, as these were strong but stretchy. Intense development has led to much more stable sailcloths which hold their shape over a wide range of wind-strengths. The technique with these modern sails is to set up the rig with an initial 'pre-bend', to give the sail its correct basic shape and to resist further bending. The rig is set up rigidly so that very fine adjustments can be made to the sail shape that were not possible with soft cloth and masts that bent freely. The modern racing dinghy rig is a sophisticated aerofoil that can be accurately 'tuned' for different wind-strengths.

Seaworthiness and safety

The first racing dinghies were open boats without any flotation devices in case of a capsize. Dinghy sailors were expected to sail within the limits of their craft and few wore life-jackets. Indeed, an early design of self-draining dinghy was rejected by Britain's Yacht Racing Association (forerunner of the RYA) on the grounds that 'It might encourage an unseamanlike attitude to capsizing.'

A more rational approach was to design dinghies so that they could survive a capsize without outside assistance. Additional buoyancy was provided, first in the form of air tanks or bags and later watertight compartments forming part of the structure of the boat. The latter only became practical with modern construction.

The next step is to get rid of the water that inevitably finds its way aboard a small boat sailing in waves. A hand-bailer is a thoroughly awkward thing to use in a dinghy and it is almost impossible to use one and sail at the same time. The brilliant solution, which seems to have been invented simultaneously by several people, was the 'self-bailer'. This suction device uses the dinghy's speed through the water to create a vacuum down which the bilge-water will flow. All sorts of clever venturi systems were tried

Above: *The very first use of a 'trapeze' in racing was by Bill Milestone, crewing for Beecher Moore on his Thames Rater* Vagabond *in 1931. Here Milestone, properly dressed in flannels and blazer, can be seen hanging on to a knotted 'bell-rope'. The idea of attaching the rope to a special belt came later.*

Left: *In classes such as the Laser, where a trapeze or sliding seat is not permitted, vigorous sitting-out or 'hiking' is needed to keep the boat upright. This calls for fitness and strength.*

Above: Buoyancy for the whole family. It is important to realize the difference between a life-jacket, designed to support an unconscious person in rough water and a buoyancy aid, such as the garments pictured here, which are easier to wear but provide a lower level of safety.

until Duarte Bello of Portugal showed that a simple wedge-shaped flap extending from the bottom of the boat worked just as well. The modern self-bailer is hinged so that it is only extended when needed and has a flap acting as a non-return valve to prevent the water from flowing back in whenever the dinghy slows down.

Even this system is rendered unnecessary if a dinghy is built with a watertight floor raised to just above the waterline so that water drains overboard of its own accord. Care is needed, however, not to give a dinghy so much buoyancy that it will float too high in the water when capsized, making it difficult to right and having a tendency to blow away from the crew.

It is surprising now to think of dinghy-races ever being run on the sea without the crews wearing any form of personal buoyancy but, in the pre-war era, no suitable garments were made. Even after the Second World War, the choice was initially between appalling waistcoats stuffed with kapok, as likely to drown you as save you, or much-prized air-crew 'Mae Wests', if you could get one. Slowly, decent buoyancy garments appeared — after a good deal of confusion about the different requirements of a 'life-jacket' designed to save someone who is lying completely helpless in the water and a 'buoyancy aid' designed to make it easier for the active sportsman to get back on board his dinghy and continue the race.

Sailing in shorts and a golfing jacket also has its limitations, so the development of specialized clothing went hand in hand with the appearance of a more active style of dinghy sailing. The big breakthrough was the 1960s' invention of the foam-rubber 'wet-suit', which made it possible to endure immersion in cold water. A more recent development is the 'dry suit', a completely waterproof garment with rubber seals where the head and limbs emerge. This specialized clothing not only makes it possible to enjoy sailing at times when the water is cold but virtually removes the risk of hypothermia.

TYPES OF DINGHY POPULAR TODAY

There are literally thousands of dinghy classes, so we list only the most important ones. In breaking them down into trainers, single-handers, high performance racing dinghies and general dinghies, it is pointed out that the borderlines between groups are not precise. This is particularly true of general two-person dinghies, which are used for racing by some and cruising by others.

Where two figures are given for sail area in the following descriptions, the first applies to mainsail plus jib (if any) and the second to the spinnaker.

CHILDREN'S BOATS AND TRAINERS

International Optimist

Length overall	7ft 7in	(2.31m)
Weight	77lb	(35kg)
Sail area	35ft²	(3.25m²)

Designed by Clark Mills, in 1947, in response to a demand for a basic 'matchbox' boat for children, the Optimist is by far the most popular children's trainer in the world — with more than 100,000 in use. It broke new ground in making the learner handle the boat *ab initio* rather than crewing for a more experienced person. Surprisingly, children as young as seven or eight take to this readily and can pick up the basics in about a week. The Optimist is also a keen junior racing class, with children up to 15 competing with great enthusiasm at up to international level. The secret of the Optimist is that it places the child firmly in control of its own destiny from the first moment of going afloat, and this proves to be a powerful incentive to learning.

Left: The International Optimist is now the most popular children's boat. As there is only room for one small child in an Optimist, the beginner has to take full charge from the first moment he or she goes afloat but, surprisingly, this ab initio *learning process works very well.*

Above: The International Cadet, designed as a miniature racing boat for two children, has brought thousands of young people into racing over the years. Unlike the Optimist the Cadet has a jib and spinnaker and is usually sailed by a teenaged helmsman with a younger child as crew.

International Cadet

Length overall	10ft 7in	(3.2m)
Weight	135lb	(61.2kg)
Sail area	50/49ft²	(4.65/4.55m²)

Designed by Jack Holt as a junior race trainer, the Cadet introduced many thousands of newcomers to sailing, including several Olympic medallists. It was purposely made too small for an adult but with all the attributes of a racing dinghy, including spinnaker, in miniature. Designed for amateur construction in plywood, thousands were built in school workshops. Not so generally used now as 20 years ago but still popular in a number of countries.

Mirror Dinghy

Length overall	10ft 10in	(3.3m)
Weight	135lb	(61.2kg)
Sail area	69/65ft²	(6.4/6m²)

Though not solely a training boat, the Mirror Dinghy has become one of the most popular first boats because of its cheapness, simplicity and all-round usefulness. Large enough to be used as a picnic-boat (the author's record is three adults, two children and a dog!) it is an ideal knockabout dinghy. Like the Cadet, from the same designer, Jack Holt, the Mirror has a small spinnaker to make racing more interesting.

***Right:** The simple, robust but sporty Topper is often used as a race trainer for single-handers but is just as attractive when used as a straightforward fun-boat.*

Topper

Length overall	11ft 2in	(3.4m)
Weight	135lb	(61.2kg)
Sail area	56ft^2	(5.2m^2)

Designed in the first instance as a one-person fun-boat, the Topper has become, in addition, a popular race-trainer for teenagers as it has sufficient sail area to have a lively planing performance. Construction in injection-moulded polypropylene makes it extremely durable and the fittings are also strong and simple. Designed by Ian Proctor, the Topper was a successful attempt to make a small boat into a competitively priced, factory product and there are plenty of these around as a result.

Pirat (Dutch)

Length overall	7ft 10in	(2.38m)
Weight	66lb	(29.96kg)
Sail area	35ft^2	(3.25m^2)

One of two dinghies of this name, the Dutch Pirat is a sensible little, flat-bottomed children's boat with a single lug-sail. Once very common in European waters, it has been replaced in many cases by the Optimist, which has a great following internationally.

Pirat (German)

Length overall	16ft 4in	(4.97m)
Weight	375lb	(170.25kg)
Sail area	108ft^2	(10.04m^2)

One of the largest dinghies to be considered a trainer, the German Pirat is a sturdy dinghy with conventional sloop rig big enough to allow the teaching of adults. It is also much used for junior racing in Germany and other European countries.

V–J

Length overall	11ft 6in	(3.5m)
Weight	No minimum weight	
Sail area	118ft^2	(10.97m^2)

Showing a completely different attitude to junior sailing, the Australian VJ is a very fast and sporty lightweight dinghy with a big sail area and bowsprit that introduces many young Australians to racing. Unlike European trainers which emphasize safety, the VJ emphasizes skill and excitement.

SINGLE-HANDED DINGHIES

Sunfish

Length overall	13ft 10in	(4.2m)
Weight	126lb	(57kg)
Sail area	86ft²	(8m²)

This rather crude 'sailing surfboard' type dinghy turns out to be probably the most popular small boat in the world, with around 200,000 sold. Intended purely as a leisure craft, it is nevertheless raced keenly, especially in the warm parts of the USA.

Laser

Length overall	13ft 10in	(4.2m)
Weight	130lb	(60kg)
Sail area	76ft²	(7.06m²)

Designed by Canadian Bruce Kirby, the Laser has become the most popular one-man racing dinghy in the world, with large fleets in virtually every country. The great secret of the Laser is that it is simply but well made with every detail carefully considered. A fast and very exhilarating dinghy in fresh winds, it demands a lot of skill and technique to race successfully. The Laser pioneered the concept of a 'manufacturer's class', in which administration was provided as a kind of after-sales service. It also eliminated the need for the measurement and certification process required for most racing dinghies, as every purchaser of a new Laser is assured of a class-legal boat, in every respect ready to race. Although it has some opponents, this system simplifies ownership.

International Moth

Length overall	11ft	(3.35m)
Weight	None specified, typically around 50lb (22.7kg)	
Sail area	85ft²	(7.9m²)

The International Moth is a development class in which complete freedom of shape is allowed within a fixed overall length. There is a maximum sail area but no minimum weight and this results in a remarkably fast little dinghy. The Moth offers a good opportunity for young designers to try out their ideas at low cost and Moth enthusiasts may change the hull of their dinghy quite frequently while retaining the rig and fittings. There used to be a split between European Moths, which tended to be narrow skiffs, and the Australian type, wide scows which were superior in strong winds. A compromise type, consisting of a relatively narrow hull with wide wings to assist sitting out, proved superior to either of the earlier models. There is also a one-design Moth known as the *Europe* or *Europa Moth*, which is a popular one-person racing dinghy that suits a lighter helmsman than the Laser.

Solo

Overall length	12ft 5in	(3.8m)
Weight	200lb	(90.7kg)
Sail area	90ft²	(8.36m²)

Designed for amateur construction by Jack Holt, the Solo is more often built of glass fibre nowadays. Popular in Britain and Holland, the Solo is slightly bigger, heavier and more stable than the Laser. It has an unusual rig with a fully-battened sail set on a stayed mast.

OK

Overall length	13ft 1½in	(4m)
Weight	158lb	(72kg)
Sail area	89ft²	(8.3m²)

Designed by Knud Olsen as a trainer for the Olympic Finn, the OK developed into a racing class on its own merits. The main similarity to the Finn lies in the bendy, unstayed rig but the hull is quite different, being of fairly lightweight, hard-chine ply construction, whereas the Finn is heavy and rounded. A fast and lively dinghy but one which — like several others — suffered from the impact of the Laser, which has been dominant in this market for some years.

Finn (see Olympic Classes)

***Top:** The Laser is easily the most popular single-handed racing dinghy in the world. An important part of its appeal is its extreme simplicity, with hardly any expensive fittings, and the fact that all Lasers are guaranteed to be the same, so racing is a real test of helmsmen rather than of boats.*

***Above:** The Solo, designed by Jack Holt for* Yachting World, *is a single-handed racing dinghy. It has the unusual combination of a stayed mast and fully-battened sail.*

Contender

Overall length	16ft	(4.87m)
Weight	228lb	(103.4kg)
Sail area	112ft²	(10.4m²)

Designed by Australian Bob Miller (alias Ben Lexcen) for an IYRU competition aimed at finding a replacement for the Finn, the Contender is a very fast and demanding single-handed trapeze dinghy. Having chosen the Contender and given it International status, the IYRU then got cold feet and never did replace the Finn. A big single-hander, looking rather similar in shape to the Flying Dutchman, the Contender places on the helmsman a high demand for athleticism and co-ordination. Although steering from the trapeze is quite easy and pleasant to windward, a fast reach can be extremely tricky. Raced at a very competitive level in a number of countries, the Contender is the boat for the single-handed racer who wants to take on a really challenging boat.

International 10 Square Metre Canoe

Overall length	17ft	(5.2m)
Weight	138lb	(63kg)
Sail area	107ft²	(10m²)

Fastest of all single-hulled small boats, the Canoe gives the impression of being impossibly difficult to sail but is in reality no more than very difficult! It is in a sense a 'one-hulled catamaran', as it consists of a very slim, easily-driven hull which is given great power by the helmsman's weight on the end of a long, sliding seat. In addition to steering and balancing a boat with very little hull stability, the helmsman has a full sloop rig to look after. The hull of the canoe is completely sealed so that recovery from capsize can be quick. The narrow hull of the canoe penetrates waves well and the boat's speed to windward compared with a conventional dinghy needs to be seen to be believed.

Below: *The International 10sq m Canoe is a racing boat for the connoisseur. One of the fastest of all small boats, it is sailed by one person who sits out on the end of a long sliding seat to give the narrow hull stability.*

TWO-PERSON DINGHIES

As there are literally hundreds of designs which fit into this category, it is only possible to list the best-known ones. The reason there are so many is that the category covers everything from homely knockabouts to high-performance racing dinghies. In between are many designs with a dual-purpose character. An example might be the well-known Enterprise, which many people race very keenly while others merely use it for family fun sailing.

Albacore

Overall length	15ft	(4.57m)
Weight	260lb	(118kg)
Sail area	125ft²	(11.62m²)

One of a series of dinghies designed by Uffa Fox for Fairey Marine, and built originally in hot-moulded wood, the Albacore is one of two still built. A sturdy dinghy that lasts for many years and has a good all-round performance, it has a fairly small but very loyal following.

Australian 12 and 18ft skiffs

The two sizes of Australian skiff are among the fastest single-hulled boats of their size in the world. They have no minimum weight and unlimited sail area, and are allowed as many or as few crew as they wish. The 18ft skiff is sailed by semi-professional crews in Sydney Harbour, where their races are a great public spectacle. Formerly, they used to carry up to five crew, all on trapezes, in order to balance the vast sail-plains used. Nowadays, with lighter construction and more efficient rigs, the 18ft skiffs have three crew, all on trapezes, standing on extension frames which project from the gunwhale. They have a variety of masts and rigs for different wind strengths. It is very interesting to see how an almost totally free rule such as this one has led to a very expensive, supercharged style of racing boat.

Cherub

Overall length	12ft	(3.65m)
Weight	150lb	(68kg)
Sail area	140/115ft²	(13.02/10.69m²)

One of the few New Zealand dinghies to gain recognition abroad, the Cherub is a very lively, lightweight design by John Spencer which includes a large, flat-cut reaching spinnaker in its sail-plan. Extremely fast in fresh winds, the Cherub needs to be sailed with great skill and co-ordination. New Zealand and Australian dinghy sailors pioneered the use of large, flat spinnakers set on long poles so they could be virtually extra-large headsails. Gybeing a Cherub calls for a well-developed technique.

Enterprise

Overall length	10ft 3in	(3.12m)
Weight	250lb	(113.5kg)
Sail area	113ft²	(10.50m²)

The first British dinghy to be sponsored by a national newspaper, the Jack Holt-designed Enterprise has survived a lot longer than the *News Chronicle*. Intended originally for amateur construction in plywood, but now universally built in glass fibre, the Enterprise is still one of the most popular boats for inland sailing due to its relatively light weight and big sail area.

Fireball

Overall length	16ft 2in	(4.93m)
Weight	176lb	(79.9kg)
Sail area	123/140ft²	(11.44/13.02m²)

Designed by Peter Milne, the Fireball is a fast and exciting racing boat with a scow hull-form. The trapeze and big spinnaker give the crew plenty to do. Produced in both glass fibre and wood, a number are still built each year by amateurs, using the stitch and tape method.

Firefly

Overall length	12ft	(3.65m)
Weight	160lb	(72.64kg)
Sail area	90ft²	(8.36m²)

Smallest of the Uffa Fox/Fairey Marine dinghies, the Firefly was intended as a one-design version of the National 12ft dinghy. Thanks to its sturdy hull construction, the Firefly became a favourite for school and college fleets. Now built in glass fibre.

Flying Dutchman

(see Olympic classes)

GP14

Overall length	14ft	(4.26m)
Weight	285lb	(129.4kg)
Sail area	122ft²	(11.35m²)

One of the best-known of Jack Holt's 'Build her Yourself' designs, the General Purpose 14ft (4.26m) was one of the most popular dinghies in the late 1950s and early 1960s, when thousands were built in school and college workshops. Although not as popular now, the GP has been kept up to date with increased sail area and modern construction. A sturdy, reliable dinghy which can be used both for racing or cruising, the GP14 has a very long life and holds its value well as a result. It was one of a number of dinghies originally launched by *Yachting World* to satisfy a demand for a versatile 14 footer.

Below: The Merlin Rocket is one of the 'development' dinghy classes, in which any hull design is permitted within certain criteria. No trapeze is permitted, which has resulted in the boat becoming extremely wide in order to make the best use of the crew's weight in providing stability.

Heron

Overall length	11ft 3in	(3.43m)
Weight	144lb	(65.4kg)
Sail area	70ft^2	(6.51m^2)

One of the first dinghies designed specifically for car-topping, the Heron has a rig which can all be fitted into the length of the hull. A modest but reliable performer that looks a little like a smaller GP14.

Hornet

Overall length	16ft	(4.87m)
Weight	276lb	(125.3kg)
Sail area	143/130ft^2	(13.29/12.09m^2)

Designed as a fast, sporty two-man racing dinghy suitable for amateur construction, the Hornet was one of Jack Holt's best designs and gave a large number of people their first introduction to high-performance dinghy sailing. Originally fitted with a sliding seat for the crew, this was later discarded in favour of the easier-to-manage trapeze system. Similarly, the fully-battened mainsail has been replaced by a conventional one and a larger jib added to boost performance.

International 14ft Dinghy

Overall length	14ft	(4.26m)
Weight	200lb	(90.7kg)
Sail area	190/190ft^2	(17.65/17.65m^2)

The first small boat to earn the title 'International', the 14ft dinghy has had quite a chequered history. In its early days, during the 1930s, it was in the premier dinghy racing class and was largely responsible for creating an entirely new breed of skilled dinghy-racing helmsmen and crews. Its rules, which permitted a wide variety of hull shapes, allowed Uffa Fox to develop the first effective planing hull. With its undecked hull and big sail area, it was always a demanding dinghy to sail. In the post-war era, the class gradually got left behind through failure to accept sensible modern developments such as self-bailers and trapezes but, instead, became a kind of 'vintage sports-car' class with superbly built, very expensive and thoroughly out-of-date designs.

In the 1980s, the class had a complete change of heart when trapezes became allowed for both helmsman and crew and a dramatic reduction in minimum weight transformed the boat into a really fast, tricky skiff along Australian lines. Now, it is again one of the most important classes in which ideas for design and construction can be tried and crews tested to the limit.

Korsar

Overall length	16ft 5in	(5m)
Weight	220lb	(99.88kg)
Sail area	158ft^2	(14.69m^2)

Popular German dinghy which is often considered a junior Flying Dutchman. Modern in design, weight and sail area, the Korsar is a good if not spectacular performer.

Lark

Overall length	13ft 4in	(4.06m)
Weight	220lb	(99.88kg)
Sail area	202ft^2	(18.78m^2)

Designed by Mike Jackson as a budget 'club racer,' the Lark is an excellent all-rounder for those who prefer a straightforward dinghy without the added complication of spinnaker and trapeze. Falling between the National 12ft and the Merlin Rocket in size, the Lark has a one-design hull shape which does not date. Considered ideal as a husband-and-wife racing dinghy.

Merlin Rocket

Overall length	14ft	(4.26m)
Weight	216lb	(98.06kg)
Sail area	190ft^2	(17.65m^2)

Conceived as a cheaper alternative to the International 14ft Dinghy, the Merlin is also a development class in which many varieties of hull shape can be tried. As the trapeze is not allowed, the modern Merlin is designed to the maximum permitted beam, so as to give the crew as much sitting out power as possible. This also gives the boats a rather odd, dish-like appearance. Very keenly raced, especially by those who are interested in the technical side of sailing.

National 12ft Dinghy

Overall length	12ft	(3.65m)
Weight	150lb	(68kg)
Sail area	90ft^2	(8.36m^2)

Created in 1936, as a cheap, two-man development dinghy class, it has been one in which a remarkable number of top sailors have had their introduction to racing. Sensible, progressive rule changes have steadily reduced the minimum weight and allowed a change from the original clinker wood construction to modern glass fibre, ply or moulded wood methods. Because of its small size, the National requires a fairly light crew and many of the most successful teams consist of a man as helmsman and woman as crew. The championship of the National 12ft Class, known as Burton Week after the principal trophy, is always one of the top dinghy events of the year and on the 50th anniversary championship in 1986, the first boat built to the class rules, *Gypsy*, sail number N1, was a keen competitor.

Scorpion

Overall length	14ft	(4.26m)
Weight	180lb	(81.72kg)
Sail area	227ft^2	(21.1m^2)

Sporty, non-trapeze dinghy with a rather narrow hull-shape.

Snipe

Overall length	15ft 6in	(4.72m)
Weight	381lb	(172.9kg)
Sail area	115ft^2	(10.69m^2)

The first ever dinghy designed for amateur construction, the Snipe is still keenly raced in some parts of the world in spite of being very heavy and undercanvassed compared to modern dinghies. It was designed in 1931 by William Crosby, editor of *Rudder* magazine who had the prototype built by a 14-year-old boy to prove it was within the scope of the average handyman; one of the first 'hard-chine' small boats.

***Above:** The sturdy Wayfarer is one of the most versatile of dinghies, being equally suited to racing or cruising. Thanks to its stability and robust construction it is frequently used by sailing schools.*

Wayfarer

Overall length	15ft 10in	(4.82m)
Weight	372lb	(168.8kg)
Sail area	296ft^2	(27.53m^2)

Most versatile of all dinghies, the Wayfarer, designed by Ian Proctor, is raced, cruised, is an ideal picnic boat and a favourite for teaching newcomers. Sturdy, stable and well-mannered, the Wayfarer has made some remarkable long-distance passages in the hands of enthusiasts and is found in the fleets of very many sailing schools. Although it is rather heavy for racing, there are keen fleets in a number of locations.

420

Overall length	13ft 8in	(4.16m)
Weight	220lb	(99.88kg)
Sail area	207ft^2	(19.25m^2)

A French design, the 420 is often used as a youth racing class because it is a good trainer for the Olympic 470. Rather undercanvassed because of its training role, the 420 is a sparkling performer in a strong wind.

470 (see Olympic classes)

5-0-5

Overall length	16ft 6in	(5.05m)
Weight	280lb	(127kg)
Sail area	146/250ft^2	(13.6/23.3m^2)

A real man's racing dinghy, the 'Five-oh' started life as the Coronet, designed by John Westell. The French Caneton Association decided they needed a completely new boat and asked Westell to adapt the Coronet slightly to their requirement. The result was a dinghy of impressive power and speed, thanks to its large sail area and wide beam. After the Flying Dutchman, the 5-0-5 is the top performing two-man dinghy and has a strong international following.

2882
K-2
92
K-2922

KEELBOATS

Day-racing keelboats were once the core of the sport of yacht racing but suffered a long, slow decline as cruising yachts and cruiser-racers gained in popularity. Having reached nearly rock-bottom, the popularity of racing keelboats is now returning and classes thought to be completely moribund, such as the International 6-metre and 8-metre classes, are now being raced again.

The disadvantage of a keelboat is that it has to be kept in the water, on a mooring, and this leads to more expense, more maintenance and more commitment generally on the part of the owner. On the other hand, keelboats tend to have a very long life, can be extremely satisfying to sail, do not normally capsize and can be raced with equal success by man or woman, young or old.

It used to be the case that every major yacht club had its own keelboat class and some very venerable ones still survive. For instance, the Seabird Half-rater Class, which sails on the English north-west coast, is more than a century old, with some of the original boats still sailing. Several of the Solent keelboat classes date from around the turn of the century and there are more like them on the east coast.

Attempts to foster international classes of racing keelboats have always proved up-hill work but the Star is certainly the most widely distributed keelboat, followed by the Olympic Soling Class. At club level, the 17ft Squib has been very successful while the hybrid dinghy-with-a-keel, the Flying 15 has always been a popular boat, especially as it is small and lightweight enough for it to be kept out of the water.

Keelboats such as the Squib or Flying 15 are one-designs with just a small degree of freedom in the layout. Some, such as the Dragon, have a one-design hull and rig but fairly wide discretion on layout, while all the boats built to the International Rule are free designs within a measurement rule.

In theory, any number of classes are possible within the International Rule, and yachts of up to 23-metres rating have been built in the past. The ones used today are the 5.5, 6, 8 and 12-metre classes. The 12-metre was used in every America's Cup match from 1958 to 1987.

Whereas most dinghies and indeed most cruisers date fairly rapidly, some of the older keelboats have a classic, ageless quality. A good example is the International Dragon, designed in 1927, which seems to be most people's idea of a pretty boat. It is also a good example of how sensible modernization of construction, layout, fittings and rig have kept alive an old design.

Many keelboat classes are still local in character, so only those with an international following are listed.

Above: The start of a race for Dragons. This traditional three-man keelboat has enjoyed a considerable revival in popularity in recent years, following a dip in fortunes after it was dropped from the Olympics. The classic Scandinavian design of the Dragon is as attractive now as when it first appeared in 1927.

International Dragon

Overall length	29ft 2in	(8.88m)
Beam	6ft 5in	(1.95m)
Draught	3ft 11in	(1.19m)
Weight	3792lb	(1721kg)
Sail area	286ft^2	(26.59m^2)

Designed by Johan Anker of Norway, the Dragon was used in the Olympic games from 1948 to 1972. After a decline, it has recovered well and is now a top international racing keelboat once again, with fleets particularly strong in Germany, Denmark and Great Britain.

Raced by a crew of three, it is a heavy, narrow boat with a very rounded entry which makes it difficult to sail well through waves. Good balance is essential and a proper understanding of rig tuning is required in order to achieve this. Glass fibre hull construction has helped to reduce maintenance costs but it is still a fairly expensive boat.

International E22

Overall length	30ft 6in	(9.30m)
Weight	3360lb	(1524kg)
Sail area	290/398ft^2	(27/37m^2)

Designed by 'Skip' Etchells in response to an IYRU competition for a new Olympic keelboat, the E22 was the pick of the bunch after the smaller Soling, which was the design chosen. The E22 is light for its size and capable of planing in strong winds. It is a faster, more modern design than the Dragon and the class aims to give first rate racing while keeping costs at a minimum. Around 600 have been built.

Opposite: For some, the idea of racing in a boat that could capsize at any moment is simply not attractive and a solid lump of metal below the hull is the reassurance that this will not happen. Racing keelboats range from huge and very expensive yachts such as the 12-metre down to the Flying 15, pictured here, which is virtually a dinghy with a keel.

Above: This historic picture shows a young Prince Charles sailing a Flying 15 with the designer Uffa Fox as crew. In the background, Prince Philip sails his own Flying 15, Coweslip. *History records that Prince Charles was the more successful of the two in this particular race.*

International Flying 15

Overall length	20ft	(6.09m)
Weight	725lb	(329kg)
Sail area	150/150ft²	(13.95/13.95m²)

Uffa Fox designed the Flying 15 when he felt he was getting too 'broad in the beam' for dinghy racing, and it is really a big planing dinghy with a ballast keel of 400lb (181.6kg) to make sure it cannot capsize. With a generous sail area and big spinnaker, the crew have plenty to keep them busy, especially as no trapeze is allowed. More than 2,600 have been built and the class is as popular as ever it was, especially in those clubs which race on fairly open water.

Star and Soling (see Olympic classes)

Tempest

Overall length	22ft	(6.7m)
Weight	1034lb	(469.4kg)
Ballast	495lb	(224.7kg)
Sail area	248ft²	(23.06m²)

Designed in response to an IYRU competition for a Star replacement, the Tempest, which was designed by Ian Proctor, has something of the same character as the Flying 15, only more so. It is a big, fast dinghy-with-a-keel but unlike the Flying 15, the crew is allowed a trapeze. Having been chosen for this role, the Tempest was used in the Olympics just twice, in 1972 and 1976, and then dropped as it was said that it did not enjoy support from sufficient nations. Since then it has declined rapidly in numbers but, like the Dragon, might eventually recover from the trauma and once again become a popular boat in its own right.

MULTIHULLS

Pacific islanders were the first multihull enthusiasts. Their development of outrigger canoes was purely practical because on the one hand reef islands demand boats of shallow draft, and on the other the islanders had no metals and therefore were prevented from developing boats with keels, even had they wanted to. All the early explorers mentioned how fast and seaworthy the native outriggers were but it took a long time for them to become accepted in northern waters.

The advantage of the multihull is that it gets its stability from width rather than weight and its disadvantage is that it is not self-righting from a capsize.

In 1876, Nathanael Herreshof developed a racing catamaran 25ft (7.60m) in length, but as *Amaryllis* tended to beat much larger yachts by an embarrassing margin this was considered 'unfair' and Herreshof was persuaded to drop his experiments. During the 1950s, the Prout brothers of Canvey Island, Essex, who were Olympic canoeists, hit on the idea of lashing two canoes together and fixing a mast in the middle. After various experiments they established a European style of catamaran with symmetrical, round-bottom hulls with centreboards, and their Shearwater design was the first to become established as a racing class.

For once alert to future possibilities, the International Yacht Racing Union established a series of restricted multihull classes, limited by length and sail area, and these are lettered A-D. After a competition, the most outstanding B Class catamaran, the Tornado, was selected as an International Class and later chosen for the Olympics. A similar exercise was carried out in the search for an International A Class Catamaran but, unfortunately, the one chosen — the Australian-designed Australis — has not caught on. Nevertheless, it should be said that there is plenty of racing in a variety of classes that fit into A Class.

The C Class catamarans are used for the International Catamaran Challenge Trophy, the so-called 'Little America's Cup'. The early years of this competition were dominated by the Hellcat series of designs by Roderick Macalpine-Downie, culminating in the famous wing-masted *Lady Helmsman*. Later, it was won by Denmark, then the USA, then Australia. Catamarans built to this class are highly sophisticated and are the fastest small boats in existence. The D Class formula has never caught on and only a few catamarans of this size have been built.

The reason that catamarans are so much faster than one-hulled boats is that their great width gives them much greater initial stability and hence sail-carrying power. If a catamaran is allowed to heel too far, it will tip right over and capsize but the same applies to unballasted dinghies so this is not a disadvantage in a day-racing catamaran. The worry about capsizing is, however, a very real one in the case of cruising and offshore racing multihulls.

As catamarans are so much faster than other small boats, they tend to be in the forefront of development of aerodynamic masts and rigs and, specifically, ones that are able to operate at a higher lift-to-drag ratio than conventional masts and sails. With this in view, streamlined, rotating masts and fully-battened sails are common on racing catamarans, in an effort to make the rig more wing-like. For really advanced racing craft, such as the C Class, wing masts are usual and these have also been developed for offshore racing multihulls.

As well as being expensive, wing masts have the disadvantage of being very impractical. It is not advisable to leave a boat unattended with a wing mast rigged, as any reasonable strength of wind is likely to send it sailing off on its own. This means that day-racing boats with wing masts have to put them up every time the boat is to be used and take them down again afterwards. An offshore multihull with wing rig can find that, even with all the sail taken down, in strong winds there is still a dangerous amount of power developed by the spar alone.

Multihulls require a different racing technique to other small boats right from the start. Not so quick at tacking but much better at lying stopped, catamarans usually line up for the start in quite an orderly fashion compared to dinghies and then shoot off with instant acceleration as soon as the starting

The IYRU Catamaran Classes

Class		
A Class (single-handed)	Max length	17ft 9in (5.48m) (excluding rudder)
	Max beam	7ft 5in (2.30m)
	Max sail area	150ft² (13.95m²)
B Class (two-handed)	Max length	19ft 9in (6.04m) (excluding rudder)
	Max beam	10ft (3m)
	Max sail area	235ft² (21.83m²)
C Class (two-handed)	Max length	24ft 9in (7.54m) (excluding rudder)
	Max beam	14ft (4.26m)
	Max sail area	300ft² (27.90m²)
D Class (three-handed)	Max sail area	500ft² (46.40m²)
	(no other restrictions)	

Below: *The Tornado is the only multihull to be used in the Olympics and is a very high-performance two-man boat. Originally built of 'tortured' ply, most modern Tornados are of glass fibre sandwich construction. The mast rotates to give a smooth airflow on to the lee side of the sail.*

Below: The Dart aims to give the thrilling performance of a catamaran at a relatively affordable price. The Dart has no centreboards and an unusual rig with no main-boom, both these features being simplifications in order to keep down the cost of manufacture.

gun goes. Because one can always get more speed by bearing off, it is easy to lose track of the true wind direction and go thundering off on a reach when you should be beating to windward. The skill is to judge the 'Vmg' (that is, the speed made good to windward) to a nicety, with the right combination of pointing and speed.

Fast multihulls never run dead downwind because it is their slowest point of sailing. Much faster progress downwind can be achieved by sailing a series of broad reaches in order to keep the apparent wind and therefore the speed up. This 'tacking downwind' is a highly-developed skill of its own.

Catamaran enthusiasts always face some difficulty in building up good racing fleets, because their boats tend to be a little more expensive than a dinghy of equivalent size and take up more space, both in the dinghy park and afloat. Because they sail so much faster, they need special courses and this is an extra burden for the race officer. The compensation is the sheer joy of flying across the water with a seemingly effortless speed that is never achieved by any other kind of boat.

C Class

Overall length (inc. rudders)	25ft	(7.62m)
Weight	No limit	
Sail area (inc. mast and boom)	$300ft^2$	$(27.9m^2)$

Although only a few dozen of these boats have ever been built, they are the most highly-developed of all small sailing craft. Ultra lightweight construction is one area of development but more important is the rig where the designer is allowed complete freedom within a maximum area. The result has been increasingly sophisticated solid or semi-solid aerofoils in which flaps and slots are used to achieve camber and twist control. The difficulty lies in making an effective, adjustable aerofoil without letting the weight become excessive.

The reason that all this effort is poured into the C Class is purely due to the International Catamaran Challenge Trophy, currently held by Australia (1987). There is virtually no racing suitable for the C Class outside this arena.

As an indication of the performance of a modern C Class, a race was recently held in Sydney Harbour in which one sailed against a selection of 18ft skiffs, generally held to be the fastest of all dinghies. The catamaran completed a 15 mile course in about half the time taken by the fastest skiff.

Dart

Overall length	18ft	(5.49m)
Weight	295lb	(134kg)
Sail area	$173ft^2$	$(16.1m^2)$

Designed by Rodney March, who was also responsible for the Tornado, the Dart is the most successful, strict one-design racing catamaran. Cleverly designed for both simplicity and high-performance, the Dart has no centreboard and the mainsail has no boom, reducing cost and complexity in both cases. It can be sailed by either one or two crew and it offers exciting performance without calling for a lot of technical expertise on the part of the crew. There is a small sister, the 14ft Spark and a big brother, the 22ft Stampede but neither of these have managed to achieve the popularity enjoyed by the Dart.

Hobie 14 and Hobie 16

Overall length	14ft (4.26m)	16ft (4.87m)
Weight	240lb (109kg)	340lb (154kg)
Sail area	118ft^2 (10.97m^2)	218ft^2 (19.6m^2)

Californian Hobie Alter, saw a market for a catamaran that could be launched from an open beach — something that is very tricky for a boat with centreboards and fixed rudders. He therefore designed a 14ft (4.26m) cat with very deep, 'banana' hulls that had sufficient grip on the water not to need boards, and with rudders that fold back if they hit the bottom. The crew sit on a raised platform to keep them reasonably dry. Though not a particularly fast boat, the Hobie 14 is a lot of fun to sail and can be mistreated fairly abominably without wrecking it. These qualities were sufficient to make it the best selling of all small multihulls.

The Hobie 16 follows the same ideas but has a much more sophisticated rig, giving it a genuinely high performance, especially as both helmsman and crew can use trapezes. It is a tricky boat to sail well due to its tendency to 'trip' over the lee hull if pressed too hard. There is also a conventionally-shaped Hobie 18, which has not had quite the same impact as the smaller boats.

Shearwater

Overall length	16ft 6in	(5.05m)
Weight	308lb	(139.8kg)
Sail area	160ft^2	(14.88m^2)

The Shearwater Mk III, designed and built by the Prout brothers of Canvey Island, was the first catamaran to become a successful racing class. Today, it looks heavy and narrow and inevitably, therefore, has been superseded by more modern designs, but it was an important pioneer that made nonsense of the belief that catamarans did not handle well enough to be raced seriously.

Tornado (see Olympic classes)

Unicorn

Overall length	18ft	(5.49m)
Weight	200lb	(90.7kg)
Sail area	150ft^2	(13.95m^2)

John Mazotti designed the Unicorn as a one-design within A Class, and it has become a popular racing class with the advantage of being able to race either as a one-design or in competition with other A Class cats. Very fine and quite delicate compared to a production class such as the Dart, the Unicorn is more of a specialist boat and extremely fast when sailed by an expert.

THE OLYMPIC CLASSES

During the Olympiads following the Second World War, the classes used in the Olympic regatta changed quite often and there was even a policy that at least one class be replaced every four years. This policy has now been abandoned in favour of stability and since 1976 the only change has been the addition of a sailboard. The Olympic programme is arranged in terms of events rather than classes, so it is possible to add to the events without changing the classes; that is, from 1988 onwards there is a women's two-crew dinghy event in addition to a mixed two-crew dinghy event — both sailed in 470s. In future, there could be a women's sailboard event.

The events and classes currently used are as follows, with all being open to either men or women except the women's two-crew dinghy.

Event	Class
Sailboard	A specially-made Division II sailboard
Single-handed dinghy	Finn
Women's 2-crew dinghy	470
2 crew dinghy	470
Large 2-crew dinghy	Flying Dutchman
Catamaran (2 crew)	Tornado
2-crew keelboat	Star
3-crew keelboat	Soling

Sailboard

Having made the courageous decision to include a sailboard in the Olympics, the IYRU has had great difficulty both in choosing which one to use and in providing a suitable competition. It was found very early in the development of sailboard racing that lighter sailors have the advantage and therefore fleets are usually broken down into weight groups. This idea was not acceptable to the Olympic authorities because it would have meant more than one set of medals — yet more 'events'. So the first time a sailboard was used — at Long Beach in 1984 — a single group of any weight sailed on a production Windglider board. The Gold Medal winner was the very light Dutch teenager, Stephan van den Berg.

IYRU Division II Sailboard

Overall length	12ft 10in	(3.9m)
Weight	39.7lb	(18kg)
Sail area	67.8ft^2	(6.3m^2)

In an effort to avoid the problems that had been associated with choosing one particular production board in 1984, the IYRU decided that for 1988 a board from within Division II

Above: *The IYRU Division II sailboard is the most recent addition to the list of Olympic craft. A drawback is that the class strongly favours sailors of light weight so that tall, thin competitors tend to be the most successful.*

Opposite: *A highly sophisticated and technically demanding dinghy, the Flying Dutchman represents for many the epitome of an Olympic dinghy. However, it is very expensive — which tends to reduce the number of countries that enter for this class.*

would be selected and then specially manufactured in Korea for use at this one event. The thinking behind this was that designs do not vary much within Division II, so it should be possible to train on any board that fits these rules. Once again, there was only a single weight class so the winner was another lightweight person.

Finn

Overall length	14ft 9in	(4.5m)
Weight	319lb	(144.7kg)
Sail area	110ft^2	(10.2m^2)

First selected for the Olympics in 1952, the Finn has kept its place as the single-handed dinghy mainly through political inertia within the IYRU. Although it is an old-fashioned design, it is a very challenging boat to sail and winning a medal in it is a truly Olympian task. Heavy, narrow and without a trapeze, the Finn calls for a lot of old-fashioned muscle and hard work but, at the same time, a finely-honed racing skill. The unstayed una rig is unlike other dinghies and calls for a long training in order to get the best out of it.

Modern rigs give more help to a lighter man, so it is not strictly necessary to be a 7ft (2.13m) tall gorilla to sail a Finn, as it used to be, but a very high degree of physical fitness is always required.

470

Overall length	15ft 5in	(4.7m)
Weight	264lb	(120kg)
Sail area	135/140ft^2	(12.5/13.02m^2)

A modern, glass fibre dinghy designed in France by Andre Cornou, the 470 was adopted in order to make the Olympics accessible to a younger, lighter and less wealthy dinghy sailor than the one who sails a Flying Dutchman. It has been successful insofar as it calls for a lightish crew and emphasizes agility and co-ordination.

Problems have centred around the construction of the boat, which tends not to have a long life in top competition. Weak class rules make it difficult to control weight distribution properly and it has taken a number of years to get the boat sufficiently tightly-controlled to fulfil its design objective. However, it is the most popular Olympic class and has succeeded in widening the entry list, which was beginning to become dangerously small by 1972.

Flying Dutchman

Overall length	19ft 10in	(6.05m)
Weight	365lb	(165.6kg)
Sail area	200/190ft^2	(18.6/17.65m^2)

A big, fast, stable dinghy that has been in the Olympic fleet since 1960. The FD requires a great deal of technical expertise and is also very expensive — this was why the less elitist 470 was added as an alternative. The class rules are quite permissive in respect of construction, layout, fittings and so on; as a result there is a considerable 'arms race', with a lot of money being expended on the latest technology.

Because it is such a big boat, it is an advantage to have a big crew and some immensely tall men are to be found at the sharp end of Flying Dutchmen. The large, beamy hull gives a rather dull ride but it is very sensitive to small tuning changes, which is why every possible adjustment is found on these boats. Although very specialized, the Flying Dutchman provides the sort of challenge which calls for a special combination of technical and sailing skills.

I
ITC
97
FD
I·10

Below: *Seeming ready to leap right out of the water, a Tornado catamaran speeds across a windswept sea. The tactics of racing these boats is very different from normal dinghy-racing, as they are slow to tack but much faster through the water. Down-wind tactics are particularly interesting as it is much quicker to sail a series of broad reaches and gybes rather than a direct, down-wind course.*

Tornado

Overall length	20ft	(6.09m)
Weight	279lb	(126.5kg)
Sail area	235ft^2	(21.83m^2)

Designed by Rodney March, the Tornado represented the 'state of the art' in multihull design in 1967, when it won an IYRU competition for a B Class catamaran. The very slim hulls were originally built using the 'tortured ply' method, in which large sheets of plywood were forced into a limited double curvature, giving a light, stiff, stressed skin. Modern Tornados are built using foam sandwich glass fibre construction compressed into moulds by vacuum bags, and they are pretty expensive as a result. The rig, with its streamlined, rotating mast, fully-battened mainsail and small jib came straight from C Class experience in the 1960s, and is a very powerful, reliable power unit.

Easily the fastest of the Olympic classes, the Tornado is a man-sized boat for two to handle and calls for a lot of strength and fitness. Because of its great speed, the Tornado requires a special extra-large course with longer reaches, and this is an extra imposition on the already hard-pressed organizers of the Olympic regatta.

Above: At Olympic level, there is very little difference in the speed of a fleet of Stars. This places a tremendous emphasis on tactics and a premium on handling, as the Star's complex rig has to be tuned with great accuracy.

Star

Overall length	22ft 8½in	(6.9m)
Weight	1480lb	(671.3kg)
Sail area	280ft²	(26m²)

The enigmatic Star was designed in 1911, and has been in the Olympics, off and on, since 1932. It has been modernized repeatedly, so that only the hull shape remains original. Anyone who sails a Star will confirm that, although so seemingly antiquated, it is a superbly sensitive boat with unrivalled racing qualities. It is especially strongly supported in its country of origin, the USA, where the championships of the class are fiercely contested. The difficulty of sailing the Star lies in controlling its very large sail area, which is set on an extremely light, bendy mast. Rather surprisingly, the Star has never been fitted with a spinnaker, although the mainsail is so large and the boom so low that the crew is not short of work on the downwind legs of a race.

Soling

Overall length	26ft 9in	(8.15m)
Weight	2280lb	(1034kg)
Sail area	233/255ft²	(21.6/23.7m²)

Designed by Norwegian Jan Linge, the Soling has been one of the IYRU's success stories. Produced by a competition to find a new 3-crew keelboat, it has settled down into a very competitive, well-controlled racing boat. It is also a well-engineered boat, designed for glass fibre construction from the outset, and has had very little in the way of structural problems. Good rules forbid the use of exotic materials and keep the costs reasonable.

Although quite fast, the speed difference between boats is not great and this places a strong emphasis on tactics and handling. To keep the crew out of mischief there is a choice of two spinnakers, which can be set depending on conditions. Racing at Olympic level in Solings is exceptionally close and can be fiercely competitive.

OFFSHORE RACING YACHTS

Jolie Brise, winner of the first Fastnet Race, in 1925, was not really a yacht at all, she was a Le Havre pilot cutter. This was a case of history repeating itself, as the earliest inshore racing yachts had been adapted working boat types which, under the pressure of competition, soon developed into pure racing machines. In the same way, the working-boat era in offshore racing was swept away for ever in 1931, when *Dorade*, designed by Olin Stephens, introduced the idea of a yacht designed purely for offshore racing.

By today's standards, *Dorade* was heavy and moderate, and she was comfortably fitted out but a whole generation ahead of the *Jolie Brise* concept. The development of offshore racing design goes in cycles; a leap forward is followed by a period of stability during which only improvements to detail are made and then there is another inspired leap forward. The *Dorade* era lasted a particularly long time and yachts being built right up to 1960 showed only detail developments.

Dorade was more or less a metre-boat type, adapted for use as an offshore racer, as Stephens had previously designed a 6-metre. Of medium to heavy displacement, she had a relatively narrow beam and a canoe body that blended very smoothly into the keel. The rudder was attached to the aft end of the keel and raked forwards to reduce the wetted surface of the keel.

The breakaway from this general theme did not come until designers such as E.G. Van de Stadt of Holland began to make lighter yachts, more like model boats. Although light, inshore racing boats such as the One-raters and Half-raters, designed around the turn of the century by Sibbick and Fay, had had model-like profiles with the rudder separated from the keel, this was never considered an acceptable feature for a large yacht — particularly one that is designed to go offshore.

Van de Stadt's *Zeevalk*, designed to the RORC rule, was an attempt to produce a light, dinghy-like yacht that would be a lot faster in strong winds than the conventional, heavy-displacement hulls. She had a hard-chine plywood hull and a pure fin keel that stuck straight out from the bottom of the

Below: Stormy Weather *was one of the first yachts designed purely for ocean racing and was an important milestone in the career of her designer, Olin Stephens. She won the Fastnet Race in 1935, and having been faithfully restored to her original condition, was again a competitor in 1987.*

canoe body without any blending in. The rudder, a balanced spade, was quite separate, and stuck out under the stern, right at the aft end of the waterline. For a number of reasons unconnected with their basic design, *Zeevalk* and her near-sister *Black Soo* never had quite the success that Van de Stadt hoped for. They were fast in strong following winds, but correspondingly slow in light ones and on average were only moderately successful.

However, light-displacement offshore boats with separate keels and rudders gradually found increasing favour. Van de Stadt was one of the first designers to favour glass fibre and his Pionier and Excalibur designs, built in England by Southern Ocean Shipyard at Poole, were among the first of the really successful series-produced, offshore racing yachts.

The decisive blow in favour of light-displacement and separate rudders was struck by the American designer Dick Carter, whose very first offshore design, *Rabbit*, won the 1965 Fastnet Race. Her hull had a wine-glass section and was very beamy, something that designers had shied away from for years. In a traditional, heavy-displacement type, beam is always considered to be a slowing-down factor and is given an appropriate allowance under the rating rule. Carter thought of his boats as going over rather than through the water and gave them a hull shape in which a lot of the stability was derived from the wide, shallow, midship section. This enabled him to reduce the ballast and lighten the whole boat.

Carter's wine-glass section had to be accompanied by a new, dinghy-like style of sailing in which the yacht is never allowed to heel over too far. Heavy, narrow boats are expected to heel and the older style of offshore yacht sailed to windward with a heel of 20 or 30 degrees whenever there was a respectable amount of wind. Carter's beamy, shallow hull shapes became poorly balanced and difficult to steer if allowed to heel anything like as much as this and were at their best if kept in the 10 to 15 degrees range.

Rabbit and her larger derivative, *Red Rooster*, were really a revelation to sail. Instead of ploughing and smashing their way through the waves, they seemed to dance lightly over them. Downwind, they were able to surf along on big waves like a dinghy and achieve speeds far in excess of the theoretical hull maximum.

After *Rabbit*, yachts with a continuous underwater profile (that is, with the rudder attached to the keel) had little chance. Even the relatively heavy designs from Stephens began to have separated rudders, the so-called 'Fin-and-skeg' profile. Stephens was able to use the results of his intensive research into 12-metre design to benefit his offshore yachts. In particular, he used the 'bustle' feature that in 12-metres had been shown to smooth out the water-flow and create the effect of a longer waterline. These heavy Stephens' yachts with fin-and-skeg profile and bustled afterbody had the benefit of being outstanding all-rounders. Not as fast as the lightweights in certain conditions, they nevertheless put in good average performances on all points of sail and this usually proves a better race-winning tactic than excelling in just one condition.

The One Ton Cup and the other level rating classes that it spawned were responsible for hotting up competition to an unprecedented extent, and design began to change more rapidly. This effect became more marked after the International Offshore Rule was introduced and designers worldwide were working towards the same ends.

Carter, followed by Doug Peterson from California and Ron Holland from New Zealand, obtained their early successes in the level rating classes and finally broke the

Above: *Rabbit, was the first successful design by Dick Carter and introduced a new style of much lighter, more dinghy-like offshore racing yacht. In order to be successful, this type of yacht needs to be sailed in a dinghy-like fashion, with constant attention to the setting and trimming of the sails.*

Right: In addition to being a star of the BBC 'sea-soap' Howard's Way, Barracuda of Tarrant *is representative of a growing disenchantment with the IOR Rule and the type of yacht it produces. Designed to be fast regardless of rating,* Barracuda *races mainly under the Channel Handicap System, where she has proved extremely successful.*

seeming monopoly that Stephens had had for so long. Their designs emphasized the role of the fin keel still further and they raised and flattened the underside of the hull in order to lengthen the keel. They also began to allow the position of the measurement points to dictate the shape of the hull. 'Bumping' was introduced as a way of making the hull locally fatter at the measurement points and yachts began to look strangely misshapen until the rule was modified so that the size of bumps could be controlled.

Changes in design went hand-in-hand with changes in construction, as designers called for ever lighter, stiffer hulls. Wood gave way to aluminium and glass fibre which, in turn, gave way to composite construction, using a variety of high-strength resins and reinforcing fibres plus lightweight core materials such as foamed plastics, balsa wood or honeycomb structures.

The rigs of offshore racing yachts have gone round in a complete circle of development. Going back to the 1930s, we find the majority of successful yachts had what is known as 'three-quarter' or 'seven-eighths' rig; that is, the forestay reached three-quarters of the way up the mast or a bit more. This gave what were considered to be the correct proportions of mainsail and headsail.

John Illingworth and others realized that headsails are more efficient aerodynamically than mainsails because the smooth airflow is not interrupted by the mast. Since the RORC rule measured jibs as if they occupied the triangle formed by the mast, the forestay and the deck, any area that overlapped the mainsail was an unmeasured or 'free' area. This led to the development of masthead rigs with large, overlapping genoas, and these became bigger and bigger, with the mainsails shrinking correspondingly until, by the mid-1970s, the mainsail was little more than a ribbon of sail-cloth while all the power was supplied by an extensive wardrobe of headsails.

This distortion of the sail-plan was finally corrected by the introduction of IOR which measured headsails more strictly and encouraged the mainsail to grow back to a sensible size one more. This happened at the same time that more dinghy racing people were coming into offshore racing and had a natural inclination towards rigs with a big mainsail and bendy mast. It was realized that a mainsail is, in fact, a much more adaptable sail as its power can be varied to a very large degree by playing with mast-bend and tension on various parts of the sail. Today's IOR yachts typically have tall, multi-spreader masts of very small section which are capable of being bent to alarming looking angles. Complex rigging is needed to hold them up, including runners and check-stays which stop the spar from going so far out of column that it collapses. Mast-head rig is still used in some instances but, generally speaking, three-quarter rig is more popular.

OTHER RATING RULES

The purpose of any rating rule is to assess the potential performance of a boat in such a way that it can be given a fair handicap. Unfortunately, it seems impossible to devise a rule that does not impose some influence on the design of yachts that are to be governed by it. Over a period of years, the IOR rule has resulted in, or at least permitted, a 'grand-prix' style of yacht, characterized by high cost, great sophistication and a relatively short racing life.

MHS/IMS

In reaction to the supposed excesses of IOR, the Massachusetts Institute of Technology set out to devise a rule that made a completely scientific assessment of the speed potential of any sort of boat. In order to achieve this, a new way of measuring the hull was devised, using an electronic probe linked to a computer, as it was thought that this would discourage designers from shaping their hulls to take advantage of the way in which hulls are measured under IOR.

When this new rule came into use, at first named Measurement Handicap System and later International Measurement System, it was found that it, too, seemed to favour one type of boat against another. This was demonstrated when a 16-year-old cruising ketch, *Holger Danske*, won the Bermuda Race, using IMS rating. Some yachtsmen found this a splendid endorsement of the new rule, others were confirmed in the suspicion that it was just a way of encouraging old clunkers to race.

Portsmouth Yardstick and PHRF

The PYS system, used for dinghy sailing in Britain for many years, is somewhat similar to the Performance Handicap Rating Formula in that they are both based on results. This was a very traditional way of arriving at handicaps: 'If Fred wins this week, slap a couple more minutes on his handicap for next week.' In reality, both systems are a lot more sophisticated than this, but human judgement plays an important part.

Channel Handicap

In the last few years, this system managed by the Royal Ocean Racing Club has been a great success in bringing back into racing owners who had given up because of the expense and intensity of racing under IOR. Instead of needing to have complete measurement carried out, the owner sends in certain key dimensions of his yacht which are then used to compute a rating using a secret formula. The element of secrecy is supposed to prevent designers from getting around the rule. Once again, however, an element of human judgement is involved, as the rule-makers admit that they juggle with the formula when it looks as if any particular boat is doing rather too well. 'Informal' systems of this kind can work well for a time, until designers discover how to outsmart them.

Safety

The organizers of offshore races take safety extremely seriously and most follow the lead of the Offshore Racing Council in laying down strict requirements for any yacht entering for offshore racing.

Races are divided into categories, from 0–4, depending on how long and arduous they are and for each there is a set of safety requirements. The basic ones, which apply to all types of race, are as follows:

- Yachts shall be self-righting, strongly-built, watertight, fully seaworthy and properly rigged.
- All heavy items such as ballast, anchors, batteries, stoves, engines and tanks must be securely fixed so that they would stay in place in the event of a complete capsize.
- Hatches and companionways must be capable of being securely closed, and remain so even if the yacht capsizes.
- Cockpits must be waterproof, self-draining and not too large in relation to the yacht.
- There must be means of closing off or plugging any holes in the hull.
- There must be lifelines right round the hull at a minimum height.
- There must be proper accommodation, with bunks, a galley with cooker, toilet, water-tank and emergency containers.
- Equipment carried on board must include at least two anchors, two fire extinguishers, two bilge pumps, two buckets, flashlights, first-aid kit, foghorn, radar reflector.
- Navigation equipment, including a compass and a spare one, and various other instruments.
- Navigation lights, including a spare set that work off a different power source.
- Storm sails.
- Emergency steering.
- Tools and spares.
- Radio telephone, radio receiver for weather forecasts and a radio direction finder.
- A life-raft of approved type, capable of carrying the whole crew, a life-jacket and a safety harness for each person.
- Two life-rings, both with self-igniting lights and one with a dan-buoy with 6ft (1.83m) pole and flag.
- A set of approved distress flares.
- A 50ft (15.24m) heaving line.
- 'Grab-bag' with emergency rations, drinking water etc.

Ocean crossing races, those in categories 0 and 1, have an even more formidable list of requirements.

Except in favoured climates such as Hawaii, ocean racing is very often cold, wet, exhausting and extremely expensive. It has been likened to standing under a cold shower tearing up five pound notes. In view of this, the reader may wonder why people do it. There is no easy answer except to say that, a bit like mountaineering, the discomfort and danger is part of the challenge and makes the reward seem even greater when the objective is finally achieved. Competing in something such as the Fastnet Race can be a very arduous business indeed, but you can certainly walk a little taller afterwards.

CRUISING YACHTS

To define a cruising yacht is exceptionally difficult as it is possible to cruise in anything from a racing dinghy to an ocean liner, but what most people understand by the term is a yacht designed in the first instance for seaworthiness and 'liveability' rather than speed. A cruising yacht is always a thing of compromise in which a mixture of conflicting requirements are balanced.

Hull design

Racing yachts achieve their performance by expensive, lightweight construction and by having very little in the way of creature comforts. A cruising yacht is bound to be heavier and therefore to have a fuller-shaped hull. It used to be thought that only the old style of hull, with the rudder attached to a full-length keel, could be considered really seaworthy but this was mainly conservatism and the majority of modern cruising yachts have a keel of moderate size and a separate, skeg-hung rudder.

Deep draught is a disadvantage in a cruising yacht, not only because it limits the areas that can be visited but because it is a great advantage to be able to 'dry out' safely alongside a wall or jetty. To this end, a reasonably long keel with a straight and substantial bottom to it is called for. A yacht with a deep fin keel is always in danger of tipping over when dried out and can only really do this safely with a special cradle.

Two recent developments in keel design have helped the cruising yachtsman. The Collins Tandem Keel concentrates a high proportion of the ballast into a thick end-plate. This has the double advantage of reducing draught by lowering the centre of gravity of the keel and of providing a substantial 'foot' for the yacht to rest on when it goes aground. The Scheel Keel does not have the pronounced wing-like end plates of the Collins keel but it does broaden out

***Right:** One way to make a boat cheaper is to use less material in building it and so the great majority of production cruiser-racers are light in weight and go over rather than through the water. A disadvantage of this type is that it is sensitive to the amount of weight carried on board and has a very lively motion in rough water.*

into a fat bulb at the bottom with similar advantages. It is suitable for bigger yachts than the Collins and is fitted to some substantial luxury cruising yachts.

Yachts which go aground on every tide are a special problem which is usually solved by fitting twin bilge keels. These ensure that the yacht will stand safely upright on the ground with no danger of falling over, but, unfortunately, the added wetted surface of bilge keels does not help performance. Ballasted centreboards or retractable keels give better performance but there is a constant danger of getting mud and stones stuck in the aperture and jamming the mechanism. Another solution for yachts on tidal moorings is to fit 'legs' to a conventional fin-keeled hull. These are props fitted to the side of the hull to stop it falling over when the water disappears. The drawback is the nuisance of fitting and removing them and some designs have appeared with legs built into the hull.

Rig

The rig of a cruising yacht must be easy to handle. Most cruising yachts are handled by families who cannot be expected to rush on deck to wrestle with enormous and very heavy headsails as soon as the wind pipes up. The fashion used to be to have a sail-plan divided up into a number of relatively small sails that were never too much to handle and as a result, ketch and yawl rigs were common on cruising yachts as small as 30ft (9.14m) overall.

This has been changed by the development of 'labour-saving' systems, particularly roller furling, and this has made life a lot easier for the cruising yachtsman. At first, rollers were only used for furling headsails completely — there was no question of setting them half-rolled. Even this was a big step forward, because it cut out the long job of dragging a big sailbag on deck, hanking the sail on and hoisting it. Now the sail can be left rolled on the forestay when it is not required, and this has the further advantage that the fore-peak is not cluttered with sailbags.

Eventually, the roller gear was made strong enough and the headsails flat enough so that these devices could be used for reefing as well. You have to be quite confident that everything is properly designed and made to do this, but when it works it is a tremendous boon to be able to adjust the sail area quickly and easily without leaving the cockpit.

A further development of this idea is the mainsail that rolls up inside the mast. The case for this is not so clear, because — with properly laid-out reefing gear — it is not difficult to adjust the area of the mainsail. The roller system is expensive and should it decide to go wrong with the sail partly rolled up, could cause a lot of trouble.

The device that makes all this labour-saving deck equipment possible is the self-tailing winch. A development of the geared sheet-winch, it has a kind of rope-gripper on top which automatically takes the slack of the rope as it comes off the winch drum. This enables the person operating the winch to use both hands to wind the handle, a job that formerly called for two people.

***Above:** Early start. Getting the mainsail cover off ready for a full day of sailing. A great attraction of the modern, glass fibre production yacht is that it requires very little regular maintenance, so that the owner is able to get as much sailing time as possible for his money.*

Self-steering

Without some kind of self-steering device, one person has to be at the helm of a yacht as long as it is underway and with a small crew, this is a considerable disadvantage. If this chore can be taken away, even temporarily, the helmsman is free to nip below to check the chart, or put the kettle on or listen to the weather forecast without needing to disturb anyone else. This makes it practical and safe to have just one person on watch which, in turn, makes it practical to cruise with, for instance, youngish children.

A lot of effort has gone into perfecting wind-vane self-steering of the type pioneered by Col. 'Blondie' Hasler and many yachtsmen still prefer this type because it does not rely on electrical power. In the past few years, however, electric 'autohelmsmen' have improved so much that they are almost completely reliable. It has been possible for many years to have a satisfactory electric autopilot for a fairly big cruising yacht with

wheel steering, provided there was a good supply of electricity available. The big development has been in the simple tiller pilots that are now available for even the smallest yachts.

These are portable and can be brought on deck as and when required. They fit on a bracket on the side of the cockpit with a push-pull arm attached to the tiller and will operate efficiently from a normal 12-volt battery for many hours. Mostly, they are controlled by means of a small internal compass but, as an extra, many offer the alternative of control by means of a small wind-vane and this is the preferable method whenever you are sailing to windward.

Below decks

Down below, a cruising yacht has to combine the functions of sitting-room, bedrooms, kitchen, bathroom, engine-room and navigation space, all within a very small space. Like houses, yachts tend to sell on the number of beds offered and for this reason there is always the temptation to fit more berths than there is really room for. For instance, yachts of only 30ft (9.14m) are routinely offered with six berths but this will result in a terrible crowding on a proper cruise — everyone needs sufficient room to stow away their clothes and it is not going to be much of a holiday if you cannot at least all sit down to eat at the same time!

Traditional cruising yachts relied mostly on 'settee berths', that is, bench seats that doubled as bunks. With beamy modern yachts, however, it is possible to fit pilot berths above and outboard of the saloon settees. These are far more comfortable and private, and make it unnecessary to stow away all the bedding before anyone can sit down to breakfast. Berths forward of the mast, although almost invariably fitted to cruising yachts, are hardly usable at sea because of the uncomfortable motion so, at best, they can only be a harbour cabin. An aft cabin, increasingly found on yachts from about 35ft (10.67m), is better because it is in the area of least motion and offers more privacy.

Engine

Petrol engines in cruising yachts are a pain in the neck. They frequently refuse to start because damp gets into the ignition system, and having petrol aboard a yacht is a constant safety worry as any escaping fumes will sink into the lowest part of the bilge and lurk there, waiting for a spark to set them off. Fortunately, there is now such a comprehensive range of marine diesel engines available that any yacht with a fitted engine can make use of one. Diesels are far safer in a boat and far more reliable, too. Only the very smallest sailing yachts, which use an outboard motor as an auxiliary, need carry petrol aboard; even then it can be in a separate tank kept outside the cabin.

The modern marine diesel can do more than one thing to earn its living. Invariably, it will be fitted with an alternator to charge the batteries and perhaps a compressor to power a fridge-freezer. Many slightly larger cruising yachts use a 'calorifier' system to obtain domestic hot water from the engine's cooling system. With an efficient system, it is only necessary to run the engine for about 15 minutes in order to heat sufficient water for a good shower.

Modern cruising yachtsmen like their comforts. Electric lighting, hot water, even hot-air central heating is more-or-less taken for granted; all this makes the modern yacht a complex piece of engineering, unfortunately with cost to match.

Cooking used to take place over a roaring paraffin burner but the great majority of yachts nowadays use bottled gas stoves. This, too, brings a possible danger as LPG — like petrol vapour — is heavier than air. It is therefore essential, and indeed obligatory in most countries, to store gas bottles in a specially designed airtight locker with overboard drains.

Maintenance

Only the very rich have paid hands these days, so the vast majority of cruising yachts spend five days a week swinging on moorings or made fast on a marina berth. When the owner, his family and friends come aboard they do not want to spend most of their weekend scraping and painting, scrubbing and mending; they want to go sailing for as many hours as possible. For this reason 95 per cent of all cruising yachts have glass fibre hulls which just require occasional cleaning and antifouling and a certain amount of wood trim on deck — preferably teak because this requires very little attention. Aluminium spars, stainless steel fittings and synthetic sails and lines require only the occasional checkover while, below-deck, varnished woodwork, laminated work-surfaces and vinyl overheads combine to form a 'wipe clean' yacht. It may not be quite so evocative as all that gleaming woodwork and shining brass of days gone by but it is certainly a great deal more practical.

Left: *Laying-up, the old-fashioned way. Wooden yachts need to be brought out of the water each winter for a fairly extensive programme of cleaning, painting and varnishing. The modern yacht can be safely left in the water all winter and then pulled out for just a few hours of cleaning and routine maintenance prior to a new season of use.*

KA
KA
919
US-41110
KA 4000

Great Sailing Races of the World

Once, yacht racing was the sport of a privileged minority. Today, it is one of the most popular of all participant sports — with competition taking place wherever there is sufficient water in which to float small boats. The pinnacle of the sport lies in the great ocean races where the toughest and most experienced sailors do battle, not only against each other but against the sea in all its moods. In the 1920s, yachtsmen who suggested racing at sea in relatively small yachts were considered madmen. Now, even a single-handed race around the world is accepted. These races represent the greatest sporting challenges in existence.

Left: *Start of the third race of the 1987 Admiral's Cup series. An event such as this represents the pinnacle of a sport the roots of which lie in the regular weekend events run by sailing clubs throughout the world.*

***Right:** The Dragon is a pre-war design that has remained up-to-date thanks to sensible modernization over the years and is still one of the most competitive racing keelboats. Sailing a Dragon well calls for co-ordinated teamwork from the three members of the crew.*

Before going on to look at some of the world's great sailing races in detail, it seems appropriate to explain how sailing races are organized, at various levels.

Club racing

Virtually every sailing club organizes races for its own members and these will be for one-design classes or mixed handicaps. The simplest kind of race to organize is one for a one-design class, the Laser single-handed dinghy for example. All that is necessary is to set a course, make the warning and preparatory signals and the start. Off go the Lasers and the first one of them to cross the finish line is the winner.

On a Saturday afternoon, the average club might have starts for half a dozen different one-design classes and perhaps one or two handicap divisions. Mixed small boats and dinghies might race using a handicap devised by the club itself or by one such as the Portsmouth Yardstick handicap system. This gives a yardstick rating to each boat according to its type, and after the race the handicapper uses a set of tables to convert elapsed times into corrected times, to find the winner.

If the club includes cruisers, it may well run a handicap class for them, based on one of the easy-to-apply rating systems such as Channel Handicap or Scandicap. These involve the owner in a little bit of homework because he has to write off to the appropriate rating authority (eg Royal Ocean Racing Club in Great Britain) and get a rating for his boat, but the cost is low and he does not need to go through a full measurement procedure. In the United States he might have his boat measured using the IMS (International Measurement System, formerly known as MHS). The measuring is done by a machine and a computer produces the rating.

Now every ambitious sailor knows that to gain experience it is necessary to go beyond his (or her) own club and enter for more important races in a variety of places. This takes us to the next level of competition.

Open meetings

Every one-design class, and most cruiser classes have an owner's association to run their affairs, and one of the most important jobs of the Class Association is to run a programme of 'Open meetings'. These are sets of races, usually run over a weekend, in which anyone belonging to the Association can take part. The organization of the weekend is handled by a local club, usually with some help from officers of the Class Association. In the great majority of cases, these open meetings are used as a means of qualifying for entry to the Regional or National Championship of the Class and this brings us to the next level.

Championships

All the popular classes have to limit the number of entries to their main, annual championships; otherwise, the organization becomes too onerous for a normal club to handle and the numbers on the starting line too many. Therefore, the Class Secretary will work out a points system which might call, for instance, for results from five different open meetings, the best 100 skippers gaining places at the National Championships.

Regional championships of a dinghy class are often run over a weekend or long weekend but the annual championship normally requires a full week and might consist of six races, the best five to count. For those who do well at this level, aspirations rise and other possibilities begin to beckon. There may be Continental or World Championships on offer, involving trips abroad, and there may also be a tap on the shoulder by a scout from one of the Olympic classes, suggesting a try-out in one of these.

It used to be the case that dinghy people, keelboat people and offshore people did not mix but, happily, nowadays there is every encouragement to crews who want to migrate upwards towards larger boats. This is because a skipper who wants to race, say, a 30-footer needs to find five others willing to sail with him, so he is constantly on the lookout for keen youngsters who have already acquired initial experience in dinghy or small keelboat classes.

World or Continental championships are the pinnacle of small-boat racing and the sailors who reach this exalted level almost always crop up in other classes or competitions after a while. Top sailors nearly always have a record of success in several different classes.

Keelboats

Day-sailing keelboats: Solings, Etchells, Dragons, the metre-boat classes, and so on, are organized along similar lines to dinghy classes, with club, area, national and world events. But moving this type of boat around is a major chore and, as a result, many keelboats never stray far from their home club. But to do well in these classes it is just as necessary to travel and the owner of a Soling, for example, which is an Olympic class, may well find himself on the road at least six or eight times a year. This obviously adds tremendously to the costs involved in campaigning a boat of this sort.

Offshore

Every seaworthy boat is capable of being rated and entering a race but, in practice, it is not worth bringing a pure cruiser up to the strict safety standards required. However, many production boats are sold as 'cruiser-racers', which means that they are considered suitable for racing — if the owner chooses to do so. The fact that the majority of offshore boats are series produced encourages the formation of one-design classes. These have the great advantage of being able to race without the considerable expense of rating

D
D
K-415

Right: *One-design offshore yachts such as this Sigma 33 make it possible to sail in a very competitive fleet without the astronomic costs of campaigning a one-off racing yacht. The Sigma owner has the option of racing either against other Sigmas or in a handicap fleet.*

and fitting out to full offshore standards.

In fact, the owner of a stock offshore design can have the best of several worlds. Let us take as an example the Sigma 33, one of the most popular 'stock' cruiser classes in Britain and one which has its equivalent in several other countries. As delivered from the builder it is capable of racing in class events against other Sigmas. In addition, the owner can easily get a Channel Handicap rating which will enable him to take part in a variety of coastal and short offshore events, competing against other types of yacht.

Finally, he can get an IOR Rating. This costs rather more but since he has a stock boat, it is not necessary to go through the full hull measurement procedure as these dimensions are already known. Provided he has all the correct safety equipment and a properly qualified crew, he can now enter for major offshore events, in competition with all the hotshots.

In theory, any club can organize an offshore race but in practice this tends to be left in the hands of a relatively few specialized organizations which are set up to do this. In most countries where offshore racing is a major part of the sport there is one club which also acts as the rating authority — the organization that carries out measurement and issues rating certificates. Examples are the Cruising Club of America (CCA) and the Royal Ocean Racing Club (RORC).

All these national clubs or associations belong to the Offshore Racing Council, which administers the rating rules and co-ordinates major world events such as the 'Ton Cups', which are actually the World Championships of the various level rating classes.

The really big events for offshore yachts, such as the Admiral's Cup, Southern Cross and Southern Circuit, require such massive organization that they are normally handled by several clubs in association with a major sponsor. Stock yachts, such as the Sigma mentioned above, are no longer in the picture, because these big international offshore championships call for specially-designed and built yachts. Because of the high technology involved, these are extremely expensive. For instance, to build and campaign a One Tonner, capable of competing in the Admiral's Cup, could easily cost £¼m.

The very high cost of campaigning a 'Grand Prix' IOR yacht means that skippers are increasingly driven towards sponsorship. In the past, it was not permitted to give a yacht a name connected with the sponsor but a gradual softening of the rules now makes this possible in most of the major competitions. However, for the meantime, sponsored yachts are kept separate in an 'open' division which in many cases is not eligible for the principal trophies. For instance, many of the yachts taking part in the 1987 Admiral's Cup series were sponsored and had names that reflected that, but as a result the yacht that had the best corrected time in the Fastnet Race was not eligible to collect the Fastnet Trophy.

In addition to what one may call 'mainstream' offshore events, there are the 'spectaculars' such as the big, sponsored ocean races which are either partly or wholly outside the normal administrative channels. But they are by no means all the same. At one extreme one may take the Whitbread Round the World Race. This is as conventional as a sponsored spectacular can be in that it is organized by a club, the Royal Naval Sailing Association, and the competing yachts are rated under the IOR system. The yachts are permitted to be sponsored but have to follow existing rules and guidelines.

At the opposite end of the spectrum, one can look at an event such as the Route du Rhum which is not organized by a yacht club

but by a commercial organization set up for the purpose. The competitors are permitted unlimited sponsorship and they are not handicapped. Many are professionals.

The hierarchy

Starting from the bottom: every yachtsman who wishes to compete in racing must belong to a yacht club which is affiliated to a National Sailing Authority. In almost every case, he must also belong to a Class Association appropriate to the boat he is racing. This organization, also affiliated to the National Authority, is responsible for ensuring that every boat is class legal and for issuing a certificate to that effect.

All National Sailing Authorities are members of the world governing body, the International Yacht Racing Union, which maintains the Yacht Racing Rules, organizes the Olympic Regatta and directly administers the International Classes. It licenses International judges, approves International Juries and liaises with inter-governmental bodies on matters of interest to yachtsmen.

Offshore yachtsmen also belong to clubs, but the IOR and IMS rating systems are controlled by the Offshore Racing Council, a world body which liaises with, but remains independent of, the International Yacht Racing Union.

Some board-sailors operate completely within the yacht club hierarchy but many never bother to join any kind of organization. There is a 'circuit' of professional board-sailors which is run by an association of manufacturers having no connection with the mainstream of yachting.

THE RACES

Every year there are many yacht races at national, continental and world championship level. So many, in fact, that it is not possible to give an individual description of all of them — even though they do represent the top level of competition for that particular class. The following is a selection of some of the best known offshore events.

MACKINAC RACE

Started in 1898, this event has a longer history than any other major race, even though it is held on fresh water. The course of 330 miles is from Chicago, up Lake Michigan to Mackinac Island and back. The lake is 350 miles long and 100 miles wide and must therefore be considered a mini-ocean in everything but name. This is the only major race which continued to be sailed during the two world wars.

BERMUDA RACE

The first Bermuda Race was held in 1906, when just three yachts sailed from Brooklyn to Bermuda (approximately 600 miles). The winner was *Tamerlane*, owned by Frank Maier and skippered by Thomas Fleming Day – editor of *Rudder* — who had suggested the event in the first place. However, the initial series of races ran only until 1910, when the event died out.

It was revived in 1923 and has continued ever since, apart from a break for the Second World War. After 1924, the race became biannual so as not to clash with the Fastnet Race, initiated in 1925. The first few races were started from New London, Connecticut and then, from 1936, the start was moved to Brenton Light, off Newport, Rhode Island, making the course length 635 miles. By that time Newport had become the premier yachting harbour of the East Coast — home of the America's Cup — and possessed all the facilities needed to support a large fleet.

It is tempting to suppose that a race from Newport to Bermuda during the summer months would be an agreeable and straightforward cruise but, in fact, the Bermuda Race has had more than its fair share of gales and presents an unusually tricky problem to the navigator, because of the Gulf Stream. This runs up the east coast of the United States like a great river, attaining a rate of up to five knots at times. The difficulty comes from the fact that somewhere along the rhumb line from Newport to Bermuda there is generally a large loop or meander in the stream. If a yacht hits the stream in just the right spot she can receive a major boost from the southward flowing meander, but if she hits it wrong she could be plugging against the current as it turns back north.

The meander is not constant and the tactics that win a Bermuda Race one year can be totally wrong next time. In the pre-war races, navigators really earned their keep as they constantly worked astro sights and compared them with dead reckoning in an effort to judge which way the stream was flowing. It is easy to tell *when* the yacht hits the stream by the increase in water temperature, but the trick is to judge its direction.

Nowadays, it is not nearly such fun because the stream can be seen quite clearly from satellite pictures which are made available to all competitors just before the start. Furthermore, the yachts are permitted to use radio fixing aids such as LORAN and Omega which do most of the navigator's work for him or her. Incidentally, it was in the Bermuda Race, in 1926, that radios were carried aboard some of the yachts for the first time. They were straightforward receivers, used to check chronometers against broadcast time signals. Today's 'black boxes' tell

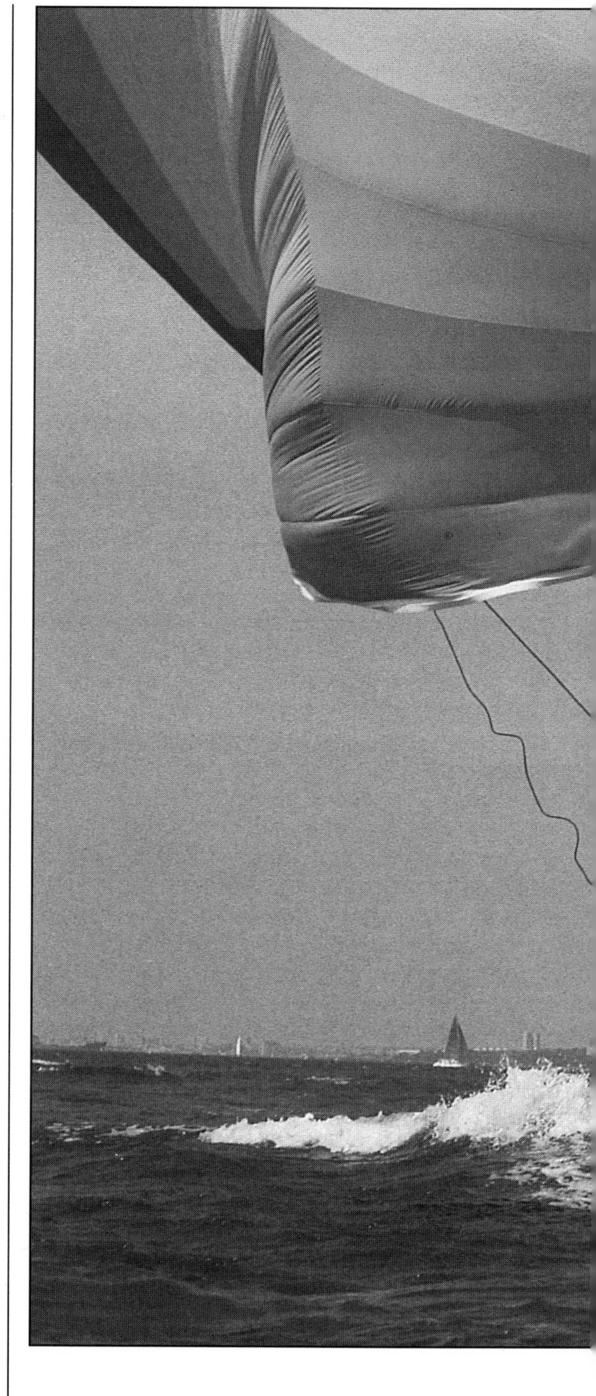

Right: *The Irish Admiral's Cup competitor* Moonduster *takes the lead during the 1983 event. This fine-looking wooden Holland design is one of the largest yachts to take part in this competition, which has been dominated in recent years by yachts of One Ton rating.*

you where you are, where you should be and what's for dinner, all at the touch of a button.

When navigators get their sums right, a yacht can be carried south by the stream at two or three knots, sailing hard on the wind into a fresh south-westerly. This wind-against-current situation makes for a very rough sea and right from 1923 the Bermuda Race had the reputation of being a wet ride. After this race one of the competing yachtsmen, Judge S.B. Coffin, remarked, 'Next time I come to Bermuda, it will be in a submarine. Then I can be under water all the time instead of half under, all the time.'

In 1930, a young naval architect named Olin Stephens sailed his own *Dorade* into second place in Class B and began an association with offshore racing that was to last for 40 years. No designer has produced more winners than Olin Stephens.

One of the greatest sea rescues in the history of yachting took place during the 1932 race. In bad weather and at night, the 78ft (23.77m) schooner *Adriana* caught fire. There was, of course, no radio transmitter with which to make a distress call in those days but, fortunately for the crew, their distress signals were seen by the British yacht *Jolie Brise*. In a superb display of seamanship her skipper Bobby Somerset managed to come alongside *Adriana* just long enough to allow ten of her crew to jump across. Tragically, one man fell between the two yachts and was lost.

When the race was revived after the Second World War, it quickly became one of the most important events in the calendar, a position it was to hold for a further 15 years — after which there began to be a far greater choice of major events. This period also saw the longest run of success ever when Carleton Mitchell won the Bermuda Race three times running in his 38ft 7½in (11.77m) centre-board yawl *Finisterre*. Mitchell was a man who believed that it was perfectly possible to combine the roles of cruising and racing. So he had Sparkman and Stephens design a beamy, seakindly yacht that was ideal for Caribbean cruising. But when he raced, he raced hard and got the best people available as crew. He could not stay with the deep-keel sloops to windward but as soon as sheets could be eased just a little, *Finisterre* would be off at maximum speed.

Mitchell's first victory was in the very windy 1956 race, when a new course record of two days, 22 hours, 11 minutes was set by the big yawl, *Bolero*, skippered by Sven Salen. But this time competitors were served up with a sharp reminder of the dangers of approaching a rocky coast in poor visibility. The cutter *Edlu*, owned by Henry Wise, misjudged her position and hit the coral reefs off the north coast of Bermuda during the night. For hours the crew clung to the rigging as breakers pounded the hull of the yacht to pieces. Just in time, dawn broke and they were spotted from the shore.

There was another even more remarkable escape in 1960, when a tropical storm hit the fleet just as most of them were nearing Bermuda. In pitch darkness and a huge sea, Jack Westin went overboard from the yacht *Scylla*, skippered by sailmaker Charlie Ulmer. Westin's good fortune lay in the fact that this was the first yacht to carry a floating strobe light attached to a life-ring. This was thrown overboard after Westin and its brilliant flash enabled the crew of *Scylla* to turn the yacht round and sail back to precisely the spot where he was clinging to the life-ring. Since then, a bright, flashing light of this type has become a compulsory safety feature for all offshore yachts.

ONION PATCH TROPHY

After the Royal Ocean Racing Club had created the Admiral's Cup in 1957, the people of Bermuda decided to copy the idea by promoting a similar series of races, with the Bermuda Race as its climax. Accordingly, in 1962 the Royal Bermuda Yacht Club presented the Onion Patch Trophy and the first event was held two years later (Onion Patch is the jocular American term for Bermuda). The idea was to have a series of short races around Newport and the Long Island Sound area before heading off to Bermuda.

After a rather slow start, the Onion Patch series began to catch on well and succeeded in attracting teams from Europe and South America, in addition to the USA and Bermuda. In 1972, a record fleet of 178 yachts started in the Bermuda Race and ran slap into the worse gale in the long history of the event. For more than 24 hours, the fleet was sailing to windward in winds of 40–50 knots which, in the open ocean, built up an enormous sea. There was a large number of retirements but the British Swan 48 *Noryema VII*, sailed in owner Ron Amey's absence by Teddy Hicks, sailed a superb race to finish first by a large margin. Conditions were so bad that *Noryema* had to make two shots at finding the finish line and a number of others hove-to offshore rather than risk attempting to approach the island in the darkness and near-hurricane conditions.

This was the first and only time that a non-US yacht has won the Bermuda Race but, unfortunately, the British team did not also win the Onion Patch Trophy because another member of the team, Sir Max Aitken's *Crusade*, carried away a lower shroud and had to heave-to for repairs.

In spite of the bad weather, 1972 was the pinnacle of the Onion Patch's success and afterwards it rapidly declined in popularity. The reason was that because some American yachtsmen felt that the IOR system gave undue advantage to pure racing types, the CCA was persuaded to commission a further, completely new rating system. This was the Measurement Handicap System or MHS (the name has since been changed to the International Measurement System) which is the most scientifically-based rule yet devised but, as far as the Bermuda Race and Onion Patch were concerned, had two drawbacks.

The first is that it went to the opposite extreme to IOR, in seeming to encourage traditional cruiser-racer types that had long been superseded in top racing fleets. In 1978, when the Bermuda Race was won by a 23-year-old, 40ft (12.19m) yawl named *Babe*, her owner Arnold Gay commented, 'We have set yacht design back 30 years.' The effect of this was naturally to discourage owners from entering in the latest racing designs, and this relegated the event to the second rank in people's minds.

Furthermore, by moving away from IOR, the organizers of the series were cutting themselves off from the mainstream of world yachting. So the net effect was that, although the Bermuda Race continues, the Onion Patch Trophy gathers dust on the shelf of the Royal Bermuda Yacht Club and instead, the Southern Circuit is regarded as the top US ocean racing series.

THE TRANSPACIFIC RACE

This race, universally known as the 'Transpac', occupies a slightly anomalous position in the world of offshore racing. It is one of the oldest races, having first been sailed in 1906 — and was for many years the longest at 2,200 miles – but it has the special feature of being virtually always downwind for the whole distance. This means that specialized downwind flyers with a poor windward performance can win this race but would not win any other; this sets them aside from the larger world of yachting.

Just three yachts set off from San Pedro, in June 1906. The winner — in a time of 12 days, five hours — was the 85ft 10in (26.16m) schooner *Lurline*, owned by H.H. Sinclair. Three more races were held in 1908, 1910, and 1912, after which the event lapsed until 1923. Entries were quite erratic for the next few years, but after 1934 it started to become a regular affair, with a steadily rising number of competitors.

Because of its specialized downwind nature, the fastest time was of as much interest as the handicap winner and big ketches and schooners that would not stand a chance in a race to windward continued to do well. In 1947, for instance, the record time was reduced to 10 days 10 hours by the 98ft (29.87m) schooner *Morning Star.* In 1961, this was reduced to nine days 13 hours by the ketch *Ticonderoga*, owned by Bob Johnson. In 1971, the same owner's *Windward Passage* reduced it to nine days nine hours.

The really dramatic increase in speed came when Californian designers began to produce specialized Transpac designs. These 'Ultra-light Displacement Boats', or ULDBs, are considered quite controversial in the sailing world because their extreme form and

Below: Ticonderoga, *thrashing to windward in a fresh breeze. This famous old yacht began her racing career in the 1930s and was still winning in the 1970s. She helped to set the fashion for 'line honours' winners, where more importance is given to finishing first than to winning on handicap.*

very lightweight construction means that their safety is a little questionable. Nevertheless, it was one of these specialized yachts, the 67ft (20.42m) *Merlin* which, in 1977, covered the course from Los Angeles to Honolulu in the astonishing time of eight days 11 hours and 45 minutes, which represents an average speed of 11 knots for the entire 2,200 miles of the course.

THE FASTNET RACE

Britain's first and greatest offshore race was inspired by the Bermuda Race. The yachting writer Weston Martyr, wrote an article describing the US event and suggesting that Britain was falling behind in the development of yachts suitable for this kind of sailing. The correctness of this assertion is shown by the fact that the first Fastnet Race, in 1925, was won by a Le Havre pilot cutter, *Jolie Brise*. It was rather as if a Grand Prix motor race had been won by a London taxi.

Martyr also suggested the course: from the Solent, around the Fastnet Rock, off the south coast of Ireland, and back to Plymouth. This course of 600 miles has the great merit of being similar in length to the Bermuda Race. It is also a course with plenty of variety, giving the competitors almost every kind of challenge.

The initial leg down Channel is straight into the prevailing south-westerly wind and, in addition, there are strong tides which must be worked to the best advantage. Three headlands which project from the South Coast: Portland Bill, Start Point and The Lizard create extra-strong tidal streams and act a bit like jumps on a steeplechase. On the outward-bound track yachts are not required to sail around the Scillies and can normally ease sheets at the Lizard and steer a north-westerly course. From Land's End onwards, the yachts are in the open ocean, with no friendly refuge to leeward. The wind has a way of veering to the west at this point, making it a rough, tough close fetch to the Fastnet Rock.

After rounding the rock, morale soars with the prospect of a fast broad reach or run back to the Bishop Rock, outer sentinel of the Scillies, which must be left to port. Before the advent of modern navigation aids, finding the Bishop was a tricky problem, especially if visibility was poor. From the Bishop, it is a headlong dash back to the finish at Plymouth, where the attractive prospect of a bath, food and beer beckons invitingly.

Just seven yachts sailed in the 1925 race, defying dire warning from many members of the yachting 'establishment' that such a race would be a recipe for disaster. In fact, over the years it has proved to be a remarkably safe event, being almost free of serious accidents until the notorious gale of 1979, when 15 people lost their lives.

The first race started from Ryde, but all subsequent starts have been from the Royal Yacht Squadron's start line at Cowes. This was a very wise move by the Squadron as it ensured that Cowes, for very many years the centre for traditional yachting, was getting in on the ground floor of this new branch of the sport. But it was not the Squadron that organized the race. In 1925, at the conclusion of the first event, most of the people involved got together to form The Ocean Racing Club. George Martin, owner of *Jolie Brise*, was persuaded to be the first Commodore.

The Fastnet was an annual race until 1931, when there was a mutual agreement to alternate with the Bermuda Race. There had been transatlantic competition from 1926 onwards, when the American schooner *Primrose IV* sailed over to compete. She was beaten by just a few minutes, by the Royal Engineers club yacht, *Ilex*. There was still a lot of criticism of the race, however. So in 1928 a minimum of 35ft (10.66m) waterline length was fixed for the Fastnet Race and the shorter Channel Race was initiated for smaller yachts. It is interesting to think that if the same minimum applied today, about three-quarters of the RORC fleet would be ineligible.

In that year, 1928, Paul Hammond's *Niña* became the first foreign winner of the Fastnet. She was an odd-looking yacht and one of the first designed to take advantage of the rating rule then in force in the United States. She was technically a schooner, but her foremast was so much shorter than the mainmast that her sail-plan was almost that of a cutter. Yet she proved to be a fast and very long-lived yacht, for she won the Bermuda race in 1962 under a totally different rule.

The much travelled *Jolie Brise*, now owned by Bobby Somerset, won the Fastnet Race again, in both 1929 and 1930, the only yacht to win this race three times. The days of the souped-up working boat came to an abrupt end in 1931, when the all-conquering *Dorade* put in her first appearance. Designed by Olin Stephens, she was the first really modern ocean racing yacht and set completely new standards of performance. Having won the Transatlantic Race, she came on to Cowes for the Fastnet and absolutely demolished the English fleet, winning by eight hours on corrected time. It was a very windy race, and resulted in a rare fatality when one of the crew of *Maitenes II* was lost overboard in storm force winds.

There was an immediate move to tighten up safety standards and, for the first time, yachts were required to have lifelines right round the deck. In retrospect, it is astonishing that this had not been thought necessary before — but inshore racing yachts had never had lifelines and specific requirements for offshore yachts were a new idea.

Yachts designed by Olin Stephens now won four times running, from 1931/7. *Dorade* won in 1931 and 1933, followed by *Stormy Weather* in 1935. *Stormy* was a kind of enlarged and improved *Dorade* and, like the earlier yacht, was a yawl because the rule in force in America favoured a yacht with more than one mast. Incidentally, *Stormy Weather* has recently been restored to her original appearance and was a competitor in the 1987 Fastnet Race, marking 52 years of sailing. The fourth Stephens' winner was *Zeearend*, another yawl similar to *Stormy Weather*, built in Holland for Dutchman Cees Bruynzeel.

Staggering from these repeated blows, British design managed to hit back in the final pre-war Fastnet race, in 1939, which was won by Isaac Bell's Nicholson-designed 63ft (19.2m) *Bloodhound*. Nicholson built three yachts to the same design, *Bloodhound*, *Foxhound* and *Stiarna*, all conforming to the 12-metre Cruiser-racer Rule. They are very handsome, successful yachts and all are still sailing. *Bloodhound* had the distinction of becoming a royal yacht during the 1960s, when Prince Philip owned her.

Also in 1939 an exceptionally keen young naval officer named John Illingworth commissioned from Laurent Giles a design embodying many of his own ideas for an offshore racing yacht. Named *Maid of Malham*, she had the novel feature of a masthead forestay that enabled Illingworth to set larger headsails. The leading sailmaker of the day, Chris Ratsey, refused to make the sails Illingworth ordered for *Maid*, saying he was 'ruining a lovely boat'. Although Illingworth did not manage to win the Fastnet, he did win the 1939 RORC points championship for the first, and by no means the last, time.

Five years of war service gave Illingworth plenty of time to clarify his ideas about ocean racing and when he went back to Laurent Giles, in 1946, he presented the designer with a very specific brief. Illingworth swept away the idea of a racing boat being a souped-up cruiser, discarding all features which did not add to performance. When I sailed with Illingworth in the 1960s, he told me that the secret was to look at every single item on board and ask the question 'Does it make the yacht go faster?' If not, remove it.

This philosophy led to the yacht *Myth of Malham*, which some yachtsmen condemned as 'an ugly machine'. Illingworth objected to long overhangs and *Myth*'s bow was so abrupt that she looked as if she had sailed into a wall and then been crudely repaired. He also knew that headsails were more efficient than mainsails and that overlap was free area under the RORC rule, resulting in the characteristic cutter foretriangle with overlapping headsails.

Myth of Malham was an outstanding success, winning the Fastnet Race in 1947 and 1949. She also introduced the era in which ocean racing became a serious sport in its own right, and was a member of the very first British Admiral's Cup team.

Partly because of the Admiral's Cup, the Fastnet has always enjoyed a very strong foreign entry. In the 21 races from 1947 to 1987, there have been nine British winners, six American, and one each from Sweden, the Netherlands, France, Australia, Brazil and Belgium. This is a very healthy situation, for nothing kills an international sporting event more effectively than complete domination by one country.

From 1957 onwards, the Fastnet Race acquired the new status of being the culminating event of the Admiral's Cup series and this emphasized the foreign challenge even more strongly than before. Since that date, the majority of winners of the Fastnet Trophy have been competitors in the Admiral's Cup for the very obvious reason that these will always be the newest and most keenly raced boats. Yet it is important to realize that the competitors for the Admiral's Cup are but one section of the entry list. For instance, the 1987 Fastnet Race had 261 entries, of which just 42 were also competing in the Admiral's Cup.

One thing that an offshore race needs is a good capful of wind from time to time to remind people that racing offshore can be a tough and potentially dangerous business. Several years of generally light winds prior to 1979 had tended to lull yachtsmen into a false sense of security and allowed them to think that in modern, well-equipped yachts a 600-mile race was not really that much of a challenge. This was also a period of very rapid expansion in sailing, when many new people were buying boats without having had the years of experience previously thought necessary before owning a boat.

Above: *Stormy Weather, which won the Fastnet Race in 1935, returned 52 years later to compete in the 1987 event. She was Olin Stephens' second successful offshore design after Dorade, which he and his brother Rod sailed to victory in the 1931 and 1933 Fastnet Races.*

Thus, the stage was set for yachtsmen to be taught a tragic lesson when the record fleet of 303 yachts set off on the 1979 Fastnet Race. It was a straightforward race to begin with, so the great majority of the fleet were already clear of Land's End when a hurricane-force gale hit the area. It was not merely the strength of the wind that was exceptional; due to some particular combination of tide and wind direction, the sea became huge and very irregular, with vicious, breaking crests rearing up at random.

Hardly a single yacht escaped damage and there were very many broken masts and rudders. A total of 24 yachts were abandoned and 15 people died in the raging sea. It was by far the worst disaster in the entire history of the sport.

Afterwards, the Royal Ocean Racing Club and Royal Yachting Association conducted a thorough inquiry which had major repercussions. One of the early findings was that although 24 yachts had been abandoned, only four of them subsequently sank. Overwhelmed by the appalling conditions, crews had abandoned ship needlessly and some had died as a result. Numerous technical lessons were learned concerning the stability of yachts, the fitting and securing of hatches and safety equipment, the design of life-rafts and many other points, but the most important conclusion reached was that there really is no substitute for experience.

In Australia, yachtsmen were accustomed to sailing in much windier conditions than prevail in Europe and many members of the Australian Admiral's Cup team reported that they had experienced conditions at least as bad before. This had made an enormous difference to the confidence with which they handled their yachts during the storm. In contrast, some British yachts had no-one aboard with experience of a severe gale and these were the crews that got into trouble. One of the most important actions of the RORC, therefore, was to place very exacting requirements for experience on competitors in this race thereafter.

The effectiveness of this action was proved in 1985 and 1986 when there was plenty of wind, though nothing quite like 1979. On both occasions a number of yachts retired — most through prudence rather than as a result of damage — and there were no serious accidents to crews. Numbers were slightly down from 1979 but the 261 starters in 1987 were all properly equipped, in every sense, to take the worst that the Fastnet Race could throw at them.

ADMIRAL'S CUP

Born from the relatively modest idea of making life more interesting for American yachtsmen visiting England for the Fastnet Race, the Admiral's Cup has become the most important series in the whole of offshore racing.

The originator was Sir Miles Wyatt who, in 1957, was 'Admiral' — a position similar to that of president in most sports clubs — of the Royal Ocean Racing Club. The Fastnet Race had been well-supported by visitors from the USA since its inception, in 1925, and Wyatt felt the club should do more for those hardy souls who crossed the wild Atlantic just to sail in a single race. He proposed a team competition for three yachts each from Britain and the USA, taking in the results of four races: the 225-mile Channel Race just before Cowes Week, followed by two of the premier races during Cowes Week — the Britannia Cup and the New York Yacht Club Cup — and finally, the 600-mile Fastnet Race. To make sure that the main emphasis was on offshore performance, the Cowes Week races would count for single points, the Channel Race double and the Fastnet triple.

Wyatt put his idea to the owners of three of the best yachts in the RORC fleet: John Illingworth and Peter Green of *Myth of Malham*, Geoffrey Pattinson of *Jocasta* and Selwyn Slater of *Uomie*, who joined Wyatt in the purchase of a silver-gilt cup costing £300. For this first event, there was no question of the Americans holding team trials, they just nominated three yachts which had already announced their intention of making the trip that summer. In the circumstances, it was a strong team: Dick Nye's *Carina* was the 1955 Fastnet winner and had two Transatlantic Race wins to her credit. She was backed up all the way by Bill Snaith's *Figaro* and Blunt White's *White Mist*.

The racing was remarkably close. The British trio took an early lead, mainly because *Figaro* did not start in the Channel Race, after which the Americans came back strongly in the two Cowes Week events. That year's Fastnet Race was one of the windiest on record, with a fleet of 42 yachts battering their way out of the Solent into the teeth of a full gale from the West. Only 12 yachts completed the course, including five of the six Admiral's Cup competitors. *Uomie* pulled out leaking badly and *Carina* had to be pumped the whole way round the course. Dick Nye had no intention of giving up, however: 'Is every man a tiger?' he would yell, chomping a sodden cigar. A chorus of 'Grr . . grr', from the crew, gave him the answer he wanted.

The beamy yawl-rigged *Carina* found just what she wanted on the run back from the Fastnet: gale-force quartering winds, and she romped home to Plymouth in 30 hours to win her second Fastnet. As *Carina* was made fast in Millbay Dock, Nye made the oft-repeated remark to his bone-weary crew, 'OK boys, we made it. You can let the damn boat sink now!' The US trio won the Fastnet Race convincingly but the overall series was won by the British team by the narrow margin of 70 points to 68.

This very first team series for offshore yachts had been both stirring and competitive and was naturally well written-up in the world's yachting magazines, with the result that interest was expressed from several countries. The RORC therefore decided to continue the competition in 1959, throwing it open to all nations. Holland and France entered teams but the Americans were not able to find three yachts that were willing to make the trip.

France's first effort was not very strong and all three of her yachts dropped out of the Fastnet Race but the Dutch made a commendable first effort, scoring 123 points to the defending team's 135.

The year that proved that the Admiral's Cup was going to catch on was 1961. For the first time, British yachtsmen commissioned new yachts especially for the Admiral's Cup and the United States were back; so, too, were Holland and France, and Sweden joined the fray for the first time, bringing the total up to six. At that time, the British team was selected by committee decision and the choice was very conservative with just one of the new yachts, Ren Clarke's Nicholson-designed *Quiver III*, being joined by old favourites *Myth of Malham* and the club yacht, *Griffin II* (the former *Yeoman III*).

They were soon shaken out of their complacency when a strong US team consisting of *Windrose* (Jacob Isbrantsen), *Figaro* (Bill Snaith) and *Cyane* (Henry Du Pont) took a commanding lead in the Channel Race, which was won by *Windrose*. Mainly thanks to the

Left: *Dismasted, with lifelines smashed and wreckage trailing over the side,* Ariadne *was abandoned by her crew during the disastrous 1979 Fastnet Race. One of the lessons learned was that it is better to stay on board a disabled yacht unless she is definitely sinking.*

Left: *A survivor about to be picked up by helicopter after abandoning ship during the 1979 Fastnet Race. A total of 15 died but many more were rescued by helicopters and lifeboats.*

efforts of *Quiver*, Britain fought back in the two inshore races but were still 13 points behind at the start of the triple-scoring Fastnet. The Dutch yacht *Zwerver* won the Fastnet Race and the British had best team points but only just, so overall the United States won by 220 points to 210.

This first overseas win undoubtedly set the competition on its feet. The British saw that they would have to take things more seriously in future, while the visiting countries understood that they had a perfectly good chance of winning.

The reaction of British yachtsmen to losing the cup was encouragingly robust. The RORC announced that it would select the team on the results of a series of races early in the season and there was a positive rush of new building. Newspaper magnate Max Aitken commissioned a 'flat-out' 48ft 6in (14.78m) cutter from Illingworth and Primrose. Lightly built in cold-moulded wood by Souters of Cowes, *Outlaw* was a sinister-looking yacht but tremendously fast to windward. Just as significant, two experienced offshore men, Derek Boyer and Dennis Miller, commissioned a 43ft 5in (13.23m) sloop from Sparkman and Stephens.

At the time, this was regarded as a slightly treacherous move as it had somehow been assumed that the British team would sail British yachts. But a couple of years before, 'S & S', as they were usually known, had designed to the RORC rule a marvellous little 24ft (7.31m) waterline boat, named *Hestia*, for a Dutch owner. *Hestia* had wiped up Class III in no uncertain terms. Boyer and Miller's new *Clarion of Wight* proved to be an outstanding all-round performer and began a long line of S & S yachts built for British owners. A former Fleet Air Arm pilot, Miller thought it was ridiculous to have to race a yacht in the dark with no instruments other than a compass. He therefore persuaded Richard Gatehouse to design an instrument that showed the yacht's heading relative to the apparent wind, the first of the world-famous range of instruments made by Brookes and Gatehouse of Lymington.

Sweden was the early leader in the 1963 series but it came down to another slugging match between Britain and the USA in the end, with the powerful British team winning by 250 points to the USA's 237. Last of six teams was West Germany, competing for the first time.

Stung by the success of *Clarion*, Peter Nicholson decided that the family firm of Camper and Nicholson needed to turn over a new leaf in order to stay in the game. In 1964 he designed for himself a 30ft 6in (9.30m) waterline boat, named *Roquette*, in which he did away with laid teak decks, heavy planking and solid cabin furniture in favour of plywood decks, a moulded hull and stripped-out interior. She was successful and reassured both Ren Clarke and Ron Amey sufficiently for them both to order new Nicholson yachts for the coming season.

Dennis Miller had the opposite reaction. *Clarion* had been fast but a bit fine-ended to shine downwind so he went back to Sparkman and Stephens with a request for a real racer. The result was the aptly-named *Firebrand*, which had many innovative features. To maximize working area and save weight, the deck was mainly flush, with a vestigial cabin top. Most of the winches were sited just aft of the mast to concentrate the weight amidships. She was masthead-rigged with solid rod rigging in place of wire. Her big genoas were made in America, by Hood.

Unexpected competition

The two Nicholson yachts, named *Quiver IV* and *Noryema III*, plus *Firebrand* were a powerful team, but they were to receive a shock from an unexpected quarter — Australia. No-one had really expected the Australians to go to the immense cost of shipping three yachts around the world but a national appeal had raised the money needed. The three yachts they sent contained a surprise too, a 13-year-old harbour racer named *Caprice of Huon*. She had been designed in 1939 by Robert Clark for a Hobart man named Chris Calvert who wanted a day-sailer to beat the local 8-metres. The war delayed construction but Calvert put aside a supply of Huon pine, a rare and almost indestructible timber. Built after the war, *Caprice* sailed successfully until 1954, when Calvert sold her to Bill Northam, who raced her in Sydney Harbour. Her third owner was Olympic medallist Gordon Ingate, who

Below: Firebrand, *designed by Sparkman and Stephens for Dennis Miller, was one of the first really dedicated offshore racing yachts and was a member of the 1965 Admiral's Cup team. Notice the very large size of her genoa in proportion to the mainsail and the bendy boom. Also, that the fashion for making the whole crew sit on the weather rail was yet to come.*

gave her an aluminium mast and thoroughly modernized her. To everyone's astonishment she won a place in the Admiral's Cup team with just a quarter of a point to spare.

There were eight teams in 1965, mostly sailing brand-new, specially-designed ocean racers, but they were all humbled by the 'wonder from down under', *Caprice*, which took first place in the Channel Race and both the inshore races. Unfortunately, she was not backed up by her team-mates *Freya* and *Camille*, both of which sailed the course of the Britannia Cup incorrectly and lost valuable points. The Fastnet Race was quite light and boring for a change and the rather short-rigged Australian yachts were underpowered. On points they took second place to Britain, but it had been a memorable first effort.

This experience only whetted the appetite of the Australians, who returned two years later (1967) with a team consisting of *Balandra*, a sister-ship of *Quiver IV*, *Mercedes III* (the first offshore yacht in which Bob Miller had a hand) and, amazingly, *Caprice of Huon*, campaigned with great verve by Gordon Reynolds. This time, the Australians really threw themselves into training. They arrived early and set up camp in a house at Cowes. Each morning they were out at dawn, running, and then after breakfast went for a full day's practise on the water. Navigators made an in-depth study of Solent tides, using an hydraulic model of the area, while tacticians went through the rules and sailing instructions line by line.

This kind of dedication was quite new and it really paid off. Although all three of their yachts were considered old-fashioned, having integral keels at a time when the change over to fin-and-skeg configuration, in which the rudder is separate from the keel, was just taking place, they managed the tremendous feat of having best team points in each of the four races and won the Admiral's Cup by more than 100 points.

Although the Admiral's Cup was now a very serious event, the Americans had still not reached the stage of being able to choose a team by trials — it still came down to 'Who's thinking of going to Europe this year?' In 1969 they were fortunate that the US designer Dick Carter had decided to build a new boat in Europe. This was *Red Rooster*, a lightweight, flat-floored 41-footer (12.50m) with a centreboard. She was a completely unknown quantity as she was not even completed until two weeks prior to the Admiral's Cup, but the US authorities picked her anyway as they could find only two other yachts ready to cross the Atlantic: Dick Nye's latest *Carina* and Ted Watson's big *Palawan*.

Initially, it looked as if that year's cup was again going to be a battle between Britain and Australia but, almost unnoticed, *Red Rooster* was getting good results in every race. Carter and his crew rounded off the fortnight's sailing by winning the Fastnet Race by 68 seconds from Sir Max Aitken's *Crusade*, giving the USA a narrow win in the Admiral's Cup from Australia. Unfortunately, there was a bitter dispute about the Fastnet result as finishing times taken on board both *Crusade* and *Red Rooster* would have given victory to the former, but the RORC decided to stick with the 'official' time taken by the lighthouse keeper on Plymouth breakwater.

Above: Red Rooster, *with designer Dick Carter at the helm. Winner of the Fastnet Race in 1969, this lightweight, flat-floored centreboarder set the fashion for much more dinghy-like offshore yachts and marked the beginning of the gradual decline of the Sparkman and Stephens influence.*

Front-page news

At the end of 1969 the leader of Her Majesty's Opposition, the Rt. Hon. Edward Heath, took his 34ft (10.36m) *Morning Cloud* to Australia and, to the surprise of all, won the Sydney-Hobart Race. Having done a little dinghy sailing, he was introduced to ocean racing by Sir Maurice Laing and quickly became engrossed in this sport, which he found gave a complete change of scene from politics. When Heath decided to build a new *Morning Cloud* and enter the trials for the 1971 Admiral's Cup, it had a profound effect on the sport as a whole. Heath became Prime Minister in 1970 and immediately his sailing activities were front-page news. Until then, the Admiral's Cup had rated only down-page treatment on the sports pages and was never mentioned on radio or TV. Heath's involvement changed all that.

In retrospect, we can see that he was not an especially good helmsman but an excellent manager who searched out the best possible people for his crew. His right-hand man was the former professional yachtsman Owen Parker, then a marine equipment supplier

Above: Ragamuffin, *the first of several yachts of that name built for Syd Fischer. Note the deep, well-protected cockpit, a feature of many Australian yachts of the period due to the much greater incidence of heavy weather in the Southern Hemisphere.*

in Southampton. Parker's memoirs were cheekily titled *Tack now, Sir!* On occasions when Heath was unavoidably absent, *Morning Cloud* was skippered by the very experienced 'Sammy' Sampson.

When *Morning Cloud* was chosen for the 1971 British team, the tabloid press attacked Heath for choosing an American design team — Sparkman and Stephens, naturally — while Harold Wilson sneeringly dubbed him 'The part-time Prime Minister'. His teammates were Bob Watson's *Cervantes IV* and Arthur Slater's *Prospect of Whitby*, facing a total of ten other teams.

There was added significance in the fact that this was the first time that the new International Offshore Rule (IOR) was used for the Admiral's Cup, finally unifying the rating system throughout the world. Of the 33 yachts taking part, 20 were designed by Sparkman and Stephens!

Both Australia and the USA had strong teams but the Americans made a critical mistake when one of their trio, *Yankee Girl*, went the wrong side of a buoy during the second inshore race. This was a really windy race and the Australian team, *Ragamuffin*, *Salacia II* and *Koolmooloo* put up a predictably strong performance, bringing them up to within 22 points of the British team.

The Fastnet Race was a classic, with every condition from calm to gale. The start was windy, but on the way down Channel the wind fell away to nothing. Then it filled in again and a full westerly gale was blowing as the leaders approached the Fastnet Rock. This was the occasion for Syd Fischer and his crew to show what an Australian crew could do when the wind was really up. With a full-sized spinnaker set in 40 knots of wind, *Ragamuffin* went careering off into the night, with her bow-wave shooting half-way up the mainsail. Finally, Fischer lost control and *'Rags'* went into a horrendous involuntary gybe and broach which ended with the yacht lying on its side, pinned down by the vanged-out mainsail and with the spinnaker threatening to dismast the yacht as it shook itself to destruction.

The real quality and determination of the Australian crew was proved when they got the yacht back on her feet again, cleared away the damage and then set another spinnaker! *Ragamuffin*'s great run back to Plymouth was sufficient to win her the Fastnet Race, the first and only win by an Australian yacht, but was not quite good enough to lift her team into first place in the Admiral's Cup. A good team performance by the British trio, led by Edward Heath, gave them victory.

New strategies

Up to this time, small-boat sailors had not had much impact on the Admiral's Cup; offshore racing was considered a highly specialized business in which experience was everything. But the barriers were beginning to go down. In England, Robin Aisher — who had won a bronze medal at the Acapulco Olympics — recruited another medallist from the same games, Ian Macdonald-Smith, and set about creating a dinghy-style Admiral's cupper. The Dick Carter-designed *Frigate* was almost completely devoid of accommodation, her gear and fittings were much lighter than usual and she was in every way an overgrown small boat.

The Germans, who had not previously been a force in ocean racing took a slightly different path. They, too, recruited the best small-boat sailors available but their three yachts were all fairly conventional designs, two from Sparkman and Stephens and one from Carter. The difference was that after receiving a design from the New York firm they then subjected it to intense study and analysis, with a view to optimizing the rating to the last decimal place. On arrival in England, their yachts were too conventional to invite much excitement and most of the attention was focused on the Australians' attractive new yachts designed by Bob Miller, *Ginkgo* and *Apollo II*, to join the already proven *Ragamuffin*.

But when the racing began it was the Germans, especially *Saudade*, skippered by Berend Beilken, who proved faultlessly steady and whose boats were never far from the top of the fleet. The Fastnet Race was plagued by light winds that year, which suited heavy yachts with a large sail area. As the fleet rounded the Fastnet, Britain and Australia were neck and neck on points but after a very slow and tiresome run to Plymouth it was the German team which had the Admiral's Cup in their grasp.

The long domination of design by Sparkman and Stephens had finally begun to wane by 1975. Two years before, the One Ton Cup had been won by *Ganbare*, designed by a laid-back Californian named Doug Peterson and the Quarter Ton Cup by New Zealander Ron Holland's *Eyghtene*. The Argentine designer Frers, who had trained under Stephens was beginning to make his mark but, in spite of this, with a record entry of 19 teams for the Admiral's Cup, 24 of the yachts were still designed by Sparkman and Stephens.

The West Germans, determined to retain the cup, had three S & S yachts, all fairly big and heavy, and all highly 'optimized'. In contrast, the British team was a 'liquorish all-sorts' affair. Robin Aisher's *Yeoman XX*, known as 'Kiss-Kiss', was the latest Peterson design, very light and flat-floored with a more salient fin-keel than ever before. Ron Amey was back with an attractive new Frers 46-footer (14.02m) *Noryema X*, while John Prentice steered the conventional route with the beautiful wooden-hulled Sparkman and Stephens *Battlecry*. This was the yacht which got her mast stuck through a hole in the Royal Sovereign Light Tower during one of the trial races, but she overcame both the damage and the embarrassment to win a place in the team.

Light winds plagued the series in 1975 and the second inshore race led to widespread criticism of holding racing in the Solent with its tricky tides and fickle winds. After 11 hours, not a single yacht had finished. Finally, *Guia III* of Italy crept across the line in the gathering dusk, just inside the time limit. This meant that the rest of the fleet had a further hour but many never made it. Second was *Yeoman XX*, putting the British team into a strong position. Germany had a really disastrous day with an 18th, a 39th and a disqualified.

The Fastnet Race was also held in light winds and was practically a repeat of 1973. The British team held together well and managed to regain the Admiral's Cup by a very large margin. After the series, arguments raged about the wisdom of holding such major races in the tricky waters of the Solent. While many supported the traditional view, others suggested, for the future, the relatively straightforward arena of Christchurch Bay, just outside the Solent.

Weather fair and foul

The year 1977 was a great one for getting a sun-tan but poor for yacht racing. After the most windless Fastnet Race on record, which took some small boats up to a week to complete, the British team consisting of *Yeoman XX*, *Moonshine* and *Marionette* retained the Admiral's Cup. The poor weather spoiled what should have been a fascinating year in which many new designers appeared with a great rush of original ideas. Boat of the year was *Imp*, designed by Ron Holland for Californian David Allen. Holland gave *Imp* a very broad, powerful stern but her main innovation was in construction. All the heavy structural loads were taken by an aluminium 'space frame', making it possible to reduce the weight of the skin considerably. Although she needed fresh breezes to shine, *Imp* won the Fastnet Race.

No-one will ever say that there was a lack of wind in 1979 — it was the year of the Fastnet disaster. There were no casualties among the 19 Admiral's Cup teams, though there were a number of retirements, mainly due to rudder failures. After several seasons of light airs there had been a general lightening of gear and there was a fashion for very light, carbon-fibre rudders. When the going got really tough, many of these snapped like carrots, leaving yachts unmanageable. Britain's chances in the Admiral's Cup had been torpedoed several days earlier, when *Morning Cloud IV* broke her carbon-fibre rudder during the Channel Race. At least she had no problem during the Fastnet Race.

Though overshadowed by the shock of 15 deaths (see page 92), the Australian performance was remarkable and fully-justified their reputation for excelling in strong winds. *Impetuous*, *Police Car* and *Ragamuffin* finished in third, fourth and 13th position, to give Australia her second win in the Admiral's Cup.

Above: Saudade, *a member of the winning German team in the 1973 Admiral's Cup, pictured at the start of the Channel Race. Notice that she is carrying a star-cut spinnaker successfully on a fairly close reach, while the other yachts in the picture are setting mainsails and genoas only.*

Controversies

The 1981 series was marked by a bombastic wager between two millionaires and the curious affair of *Victory of Burnham*'s rating. The wager was between Australia's Alan Bond and Britain's Peter de Savary. These two agreed to a match-race between Bond's *Apollo V* and de Savary's *Victory of Burnham* for a wager of £10,000 in gold coins on each side. As it happened, there was no wind and the race ran out of time.

Victory of Burnham, designed by Ed Dubois, was the crew-training boat for *Victory*'s America's Cup challenge. When she appeared at the beginning of 1981, she was not only fast, she had a remarkably low rating of 33.1ft. At that rating she was practically unbeatable and other designers scratched their heads, wondering how Dubois had done it. She was measured again prior to the Admiral's Cup, with the same result. There were plenty of grumbles but no-one could put their finger on anything wrong. During the series, *Victory*, with Phil Crebbin as skipper, sailed outstandingly well and was second-best individual yacht to New Zealand's *Swuzzle Bubble*, by a single point.

The following year, when *Victory* was sailing in the SORC series under new ownership, she was protested for her rating and

measured yet again. This time, major differences were found in the hull measurements, putting the rating up to 34.5ft. To say there were raised eyebrows would be an understatement: the chorus of 'I told you so' was deafening and easily reached from Florida to St James' Place, where the RORC decided to re-score the whole 1981 Admiral's Cup as if *Victory of Burnham* had had the higher rating. To their relief, they found that Britain would still have won the cup, though how the original mistake had passed through so many checks has never been properly explained.

Another controversy surrounded the Italian team, on which all three skippers were American sailmakers. There were dark mutterings about 'hired killers' and for future events there would be a new rule requiring at least half of every crew to be nationals of the country they were representing, including the No. 1 helmsman.

'Mumm' was the word in 1983 when, thanks to an exclusive sponsorship deal, the event officially became known as the 'Champagne Mumm Admiral's Cup'. It was also a year of deep embarrassment for Great Britain which, for various reasons, had the weakest team for many years. It was also the first year in which an Olympic course race was held in Christchurch Bay.

The West Germans not only had great experience of the event by now, they also had home-grown designers. Freidrich Judel and Rolf Vrolijk designed two of their team, *Pinta* and *Outsider.* These were built using the most advanced composite construction yet seen, with pre-impregnated cloths of Kevlar and carbon fibre being laid up under heat and pressure in an autoclave to give hulls of unprecedented lightness and stiffness. The third member of the team was *Sabina*, built in aluminium to the designs of the Dutchman Jac de Ridder.

This combination simply overpowered the opposition and Germany were the winners by an unprecedented 367 points from the runners-up, Italy. Britain finished a lowly eighth, her worst ever performance.

Superior yachts

An effect that had become more and more pronounced was the superiority of yachts built for the One Ton Cup competition. Because this is run without handicap, tiny differences between the boats are immediately obvious and the racing acts as a kind of design forcing-house. This effect was clearer than ever in 1985, when the One Ton Cup was held at Poole shortly before the Admiral's Cup. The winner in a very hard-fought series was *Jade*, designed by Rob Humphreys and owned by an American living in England, Larry Woodell. She was joined in the British team by *Panda*, owned by Peter Whipp, and *Phoenix*, which got into the team in the most extraordinary manner. Graham Walker had started the season with a fine new one-tonner, named *Indulgence*, with a strong crew headed by Harry Cudmore. But in an early-season race she hit a submerged wreck and sank. Walker then made an agreement with Lloyd Bankson, owner of the mediocre trialist *Rubber Duck*, to take over his boat. Cudmore and company worked wonders to raise the performance of this boat, transforming her into *Phoenix*.

Jade was clearly the yacht of the year but, to a degree, this proved to be her undoing. She was 'the boat to beat' after the One Ton Cup, with every skipper in the fleet just waiting to have a crack at her. Team-mate *Panda* seemed still to be fighting over an old score from the One Ton Cup and got involved in two

Left: *The German Admiral's Cup competitor* Pinta *on an easy spinnaker reach at the start of the 1981 Channel Race. The brownish colouring of the mainsail indicates that it is made from Kevlar, one of the new high-strength fibres that have become increasingly important in sailmaking.*

protests, losing points on both occasions. In the end, though, it was a simple gear failure that crippled the British team when a shroud broke on *Jade* in the windy Fastnet Race, partly dismasting her.

In contrast, the German team — as well as having three excellent boats — had it dinned into them by their manager Michael Iwand that they must stay clear of trouble, at all costs. This they did and *Diva*, *Outsider* and *Rubin* were justly rewarded for their endeavours by a third German win.

Every single Admiral's Cup competition is more competitive than the last. More and more effort is poured into design, construction, fitting-out, sail-making and managing a team, with the result that the costs of running a campaign have soared into the hundreds of thousands of pounds. With this kind of pressure, sponsorship becomes unavoidable and it was a relaxation of the rules on advertising prior to the 1987 series that gave New Zealand a sporting chance at last. There have been New Zealand teams at various times back to 1975, but the effort of getting a first-class team together and sending it to England was almost beyond the ability of a small country. A freer approach to sponsorship made this possible and New Zealand design had already been proved at world level in events such as the One Ton Cup.

The 1987 series was exceptional in that at least six teams looked like potential winners, with Britain, Australia, Ireland, Germany and USA being the front runners. Even Denmark had a wonder-boat, with the jaw-cracking name of *Original Beckmann Pletfjerner.* But in a year in which the competition showed signs of becoming almost oppressively technical in nature, the added ingredient that the Kiwis had in abundance was sheer natural ability at boat-handling. They showed that complete confidence and natural talent still count. The applause for the victors was never more genuine than when New Zealand won the Admiral's Cup for the first time.

SYDNEY–HOBART RACE

The third in the trio of great ocean races, the Sydney–Hobart is also the youngest, dating back to 1945 when John Illingworth, then still a serving officer in the Royal Navy, suggested a race to Tasmania over the Christmas holidays. This was in response to an invitation from members of the Cruising Yacht Club of Australia, who had planned to cruise to Hobart. Illingworth even bought a locally-built yacht, the 34ft 9in (10.59m) *Rani*, so that he could compete.

Eight yachts rose to Illingworth's challenge and were treated to a short, sharp lesson in what ocean racing meant. On the second night out, a southwesterly gale hit the fleet and most of them hove-to or ran for shelter, but *Rani*, the smallest boat in the fleet, kept battering on. When the fleet finally struggled into Hobart, the crew of the first Australian finisher, the 52ft (15.84m) cutter *Winston Churchill* was astonished to find that *Rani* had already been there for 17 hours and was handicap winner by 29 hours.

It was a lesson that Australian yachtsmen were never to forget. Their habit of caution had grown from the fact that winds are generally stronger in the Southern Hemisphere but — once Illingworth had sown the seed — Australian offshore sailors soon became the toughest and most experienced in heavy weather of any in the world. In fact, Australians soon gained the reputation of being win-or-bust sailors and one of the first of many was Vic Meyer who ordered an 'indestructible' 57ft (17.37m) steel cutter, designed by Sydney engineer Alan Payne. *Solo* was the most successful yacht in the region during the late 1950s and early 1960s. She won the Hobart race in 1956 and 1962 and 'line honours' (first yacht home but not handicap winner) in 1958 and 1959. She won the 30 miles Montagu Island Race five times running. Meyer had the reputation of never taking down a spinnaker until it blew out, which would be the signal to hoist another, slightly smaller one.

For much of the 1960s, the race was dominated by the Halvorsen brothers, who designed, built, fitted out and raced their own boats. The best-known of these was *Freya*, another really bullet-proof boat which was also a member of the first Australian challenge for the Admiral's Cup. She won the Hobart Race in 1963, 1964 and 1965, the only yacht to win this event three times (and in consecutive years).

A special feature of the Hobart Race is that it is of great interest to the Australian public. In England, the average man in the street in Neasden has probably not even heard of the Fastnet Race, but the average Australian downing a pint in Wagga Wagga knows all about the Hobart Race — which is given a lot of media attention there. But he cannot really be doing with handicap results because they do not make a lot of sense unless you are really into the subject. So for this race, 'line honours' — the first boat to finish — became of equal, or perhaps even greater importance than the handicap result.

For this reason there has always been a special magic about being the first yacht into Hobart and there have always been entries for whom this was the main goal. The first was the 65ft (19.81m) Fife cutter *Morna*, which was first home in 1946, 1947 and 1948, on the last occasion setting a course record of four days, five hours, one minute. She was then bought by the brothers John and Frank Livingston, who renamed her *Kurrewa IV* and took 'line honours' in 1954, 1956, 1957, and 1960. In the 1957 race they lowered the course record to three days, 18 hours, which remained the best time until 1962. After 1960, the beautiful but elderly *Morna/Kurrewa* was no longer able to stand up to the battering of a Hobart Race and retired gracefully.

Above: *The Halvorsen brothers'* Freya *is the only yacht to have won the Sydney–Hobart Race three times running (1963/4/5). Notice how her deep cockpit and narrow decks encourage the whole crew to crowd into the cockpit area when their weight would be more useful on the weather rail.*

After this, the record for the Sydney–Hobart race became an international goal, with the big, ocean-girdling maxis making it one of their targets. The first of these was American Huey Long's first *Ondine* which, in 1962, reduced the course record to three days, three hours, 46 minutes. In 1971, three big American yachts were in on the act: Jim Kilroy's *Kialoa II*, Huey Long's *Ondine II* and Ted Turner with the converted 12-metre *American Eagle*. *Kialoa II* had the best time in the fleet but it was not a windy year and the record eluded her.

In 1972, an extraordinary 72ft (21.95m) ferro-cement yacht named *Helsal* made her appearance. Ferro is normally only thought suitable for heavy cruising yachts but designer Joe Adams persuaded the owner, Tony Fisher, to build *Helsal* with steel pipes embedded in the cement as stringers. Steel cables were inserted into the stringers and were used to post-tension the structure after curing, a technique invented for bridge-building. That year, Fisher was also helped by favourable winds and cut a remarkable two-and-a-quarter hours from *Ondine*'s record. Two other yachts, *Apollo* and *Siska II*, were also at the finish line inside the record.

San Francisco millionaire Jim Kilroy was back in 1975, with a new 79ft (24.08m) *Kialoa*. Again, the conditions were kind; a total of nine yachts surpassed *Helsal*'s time, with *Kialoa* setting the new bench-mark of two days, 14 hours, 36 minutes.

SOUTHERN CROSS CUP

In 1967 Australia won the Admiral's Cup for the first time and this provided the impetus to create an 'upside-down' Admiral's Cup in Australia, to be held the following Christmas. Shipping a team of three yachts from Europe to Australia is an enormous commitment, of course, but the same had always been true for Australian teams coming to Cowes, so British yachtsmen felt a strong moral obligation to make the trip if they could. Unfortunately, plans for the first event were wrecked by a dock strike in Britain which not only made it impossible for the British team to get to Australia but also left two of the victorious Australian yachts marooned in Europe.

One result of this was to allow Australian states to enter teams, in order to bulk up the numbers, and the only real overseas competition came from New Zealand. Eric Tabarly had sailed out to Australia with *Pen*

Duick III, but he could not find two more French yachts to make up a team. New Zealand had one outstanding competitor in *Rainbow*, a one-tonner sailed by sailmaker Chris Bouzaid. She sailed an outstanding Hobart race in strong winds and was the first overseas yacht (Illingworth had won in an Australian yacht) to win this race but, on points, the New South Wales team of *Mercedes III*, *Calliope* and *Moonbird* were the first winners of the Southern Cross Cup.

The format was similar to the Admiral's Cup, with a mixture of short and medium length races in the Sydney area prior to the Sydney–Hobart Race itself; this, like the Fastnet Race, counts for extra points in the series. One problem faced by the organizers was the vast fleet of spectator boats. Sydney is one of the world's most boat-conscious cities and during the Christmas holidays, everything that can float goes out to watch the races; at times, it is really difficult

for the Southern Cross competitors to find their way through the milling fleet of boats.

In 1969, a British team consisting of Sir Max Aitken's 62ft (18.89m) *Crusade*, Arthur Slater's 41ft (12.50m) *Prospect of Whitby*, designed by Sparkman and Stephens, and Rodney Hill with a stock S & S 34, *Morning After*, finally made it. But a lot of the media attention was focused on the British team reserve, *Morning Cloud*, the first yacht of that name owned by Edward Heath. And rightly, too. When the time came for the Sydney–Hobart Race, Heath and his navigator Anthony Churchill decided to follow the advice of John Illingworth, whose game plan had been 'Ignore the weather forecasts — go out to sea'. Heading well out from the New South Wales Coast, they picked up a favourable northerly breeze which carried them most of the way across the Bass Straight before a strong southerly gale swept in. *Morning Cloud*, one of the smallest yachts in the fleet, then made an outstanding job of beating down the coast of Tasmania to Hobart, winning the race on handicap from a hot, 79-boat fleet.

The British team also did well but were just beaten on points in the series by the New South Wales team. That year also saw the first appearance of a West Australian named Alan Bond who, in effect, said, 'To hell with the handicap — let's get there first.' To help him in this ambition he hired an ambitious young small-boat designer named Bob Miller, who designed for him a 57ft 4in (17.47m) ultralightweight, giant dinghy, named *Apollo*. She was barely ready for the 1969 race but had a tremendous duel all the way to Hobart with Sir Max Aitken's *Crusade*, which beat her by a scant 18 minutes. This was Alan Bond's first foray into a major yachting event and the beginning of a story which reached its climax when *Australia II*, designed by the same Bob Miller (who meanwhile changed his name to Ben Lexcen) won the America's Cup.

The yacht that changed Australian ocean racing was *Ragamuffin*, designed by Sparkman and Stephens for Syd Fischer, in 1968. Fischer, who made his money in the construction industry, was an all-round sportsman who had been a rugger player and surf-boat helmsman before taking up sailing. After several seasons learning the ropes, Fischer was ready for the big time and pestered Sparkman and Stephens incessantly to get exactly what he wanted. Fischer and his sailing master, Graham Newland, put a great deal of new thought into the layout. Built in cold-moulded wood by Cec Quilkey, *Ragamuffin* was a super-boat from the start and raised the standing of Australian yachtsmen to a new level. Oddly enough, the one race that *'Rags'* never did manage to win was the Sydney–Hobart, but among her many successes was membership of the winning Southern Cross team, in 1969.

1971 was the year that saw the emergence of New Zealand as one of the top nations in offshore racing. Always a nation of outstanding small-boat sailors, New Zealand had not previously had the resources for a major international challenge, but Chris Bouzaid's victory in the 1967 Sydney–Hobart started the ball rolling. He then shipped his one-tonner *Rainbow II* to Europe, where he had two successive shots at the One Ton Cup, winning outright at the second attempt. In those days, the cup was defended by the winner's club so the next One Ton Cup, in 1971, was held in Auckland. But to the fury of the Kiwis, it was won by Syd Fischer who made a last-minute entry in a chartered yacht, *Stormy Petrel*.

As a result, the New Zealanders put a maximum effort into the 1971 Southern Cross, sending a team of three one-tonners: *Pathfinder*, *Wai-Aniwa* and *Runaway*. They ran into strong opposition both from the NSW team and from the British trio of *Morning Cloud*, *Prospect of Whitby* and *Cervantes IV*. In one of the inshore races, Chris Bouzaid caused a furore by setting a large, light headsail at the same time as the spinnaker — something which most yachtsmen felt was outside the rules. But after a marathon protest hearing, the sail was declared legal. Subsequently, this style of sail, variously known as a 'big boy' or 'blooper' became universally used on IOR yachts as it not only adds sail area but counter-balances the spinnaker, making downwind steering easier.

After the short races, the British team had a 200-point lead and were looking very strong in the early stages of the Hobart Race. Approaching Tasmania, however, they ran into calm while the three smaller New Zealand yachts came boiling up astern on a fresh north-westerly. In the relatively short distance remaining, there was no way that the British could shake off the New Zealanders, who finished with an unprecedented first, second and third to take the series.

The New Zealanders led the world in producing compact, well-trained teams, all sailing the same size of boat. Lacking the resources of the larger sailing nations, it made sense for them to concentrate their efforts on one-tonners. In the 1980s, yachts of 30.5ft rating (the new One Ton Cup rating) tended to dominate events such as the Admiral's Cup and Southern Cross so that rules had to be introduced to oblige teams to have at least one larger boat. Before this happened, Britain had one more win in the Southern Cross — the 1986 event.

When the IOR fixed 70ft as the maximum possible rating, a 'maxi' class of yachts around this rating started to emerge and has increased steadily since. These big offshore yachts, which are generally about 80ft (24.38m) in length overall, have had some tremendously exciting duels in the Sydney–Hobart event. In 1982, for instance, *Condor of Bermuda*, *Apollo II* and *Helsal IV* ran into the Derwent River with only a few minutes

Left: Morning Cloud, *the first of four yachts of this name owned by Edward Heath. She was reserve member of the 1969 British team for the Southern Cross Trophy and was the surprise winner of the Sydney–Hobart Race, the first British yacht to achieve this.*

NIRVANA

separating them. Finally, *Condor* and *Apollo* crossed the finish line just seven seconds apart, after 630 miles of racing.

There was a more controversial finish by the maxis the following year, when *Condor* and *Nirvana* sailed neck and neck towards the finish in light airs. Picking up a puff of wind, *Condor* tried to squeeze between *Nirvana* and the shore, while the latter headed up to 'close the door'. With a crunch, *Condor* went on the rocks and stuck there for several minutes. *Nirvana* was first to cross the finish line but in the protest room *Condor* came out on top, after helmsman Ted Turner successfully pleaded that his call for water had been a legitimate one.

The Sydney–Hobart Race, and later the Southern Cross series, really launched Australia into the world of ocean racing, and 40 years of competition have paid dividends. Today, Australian designers, builders and, particularly, offshore sailors, are among the best in the world. With New Zealand, Japan, Hong Kong and perhaps other Far Eastern countries joining in, Australia's great bluewater classic should have a secure future.

SOUTHERN OCEAN RACING CONFERENCE

Not a race but a series, the 'SORC' is the top US offshore racing event and grew over a period of years rather than being created at any one moment. It peaked in popularity in the 1970s, since when a mixture of rising costs and disagreements about courses and rating rules triggered a decline.

A colourful character named Gidge Gandy suggested a race from St Petersburg, Florida, to Havana, Cuba, and this was inaugurated early in 1930. The race, a little under 300 miles in length, was won by Garner Tullis' *Windjammer* in a small fleet of about a dozen yachts which seemed to have raced without handicap. It was very much a 'fun' event, with after-race entertainment in Havana high on the agenda. Apart from various gaps due to wars, revolutions, etc., this race was run annually until the Cuban Revolution of 1960.

Four years later, the Miami Yacht Club began a race to Nassau in the Bahamas. The 176-mile course has three legs: from Miami to Great Isaac Key, thence to Stirrup Key, then to the finish at Nassau. As this cuts directly across the Gulf Stream it can be an extremely rough race if the weather happens to be windy. It was very windy for the inaugural race, in 1934, when only three of 12 starters reached the finish.

It was becoming fashionable in the late 1930s for the 'snow birds' from the Eastern States to fly down to Florida after Christmas to avoid the worst of the winter and eastern yachtsmen began sending their yachts down to Florida to take part in these two races which were normally held during February. In response, the two organizing clubs decided to create a co-ordinated five-race series, starting with the short Lipton Cup off Miami, followed by the Miami–Nassau, the Governor's Cup off Nassau, the St Petersburg to Havana and, finally, Havana to Key West. From 1941, it was decided that the whole event was to be run under the CCA rule.

This splendid plan was still-born because of the Second World War but the idea was revived in 1947, when it became known as 'The Winter Circuit'. Later, all the clubs involved formed a joint organizing committee and this was responsible for the ponderous title 'Southern Ocean Racing Conference'.

After the demise of the race to Havana, a new course was instituted from St Petersburg

Above: *Bob Bell's big Holland-designed maxi* Condor *ranges constantly around the world, taking part in all the major offshore racing series.*

Left: *Marvin Greene's beautiful maxi-yacht* Nirvana, *which holds the course record for a number of major races including the Fastnet Race and Bermuda Race. Although comfortably fitted out below she still manages to be outstandingly fast.*

to Venice, a short way down Florida's West Coast but, in 1973, the club there made such an almighty mess of timing the finish that the race was allowed to lapse and another short 'warm-up' race round Anclote Key was substituted. At the same time, it dawned on the organizers that the whole thing was back to front, and from 1961 the series began at St Petersburg and ended at Nassau. A new, 400-mile race from St Petersburg to Miami via Rebecca Shoals had the effect of moving the entire fleet from the West to the East Coast.

The popularity of the series increased steadily through the 1960s, with 100 yachts taking part in the 1969 Miami–Nassau. And in 1974, a new race — the 'Ocean Triangle' — was instituted. This is a 130-miler, starting from Miami, crossing the Stream to Great Isaac Key, then back across the Stream again to Fort Lauderdale and down the coast to the finish at Miami.

The very first winner of the 'Winter Series', in 1947, was the 45ft (13.72m) Sparkman and Stephens yawl, *Revonoc*, owned by Harvey Conover. She won a very windy Miami–Nassau race in which the 72ft (21.95m) *Tioga* was dismasted and a man was lost overboard from *Windy*.

During the 1950s, the series was dominated by Carleton Mitchell, first with *Caribbee* and later with his famous 38ft 7½in (11.77m) yawl *Finisterre*, in which he won the Bermuda Race three times and the SORC three times. After that, Mitchell got a bit bored with the series and was in the habit of sailing in the Miami–Nassau and then going off for a Caribbean cruise rather than chase the fleet to the West Coast.

Up to the beginning of the 1960s, all offshore yachts were individually designed and built; there was no such thing as a production yacht. Things began to change in 1961, when St Petersburg boatbuilder Charley Morgan boasted that he could beat the fleet with a glass fibre boat, a material which at the time was mainly used for small powerboats. Dinghy sailor Jack Powell took him at his word and Morgan built a 40ft (12.19m) yawl named *Paper Tiger*, which proved she was nothing of the sort by winning the circuit outright.

The glass revolution really got underway in 1964, when the SORC winner was *Conquistador*, a stock Cal-40 owned by Fuller Calloway. Ted Turner had his first introduction to offshore racing in one of these very successful boats, *Vamp X*, winning the circuit at the second attempt. It is ironic that this very healthy development did not last; as racing became more intense, in the late 1970s, it once again became imperative to have an individually — and very expensively — built boat to have a chance of winning.

Big boats have always played an important part in the SORC. The yacht that started this was the 72ft (21.95m) ketch *Tioga*, designed by L. Francis Herreshof, son of the great 'Captain Nat' Herreshof. Owned originally by Henry Noyes, she began her racing career in the late 1930s — when she was almost always the first to finish whether or not she won a race on handicap. After the war she was bought and modernized by Bob Johnson who changed her name to *Ticonderoga*. 'Big Ti', which carried a crippling rating under the CCA rule, really set the fashion for 'line honours' yachts, which were seldom the winners on handicap but were first to finish.

When *Ticonderoga* began to get elderly, Bob Johnson commissioned the English designer Alan Gurney to design a replacement — a flat-out, beat-the-fleet boat. The result was the epoch-making *Windward Passage*, a superlight 73ft (22.25m) flyer built of laminated spruce. On her debut, in 1969, she broke the course record for every race she entered — including knocking three-and-a-half hours off the previous best time for the Miami–Nassau. This marvellous boat really showed the world what a big, light, modern yacht could do and, together with the Dutch yacht *Stormvogel*, began the trend towards maxi-raters. Almost incredibly, *Windward Passage* was still winning races in the late 1980s, after a lot of loving care and modernization by Bob Johnson's son, Frank.

The SORC reached the pinnacle of its success in the early 1970s, but the seeds of decay were beginning to sprout. The fleet results began to be dominated by the new breed of hot one-tonners that the IOR had created and this led to dissatisfaction from owners of older, outclassed yachts. In 1976, therefore, the fleet was divided into 'old' and 'new' divisions. But this only made things worse, because the 'old' owners soon found that they had effectively consigned themselves to the junk heap; all attention was focused on the new boats each year.

A further problem was that, whereas owners and crews had previously lived on board their yachts during the SORC, the modern, stripped-out racers were so uncomfortable that everyone had to sleep ashore in hotels, not just in one expensive resort but in three different ones. This made the whole exercise extremely costly and logistically difficult as every yacht needed to be followed around by a truck-load of personal gear and equipment. Furthermore, the 'conference' of organizing yacht clubs is quite an unwieldy affair and the handling of the series is ponderous and expensive as a result.

By 1985, the fleet was down to 75 boats and it sank again in 1987, when the new IMS measurement system was introduced. However, it is still too early to tell whether this will revive the series. It is possible that a more compact series based on just one centre might prove more popular than the dispersed SORC. That there is demand for a top-class series early in the year is certain, because the US fleet is so spread out during the summer that it never comes together in one place.

OTHER MAIN EVENTS

It has been shown again and again that what yachtsmen like to do is to get away from their jobs for about two weeks at a time, to sail in a series of races, some short, some long, that offer variety, interest and challenge. The Bermuda Race grew into the Onion Patch Series, the Fastnet into the Admiral's Cup, the Sydney–Hobart into the Southern Cross and the Miami–Nassau into the SORC. Seeing this successful formula in action has encouraged other sailing clubs to create similar events. The main ones are briefly described here.

SARDINIA CUP

The Costa Smeralda is the Aga Khan's exclusive resort for the very wealthy on the north-east coast of Sardinia. It operates on the principle of every facility being the best available — with prices to match. The Yacht Club Costa Smeralda at Porto Cervo is very splendid but had little *raison d'être* until 1978, when it was decided to create a new event with the same criteria as the Admiral's Cup, to be run on 'even' years (the Admiral's Cup has always been run on odd-numbered years — see *The Major Records*).

Initially, a great deal of money was poured into the event to 'prime the pump'. Yachts were shipped to Sardinia free, air tickets were handed out to journalists and so on but nowadays most of that has disappeared. The great appeal of the event is that if all goes well it can be a fortnight of first-class racing in Mediterranean sunshine, with the spectacular scenery of Sardinia as a background. There are five events (originally four): three of these are inshore races off Porto Cervo, a short offshore to Asinara and back, and a long race to Les Isles Porquerolles, on the French coast, and back.

The problem with Mediterranean weather is that it tends to extremes: no wind or too much. This is particularly true in the Straits of Bonifacio which have to be threaded twice on the long race. If a 'Mistrale' wind blows from the north it funnels through the straits, increasing a strong wind still further. In 1980 the long race was distinctly visceral, with the fleet battling back from the French coast in 50 knots of wind. Next time, in 1982, the opposite applied and there was so little wind that the programme was not completed.

Though very clearly an 'artificial' series, created from nothing in a place with no background of sailing, the Sardinia Cup at its best can be tremendously attractive, so any owner who announces the intention of entering is usually deluged with enthusiastic volunteers for crew. This being so, the series will undoubtedly continue to be popular but, because of its very variable nature, it will continue to be regarded as a holiday event rather than a really top racing occasion.

Above: This picture of the American yacht Scarlett O'Hara *surfing off an ocean swell under spinnaker shows just why the Clipper Cup (now Kenwood Cup) has become such a popular series. Hawaii offers almost perfect sailing weather for much of the year.*

KENWOOD CUP (FORMERLY CLIPPER CUP)

If you were a rich but very busy man who had just spent $1m on a new racing yacht, what you would like to be assured of on your two-week holiday would be really superb weather. There is probably nowhere in the entire world more likely to provide it than Hawaii. This is why Dennis Conner chose to do all his training for the 1987 America's Cup there. For the sailor, Hawaii would seem to have virtually everything: reliable strong winds, warm water and semi-tropical temperatures. It is a long way from the traditional centres of sailing, but quite accessible from the whole US West Coast and not impossibly far from New Zealand, Australia, Japan and Hong Kong.

The other big attraction of a series based on Hawaii is that it provides an ideal course for a long race: the 775-mile Around the State Race round all the islands of the Hawaii group. Modern offshore racing yachts, from one-tonners upwards, romp round a 600-mile course such as the Fastnet in two to three days so a rather longer event is attractive, especially in reliable winds.

The Clipper Cup series, sponsored initially by Pan American World Airways, began in 1978 when Dick Gooch of Waikiki Yacht Club set out a plan for an Admiral's Cup style five-race series. The event has gone from strength to strength ever since. Rather like the Southern Cross series, more than one team per country is allowed and, in addition, all the races are open to individual yachts. Another of Gooch's good ideas was to handicap the races on time-on-distance, which always tends to favour larger boats, and not to have an upper limit on rating. Thus, the big maxi-yachts have been attracted to the series and teams are often formed from a maxi, a 50-footer and a one-tonner.

The first series had six teams: two each from Australia, New Zealand and the USA, with Australia 'A' — consisting of *Ragamuffin* (Syd Fischer), *Magic Pudding* (John Karrasch) and *Big Schott* (Marshall Phillips) — the winners. One thing that came out of this first series was wonderful pictures of yachts surfing down sparkling waves in the brilliant sunshine, with the result that 11 teams signed up for the next event, in 1980, and the same number for the one after that, in 1982. It is interesting to see the composition of teams in 1982: three from the USA, three from Australia, three from Japan and two from New Zealand, making this a veritable Pacific Admiral's Cup. The top individual yacht that year was the 39ft (11.88m) *Tobiume* from Japan, a completely new nation in the sport of offshore racing.

The tremendous cost of getting a three-yacht team to Hawaii prevented European countries from entering this event until 1988. In that year the Kenwood Company offered a generous travel grant to the top-scoring European team in the previous year's Admiral's Cup. This grant enabled a British team to compete for the first time.

THE TON CUPS

Handicap racing is all very well, but there is a certain frustrating quality about a race in which you may hardly see the other competitors and will not know the result until someone ashore has done a lot of sums. Furthermore, every sailor knows that nothing sharpens up technique more than a one-design race in which all boats are equal and the first home wins.

Frenchman Jean Peytel had the brilliant idea of organizing boat-for-boat racing for offshore yachts, declaring a fixed maximum rating level within which all competitors would race without handicap. In 1965, Peytel's Club — the Circle de la Voile de Paris — re-awarded a famous old trophy known as the 'One Ton Cup' for a series of races to be sailed at 22ft RORC rating. The name of the trophy has caused a good deal of confusion. It got its name from the fact that it was originally for keelboats rated under the 19th-century tonnage rating system, for keelboats of one ton rating. Later, after these boats had died out, it was used for racing in International 6-metres and finally for offshore yachts rating 22ft. The term 'One Ton' has no technical significance today — it is just the name of the trophy.

Peytel's idea was an immediate success and a regatta for yachts of this size has been an annual event ever since. Soon there was a demand that the idea be extended to other sizes of yacht and so, in 1966, a second 'level rating' class was established at 18ft rating. The trophy for this is actually the Lord Granard Cup but, inevitably, it became known as the Half Ton Cup. The idea continued to find success and more level-rating classes were established until eventually, using the vernacular, the classes were: Mini-Ton, Quarter Ton, Half Ton, Three-quarter Ton, One Ton and Two Ton. The last-named was only partly successful and lapsed after 1981.

One of Peytel's excellent ideas was to structure a well-balanced regatta consisting of a mixture of Olympic Course races, middle- and long-distance races so that the competitors should receive a thorough test in a variety of conditions. This format found wide support and is now used in practically all major series for offshore yachts.

The establishment of the ton cups had an influence far beyond the actual racing. Yachts of those sizes became more highly developed and popular and as a result all racing tended to concentrate gradually into a series of rating bands around the various ton cup limits. Even production yachts tend to fall into appropriate size brackets.

All the ton cups have been converted from the original RORC ratings to IOR ratings and there have also been adjustments of the rating limits from time to time. The current One Ton Cup rating of 30.5ft IOR has the special significance that it is also the lower limit for yachts taking part in the Admiral's Cup. As a result, these yachts — which are eligible for what are probably the two most competitive series in the calendar — have become more highly developed than any other.

The winners of every ton cup series so far are given separately. It would be impossible to give any worthwhile description of so many races individually.

THE OCEAN SPECTACULARS

So far we have looked at conventional ocean races and series, run at regular intervals by yacht clubs using widely-accepted rules. During the past 30 years, however, new events have brought fundamental changes to the sailing scene by encouraging new types of boat and new forms of competition. The most influential of these is the Single-handed Transatlantic Race.

THE SINGLE-HANDED TRANSATLANTIC RACE (OSTAR)

Col H.G. 'Blondie' Hasler was an innovator who made very important contributions to yacht design. In the early post-war years he raced in the Royal Ocean Racing Club's events, sailing a 30 sq metre: a light, slim, long-ended Scandinavian 'Skerry cruiser' that was the very opposite of the deep, heavy cruiser-racers then in vogue. However, he became bored with this form of racing because he felt that all rating rules tend to preserve the *status quo*, whereas he was interested in change.

Hasler therefore thought of a race in which the only handicap would be the human factor. He reasoned that if the sole restriction was that only one person could be aboard, this would force the development of yachts that were both seaworthy and easy to handle. When he suggested a single-handed race across the Atlantic, most yachtsmen strongly opposed it on the grounds of safety. But Hasler had two powerful allies: Francis Chichester and Chris Brasher of *The Observer* Sunday newspaper. In the Royal Western Yacht Club of England, they found an organization willing to brave the criticism of conventional yachtsmen and act as organizer.

Hasler and Chichester said they would race across the Atlantic for a wager of half-a-crown (2 shillings and sixpence in old currency) but as only the English knew what this meant, they raised the stakes to 5 shillings (today's 25p). The first race was fixed for June 1960, to start at Plymouth and finish in New York (changed to Newport, Rhode Island for subsequent races). True to Hasler's concept, there were no restrictions whatever on the type of boat.

There were just five competitors but the most interesting yachts were those of Hasler and Chichester. Hasler had been tinkering for several years with *Jester*, a 25ft (7.62m) Scandinavian Folkboat, which was a basically seaworthy, reasonably fast small boat. In place of the conventional cockpit and cabin-top, *Jester* was completely decked-over as Hasler planned to remain inside the cabin most of the time and sail the boat by 'remote control'. His most striking innovation was to replace the conventional sloop rig with a single, fully-battened, Chinese junk-style sail set on an unstayed mast. This has two great advantages: it is semi-balanced, having area ahead of the mast as well as abaft and so needs only light control forces, and it is uniquely easy to reef. On being lowered, each segment of sail simply folds down on to the one below, like a Venetian blind. Hasler could do this without going on deck — by a series of control lines leading into the cabin through small holes.

His second area of study was self-steering. At that time, it was not possible to consider an electronic 'auto-pilot' for a small sailing yacht but Hasler designed a wind-vane-controlled steering system that used the power of the water flowing past the boat to amplify the power from a relatively small vane, thus providing the extra power needed to operate the yacht's normal rudder.

Chichester's *Gipsy Moth III* was a larger, much more conventional yacht than *Jester*. With a length of 39ft (11.88m) and a conventional sloop rig, she was quite heavy at 13 ton (13.21 tonne) and many people doubted that 58-year-old Chichester would be able to handle her effectively. For his self-steering, he relied on a more basic system than Hasler. The rudder was directly connected to a wind-vane and Chichester found that he needed

***Above:** 'Blondie' Hasler's highly individualistic little 25ft (7.62m)* Jester *was the test-bed for his experiments with both self-steering and junk rig. Both can be seen in this picture of* Jester *as she set off on her seventh Single-handed Transatlantic Race.*

Right: The Newick-designed trimaran Three Cheers, *in which Mike McMullen put up a tremendous performance to finish second in the 1974 Round Britain Race. Tragically, both yacht and skipper disappeared during the 1976 Single-handed Transatlantic Race.*

Right: The extraordinary Vendredi 13, *which was an attempt to create an enormous but very easily-handled yacht capable of challenging the big multihulls in the Single-handed Transatlantic Race. She very nearly succeeded.*

a sizeable vane to get enough power. His 'Miranda' system ended up as virtually a full-sized mizzen, complete with reefing; a bit crude, but it worked.

The other competitors were: *Eira*, a conventional Folkboat sailed by Valentine Howells; *Cardinal Vertue*, a 25ft (7.62m) Vertue Class sloop, sailed by David Lewis, and *Cap Horn*, a lightweight 21ft (6.40m) centreboard sloop, entered by Frenchman Jean Lacombe. As well as having the smallest boat, Lacombe was five days late starting — due to technical problems.

Among the many problems these pioneers faced was which route to take. Chichester chose the shortest, so-called 'Great Circle' route, which carried the disadvantage of being directly into the prevailing westerly winds. Hasler, knowing he had a slower boat, chose a daring northerly route in the hope of finding favourable winds on the northern side of the Atlantic depressions. This route is longer, colder and involves the risk of running into ice. You need to look at a globe to understand why the direct route from Plymouth to New York goes so far north: following this route involves making a landfall at Cape Race on the coast of Newfoundland and then heading south-west down the US East Coast.

The winner of this first race, by a full 8 days, was Francis Chichester sailing *Gipsy Moth III*. This represented a triumph for toughness, determination and resilience but not a vindication for Hasler's concept, for the main lesson learned was that the bigger boat won. Chichester had had to work himself to the point of exhaustion, steering, navigating, changing and setting sails and carrying out all the other tasks involved in racing a yacht. Hasler had almost been able to relax in his cosy cabin and only had to steer by hand for one hour in 48 days. Nevertheless, Chichester won thanks to his larger, faster yacht.

When the second race was planned four years later, the committee introduced a handicap procedure and decided to declare both an elapsed and a corrected time winner. Later in the history of the race, it was found necessary to impose an overall length limit and within this, several classes defined solely by overall length were established. This is probably as free a system as can be devised without a complete free-for-all.

Innovations

The 1964 race brought two greatly significant innovations: the first yacht designed and built specially for the race and the first multihulls. French naval officer Eric Tabarly had been inspired by the first race and decided to enter the fray in 1964. At first, he planned to use a stock, light-displacement racing yacht of 31ft 6in (9.60m) overall length but, after getting some experience with this, decided to sail a larger boat. Together with the builder, Constantini, he designed a lightweight 44ft (13.41m) ketch, built in plywood. Because of the lighter displacement, *Pen Duick II* only needed about the same sail area as *Gipsy Moth III* but her extra length gave her added speed. Light-displacement boats tend to involve harder work as their small sail area needs constant adjustment, but Tabarly was a much younger, stronger man than Chichester.

Seagoing multihulls were only just beginning to make their apperance in European waters and most yachtsmen viewed them with suspicion; their speed potential was undoubtedly high but their safety was questionable due to the lack of self-righting ability. To overcome this drawback, the English designer Michael Henderson designed a catamaran with ballast keels — like a double yacht. This achieved the aim of self-righting at the sacrifice of some speed potential.

Henderson's *Misty Miller* was one of three multihulls entered for the 1964 race. The others were *Folâtre*, a fairly basic Piver-type trimaran entered by Derek Kelsall, and David Lewis's *Rehu Moana*, which was not a racing boat, having been designed to sail around the world. All three performed pretty poorly.

Before this race, Chichester said that his ambition was to cross the Atlantic in 30 days, which he did — with just three minutes to spare. But Tabarly beat him to Newport by almost three days. Apart from making Tabarly a national hero in France, this result confirmed that the 'OSTAR' would most likely be won in future by a long, light boat specially designed for the race, with a rig that was as easy to handle as possible.

The 1968 winner, Geoffrey Williams, followed this line of thinking — but with an added innovation. His yacht, *Sir Thomas Lipton*, designed by Robert Clark, was 56ft (17.06m) overall, of moderately light displacement and ketch-rigged with a cutter fore-triangle to divide the sail area into portions which one man could handle. She was an extremely attractive and logical boat, and she could receive advice about the best route to take by radio telephone. Williams arranged with English Electric Computers that they would get the latest weather forecasts from the Meteorological Office each day, calculate the most favourable course and pass this information on to him.

In conventional racing, this would not be allowed as it was a clear case of 'outside assistance', but the OSTAR had no rule against this kind of thing. The weather forecasting proved to be of crucial assistance to Williams, who was advised to sail north in order to avoid a deep depression which caused serious problems for many other competitors including one direct rival, the South African Bruce Dalling, whose *Voortrekker* was similar in size and concept. There was some resentment about Williams' victory and outside assistance was banned for future races. But modern technology made this irrelevant shortly afterwards, with the arrival of the 'Weatherfax' system that allows yachts to receive complete forecast maps by radio.

In 1964, multihulls had been 'knocking at the door', and in 1966 Derek Kelsall won the first Round Britain Race, sailing a trimaran of his own design. Eric Tabarly was convinced of the type's potential and his entry for 1968 was the extraordinarily-advanced 67ft (20.42m) aluminium trimaran, *Pen Duick IV*. This was potentially a much faster boat than *Sir Thomas Lipton* but Tabarly had left himself insufficient time to sort out teething problems, particularly with the complex self-steering system. He had to retire from the race after colliding with a ship.

The banner for multihulls was then taken up by Tom Follett, sailing the attractive little proa, *Cheers*, designed by Dick Newick. This minimal craft was 40ft (12.19m) long but so slim and light that there was only just room for Follett to squeeze into the larger of the two hulls. She was intended to be a modern version of the true Melanesian multihull, consisting of a canoe hull with one balancing outrigger which always remained to leeward. Instead of tacking, a boat of this type stops and reverses direction.

This is not the best craft for slugging to windward in the North Atlantic, so Follett took the southern route, sailing south to the Azores before crossing the Atlantic in the Trade Winds. This gamble nearly paid off, as *Cheers* reached the finish only 28 hours after the winner. Furthermore, Follett had enjoyed a pleasant trip in sunny latitudes while Geoffrey Williams and Bruce Dalling (first and second respectively) had battled against the worst that the North Atlantic could throw at them.

The 1968 race attracted a lot of adverse comment through the activity of some very cranky, unseaworthy entries. Critics of the event said it was wrong to encourage people to set off alone in unsuitable craft, only to be rescued at considerable public expense. Hasler had said that any single-hander who got into trouble in mid-Atlantic 'should be prepared to drown like a gentleman', but this proved a pious hope. Edith Baumann of West Germany and Joan de Kat of Belgium had to be rescued after their poorly-designed trimarans fell to pieces, while Marc Cuiklinski of France was picked up from his sinking yacht after the rudder had broken off.

Clearly, there were just two possible lines of development for this race: multihulls or even-larger monohulls. By 1972, the development of sail-handling equipment such as roller-reefing and better winches made it feasible for a single-hander to manage a much larger sail area than hitherto, so designers turned their thoughts to a huge but very light monohull with reasonably small sails. The French yachtsman Jean-Yves Terlain had the most ambitious ideas, and joined forces with the American designer Dick Carter. Together they devised the astonishing 128ft (39.01m) *Vendredi 13*. Carter believed that waterline length was all-important and set out to create the slimmest, most easily-driven hull possible

on this enormous length. To drive it, he planned a rig with just three boomed jibs so that, instead of reefing, Terlain could just lower one or two of the sails. Excellent to windward in strong winds, *Vendredi 13* was a poor performer in light or following winds and an attempt was made to mitigate this weakness by giving her big, lightweight genoas which could only be set in gentle conditions.

Terlain would probably have won but for some minor gear failures and light winds near the finish. The winner, in the new record time of 20 days, 20 hours, was Alain Colas, sailing *Pen Duick IV*, bought from Eric Tabarly. Colas had been sailing this boat almost continuously for more than two years and had the big trimaran fully sorted-out. In the rush to complete a new boat, this all-important factor is frequently overlooked.

***Below:** The 'ultimate monster'* Club Mediteranee*, seen from the air, setting four mainsails and three jibs. Gear failure prevented her from winning the 1976 Single-handed Transatlantic Race and afterwards an upper limit of size was brought in to ensure that yachts of this size could not compete again.*

Tragedy touched the race in 1972, when Sir Francis Chichester entered — against all advice — sailing his latest boat, *Gipsy Moth V*. He was clearly unwell and hardly able to handle the boat at the start. After a few days he radioed that he was turning back and, in a worthy but misguided attempt to help him, a French weather-ship damaged *Gipsy Moth*'s rigging while trying to go alongside. Then an American yacht tried to come to the aid of Chichester and was hit and sunk by the French ship, with the loss of seven lives. Chichester was eventually rescued by the Royal Navy but died shortly afterwards.

The 1976 race proved that Hasler's original concept had got completely out of hand and the future of the race was placed in doubt. The 1972 winner, Colas, concluded that the *Vendredi 13* concept had been correct but had not been taken to its logical conclusion. When he announced his plan to build a vessel of 236ft (71.93m) for the following race, he was roundly criticized by Eric Tabarly, who wrote, 'His boat adds nothing new to naval architecture. It is quite uninspired, being merely an enlarged version of *Vendredi 13*, with all her defects as well, multiplied by two.'

Remarkable feats

Following the 1972 race, Colas had made a marvellous round-the-world voyage with *Pen Duick IV*, renamed *Manureva*, but on his return he suffered a serious accident in which half of one foot was torn off. As he fought to regain his fitness and struggled to find the backing to build his enormous yacht, Colas became a lonely, embittered figure.

He did succeed in getting the monstrous *Club Mediterranee* built, and sailed her single-handed across the Atlantic, but he did not win for the usual reason — lack of preparation time. A basic design fault in the four masts caused the halyards continually to chafe through and break. Eventually, he was forced to put into St John's, Newfoundland, for repairs. He then needed the help of a gang of men to get his huge vessel back out of the harbour again. This was against the rules and he was given a time penalty.

Meanwhile, the winner for the second time was Eric Tabarly, sailing his 73ft (22.25m) ketch *Pen Duick VI*. This conventional, big IOR boat was designed for the Whitbread Round the World Race and not really suited for single-handed sailing (the normal racing crew was 18 men!). That Tabarly managed this feat was a tribute to his tremendous toughness and experience rather than to the design of the yacht.

The 1976 race encountered very bad weather and several big multihulls were knocked out. *Kriter III*, the former *British Oxygen*, broke up and sank, while Mike McMullen and his trimaran, *Three Cheers*, disappeared and were never found. This made the performance of Mike Birch, who finished in third place in the very light 31ft (9.45m) trimaran, *The Third Turtle*, very remarkable.

Above: The trimaran Fleury Michon, *sailed by Philippe Poupon, was the first to finish the 1984 Single-handed Transatlantic Race but had victory snatched away due to the fact that Yves Fauconnier was given a time allowance for attempting to rescue another competitor.*

The Royal Western Yacht Club, organizers of the race, reacted to the events of 1976 by fixing a maximum size of 56ft (17.06m) and a maximum fleet of 110 boats. This was the end of the concept of a 'no holds barred' race.

The American multihull designer Dick Newick finally hit the jackpot in 1980, when Phil Weld was the winner with *Moxie*. Weld, a retired newspaper proprietor, was one of the few to have capsized a multihull in mid-ocean and lived to tell the tale. On his way from America to take part in the 1976 race, his trimaran *Gulfstreamer* had been flipped over by an unlucky wave but he and a companion had lived in safety — if not comfort — inside the hull of the upturned yacht for several days until spotted. This showed that a multihull capsize was not necessarily fatal, provided the boat was suitably designed.

Moxie, at 51ft (15.54m) built well below the new 56ft (17.06m) limit, was designed with roller-reefing headsails because Weld figured that, as the oldest competitor in the race, he needed some labour-saving aids. He was one of the best prepared, having been sailing fast multihulls for more than ten years and he had almost no technical trouble. He also predicted that the first boat home would take 18 days — a time that he bettered by 48 minutes; this was less than half the time that Chichester had taken in 1960, when he was about the same age as Weld in 1980. This indicates the enormous progress that had been made in design in just 20 years.

By 1984 the 'OSTAR' was no more, as *The Observer* newspaper had severed its connection with the event and was replaced by the brewers Carlsberg. As the two-handed transatlantic tends to be called the 'Two-STAR', wags began calling the single-handed race the 'Carlstar'. By now the maximum size had been increased to 60ft (18.28m), so as to fit in with various other races and the fleet was divided into five classes, by overall length.

As there was no longer any real doubt that multihulls would win this race in future, the front-runners were all trimarans at or near the maximum size. The first boat to finish was the 56ft (17.06m) *Fleury Michon*, sailed by Philippe Poupon in a new record time of 16½ days. However, because Yves Fauconnier had spent time rescuing fellow Frenchman, Philippe Jeantot, whose *Credit Agricole* had capsized, he was awarded compensatory time and declared the winner.

It is a race of genuine innovation, with new developments such as hydrofoils struggling to reach the top, and it is to be hoped that this relative freedom to experiment will continue.

Poupon was more than revenged in 1988 when, partly due to favourable winds, he smashed his own record with an astonishing time of 10 days, 9 hours, 15 minutes, the fastest east-west crossing of the Atlantic by any type of sailing craft with any number of crew. The first 11 finishers broke the previous record in this exceptionally fast race.

Above: Derek Kelsall's trimaran Toria was a 'breakthrough' design when she won the first Round Britain Race in 1966. Notice how her weather float is clear of the water, adding to stability and reducing wetted surface area. Her rig was her least satisfactory feature.

ROUND BRITAIN RACE

Col. Hasler, initiator of the Single-handed Transatlantic Race, had a further idea up his sleeve: a race around Britain and Ireland, starting and finishing at Plymouth. Furthermore, it was to be run in stages, with compulsory 48-hour stops at four points: Cork, Barra in the Hebrides, Lerwick in the Shetlands and finally Lowestoft, most easterly point of the British Isles. Britain is a small nation, but a line around it is 2,000 miles in length and by forcing the yachts to keep close to the coast, much more difficult navigational problems are presented than in an offshore course. Because of the stops, this is also a very social race, with rivals able to meet up in harbour and drown their aggressions in a pint or two of beer. At least, this was so until the fastest boats became so fast that the slower ones never see them after Cork.

The first race was held in 1966, when multihulls were still the big novelty. Derek Kelsall's 40ft (12.19m) *Toria* was a real trend-setting boat. Unlike cruising trimarans, which normally have solid wing-decks connecting the three hulls, *Toria* was joined together only by stout crossbeams. The remainder of the space between the hulls was occupied by netting, and this enormous weight saving had the further advantage that the waves were less likely to damage the underside of the boat. The two outriggers were raised relative to the main hull so that while one was in the water, the other would be up in the air. This reduced the area of wetted surface and made better use of the windward hull's weight.

Toria had a rather unsophisticated sloop rig and was lucky to find generally favourable winds in 1966. Kelsall and Martin Minter-Kemp cruised her around Britain with very little fuss in the fast time of 19 days (not counting the stops). The boat that should have given her a hard time, the 40ft (12.19m) catamaran, *Mirrorcat*, was delayed at the start with technical problems and never managed to catch up.

This race has only once been won overall by a monohull. This was in 1970, when Leslie Williams and Robin Knox-Johnston were first home in the 56ft (17.06m) *Ocean Spirit*. The leaders ran into very tough conditions off the north-west of Scotland (they usually do) and these two strong and experienced sailors were able to drive their solidly-built yacht harder than the multihulls. The winners took a day longer than *Toria* had in 1966.

Robin Knox-Johnston cropped up again in 1970, as co-skipper with Gerald Boxall of the 70ft (21.33m) catamaran, *British Oxygen*. Designed by Roderick Macalpine-Downie, who had had such success with smaller day-racing catamarans, 'BO' was the first really big and powerful multihull. Her speed potential was exceptional but the deck-gear available at the time was not really adequate, so Knox-Johnston and Boxall spent a lot of time either repairing things or wrestling with technical problems.

Her main rival was Mike McMullen's considerably smaller and lighter 46ft (14.02m) trimaran, *Three Cheers*. These two fought out a tortoise-and-hare contest, with *Three Cheers* going ahead when *British Oxygen* had problems and the latter then thundering past again when everything was working. *British Oxygen* was finally the winner by a small margin in the best time so far, 18 days.

Chay Blyth teamed up with Rob James for the 1978 race and they were first home, in 21 days, sailing the 54ft (16.46m) trimaran, *Great Britain IV*. Light winds made this a slow race even though the speed potential of the winners had been higher than ever.

The current record for sailing around Britain and Ireland was set by Rob and Naomi James in 1982, when they raced the 60ft (18.28m) trimaran, *Colt Cars GB* around in the astonishing aggregate time of eight days, 16 hours, three minutes. This was an example of everything going right: a fast boat, skilled crew and favourable weather conditions — for most of the time. The following year James tragically lost his life when he fell overboard from this boat, off Dartmouth.

The weather was again very tough for the 1985 race (the four-year cycle having slipped a year because the programme was getting so crowded). As far as Lerwick, there was a tremendous battle between two exceptionally fast 60ft (18.28m) trimarans: *Apricot*, sailed by Tony Bullimore and her designer-builder Nigel Irens, and *Paragon*, sailed by Mike Whipp and David Alan-Williams. *Apricot* had a wing mast which gave her superior performance in light-to-medium conditions, whereas *Paragon* was lighter and beamier and very fast in a strong breeze. Whipp and Williams were leading at Lerwick after Bullimore and Irens had problems with a broken main halyard. Heading south, *Paragon* hit a severe gale with exceptionally rough seas off the north-east corner of Scotland and suffered a severe structural failure of her main crossbeam. Her crew were just able to get the damaged yacht into Peterhead intact, leaving *Apricot* to win the race in nine days, seven hours, 33 minutes.

Many yachtsmen have found this race to be a great challenge and enormous fun, even if they are well out of the limelight. There are a number of classes for yachts of different sizes, and for production boats, in order to maintain the interest for owners of these boats. The race takes the fleet to areas where yachts would otherwise hardly ever go, such as the Shetlands — where the public take great interest and welcome competitors into their homes to recuperate. For these reasons, this popular race seems certain to continue.

WHITBREAD ROUND THE WORLD RACE

It was almost inevitable that someone would start a yacht race around the world. The question really was; when and in what form? During 1968/9 *The Sunday Times* offered their Golden Globe for the first yachtsman to sail single-handed around the world without stopping, but as the various competitors started from different places and at different times, it can hardly be called a race. There was only one 'finisher', Robin Knox-Johnston, sailing *Suhaili*.

***Below:** The first Whitbread Round the World Race was won by the stock Swan 65* Sayula, *owned by Mexican washing-machine magnate Ramon Carlin. She suffered a complete capsize in the Southern Ocean but survived without major damage.*

K
3566
F 5999

In 1969, publisher Anthony Churchill put forward the idea of a proper race around the world, but although there was plenty of interest from potential competitors he could not find a big enough sponsor to back the event. Fortunately, the Royal Naval Sailing Association was already in discussion with brewers Whitbread about a possible 'spectacular' race so, eventually, Churchill handed over his ideas to the RNSA, who agreed to organize the race.

Churchill's idea was that it should be an event for conventional ocean racing yachts, with full crews. No multihulls, no single-handed heroes, just properly designed and equipped big yachts, rating between 33 and 70ft IOR! This, and the solid reputation of the RNSA, gave the race an aura of respectability from the start. Stops were planned at Cape Town, Sydney and Rio de Janeiro.

In spite of this feeling of respectability, what was being suggested was actually extremely audacious. The small number of yachts that had sailed around the world south of the three great capes (Good Hope, Leeuwin, Horn) had done so in reasonably safe latitudes, but competitors in a real race would be tempted to sail the shortest possible course. It is impossible to sail a Great Circle course from Cape Town to Sydney, or Sydney to Cape Horn, as this would pass across Antarctica. The shortest practicable course would be along the ice limit between 60° and 70° south latitude — well within the range of drifting icebergs. Racing in these high latitudes, in conditions of extreme cold, perpetual westerly gales and with the considerable risk of hitting icebergs ever present was not easy to contemplate.

Nevertheless, there were 20 entries for the first race, which started in September, 1973. These were a mixture of already-available stock yachts, such as the Sparkman and Stephens-designed Swan 65s, and some specially designed for the race. The biggest British entry was the 80ft (24.38m) *Great Britain II*, skippered by Chay Blyth, while her main rival appeared to be Eric Tabarly, with his black 73-footer (22.25m) *Pen Duick VI*. But the French challenge proved short-lived, as *Pen Duick VI* was dismasted before even reaching the first stop. Although she was re-rigged and gamely continued the race she was never in the hunt.

Disaster

Worries about the safety of the event were confirmed during the leg from Cape Town to Sydney, which claimed three lives. Paul Waterhouse went overboard from the Italian yacht *Tauranga* when the spinnaker sheet threw him off balance. Dominique Guillet was washed off the foredeck of *33 Export* and Bernard Hosking fell overboard from *Great Britain II*. In each case, with the yacht running fast in strong winds and big seas, it was exceptionally difficult to turn back and search quickly enough to have a reasonable chance of success. Survival time in very cold water is only minutes.

The Mexican-owned Swan 65 *Sayula* was turned completely over on this leg but, although there was total chaos on board and a good deal of minor damage, the yacht was strong enough to survive and went on to be the handicap winner of this inaugural event. *Great Britain II* was the first boat home, in 144 days.

In spite of the loss of three lives, most of the crews who had taken part in the first Whitbread Round the World Race felt that it was both enormously challenging and satisfying. For the second race, in 1977, designers, builders and skippers had a better idea of what was required and it was clear that meticulous preparation was essential.

The British owner Nick Ratcliff took the bold step of rigging a Swan 65 as a sloop. The dismasting of *Pen Duick VI* suggested that this was risky but it gave the promise of higher performance. Another big sloop, the 79ft (24.08m) *Heath's Condor* was dismasted on the first leg, just as *Pen Duick* had been. The race then became a thrilling battle between newcomer Cornelis van Rietschoten's 65ft (19.81m) aluminium ketch, *Flyer*, and Ratcliff's *King Legend* with the Dutchman's yacht the handicap winner by a small margin. *Great Britain II* was again first home, in 134 days.

For the 1981 race, van Rietschoten returned with a new 77ft (23.47m) *Flyer*, with a sloop rig. This was again a very strong, unextreme all-rounder and it was left to New Zealander Peter Blake to try a breakthrough approach with the 68ft (20.72m) *Ceramco New Zealand*, a wide, shallow, downwind flier, designed to go planing away down the great rolling seas of the Southern Ocean. But Blake, who had sailed aboard *Heath's Condor* in the previous race, suffered the same fate a second time when *Ceramco*'s tall rig came crashing down.

Re-rigged, *Ceramco* got the hoped-for sleigh-ride through the 'Roaring Forties' on leg two but just failed to beat *Flyer* to Auckland (which had become the second stopping point after the initial race), so proving how difficult it is for a yacht designed for one particular condition to beat an all-rounder, even in such an unusual race.

Flyer's success in this race was total: she was first home in every leg and won the race on both elapsed and corrected time. She also set a remarkable new record of 120 days, six hours for the circumnavigation.

'Conny' van Rietschoten was an amateur, spending his own money, and he decided to quit while he was ahead in face of the immense sums of money required to build a competitive boat for the 1985 race, in which most of the 14 yachts entered were specially built and heavily sponsored. One that was not, was *Drum* — a yacht with a short but extraordinary history. Originally to be named *Colt Cars*, she was being built for Rob James,

Left: A vast spectator fleet turns out to see the competitors in the 1977 Whitbread race on their way. Great Britain II *and* Pen Duick VI *are the two deadly rivals in the picture.* Pen Duick *eventually dropped out, after being dismasted twice.*

***Above:** With double-reefed main and small jib, the maxi-yacht* Drum *beats out of the Solent at the start of the 1985 Fastnet Race. Approximately 24 hours later, her keel fell off and she capsized, miraculously without loss of life. In spite of this accident she was rebuilt in time for the Whitbread Round the World Race that year.*

who lost his life when he fell overboard from the trimaran of the same name. Then there was a board-room shuffle within the Colt company and construction was abandoned. Pop star Simon Le Bon bought the hull and had it fitted out for the 1985 race, but while sailing in the Fastnet Race the keel broke off and *Drum* capsized.

Even this did not discourage Le Bon, who put even more of his own money into the project so that the boat could be rebuilt in time for the race. Practically all of the front-runners had been built using the latest composite construction methods and this was nearly their undoing, for these stiff but light hulls proved to be dangerously brittle under extreme conditions and a number of them suffered structural defects, particularly *Côte d'Or*, the maxi-yacht sailed by Eric Tabarly.

Peter Blake was back with *Lion New Zealand*, like *Drum* designed by Ron Holland and with a similar hull form. This was more of an all-rounder than *Ceramco* but, ironically, this time Blake was beaten by a more extreme design, *UBS Switzerland*, designed by Bruce Farr for Pierre Fehlmann. The Swiss Fehlmann was not only extremely experienced but he exercised strict control and left nothing to chance. *UBS Switzerland* was first yacht home, in the new record time of 117 days, one hour, while the handicap prize went to the very-keenly sailed 57ft 9in (17.60m) French yacht, *L'esprit d'Equipe*.

For the future, the race faces two problems: the enormous cost of the yachts and the fact that for political reasons the course is to be changed for a second time. A stop-over at Cape Town is no longer acceptable so, in 1989, the course will include a kind of ocean zig-zag in the Atlantic, with Punte del Este, Uruguay, being visited both on the way out and on the way home.

MORE SHORT-HANDED RACES

Here we look at some of the more important, newer short-handed races that have been run at least twice and may reasonably be expected to continue.

ROUTE DU RHUM

When the organizers of the Observer Single-handed Transatlantic Race limited entries to a maximum of 56ft (17.06m), there was a good deal of dissent, particularly in France, where a number of large, specially-developed boats had no event to compete in. This provided an opportunity for Frenchman Michel Etevenon to promote a new race without limits. Furthermore, by having the start at St Malo and the finish at the French Caribbean island of Guadeloupe, the race could be completely French in character. At 4,000 miles, it was rather longer than the OSTAR, but the latitude of Guadeloupe makes it much more attractive for the participants to take a southerly route.

The first event took place in 1982, and was notable for two accidents and an extraordinary finish. The first accident was alarming but fortunately non-fatal. Marc Pajot, sailing the 75ft (22.86m) catamaran, *Paul Ricard*, lost control while hoisting the spinnaker at the start and ran straight over a small cruising yacht. Both boats were damaged but luckily no-one was injured.

The second, much more serious accident has not been explained to this day. Alain Colas had entered in *Manureva*, the former *Pen Duick IV*, in which he had won the 1972 OSTAR and subsequently sailed around the world. No-one could be more experienced or know his boat better, yet Colas simply disappeared. Whether he capsized, or collided with a ship or whether the well-used trimaran suffered a structural failure that he could not cope with remains a mystery.

The very experienced French helmsman, Michel Malinovsky, was convinced that it would be possible to win in a highly efficient monohull. His slim, ultra-light 70ft (21.33m) cutter, *Kriter V*, was an attempt to strike back against the multihulls — and nearly succeeded. Malinovsky took the shorter, northern route, relying on his deep-keeled cutter to excel to windward. Meanwhile, Canadian Mike Birch, sailing the Newick-designed trimaran *Olympus Photo*, took a big swing to the south into the Trade Winds, and Phil Weld aboard *Rogue Wave* went straight down the middle, following a rhumb line course.

As the leaders converged on Guadeloupe, *Olympus Photo* was slightly ahead but, in a light wind, *Kriter V* crept up to take the lead, Working around the island's southern tip, the monohull proved faster, close-hauled in a light breeze, but when victory seemed in sight the breeze freshened and the trimaran came storming up again. The two raced neck and neck for the finish at Pointe-a-Pitre but, as the morning wind grew strong, Birch's *Olympus Photo* finally leaped ahead, to finish first by just 98 seconds after 4,000 miles. The winning time was 23 days, six hours.

By the second race, in 1982, new ideas were being tried to improve on the basic multihull theme. Eric Tabarly's *Paul Ricard* replaced the righting moment of the trimaran's outriggers with hydrofoils, offering the double bonus of lower resistance and of the whole boat being partly lifted from the water when sailing really fast. But Tabarly has had endless technical problems with this concept and despite determined efforts has yet to win a major ocean race in this boat.

As an alternative to either catamaran or trimaran, a proa offers the advantage that the main weights can be offset to one side, giving more stability for an equivalent all-up weight. Guy Delage sought to go one step further with a proa of enormous beam in which the heeling moment of the rig was counter-balanced by water-ballast in an outrigger

Below: The Newick-designed trimaran Olympus Photo, *in which Mike Birch had an extraordinary duel with the big monohull* Kriter V *in the 1982* Route du Rhum *race. The two yachts raced neck and neck for the finish, after 4,000 miles of racing, with* Olympus Photo *winning by just 98 seconds.*

carried on the windward side. Furthermore, the outrigger pivoted so that the fore-and-aft trim of the boat could be adjusted. Things went hilariously wrong for Delage at the start of the race, when the pivoting mechanism went haywire. *Rosieres* gracefully folded up, rolled over and sank.

Marc Pajot had a new 65ft 7in (20m) aluminium catamaran, *Elf Aquitaine*, fitted with a sophisticated but heavy wing mast. Although a tremendously fast boat, the terrible wracking strains that a big multihull endures as it leaps and pounds through the ocean swells began to take their toll and ominous cracks appeared in *Elf*'s main crossbeam. Pajot strapped up the beam with criss-crossed wires which just held to the finish. In spite of having to stop to make

Left: Night-time finish for Britanny Ferries GB *as she wins the 1981 Two-Star race. Her co-skippers Chay Blyth and Rob James can be seen in the cockpit of the 65ft trimaran.*

repairs, he was the winner in just over 18 days.

The third race, in 1986, was again overshadowed by tragedy. Shortly after the start, a severe gale hit the fleet — causing a large number of casualties and retirements. The British 60ft (18.28m) trimaran, *Apricot*, sailed by Tony Bullimore, was wrecked while trying to enter Brest harbour but, fortunately, Bullimore was able to scramble ashore. Much more seriously, the big 80ft (24.38m) catamaran *Royale* capsized and her skipper, Loic Caradec, was drowned. The winner of the race was Philippe Poupon, sailing his new Nigel Irens-designed, 75ft (22.86m) trimaran, *Fleury Michon VII.*

By 1987, the sport of racing big multihulls single-handed had become a more dangerous activity than grand prix motor racing. Fast, spectacular and very risky.

DOUBLE-HANDERS

Partly in response to the dubious safety record of single-handed races, two double-handed races were created. The first was the Transat en Double which is double in more than one sense. A crew of two is allowed and the course is a double crossing of the Atlantic — Lorient to Bermuda and back!

TRANSAT EN DOUBLE

First held in 1979, this race was marked by an extraordinary duel between Eric Tabarly and Marc Pajot, in the hydrofoil-stabilized *Paul Ricard*, and Eugene Riguidel and Gilles Gahinet in the trimaran *VSD.* Tabarly and Pajot looked easy winners when they reached Bermuda well ahead, whereas *VSD* had serious damage to her hull and rudder and had to spend half a day in St George's Harbour having emergency repairs. But after leaving Bermuda more than 60 hours behind *Paul Ricard*, *VSD* found a better wind and rapidly closed the gap. They ran neck and neck for the finish with first one then the other taking the lead. Finally, *VSD* made it by just six minutes, after a race lasting 34 days.

This race was repeated in 1983, when the 66ft (20.11m) catamaran, *Charente Maritime*, sailed by Pierre Follenfant and Patrick Fountaine won in 22 days, nine hours. Eugene Riguidel was sailing the largest multihull built so far, the 90ft (27.43m) trimaran, *William Saurin*, but she proved somewhat clumsy and came second. After this, escalating costs and common sense gradually reduced the size of big multihulls, first to 80ft (24.38m) and later to 75ft (22.86m) overall.

TWO-STAR

Not to be outdone, *The Observer* and Europe I Radio backed a two-handed race from Plymouth to Newport, the same course as the OSTAR, the first race being held in 1981. An amazing 103 yachts entered and the winner was *Brittany Ferries GB*, sailed by Chay Blyth and Rob James. The 65ft (19.81m) trimaran had been specially designed for this race by John Shuttleworth and was an excellent and very fast boat that was unfortunately lost in the Atlantic the following year when being prepared for Blyth's New York to San Francisco record attempt. Blyth and James crossed the Atlantic in just 14 days, 14 hours, which only goes to show how much faster two men can push a boat than one can.

The race was repeated in 1986, when the winner was the 80ft (24.38m) catamaran,

CREDIT AGRICOLE
LES SABLES D'OLONNE

Royale, sailed by Loic Caradec and Olivier Despaigne in a new record time of 13 days, six hours, 32 minutes. Later that year, Caradec lost his life when *Royale* capsized in the Route du Rhum race.

THE BOC CHALLENGE — AROUND ALONE

It is always a bit risky to describe any kind of race or event as being 'The Ultimate Challenge'. As soon as one man has climbed Mount Everest you are sure to find that another will climb it twice, with one hand tied behind his back. Nevertheless, it is difficult to think of a more arduous sailing competition than the single-handed race around the world that is sponsored by British Oxygen.

It has been sailed twice, in 1982/3 and 1986/7 (following the example of the OSTAR, most big ocean races are run at four-year intervals). It is an interesting hybrid event, being run without handicap, but with the boats divided into classes by overall length. This is a similar concept to the Single-handed Transatlantic, except that the BOC race is for monohulls only — as multihulls were considered too risky for such a course.

Both races have been won by the same remarkable French sailor Philippe Jeantot, each time sailing specially designed and built yachts, named *Credit Agricole*. On the first occasion he sailed around the world in 159 days, two hours and, in the second, in 134 days, five hours. This is 10 days faster than the fully-crewed 80ft (24.38m) *Great Britain II* in the first Whitbread Race. This points to the sophistication of the yachts built for the second BOC race, which has a top limit of 56ft (17.06m) overall, and to the extraordinary skill and determination of Jeantot.

The first race was marked by two remarkable rescues, both of which were made possible by modern electronics and particularly the ARGOS satellite position-fixing system. The yachts in this, as in a number of the major offshore events, carry transponders which are interrogated by an orbiting satellite. This passes back their position to a ground station several times per day and in time of trouble there is a 'panic button' on the transponder which enables the race organizers to know that a competitor needs help. One of the yachts in the second race lost his ARGOS beacon overboard and it bleeped away in the middle of the Pacific for several weeks!

Shortly after leaving Cape Town on the second leg of the first race, American competitor Tony Lush found out that the keel was in danger of falling off his yacht *Lady Pepperell*. He pressed the 'panic button' and was picked up within 24 hours by fellow American Francis Stokes, just before *Lady Pepperell* sank. Much more dramatically, Frenchman Jacques de Roux's *Skoiern III* was pitch-poled (capsized end-over-end) in the Southern Ocean, 1,800 miles away from land. The yacht was dismasted and half-sunk and De Roux himself suffered concussion.

The ARGOS beacon saved him by sending out a distress signal, together with his position. A world-wide chain of amateur radio enthusiasts was called into play to pass on the information to other competitors and Englishman Richard Broadhead, sailing *Perseverance of Medina*, beat back against the prevailing wind towards De Roux's reported position. In a most remarkable sea rescue, Broadhead found De Roux in the trackless wastes of the ocean in just 47 hours and rescued him. *Skoiern III* sank four hours later. Sadly, this is a story without a happy ending; De Roux was a competitor in the second race, in which he was lost overboard while only a short distance from Sydney.

This is an event about which it is possible to have very mixed feelings. The sailors are heroic, the boats fascinating and the game a very dangerous one. But human nature being what it is, competitors will always want to try themselves against 'The Ultimate Challenge'.

Above: *This aerial picture of* Biscuits Lu *shows her fully battened mainsail and two headsails, both set on roller furlers. Notice also that radar is fitted as a protection against ice when sailing in high southerly latitudes in the BOC Race.*

Left: *Winner of the BOC Challenge single-handed round the world race,* Credit Agricole III *is a highly specialized design for this most demanding race. Note the small, protected cockpit, bulging topsides concealing ballast tanks, and twin rudders.*

The America's Cup

No sporting trophy has a longer or more extraordinary history than the America's Cup, which dates back to 1851 — the year of the Great Exhibition in London. Determined to cock a snook at the old world, a group of rich New York businessmen led by Commodore John Cox Stevens of the New York Yacht Club built the schooner *America* and, with her, inflicted a humiliating defeat on the combined fleet of the Royal Yacht Squadron.

Between 1870 and 1980, 24 challengers tried, unsuccessfully, to wrest the trophy from the vice-like grip of the New York Yacht Club. In the process, they spent millions of dollars and built the most fabulous racing yachts that the world has ever seen.

Seldom free from controversy, the battle for the cup has frequently boiled over into bitter accusations of partiality and bad faith. But finally, in 1983, the New York Yacht Club was forced to unbolt from its plinth the most famous trophy in sport, and hand it over to John Bertrand's victorious Australian team. And so started a new era in the history of the trophy, in which corporate sponsorship enters the scene and the future of whole cities is thrown into the ring.

Left: *Flags fly and crowds press forward, as* Stars and Stripes *glides into her berth at Fremantle following the final race of the 1987 America's Cup contest, which she won by four races to nil. With this crushing victory, Dennis Conner avenged his 1983 defeat at the hands of the Australians.*

The building of the schooner yacht *America* and her visit to England in 1851 took place against the background of the headlong development and industrialization of America. Great Britain was the most powerful nation in the world but America was growing at a phenomenal rate. The West was being opened up and the California gold rush was in full swing. Railways were pushing out from the industrial cities and the clipper-ship era was at its height.

It was a time of boldness, innovation and ruthlessness in which great fortunes were made — and lost. To give a single example of the boom conditions that existed in 1851, the year that *America* was sailed to England, Donald McKay (a Scots-born American who designed and built the best-known American clipper-ships) built the clipper-ship *Staghound* in only 60 days. She loaded in New York for San Francisco, taking cargo at the unprecedented rate of $60 per ton and after delivering it continued across the Pacific to China where she loaded tea for New York. In this single round trip she covered her building and running costs and made a handsome profit of $50,000.

John Cox Stevens was a member of a highly successful family with interests in shipbuilding, ship-owning and engineering. They also owned all the land where Hoboken, New Jersey now stands and made a fortune from developing it. John and his brothers were magnates with all the trappings of wealth — big houses, servants, strings of racehorses and yachts. John Cox Stevens built, ordered and tinkered around with a number of yachts, the best known of which was *Maria*, a 110ft (33.5m) centreboard sloop which his brother Robert designed and John continually altered and occasionally raced.

The New York Yacht Club

The club was founded at a meeting on board John Cox Stevens' schooner *Gimcrack* in 1844, and seems to have been among the first half dozen such organizations anywhere in the world. There was already a club in Boston but the great wealth of New York helped it to take a dominant position.

The America *Syndicate*

By far the best known yacht club in the world was the Royal Yacht Squadron (founded 1815) whose members regarded themselves as a civilian adjunct of the Royal Navy. Membership included noblemen and members of the landed gentry, although there were also some pretty rough diamonds on the English side of the Atlantic. Among these was Mr Joseph Weld (an early member of The Yacht Club — later Royal Yacht Squadron) who claimed that his cutter *Alarm* was the fastest sailing yacht in the world.

The atmosphere in the United States of America was one of 'Anything you can do, I can do better', so it was practically inevitable that there should be a challenge or contest between yachtsmen of the two countries, although there were lengthy arguments both by private correspondence and in the newspapers about what form it should take.

The trigger appears to have been provided by The Great Exhibition, to take place in Hyde Park, London in 1851.

At a time when the Exhibition was intended to show that everything British was best, John Cox Stevens conceived the idea of building a yacht which would demonstrate the superior standards of design and construction which he felt were being achieved in America. Having built the yacht, he would sail over to England and challenge all-comers to a race which he felt would be the ideal way of cocking a snook at the 'Old Country'.

Partly through a gambler's instinct for spreading the risk of the project and partly because he thought it would be more fun to tackle with a group of friends, he formed a syndicate of owners. The members, in addition to Stevens, were his brother Edwin; Hamilton Wilkes, a banker, yachtsman and Vice-Commodore of the NYYC; James Hamilton, a politician; John K. Beekman Finlay, a friend of the Stevens and George Schuyler, another rich man with shipping interests, who was to play a key role.

Building America

The yard chosen to build the new yacht was that of William H. Brown, mainly because the Stevens wanted Brown's foreman George Steers as designer; Steers had designed some extremely successful New York pilot schooners as well as John Cox Stevens' own *Gimcrack*.

Steers' work combined the tradition of the Baltimore Clippers — fast brigs and schooners of the War of Independence — and new ideas pioneered by the clipper-ships. The Baltimore clippers were small despatch-boats,

Right: *George Steers, who based the design of the schooner* America *on the New York pilot schooners for which he was already well-known. He missed the famous race round the Isle of Wight in 1851, after quarrelling with the owners, and was never given proper credit for his part in the yacht's success.*

blockade runners, smugglers and slavers. They developed a very deeply vee'd 'sharp' hull form with up to 30 degrees deadrise which, combined with a huge sail-plan, gave them superiority over contemporary warships, especially to windward and in light winds. They were fast but not designed to carry a heavy cargo and used a rig that was not practical for long ocean voyages. The hull-form, though deep, narrow and sharp, was still basically the old 'cod's head and mackerel tail' shape.

The Baltimore ships had been responsible for great improvements of the sail-plan. Square-sails, best for running down wind, were gradually replaced by more fore-and-aft sails. This resulted in brigs and schooners which had a far greater ability to sail to windward. The masts were sharply raked aft in order to stop the bows from burying, leading to a characteristic 'rakish' appearance.

Until the early 19th century, the main requirement of an ocean-going cargo ship was to carry a lot of weight and arrive in one piece so they were beamy, flat-bottomed and full-ended. The sudden increase in commerce brought a demand for more speed and American builders were among the first to build much narrower ships, with finer ends.

The New York pilot schooners were expected to be both fast and seaworthy so George Steers' designs had a hollow, knife-like bow and some of the deepness of hull that gave good windward ability. His own most important contribution was to blend the sharp bow into a broad, squared-off stern that gave power and stability as well as increasing the deck-space and accommodation. Schooner rig was used with the raked masts inherited from the Baltimore tradition.

The Stevens syndicate awarded William Brown an extraordinary contract in which he was to be paid the generous figure of $30,000 to build a yacht 'faster than any in the United States brought to compete with her'. The syndicate retained the right to reject the new yacht if she did not prove faster than anything on her own side of the Atlantic or if she was beaten in England.

George Schuyler was appointed to deal with the builder and seemed to delight in tightening the screw on Brown. When the launching was delayed, Schuyler demanded a discount of $10,000 and forced Brown to pay for the trials.

The vessel that Steers designed and Brown finally delivered was as follows:
Length overall: 102ft (31.09m)
Length waterline: 90 ft (27.43m)
Beam: 22ft 6in (6.86m)
Draught: 11ft (3.35m)
Displacement: 170 ton (172.76 tonne)
Sail area: 5,263 sq ft (488.9 sq m)
Rig: two-masted schooner

She was framed with white oak, locust, cedar, chestnut and hackmatack and planked

***Above:** This rather exaggerated contemporary illustration of* America *gives some idea of the sense of surprise and awe which she created, rather as the latest fighter-plane might today. In her own country she was referred to as 'A low, black schooner', while a British newspaper called her 'A suspicious-looking craft'.*

in 3in (75mm) white oak, copper fastened. The hull was copper-sheathed to 6in (150mm) above the waterline. And all her sails were of machine-woven cotton duck, far superior as a sail-cloth material to the flax canvas still used in England at that time.

Captain Dick Brown was given command of *America* and on 21 June 1851 she sailed from New York with a crew of 13 that included George Steers, his brother James and their two sons; but the owners preferred to travel over by ship. Twenty days later, the Steers brothers arrived at Le Havre.

America *comes to Cowes*

In Le Havre, *America* was slipped, scrubbed and painted ready for her foray to Cowes. Her building and the reason for her visit had been well written-up in the newspapers, and the Commodore of the Royal Yacht Squadron, Lord Wilton, wrote inviting Stevens and other members of the New York Yacht Club to visit the RYS clubhouse but avoided any mention of a race. Nevertheless, Wilton knew what Stevens had in mind and the club had already taken one step to accommodate him. A new race round the Isle of Wight had been initiated in 1850, when it was won by the famous old *Arrow*. When the club committee met in May 1851 they voted to race again for an 'Ordinary 100 guineas cup' but added the new condition that the race was open 'to any yacht from any nation'.

The Stevens brothers and Colonel Hamilton, who had been staying in Paris, joined the yacht at Le Havre at the end of July and sailed for Cowes.

On a typical August day, with light winds and fog, *America* anchored for the night off Ryde. In the morning, one of the crack English cutters, *Lavrock* came to meet her. This was the first chance for *America* to try out against an English yacht and although the wind was light and *America* was laden with cruising gear, she overhauled the cutter and beat her back to Cowes. Quickly the rumour spread that the Yankee yacht was invincible, on the slight grounds of this brief encounter.

Shortly after *America* anchored at Cowes, a welcoming party arrived from the Royal Yacht Squadron, led by Lord Wilton and including the 83-year-old Marquis of Anglesey, who stumped around the deck on his wooden leg and peered over the bow and stern before making his famous remark, 'If she is right then all of us are wrong.'

The challenge

There followed a period of some awkwardness and embarrassment. Stevens had imagined that the English yachtsmen were just waiting to challenge him to a match-race but although he was politely welcomed to the clubhouse, nobody mentioned racing. When he enquired about the Royal Victoria Yacht Club regatta at nearby Ryde he was told *America* was not eligible because she was owned not by a single person but by a group.

Apparently, he then attempted to enter *America* for the Queen's Cup, presented by Queen Victoria in 1838 and the premier yachting trophy for competition in British waters. It would have been a worthy prize for *America*. However, the annual race for the Queen's Cup was run under a time allowance and it seems that Stevens objected to the handicap worked out for *America*, and declined to compete.

Stevens then made his own challenge. He offered to race any schooner, and later any yacht of any type, for the wager of 10,000 guineas — more than double the cost of *America*. The challenge was greeted by a shocked silence; although yachtsmen did place wagers in addition to racing for trophies and prize-money, one of this size was unprecedented and excessive.

His challenge met with only one response, from the longshoremen of Great Yarmouth, Norfolk who offered to pit one of their beach yawls against *America* for a wager of £200; this was not taken up. However, Stevens did achieve publicity. *The Times* said that the English yachtsmen were behaving like pigeons paralysed by the sight of a hawk and demanded action but no-one was willing to place his head into the noose.

America had done nothing but swing to her anchor since arriving at Cowes and her crew were restive. Also, although Stevens, his brother and Colonel Hamilton were welcomed to the Squadron as 'owners', Steers and the others were not and felt slighted. Finally, the Steers brothers and one of the sons departed, leaving only George's 15-year-old nephew Henry to represent the family.

Stevens realized that his only option was to enter a normal fleet race. The first available was the 'open' race round the Isle of Wight on 22 August. Unlike the Queen's Cup there was to be no time allowance for this race and as it was for the already-existing 100 guinea cup the 10,000 guinea wager could be conveniently forgotten. (The idea that the trophy was presented by Queen Victoria is completely false, and seems to have resulted from confusion with the Queen's Cup.) Lord Wilton, on behalf of the RYS, was pleased to accept the entry of *America* and even waived the rule against syndicates and another against booming out foresails (*America* had to boom out in a light wind because her sails fell towards the centre-line, due to the raked masts).

The Race

As the *America* affair had become something of a *cause célèbre*, large crowds of spectators gathered. There were 14 entries — more than the previous year — and the Queen herself boarded the Royal Yacht with Prince Albert to view the contest.

The entries included the two champions *Alarm* and *Arrow* in addition to a fleet which ranged from the impressive 392-ton *Beatrice* to the 47-ton cutter *Aurora* — all of them to sail without handicap.

As was the custom the race started at anchor, with the warning gun being the signal to hoist sails and the starting gun to weigh anchor. *America* was the last to get away, because she tended to over-run her anchor when her sails were hoisted.

The course was clockwise around the island and in the light south-westerly *America* soon caught up and passed the entire fleet. There was then a muddle about the course. The English yachtsmen knew that they had to sail round the Nab lightship — to the east of the island — but Stevens did not. Apparently, he had not been given the appropriate programme. In the lead, he therefore directed that *America* sail straight for Bembridge, the south-eastern point of the island. The Nab was not then as far out to sea as the present Nab Tower but rounding it still involved a detour of several miles, giving *America* a big lead.

Worse was to follow. The cutter *Arrow*, potentially one of the fastest English yachts, went aground while tacking up the southern shore of the island and Joseph Weld's *Alarm* retired from the race to 'stand by' *Arrow* although her crew was in no danger. Later, two more English yachts collided, putting each other out of action. But it seems highly likely that *America* would have won even if the English had not scuttled themselves so effectively, because her cotton sails were much better than the English flax ones which had to be continually drenched with water to tighten them.

America was the decisive winner, although the smallest competitor in the race, the cutter *Aurora* was reported to have been catching up towards the end. In retrospect, *America* had luck on her side that day but it is also clear that she did indeed represent a technical advance over European shipbuilding of the period. A few days after the race, Stevens found an English yachtsman willing to take him on in a one-for-one match. Robert Stephenson bet a modest 100 guineas that his *Titania* could beat the Yankee schooner. This time sailing in a strong wind, *America* won the race by an enormous margin.

Above: *The America's Cup. Made by Garrards of London for the Royal Yacht Squadron, and referred to in their records as an 'ordinary' 100-guineas, 134oz silver cup, it has become the most celebrated trophy in sport. The New York Yacht Club drilled a hole in the base so that it could be firmly bolted down to its plinth.*

The aftermath

It has never been clear whether the Royal Yacht Squadron intended the '100 Guineas Cup' to be won outright or whether it was supposed to be a perpetual trophy. Stevens had no doubt that the 134oz sterling silver jug was now the property of the *America* syndicate and took it back to New York.

He and his friends were quite unsentimental about their now-famous yacht. Just days after the race with *Titania* they agreed to sell *America* to Lord John de Blaquiere.

It took some time for the members of the syndicate to decide what to do with the cup, which we may now call 'America's Cup'; they even considered melting it down to make commemorative medals. But eventually the idea of entrusting it to the New York Yacht Club as a perpetual trophy had crystallized.

John Cox Stevens resigned as Commodore of the club in 1855 and died in June 1857. The following month the remaining members of the syndicate handed over the cup to the club, together with a 'Deed of Gift' (see panel) signed by all of them, including Hamilton Wilkes who had died in 1852. This indicates that they had planned to hand over the cup on their return from England but then put it 'on ice' for five years.

Having received the cup, the New York Yacht Club wrote to all the principal yacht clubs of the world that they knew about, inviting challenges and promising 'A liberal, hearty welcome and the strictest fair play.' But almost immediately, America was plunged into civil war so there matters rested until the war ended in 1865.

THE 'DEED OF GIFT'

The terms under which the America's Cup was handed over to the New York Yacht Club are described in a 'Deed of Gift' which has been the subject of discussion and argument ever since. The original document has been superseded twice and the 'Third and final' deed of 1887 has been added to several times in order to describe in detail both the type of yacht that can be entered and the form of the competition. The spirit of the original gift endures, however, particularly the fact that it is to be a perpetual challenge trophy for competition between yacht clubs of foreign countries.

The original deed reads as follows:

'Any organized yacht club of any foreign country shall always be entitled through any one or more of its members, to claim the right of sailing a match for this cup with any yacht or other vessel of not less than thirty or more than 300 tons, measured by the custom-house rule of the country to which the vessel belongs.

'The parties desiring to sail for the cup may make any match with the yacht club in possession of the same that may be determined upon by mutual consent; but, in case of disagreement as to terms, the match shall be sailed over the usual course for the annual regatta of the yacht club in possession of the cup, and subject to its rules and sailing regulations — the challenging party being bound to give six months' notice in writing — fixing the day they wish to start. This notice to embrace the length, custom-house, rig and name of the vessel.

'It is to be distinctly understood that the cup is to be the property of the club, and not of the members thereof, or owners of the vessel winning it in the match; and that the condition of keeping it open to be sailed for by yacht clubs of all foreign countries upon the terms above laid down, shall forever attach to it, thus making it perpetually a challenge cup for friendly competition between foreign countries.'

The points to particularly notice about the deed are firstly that it is a competition between yacht clubs, not individuals. This is often overlooked when so much attention is focused on the owners and helmsmen involved and has become even more important recently when various challenging or defending groups have sought to make legal agreements giving them control of the commercial aspects of the America's Cup: marketing, sponsorship, television rights and so on. Following the 1987 series, some impatience was shown by several of the challenging groups with the role being taken by clubs and there was a suspicion that in future 'Clubs of convenience', that is, ones of little real substance, controlled by the challenging group, would begin to appear.

Size of vessel

The original deed gave only the most sketchy definition of what a challenger should be like, using the phrase 'custom-house rule'. In this form, tonnage normally refers to the cubic capacity or cargo-carrying ability of a ship; no mention is made of handicap or rating. Subsequent versions define the maximum and minimum size of competing yachts by waterline length but still do not precisely specify the form of measurement to be used.

Definition of 'Match'

Perhaps the most contentious issue of all has been the definition of a 'Match' and arguments raged for more than half a century. The document decrees that 'The parties . . . may make any match . . . by mutual consent.' This implies that the challenger and defender must reach a consensus about a) the type of yacht to be used and b) the type of race to be sailed. When consensus on such points is lacking, trouble begins!

George Schuyler, the last surviving member of the syndicate, was asked to agree to a second deed in 1881 and the cup was returned to him. He re-presented it with a new document in January the following year and the next three challenges, 1885, 1886 and 1887, were held under its terms.

Following the 1887 challenge, a 'Third and final' deed of gift was prepared by club officials and this much longer document created a great deal of trouble. Its most contentious feature was the requirement for all dimensions of the challenge yacht to be supplied 10 months in advance. In the opinion of many, this made it impossible to challenge with any hope of victory as the defenders would always have the advantage of being able to out-design the challengers in the intervening 10 months.

In a letter printed in *Forest and Stream* an American lawyer, Mr Stinson Jarvis, argued that both the second and third deeds were illegal; the original owners (the *America* syndicate) having irrevocably handed over the cup into trust, it was, in fact, illegal for the trustees (the New York Yacht Club) to hand it back to Schuyler.

The 1887 deed has had two more series of alterations sanctioned by the Supreme Court of the State of New York, on 17 December 1956 and 5 April 1985. The first reduced the minimum waterline length to 44ft (13.41m) in order to accommodate yachts of the International 12-metre class and removed the requirement to sail to the event while the second changed the permitted dates to take account of a series in the Southern Hemisphere.

CHALLENGES FOR THE AMERICA'S CUP

In 1886 the American schooner *Sappho* sailed over to England and in a race over the same course as the original 1851 event was beaten by four English schooners, including Mr James Ashbury's 98ft (29.87m) waterline *Cambria*. (Since the visit of *America* British designers had taken the lessons of that famous race to heart and schooners had become the most popular type.)

Emboldened by this event Ashbury decided to have a shot at regaining the America's Cup but first he had to achieve 'mutual consent' about the form of the contest. A full year was passed in voluminous correspondence between Ashbury and the New York Yacht Club in an effort to reach agreement, with little success.

1870: Cambria *v* Magic *and others*

Ashbury had two main complaints: that the Americans expected *Cambria* to race against not one but an entire fleet of yachts and that centre-boarders would be allowed. Although the norm in the shoal waters of the New York area, beamy, shallow vessels with a retractable keel were considered unseaworthy by the British who preferred deep, narrow yachts. Ashbury made little impact on the New York Yacht Club whose members felt that any challenger ought to endure the same kind of difficulties that *America* had faced in England.

As threatened, *Cambria* was made to race against 17 American schooners over a course of about 35 miles, starting in New York Harbour. Here, *Cambria*, one of the largest yachts in the fleet was at a big disadvantage compared to the shallower local boats and was hardly ideal for short-tacking through the Staten Island Narrows.

It was also soon apparent that few of the American skippers had any concept of the rule of the road, or didn't care. Six times *Cambria* was forced to take avoiding action when she was on starboard tack and held right of way. A collision with the schooner *Tarolinta* carried away part of her rigging and one of the topmasts came crashing down, striking Ashbury.

Below: *During 1896, the American schooner* Sappho *crossed the Atlantic to compete against English yachts and was beaten by four of them in a race round the Isle of Wight. Here, she is seen with James Ashbury's 98ft waterline* Cambria, *which became the first challenger for the America's Cup in 1870.* Sappho *was one of the two defenders in the 1871 match.*

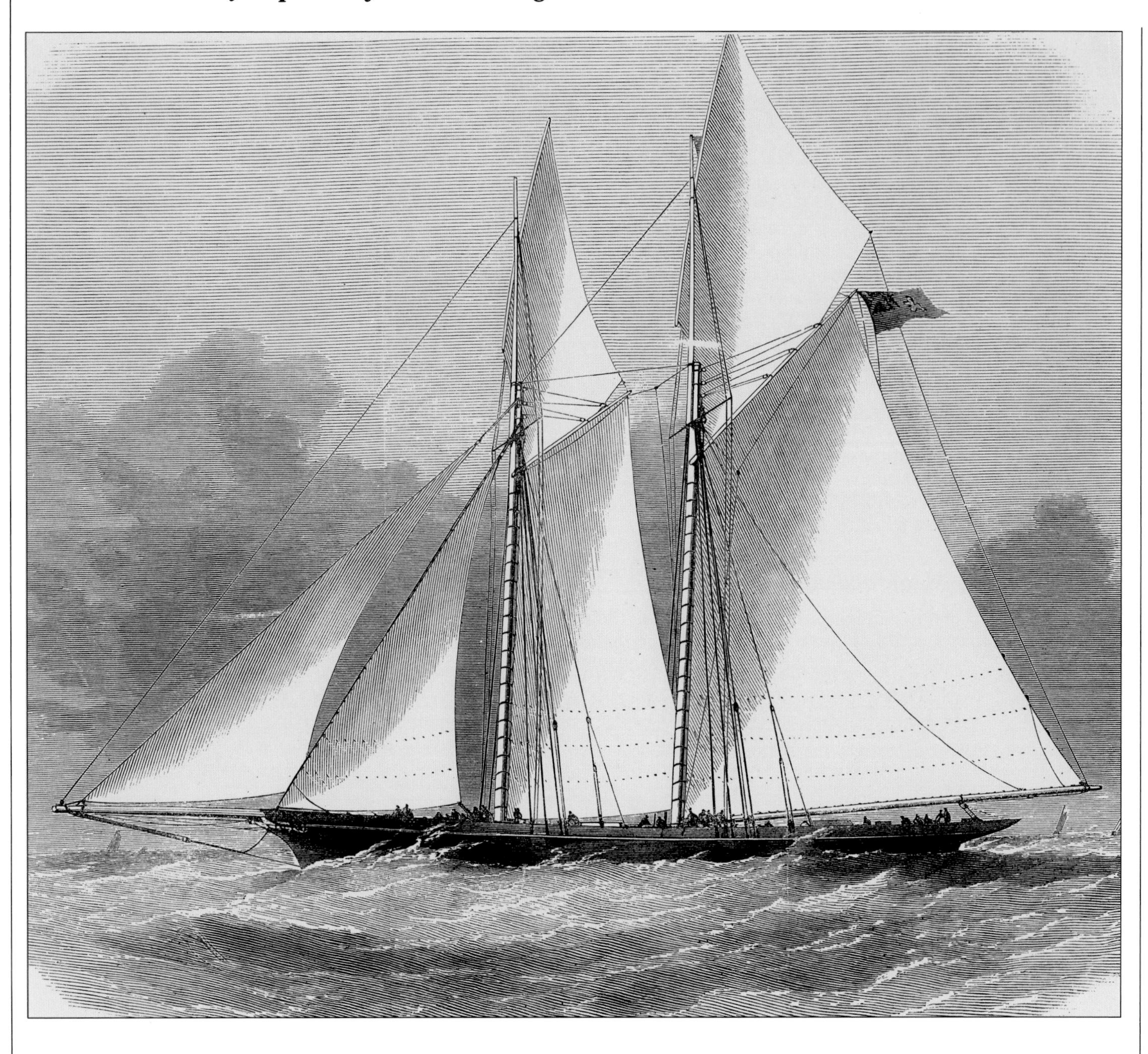

Above: Livonia *was the yacht used by James Ashbury for his second challenge in 1871. Although considerably larger than* Cambria *she was not more successful. This was partly because the Americans allowed themselves to choose from a selection of yachts, depending on the weather. Nevertheless,* Livonia *won one race and was leading in another when there was confusion over which way a mark should be rounded.*

The winner by a large margin was the 79ft (24.08m) waterline schooner *Magic*, one of the smallest yachts in the race.

On any interpretation of the rules, Ashbury should have been offered a re-sail, *Cambria* having been not merely obstructed but physically disabled. Surprisingly, however, he decided to forget the whole business and as a result he earned himself a reputation for good sportsmanship.

1871: Livonia *v* Columbia *and* Sappho

Following the 1870 débâcle, Ashbury ordered a new yacht from Ratsey of Cowes and began a steady fusillade of correspondence directed against the New York Yacht Club. It was manifestly unfair, he claimed, for the challenger to face a whole fleet and also for a proper seagoing vessel, which had just crossed the Atlantic, to compete against centreboarders built purely for the purpose of taking part in inshore racing.

The New York Yacht Club consulted George Schuyler, the surviving member of the *America* syndicate and he sided with Ashbury, saying that a contest such as the one held in 1870 'renders the America's trophy useless as a challenge cup'.

Finally conceding that the challenger should face just one defender, the NYYC nevertheless stacked the odds heavily in its own favour by claiming the right to choose the defending yacht on the morning of each race. Ashbury immediately responded with a proposal for a series of 12 races during which he would represent a different yacht club on each occasion.

He kept up a constant barrage of letters, cables and interviews in the popular press even after his arrival in New York and the NYYC deeply resented being portrayed in such an unfavourable light. Finally, it was agreed to sail a series of seven races, four wins to decide, over a selection of courses, some inshore and some in the open sea.

Ashbury's new yacht, the schooner *Livonia*, was considerably larger than *Cambria* at 106ft (32.31m) waterline and 127ft (38.71m) overall and with the enormous sail area of 18,000 sq ft (1,672 sq m) but she proved to be a disappointing performer.

The first race was held over the inshore course in light conditions and the Americans selected the 96ft (29.26m) waterline centreboard schooner *Columbia* as their representative. She was a much better boat under the conditions and won easily.

Columbia was selected again for the second race even though the wind was now strong. The programme did not say on which side the windward mark should be rounded so the owner of *Columbia*, Mr Franklin Osgood, went aboard the committee boat to find out and was told he could round it either way but, incredibly, this information was not communicated to Ashbury who assumed that he should leave the mark to starboard. Apparently, this was the custom in England in the absence of specific instructions.

The heavy, deep-draught *Livonia* went well to windward in the strong wind and reached the windward mark just in the lead. Leaving it to starboard, *Livonia* had to bear away and gybe, quite a tricky manoeuvre in a strong wind whereas the Americans left the mark to port, tacked and eased sheets putting themselves in the lead for the run home.

Ashbury protested and the protest was refused. In a welter of mutual accusations each party was left claiming that they had won, when a re-sail would have settled the matter without such discord.

The next day, the Americans were uncharacteristically disorganized. They had intended to sail one of their other schooners but they all had problems of one sort or another so *Columbia* had to serve again even though she had suffered breakages in the previous race and her skipper had been injured.

The weather was heavy again and *Columbia* was sailed with too much canvas which led to her broaching and wrecking the steering gear. *Livonia* was the winner without argument.

For the next two races, the Americans fielded *Sappho*, which won easily on both occasions. By the NYYC's reckoning, they had now retained the trophy by four races to one whereas Ashbury claimed he had won the disputed second race and that the score was now 3-2. He therefore sailed over the course twice more, without opposition, and claimed he had won 4-3. Would the club please hand over the trophy? They would not. Ashbury then left in an unpleasant atmosphere that was to poison relations between yachtsmen of the two countries for years.

These two initial challenges set a pattern that has often resurfaced during the long history of the America's Cup: high-handedness on the part of the New York Yacht Club coupled with unreasonable or disingenuous behaviour by the challenger.

THE CANADIAN CHALLENGE

Five years later, when the next challenger appeared, it was from the unexpected direction of Canada. From a sailing point of view, both of the two Canadian challengers were no-hopers but considerable progress was made towards making the America's Cup a more soundly-based and worthwhile competition.

1876: Countess of Dufferin *v* Madeleine

Countess of Dufferin was the product of a Toronto fishing-boat builder, Alexander Cuthbertson, who was really a bit out of his depth in challenging the New York Yacht Club's now well-established fleet of racing yachts. The challenge was for the best of three races and the club selected a single representative, the schooner *Madeleine*.

One reason was that she was virtually the same size as the Canadian yacht at 95ft (28.95m) waterline, 106ft (32.31m) overall and as a result there was only a small handicap factor. Furthermore, the two yachts were both under weigh before the start so that the contest looked more like a modern yacht race for the first time.

In the event, *Countess of Dufferin* proved to be no match for *Madeleine* and lost in two straight races.

1881: Atalanta *v* Mischief

Alexander Cuthbertson was the designer and builder of a further Canadian challenge five years later. Again it was a failure but two further and very important changes were made to the conditions by the New York Yacht Club.

The first concession was that there should in future be a single defending yacht for the entire series of races. On this occasion they chose the 67ft (20.42m) sloop *Mischief* after a set of defender trials — another first.

That both challenger and defender were so small had to do with Cuthbertson's lack of financial resources but the fact that they were sloops of relatively moderate design was a reaction to the capsize while at anchor of the schooner *Mohawk* at the time of the *Countess of Dufferin* challenge. *Mohawk* had been a very shallow, beamy centreboarder with an enormous rig and the accident finally convinced the Americans that this type of yacht was not really seaworthy.

A pioneering iron-hulled yacht, *Mischief* was similar in size to Cuthbertson's second effort which, like his first, was judged to be somewhat unsophisticated for the task facing her and she too was beaten in straight races. *Mischief* was designed by the then Secretary of the New York Yacht Club, A. Cary Smith and, oddly enough, she was owned by an

Right: Puritan, *designed by Edward Burgess, was a successful compromise between the shallow, beamy American types of yachts and the deep, narrow British ones. She was also the first Boston yacht to defend the America's Cup. In 1885, she beat Sir Richard Sutton's* Genesta *in a contest that was mercifully free from disputes or incidents.*

Below: The 'Plank-on-edge' cutter Galatea *was similar in design to* Genesta, *and no more successful. Lt. and Mrs William Henn lived aboard the yacht along with animals, lots of potted plants and good, solid Victorian furniture. The weight of all this bric-a-brac could hardly have helped* Galatea's *racing performance.*

Englishman, Joseph Busk, who was a member of the club. So the America's Cup has been won by an Englishman at least once.

Although the *Atalanta* challenge was looked upon as a bit of a joke, Alexander Cuthbertson deserves credit for being the only man to design, build, own and race an America's Cup challenger.

Following his second defeat, Cuthbertson announced his intention of having another crack with *Atalanta* the following spring. The committee of the New York Yacht Club felt that it would lower the standing of the trophy if a defeated yacht could challenge again after such a short time.

George Schuyler was therefore asked to write a new Deed of Gift which he handed over in 1882. It embodied the following new points: a single yacht to be named as defender (which the NYYC had already conceded), the challenging club must be one which holds its annual regatta on the sea or 'an arm of the sea', a losing yacht may not challenge again for two years and finally, a challenger must sail 'on its own bottom' to the place where the races are held.

The last points were specifically anti-Cuthbertson who came from the Great Lakes (fresh water), wanted to challenge again almost immediately, and whose yacht had been towed down the Erie Canal by a team of mules.

The 'arm of the sea' phrase resurfaced in 1986 when the Heart of America syndicate asked that Lake Michigan be considered to be an extension of the ocean. The answer was affirmative, so presumably any navigable waterway which eventually runs into the sea can be considered an 'arm'. (Since 1956 challengers are no longer required to sail to the event.)

THE PLANK-ON-EDGE ASSAULT

The next two challenges were both inspired by the English designer J. Beavor Webb and, in fact, he proposed a double challenge by two yachts of his design. His idea was that Sir Richard Sutton's cutter *Genesta*, representing the Royal Yacht Squadron, should have the first crack, in August, and that if she failed Lt. Henn's *Galatea*, representing the Royal Northern Yacht Club, should make the attempt two weeks later.

The New York Yacht club accepted the *Genesta* challenge immediately but proposed that Lt. Henn and *Galatea* should wait for a further year. The club was worried by the Beavor Webb challenge which came at a time when design ideas on opposite sides of the Atlantic were polarized to an unprecedented degree. In spite of the *Mohawk* disaster, wide, shallow centreboarders were still the norm in the USA whereas in Britain, thanks partly to a belief that yachts should be deep and heavy and partly to the measurement rule then in use, extremely deep and narrow cutters were the fashion.

During 1881, one of these 'plank-on-edge' cutters, the 46ft (14.02m) *Madge* designed by G.L. Watson of Scotland, had been shipped over to the USA and had enjoyed a very successful racing season, winning seven out of eight races and this gave the Americans a healthy respect for the type, so different from their own yachts.

With hindsight it is easy for us to see that the trend towards such excessively narrow hulls — *Genesta* had only 15ft (4.57m) beam on a waterline length of 81ft (24.69m) — was a design dead-end but the cutter rig was certainly preferable to the schooner for racing. The broad spread of canvas set on the two masts of a schooner serves well on a reach when all the sails can get a clear wind but on either a beat to windward or a dead run, the sails blanket each other while the same area of sail set on a single mast can all be made to work.

Taking the new cutters seriously, the NYYC appealed to other American clubs to help with the defence by building yachts of their own and this suggestion was taken up by the Eastern Yacht Club of Marblehead, the most prominent club in the Boston area. J. Malcolm Forbes was the main backer, Charles J. Paine the manager and the club secretary Edward Burgess, the designer.

1885: Genesta *v* Puritan

Burgess had been a teacher of entomology before turning to yacht design, had sailed since he was a boy and had a sharp, inquiring mind. He had also spent a summer in England so was well aware of the current trends of design there. Therefore his design

for *Puritan* was a compromise between British and American types. Cutter rigged, she was much beamier than *Genesta* at 23ft (7.01m) on an 81ft (24.69m) waterline but narrow by American standards. She was relatively deep-draught at 8ft 8in (2.63m) with centreboard raised or 20ft (6.09m) with it down. In comparison *Genesta* had a deep, fixed keel drawing 13ft 6in (4.11m). Initially regarded as a compromise, *Puritan* silenced her critics by beating the New York Yacht Club's trialist *Priscilla* and so earned the right to defend the cup.

To everyone's relief, Sir Richard Sutton proved to be a gentleman and a sportsman. In the first race, *Genesta* with right of way, put her bowsprit clean through *Puritan*'s mainsail, ripping it to pieces. *Genesta* could then have claimed the race by simply sailing over the course but Sutton declined to do so remarking that he had come for a race, not a walk-over.

Puritan then won in two straight races (the best of three then being the rule), once in light wind and once in heavy, but the second race was a real contest with the lead changing hands several times.

The important thing was that it had been a good, fair contest without the ill-feeling that had marred the Ashbury challenges.

1886: Galatea *v* Mayflower

The challenge of Lt. William Henn RN (rtd.) was slightly comical because he did not appear to take the racing too seriously. Unusually for those days, he and Mrs Henn lived aboard the yacht together with at least one dog and a monkey named Peggy. The interior was like a typical Victorian home complete with rugs, drapes, mirrors and potted plants.

At first the Americans thought this was an elaborate ploy to lull them into a false sense of security but it turned out that Henn really was a cruising man at heart. It seems likely that *Galatea*'s designer, Beavor Webb, had pushed him into the challenge.

Galatea proved no match for the new *Mayflower*, designed as before by Edward Burgess and campaigned by Charles Paine, a first-class yacht manager.

THE GREAT SCOT

In Edward Burgess, America had discovered one of the first truly great yacht designers unrivalled on the other side of the Atlantic until Scotland's George Watson came on the scene. Watson was that rare combination of scientist and artist that seems necessary in yacht design and his masterpiece, the royal yacht *Britannia*, was perhaps the greatest-ever synthesis of beauty and efficiency.

1887: Thistle *v* Volunteer

The British had at last done away with the measurement rule that produced the plank-on-edge cutters by penalizing beam excessively and Watson's 108ft (33.52m) cutter *Thistle*, designed for a Royal Clyde Yacht Club syndicate headed by James Bell, had a beam measurement of 20ft 3in (6.17m), only 3ft (0.9m) less than Burgess' *Volunteer*. Both also had graceful clipper bows and overhanging counters and similar rigs. The main difference was that the American yacht had a centreboard and the British one a fixed keel.

George Watson had had *Thistle* built 'under wraps' and supplied just the bare dimensions, as required by the deed of gift.

Right: Volunteer, *the third defender designed by Edward Burgess, fairly easily disposed of George Watson's first challenger,* Thistle. *When the latter was found to be 1ft 5in (43cm) longer than her declared waterline length, there was talk of cancelling the match and a further revision of the Deed of Gift was made that required the challenger to give the dimensions of his vessel 10 months prior to the match.*

Left: *The Scottish naval architect George Watson designed four challengers for the America's Cup between 1887 and 1901. His yachts were both fast and beautiful but he had the misfortune to come up against the greatest designer of them all — Nathanael Herreshof.*

When *Thistle* was measured in New York, it was discovered that her waterline length was not 85ft (25.90m) as Watson had declared but 86ft 5in (26.34m). This minor discrepancy, the result of a change of ballasting, and one which could easily be coped with by an adjustment of the handicap, sent the Americans into a fury. There was talk of cancelling this match and once again it was George Schuyler, now aged 76, who was called in to calm things down.

When it came to the actual racing, *Volunteer* won fairly easily, highlighting the difference between a boat that had been thoroughly tuned-up by a season of racing in her home waters, and one that had just sailed across the Atlantic and had had little time or opportunity for tuning. Also, Paine was obsessive about detail, constantly improving gear and rigging whereas the British tended to leave that kind of thing to professional designers and skippers.

Souvenir of the
AMERICA CUP
YACHT RACES.
With Photographic Reproductions
of all the
CHALLENGING & DEFENDING YACHTS
from 1851 to 1903.
Macdonald & Co., Ornamental Printers to the late Queen Victoria, 2 Bothwell Circus, Glasgow.

THE ILL-TEMPERED EARL

Even while the *Thistle–Volunteer* match was taking place, the New York Yacht Club decided that they would further update the Deed of Gift to plug 'loopholes'. The new deed made reasonable and sensible changes in the course to be sailed and the length of notice needed for a challenge but plunged the club into controversy by requiring a full list of accurate dimensions of the challenging yacht to be supplied at the time of the challenge. The NYYC also inserted a clause that centreboard yachts 'would always be eligible'.

This new deed was greeted with a storm of criticism from both sides of the Atlantic, particularly Britain where it was felt that the NYCC was simply trying to stack the odds in its favour. Supplying a list of dimensions a full ten months in advance of a challenge meant that the defenders would always have sufficient time to respond to the challenger's design initiative.

A potential challenger waiting in the wings was Windham Thomas Wyndham-Quin, 4th Earl of Dunraven. Like others before and since he launched a tirade of letters and articles in newspapers and magazines in an effort to change the New York Yacht Club's stance. Eventually the club conceded that the next challenge could be conducted according to the *old* deed of gift but if successful, the *next* challenge would be controlled by the *new* deed. This amounted to telling the Royal Yacht Squadron how they should conduct themselves if they ever managed to get their own trophy back.

After a great deal of negotiation, the NYYC accepted a challenge from the Royal Yacht Squadron to be made by a new yacht designed by George Watson and owned by the Earl of Dunraven. The waterline length of 86ft (26.21m) was the sole detail supplied.

1893: Valkyrie II *v* Vigilant

There now enters the story, probably the greatest genius in the history of yacht design: Nathanael G. Herreshof. A brilliant draughtsman, inventor and engineer who also had a thorough grasp of the mathematical effect of the rating rule, 'rule-cheater' was the accusation often hurled at Herreshof whereas all he ever did was take full advantage of the opportunities presented. Specifically, he saw that in a rule where waterline length was the most important measurement, an enormous increase in effective sailing length could be achieved by designing a long, overhanging bow and stern. He also made a clear distinction between hull and keel. His hulls were like gigantic canoe shapes to which a purely external ballasted fin keel was added.

New York banker C. Oliver Iselin ordered *Vigilant* from Herreshof to fend off the challenge by Dunraven's Watson cutter. The racing in this first Dunraven challenge was relatively free from controversy. In the first race, *Valkyrie II* was leading when the wind died and the race was abandoned. Then two light-wind races were both won by the defender but the next was a real contest.

After a long beat to windward in a strong wind, the Watson boat reached the turning mark two minutes ahead. On the run to the finish both crews abandoned caution and piled on sail. Both suffered broken gear and torn sails but *Valkyrie II* blew out both her spinnakers, allowing *Vigilant* to take the lead — and the series.

Afterwards, Dunraven issued a press statement claiming that the races had not been a true trial because of ballasting differences between the two yachts and because the spectator fleet had got in the way. The latter point has been a particularly irritating thorn in the flesh of many a challenger.

1895: Valkyrie III *v* Defender

This was the most acrimonious and ill-tempered series in the history of the America's Cup — at least until 1988!

George Watson saw that to out-design Herreshof he would need a really extreme design, so *Valkyrie III* had more beam, more depth, more ballast and more sail area than ever before. But Herreshof matched him with a design that was truly modern in concept with a pure fin keel of enormous depth slung beneath the shallow hull.

What rankled with the challengers was that *Defender* was built in a manner that would have been practically suicidal for a yacht that had to sail across the Atlantic. She had steel framing, bronze plating up to the waterline and aluminium topsides. The galvanic corrosion was terrific and her sailing life lasted only months. She was a pure racing machine to a degree that was not really possible for the challenger.

The first race, in a light wind, was won by *Defender* after which Dunraven demanded a re-measurement because he suspected that Iselin had been altering the ballasting of the American boat. The measurements proved to be virtually unchanged but the next race was marred by a collision before the start.

Both yachts had to alter course to avoid a steamer, and when they converged again *Valkyrie III* — being to windward — should have kept clear but in luffing up her boom fouled *Defender*'s rigging, causing damage to the topmast. *Valkyrie* finished ahead but *Defender* protested and her protest was upheld, reversing the result.

Dunraven made a completely different interpretation, blaming *Defender* for luffing up. He also complained about interference by spectator boats and said that he would not take part in any more races if they could not be controlled. He was as good as his word for immediately after starting the next race, *Valkyrie* retired, giving *Defender* a walkover.

Left: *A souvenir programme of the 1903 match, superimposed over the lines of George Watson's 1895 challenger* Valkyrie III. *It was the match between* Valkyrie III *and* Defender *that led to such bad feeling that the Earl of Dunraven was removed from honorary membership of the New York Yacht Club.*

***Right:** The first of Sir Thomas Lipton's challengers,* Shamrock, *racing with* Columbia. *The latter was skippered by the peppery little Scots-American skipper Charlie Barr, who was to prove the most effective of all the professional skippers who have been involved in the America's Cup.*

After the series, Dunraven claimed that Iselin had cheated by increasing the waterline length of *Defender* by secretly adding ballast during the night and removing it again before the re-measurement. Dunraven was an amateur designer himself and made this claim on the basis of his own observation that a fitting on *Defender*'s hull was closer to the water on that day.

This insulting attack prompted the New York Yacht Club to appoint a technical commission which, after a lengthy investigation completely exonerated Iselin. Dunraven was unconvinced and refused to apologize. The committee responded by summarily removing him from honorary membership of the New York Yacht Club and the regrettable business rumbled on for years.

ENTER 'SIR TEA'

Such was the bad feeling resulting from the Dunraven challenges, that no English yacht club wished to make a challenge and a Mr Charles Rose who initiated a challenge through the Royal Victoria Yacht Club was pressured to withdraw. This impasse continued until 1898 when a challenge was received from the Royal Ulster Yacht Club, naming Sir Thomas Lipton as the sponsor.

Born of poor Irish parents in a Glasgow slum, Lipton had built up a world-wide grocery business founded on the humble beverage, tea. He knew little about sailing and never tried to run the show as Dunraven had but he had a keen appreciation of the value of publicity at a time when advertising still consisted mainly of bill-boards or disingenuous little panels in newspapers. Lipton was well ahead of his time in realizing that if his name became well known and well thought of throughout the United States it would be sufficient to cause people to walk into his stores — what the modern advertising industry calls 'corporate awareness'.

However, this does not explain how Lipton got caught up in the America's Cup. There are suggestions that the Prince of Wales put him up to it, as a way of healing the rift between Britain and America, and also that the Marquis of Dufferin — Governor-General of Canada at the time of the two Canadian efforts — had played a role.

1899: Shamrock *v* Columbia

Like the English yacht clubs, George Watson had had enough of the America's Cup for the time being and anyway was busy designing grand steam yachts for millionaires. So another Scottish naval architect, Will Fife of Fairlie, was pressed into service to design the first of Lipton's Shamrocks. He was a fine designer but not brilliantly original like Herreshof and the first *Shamrock* was very much in the *Defender* mould, a big, beamy dish with deep keel and long ends, built of bronze with aluminium topsides. As a concession, she was allowed to be towed across the Atlantic rather than sail.

In New York, meanwhile, Oliver Iselin went into partnership with J. Pierpont Morgan, then perhaps the richest man in the world, and ordered Herreshof to build a defender regardless of cost. Competing in the America's Cup had never been a cheap business, but this was the period during which super-rich men were prepared to spend whatever it took to secure victory.

As before, Herreshof was one step ahead in the technology race. *Columbia* was even bigger than *Shamrock*, with even longer overhangs and considerably lighter. Although still rigged as gaff cutters, both yachts had hollow steel spars and during the summer *Columbia* broke a mast and *Shamrock* a gaff.

A new course was used for the first time: 15 miles to windward and return, followed by a triangle with ten mile sides followed by a second windward-leeward shuttle. A further improvement was that an Act of Congress gave revenue cutters power to clear the course of spectator vessels. The series was to consist of up to five races.

In addition to being lighter, *Columbia* was better tuned and had a better skipper; the great Charlie Barr was more than a match for Lipton's skipper Archie Hogarth. *Columbia* won in three straight races, in both light and heavy conditions, but although he had resoundingly lost, Lipton won an enormous amount of goodwill as a result of his amiable, gregarious and sportsmanlike manner. He also announced that he would be back.

1901: Shamrock II *v* Columbia

For his second challenge, Lipton persuaded George Watson to come out of retirement and he had two innovations up his sleeve. One was tank-testing, a technique hitherto used only for ships and the second a new bronze alloy named immadium which was stronger and stiffer than anything available before. She was bigger than any previous challenger at 89ft 3in (27.2m) waterline, 137ft (41.76m) overall and with an immense sail area of 14,000 sq ft (1,300 sq m).

On the new yacht's trials, however, she had difficulty in beating the previous *Shamrock* and suffered a complete dismasting with the newly crowned King Edward VII on board. The King, who adored sailing, was not especially concerned but the British public viewed the incident with alarm.

Across the Atlantic the Americans were having their own problems. A new Herreshof had been commissioned but for once 'The Wizard of Bristol' seemed to have come up with a dog. *Constitution* was unable to better a re-fitted *Columbia*. Furthermore, the New York Yacht Club were distracted by a bitter and protracted wrangle with Bostonian Thomas W. Lawson, who wanted to defend the cup without being a member of the club.

This quarrel raged on for months until Lawson was allowed to enter his yacht *Independence* into trials with *Columbia* and *Constitution*. The Boston yacht was badly beaten and in a rage Lawson had her broken up — just three months after her launch.

The new *Constitution* was given little chance in the trials thanks to the extremely aggressive tactics of Charlie Barr, the professional skipper of *Columbia*, backed up by Oliver Iselin, her equally experienced and pushy manager.

Barr, who commanded three successful defenders, knew every trick in the book. An important part of his success was that he had complete command whereas Edward Sycamore, skipper of the challenger, was always being given conflicting advice by the 'gentlemen' on board. This was crucial in the third race of the series which *Shamrock II* was leading at the beginning of the final beat. Believing he had the faster boat, Sycamore allowed Barr to push him over to the less-favoured side of the course when he should have clamped on to his weather like a limpet. Barr gradually closed the gap and after a 30-mile race the two yachts crossed the line just two seconds apart. *Shamrock II* was ahead but owed the American yacht 43 seconds on handicap and so lost the race and the series.

This very close series encouraged Sir Thomas Lipton to try once again.

1903: Shamrock III *v* Reliance

This final match before the Great War was also the last to use the rule that measured only waterline length and sail area. Overall length, depth and displacement were completely free. Herreshof himself had already played the central role in devising the 'Universal Rule' that included displacement and measured length in such a way that the ends of the hull were taken into account but for the America's Cup it was felt that the most open rule possible should be used.

Unfortunately, it was inevitable that a designer like Herreshof would exploit every possibility, producing a boat that virtually everyone agreed was a monster.

Reliance was the largest yacht ever built for the America's Cup and the most extreme in every way. On the maximum permitted waterline length of 90ft (27.43m), Herreshof extended the overhanging ends to a gigantic 145ft (44.19m). Her rig, 175ft (53.34m) in

Below: This Charles Dixon painting shows Shamrock II *and* Columbia *racing neck and neck for the line in the 1901 match. This time, the challenger had the faster yacht but skilful tactics by Charlie Barr saved the day for the Americans.*

height, supported 16,159 sq ft (1,500 sq m) of sail. Her topsail alone was bigger than the entire sail area of the modern 12-metre.

She had so much sail area that she dipped her lee rail into the water in only 12 knots of wind. To control her vast sails, Herreshof designed geared winches and a crew of more than 60 was needed. She was built of a combination of steel, bronze and aluminium and doomed to a very short life due to corrosion.

The whole concept of *Reliance* had an element of overkill and it is difficult to see how Lipton could have gone one better. He should have given George Watson another chance for he now understood that a completely no-holds-barred approach was required. Instead, for some reason Lipton returned to Fife, a fine designer but not a visionary.

Fife rightly said that the new boat must have a trial horse to work up against in America, something that previous challengers had always lacked, but for some reason persuaded Lipton to use his old design, *Shamrock I* rather than *Shamrock II*.

Shamrock III got off to a bad start when she was dismasted on her early trials in England, resulting in the death of one of her crew, and when she did reach the United States she was clearly not in the same class as the mighty *Reliance*. She was soundly beaten in three straight races, and never finished the last one due to getting lost in the fog. It was a poor showing and Sir Tommy Lipton was quite embittered by the result. When someone remarked that at least his yacht looked good he snapped back that he would rather have the ugliest boat in the world if it was as fast as *Reliance* had proved to be.

1920: Shamrock IV *v* Resolute

Lipton said he wanted a boat that was ugly but fast and he got it when he finally broke away from his Scottish naval architects and went to Charles E. Nicholson, head of the famous Camper and Nicholsons yard at Southampton.

It was agreed that the new Universal Rule would be used and this provided for a series of classes at various rating levels. Lipton

Above: *The launching of* Shamrock III *at the yard of Dennys of Dunbarton on the Clyde. This picture gives a good impression of the extraordinary size and depth of the yachts used for the 1903 match. The defender,* Reliance, *was the largest yacht yet built for the America's Cup at 145ft (44.19m) overall and had a staggering 16,159 sq ft (1,500 sq m) of sail.*

proposed to use the 'J' Class rating of 68ft but for reasons best known to themselves the New York Yacht Club wasted a lot of time before finally agreeing to sail in yachts of 75ft (22.86m) waterline, which would be roughly similar in size to 'J' Class.

Nicholson was a brilliant, up-to-date designer and in his first effort produced a fast, efficient, ugly brute but apparently did not understand the sail area part of the rule as well as he should have because *Shamrock IV* ended up with a handicap of seven minutes compared to the defender. She was one of the most lightly-built large racing yachts ever, with three thin skins of cedar, spruce and mahogany on light, laminated wood frames and stringers with deep web-frames of a plywood-type material called 'Navaltum'.

Shamrock IV was crossing the Atlantic for a match planned for autumn 1914 when war was declared. She continued to New York and was laid up in dry dock to await the end of hostilities. A full six years passed before the world was again a sufficiently secure place to concern itself with international yachting contests and it could well be that this delay was fatal to the challenger, for while *Shamrock IV* was gathering dust in dry-dock, the yacht built for the defence, *Resolute*, was out sailing.

Furthermore, during all this time, she was sailed by the same man, Secretary of the US Navy, Charles Francis Adams. With the change to a smaller boat and the death of Charlie Barr, the era of the great professional skippers was over and amateurs took the helm. The Lipton team also appointed an amateur helmsman, Sir William Burton. His wife was the time-keeper, Claud Hickman the navigator and the designer Charles Nicholson, himself a first-class helmsman, was the technical adviser.

In the first race, *Resolute*'s gaff jumped off the mast and broke and she was forced to give up. In the second, Burton surprised the Americans by out-smarting Adams on a patchy, variable day to win by 2½ minutes on corrected time.

The next race was held in another light wind, when *Resolute* proved she had better pointing ability and was two minutes up at the windward mark. On the run, *Shamrock* with her big sail area pulled ahead but although she finished first, the American yacht was winner on handicap. In the lead by two races to one, the British felt they could administer the *coup de grâce* if they had a strong wind so they were very disappointed when the committee made the decision to cancel the racing when it did blow.

The next two races were in a steady light wind where *Resolute*'s close-windedness and lower handicap allowed her to win both.

This was the last race held in gaff-rigged yachts and the last on handicap which was so confusing to the onlooker; it was also the last held off New York where the autumn weather was unpredictable.

1930: Shamrock V *v* Enterprise

Thirty years after his first challenge, Sir Thomas Lipton was still obsessed by the notion of winning the America's Cup. Although approaching 80 years of age he decided to wait until the Americans agreed to make the contest less one-sided. Eventually, the New York Yacht Club agreed to a 'scantlings rule', that is, to have the yachts built under survey to meet the minimum standards of strength and weight as laid down by Lloyd's Register.

They in turn insisted on moving the event to Newport, which Lipton had resisted as he felt the races would receive less public attention if moved away from New York.

The big obstacle for the British this time, was the American helmsman Harold Vanderbilt. Extremely rich, he was also a passionate and highly-organized sportsman. It was he who invented the game of contract bridge and wrote the yacht racing rules in the basic form that we know today.

The key to his defence was efficient organization. The crew wore numbered shirts corresponding to their jobs on board and the afterguard were each given specific responsibility in areas where they excelled.

***Right:** The launching of* Endeavour *which in 1934 came closer than any other British challenger to regaining the America's Cup. T.O.M. Sopwith poured money and technical expertise into the first* Endeavour *but received a serious set-back when most of his professional crew went on strike and were sacked.*

Enterprise, designed by William Starling Burgess, embodied very important innovations. She had the first-ever light-alloy mast (built by an aircraft company) which was 2,000lb (907kg) lighter than the equivalent wooden mast. Another innovation was her 'Park Avenue boom', triangular in section with a wide, flat top on which a large number of transverse tracks were set with sliders having adjustable stops on them. The foot of the mainsail was attached to these sliders and an exact aerodynamic curve could be created by setting the stops correctly.

Although *Shamrock V*, designed by Charles Nicholson, was fast she did not have a realistic chance against *Enterprise*. She was commanded in an old-fashioned way with her professional skipper, Ned Heard, taking the helm. She was seriously under-winched and her badly set-up rig had much more sag in the forestays than the defender had.

Shamrock V failed to win a single race. It was a sad and disappointing ending to the Lipton era but during 30 years he had seen the contest raised to an exceptional standard of sportsmanship and competitiveness. At over 80, Lipton was planning a further challenge when he died a year later.

THE AIRMAN

With the death of Sir Thomas Lipton an entirely different 'Tommy' arrived on the scene: T.O.M. (later Sir Tom) Sopwith. The famous First World War aircraft designer and builder was a talented amateur helmsman and had raced a 12-metre for some years. He seemed to have all the qualities needed for a really convincing challenge: he was rich, a forceful manager, a good sailor and had a proper grasp of the technicalities of design. After Lipton's death, Sopwith raced *Shamrock V* for a season before ordering a new J-Class from Charles Nicholson.

1934: Endeavour *v* Rainbow

Nicholson, with the experience of *Shamrock V* behind him was now handling the J-Class rule with confidence and *Endeavour*, as the new yacht was named, was his masterpiece. Measuring 83ft 3in (25.39m) waterline length, she was built of steel and was a strikingly beautiful and efficient yacht. Sopwith unleashed his own aeronautical expertise on the rig and a team under Frank Murdoch

went to work on the hollow welded and rivetted steel mast, rod rigging, hollow tubular spreaders, geared sheet winches and many other details. Sopwith was determined that *Endeavour* would be technically up-to-date in every department.

Both Sopwith and Nicholson later claimed to have come up with the idea of a four-cornered or 'quadrilateral' jib with two sets of sheets. This was made in secrecy and Nicholson urged Sopwith to sail far out to sea before trying it but the latter was spotted in the Solent and the details were passed on to America.

Meanwhile, America was a nation still shattered by the effects of the Great Depression. Eventually, Harold Vanderbilt put together a syndicate of 18 people and ordered an 'austerity' J-Class from Starling Burgess that had to use as many fittings and sails as possible from *Enterprise*. *Rainbow* proved less than outstanding and in trials lost race after race to *Yankee*, a J-Class built for the previous defender trials and up-dated by Charles Francis Adams. Even after a lot of work to bring *Rainbow* up to scratch, she only just won selection.

Crew problems

Both challenger and defender had problems with their professional crews. *Rainbow*'s mainly Norwegian crew struck for more wages. With typical lack of ceremony, Vanderbilt sat down with representatives of his crew and worked out an agreement.

Sopwith ran into more serious difficulty with *Endeavour*'s crew. Most were Essex fishermen who went 'yachting' during the summer season. When this ended, Sopwith offered them the same rates of pay for the trip to America but the men said that if they were away until the end of October their places on the fishing boats would be taken by others and they would not be able to live through the winter. Sopwith refused to pay them for the whole winter and most of the crew went on strike just a week before *Endeavour* was to leave for her transatlantic passage.

Sopwith refused to negotiate and those who went on strike were sacked. They were replaced by a group of young amateur yachtsmen recruited through the Royal Corinthian Yacht Club who were enthusiastic but lacked the toughness and experience of the hard-handed fishermen. Sopwith's determination to be nobody's fool thus resulted in him going to the America's Cup with a less than ideal crew and the incident certainly points to vital differences in management style between the two sides.

'Battle of the bath-tubs'

When *Endeavour* arrived in Newport, the Americans found out that Sopwith was no kindly old gentleman in the Lipton mould. As soon as his representatives were allowed to inspect *Rainbow* (each side had the right to inspect the other) he protested that the American yacht had been stripped out in defiance of the rules. The New York Yacht Club was forced to concede the point after which most of *Endeavour*'s accommodation was torn out. Even so, *Rainbow* was much the more stripped-out yacht.

The racing

Sopwith dealt the defenders an even more telling blow in the first race. *Rainbow* led at the windward mark but on the run *Endeavour* sailed straight past to win by 2 minutes, 9 seconds.

The second race was held in a fresher wind. *Endeavour* had the better start and after a hard-fought race won by 51 seconds.

Now two-nil up in the best-of-seven series, Sopwith was within sight of winning the America's Cup and as the third race got under way it looked as if he had this one in the bag as well. *Endeavour* was six minutes ahead at the turning mark. The wind changed and the position looked so hopeless that Vanderbilt gave the helm of *Rainbow* to wily old Sherman Hoyt and went below.

Hoyt had often sailed against Sopwith and knew that he always covered tenaciously when leading so he pointed up sharply on to a heading nearly 90 degrees above the course to the finish. Sopwith, apparently forgetting that he only needed to head up slightly to stay between his opponent and the finish, panicked and tacked in order to get directly in front of *Rainbow*. This only slowed *Endeavour* down and after crossing *Rainbow*'s bow Sopwith made a bad tack and was forced to make yet another.

Too late, Sopwith realized he had been hoodwinked into sailing *away* from the finish and *Rainbow*, well ahead, finished 3 minutes 25 seconds clear.

At the start of the fourth race, both yachts manoeuvred aggressively and there was an incident in which each skipper considered that a rule had been infringed and that he was in the right. But Sopwith did not hoist a protest flag because he wanted to win fair and square and Vanderbilt because he had been told by the NYYC committee to avoid involvement in disputes.

Sopwith still sailed an excellent first leg and was a few seconds ahead at the windward mark. Just after the mark, *Rainbow* came up on to *Endeavour*'s weather quarter and Sopwith luffed to stop her overtaking. Vanderbilt did not respond to this perfectly legitimate manoeuvre and Sopwith had to bear away sharply to avoid a collision.

Sopwith did not order a protest flag to be hoisted immediately, firstly because he still wanted to win without a protest and secondly because in England it was only necessary to show a flag 'when next passing the Committee Vessel'.

Rainbow crossed the line first and as she did so, *Endeavour* hoisted her protest flag. There then followed a much misunderstood furore. At the hearing, Sopwith entered *two* protests; one relating to the incident on the starting line and one for the luffing incident. After discussion, the NYYC protest committee refused to hear either protest because *Endeavour*'s protest flag had not been hoisted 'immediately following the incident'.

Sopwith was furious and the press and public opinion sided with him. 'Britannia rules the waves; America waives the rules' screamed the headlines. In fact, the protest committee knew that if the start line incident went to a hearing, Sopwith would lose and this made the second protest irrelevant. They therefore used what they hoped would be a tactful device to avoid a hearing. Unfortunately, their actions were misunderstood and so once again bitter accusations of unfairness were hurled at the NYYC.

With the score now at two wins each in a best of seven series, there was everything to play for but the British crew, who had held the initiative in the first two races, were now rattled and starting to make mistakes. Vanderbilt had borrowed a good spinnaker from *Yankee* together with Frank Paine, one of the few people who knew how to set the new 'parachute'-style sails. He also added ballast and to match this *Endeavour*'s crew put in 3½ ton (3.56 tonne) on the lay-day which left them very tired.

The Americans won the fifth race by better spinnaker work and this was the only time that *Endeavour* was decisively beaten on the water.

The sixth race had to be a cliff-hanger. After aggressive pre-start manoeuvres which led both yachts to hoist protest flags (both later withdrawn) *Endeavour* won the start and took the lead. On the reach *Rainbow* caught up but Sopwith luffed up head to wind and maintained his lead. On the next beat *Endeavour* set too big a headsail and *Rainbow* overtook. At the beginning of the final run to the finish *Endeavour*'s rapidly tiring crew fumbled the spinnaker hoist but once it was setting they started to overhaul *Rainbow* rapidly.

With *Endeavour* almost alongside, Vanderbilt seemed ready to throw in the towel and even Sherman Hoyt said 'It looked all over for us.' But once again, in an apparently hopeless situation, Hoyt was given the helm and set about luring Sopwith into making a fatal error. He asked *Rainbow*'s brilliant navigator, Zenas Bliss, to give him a heading to a point one mile *downwind* of the finish and headed in that direction.

Just as he hoped, Sopwith followed, slowing *Endeavour* right down as he tried to take *Rainbow*'s wind. In an effort to cross *Rainbow*'s stern, *Endeavour* had to sail even further by the lee and the defender slowly began to pull clear. *Rainbow* crossed the line first by 55 seconds, retaining the America's Cup by the closest-ever margin.

In retrospect it seems incredible that Sopwith should have failed for the second time to realize that he had only to sail straight towards the finish to win. But it is very easy in the heat of battle for the helmsman to lose track of position and that is where Vanderbilt had the crucial advantage of a better tactician (Hoyt) and better navigator (Bliss). However, on this one occasion, the British challenger was clearly the better boat and a little more coolness would have won the day.

1937: Endeavour II *v* Ranger

Sopwith had come within a whisker of success so it was only to be expected that he would try again. Nicholson, who had produced such a good design in *Endeavour* could be expected to improve things still further and it was decided to spend a full season tuning up against the previous boat. There was every reason to suppose that with such preparation *Endeavour II* could succeed.

But the yacht that *Endeavour II* came up against was a veritable super-boat. Nicholson had swapped the lines plan of *Endeavour* for those of *Rainbow* and the Americans had handed these on to Professor Davidson of the Stevens Institute of Technology in Hoboken. Davidson was the world leader in the tank-testing of model hulls.

To design his new yacht Vanderbilt formed a team consisting of Starling Burgess and the Stephens brothers, Rod and Olin. Olin had already made a name for himself with outstanding offshore racing designs which set completely new standards of performance and had also designed fast day-boats. Rod was the expert on rigging, fittings and every kind of seamanlike detail.

Below: Endeavour II *setting a quadrilateral jib on trials in the Solent. The last America's Cup challenger to be designed by Charles Nicholson, she had the misfortune to be pitted against the super-boat* Ranger, *the last and incomparably the fastest of the J-Class.*

They prepared four models for testing and model 77c chose itself. The design was so radical that Burgess confessed that without the reassurance of the tank results, they would not have had the nerve to build *Ranger* and Nicholson called her the biggest advance in design in half a century.

Both challenger and defender were built to the maximum 87ft (26.51m) waterline length possible under the J-Class rule with an overall length of 135ft (41.14m) but *Ranger* was slightly heavier and considerably more powerful. With her curious snubbed bow and flattened-off stern she was ugly but the most efficient sailing machine yet built.

From the first moments of the first race in the 1937 America's Cup match there was very little doubt about the outcome. *Ranger* won by the crushing margin of over 17 minutes. In the next race she won again, by 18 minutes 32 seconds. Afterwards, Sopwith had *Endeavour* re-ballasted and re-polished in an effort to redress the balance but *Ranger* was still the easy winner of both the following races.

With re-armament gathering pace in Europe, this was the end of the America's Cup for the time being and also the end of the 'big class'. Although they were often accused of being over-developed monsters, the J-Class were superlative racing machines that represented the absolute pinnacle of what could be achieved at the time in design, construction, sparmaking, sailmaking and many other branches of the sport. Literally hundreds of technical advances such as aluminium masts, synthetic sailcloth, geared sheet-winches, ball-bearing blocks, electronic instruments, streamlined rigging and many more improvements, flowed down from the J-Class into yachting as a whole.

Perhaps even more important, the mighty 'Js' provided a superb spectacle and were a truly evocative expression of the sporting achievements of man. Nothing that followed could ever be quite so impressive.

THE POST-WAR ERA

Before beginning the story of the post-war challenges for the America's Cup, there is just one loose end from the pre-war era. After the 1937 event Harold Vanderbilt realized that the J-Class had reached its apotheosis and would never be used again. He therefore ordered a boat built to the International 12-metre rule, to be designed by Olin Stephens. Some years before, it had been agreed that the American 'Universal Rule' would be used for big yachts while the European 'International Rule' would be used for smaller ones.

The 12-metre that Stephens designed for Vanderbilt was named *Vim* and outclassed everything else afloat. Like *Ranger* she was much more modern in hull-design, mast, sails, fittings, the lot. Vanderbilt had her shipped over to England for the 1939 summer season where she achieved 21 wins in 27 races. Shipped back to the States, she raced with equal success in 1940, after which she was laid up for the duration.

Post-war discussion

As the world crawled out of the nightmare of the Second World War, thoughts turned to a possible resumption of the America's Cup. There was no international racing taking place in day-sailing yachts but ocean racing was proving a dynamic and fast-growing sport. Captain John Illingworth, the leading figure in British ocean racing and Commodore of the Royal Ocean Racing Club, struck up a discussion with the then Commodore of the New York Yacht Club, De Coursey Fales. By 1948 they had a tentative agreement to promote a contest using largish ocean racers built to the International Cruiser-Racer Rule. Their concept was for a pure-bred racing yacht that would still have a future as a cruiser-racer when it became out-dated.

The yachting establishment of both Britain and America poured cold water on this idea. The America's Cup, it was felt, should be contested in top-class, pure-bred racing yachts. So in 1956, when Henry Sears and Sir Ralph Gore, Commodores respectively of the New York Yacht Club and the Royal Yacht Squadron entered discussions, they centred around traditional day-racing yachts that were built to the International 12-metre rule.

To make this possible, a further revision of the Deed of Gift was necessary, reducing the minimum waterline length to 44ft (13.41m) and removing the stipulation that the challenger must sail to the race venue. There was also a lengthy set of 'Sailing Regulations' which describe measurement, courses, number of races and so on.

The way was now clear for the first challenge in yachts of the International 12-metre class and a syndicate was formed under the chairmanship of Hugh Goodson. In June 1957 a challenge was issued through the Royal Yacht Squadron and this was taken up by the New York Yacht Club, which agreed to a series the following autumn.

1958: Sceptre *v* Columbia

The British syndicate was in trouble from the very start; they were basically 'yesterday's men' — middle-aged gentlemen who had been keen yachtsmen in the 1930s.

Britain's young, keen, ambitious sailors were racing either in dinghies or offshore; day-racing keelboats were a dying breed.

According to Captain John Illingworth, the syndicate's first major mistake was not to appoint a qualified technical adviser. Instead, they invited four designers to submit two designs each which were sent to the Saunders Roe testing tank at East Cowes for evaluation.

The Saunders Roe tank was fairly primitive and lacked a wave-making facility. The tests revealed little difference between the models but one of the designs by the Scottish naval architect David Boyd was slightly superior and the syndicate decided to go ahead with this design.

Boyd's design, which was to receive the name *Sceptre*, was an interesting and unusual one. She was a classic, streamlined tadpole shape: full and rounded in the forebody and tapering away to a cone. Her resistance in smooth water was very low but testing in waves would have shown that she had a tendency to pitch and plunge badly.

Where *Sceptre* was an undoubted success was in layout. Boyd gave her a large open crew cockpit which provided better working conditions, lower centre of gravity, and a better view for the helmsman.

Crew selection was haphazard and because there was an upper age limit of 30, most people who were really well-qualified got passed over. The rig was terrible, with a mast like a tree-trunk and a mainsail that was attached to the mast by sliders instead of a luff-groove. Sails, in the relatively unfamiliar Terylene were not in the same league as the Dacron ones being made by Hood in the USA and the gigantic Herbulot spinnakers were not the successful secret weapon they were expected to be.

Worst of all was the lack of a good trial horse. The only other 12-metre available was the pre-war *Evaine*. To everyone's horror she gave *Sceptre* a hard time, beating her on many occasions. Only after extensive tuning up and only then in smooth water did the new boat look faster.

America takes up 12-metre racing

Just as in Britain, there was no 12-metre racing in the USA in the 1950s but once the British challenge was received, things began to move fast. Three syndicates were formed and each ordered a new 12-metre from different designers. In addition, John N. Mathews who owned the pre-war *Vim* had her thoroughly overhauled.

The new boats were: *Columbia* designed by Olin Stephens for a syndicate headed by Henry Sears, *Weatherly* designed by Philip Rhodes for Henry Mercer, Cornelius Walsh and Arnold Frere, and *Easterner* designed by C. Raymond Hunt for Chandler Hovey. The trials series between the four yachts was extensive, testing and towards the end, almost unbelievably close.

Easterner and *Weatherly* eventually fell by the wayside because they were not campaigned seriously enough.

The final trials between *Columbia* and *Vim* were classic, with the average winning margin a mere 32 seconds. The pre-war *Vim*,

Below: In 1958, Columbia *ushered in the modern era of racing for the America's Cup in 12-metres when she trounced the British challenger* Sceptre *in straight races. This was also the beginning of an era in which American technical superiority seemed so great that taking the trophy from them began to appear an impossible task.*

aggressively sailed by Emil 'Bus' Mosbacher, was an almost perfect match for the newer *Columbia*, sailed by either Cornelius Shields or Briggs Cunningham. Eventually, the newer boat showed a tiny superiority.

This tremendous series of races provides the clue to American success for the next 20 years. The defender was always selected by a genuinely competitive process during which both yacht and crew were honed and refined to perfection over many weeks of competition. In contrast, the challenger was so often a one-boat affair which had not been tested in the fire of genuine competition and not until 1983 was this balance changed.

The series

Few expected that the actual challenge series would be such an embarrassing débâcle for the British. The first race was held in a light breeze and a smooth sea — conditions which should have suited *Sceptre* yet after a very even start *Columbia* sailed away into an enormous lead of seven minutes 40 seconds at the first mark.

Columbia won the second race — again in a light wind — by 11 minutes 27 seconds and the British could now only pin their hopes on strong winds. But when they got them for the third race, *Sceptre*'s helmsman Graham Mann found that she plunged and slammed so badly in the swell that he was unable to point up as high as *Columbia* which completely outclassed her to windward. The final race, again in a fresh breeze, was a similar story with *Sceptre* losing by a margin of just under seven minutes.

This disappointing beginning to the modern era of America's Cup races made it clear that there was an enormous technical gap between Britain and America and in future it would be hard to gain support for a British challenge.

The postscript to the *Sceptre* story is that following her defeat in 1958 she was bought by Eric Maxwell who brought her up to date for use as a trial horse for the 1964 challenge. Better than that, in the 1967 New York Yacht Club cruise she beat many of the current American 12-metres!

1962: Gretel *v* Weatherly

British yachtsmen decided they must pull themselves together and a new grouping was formed around the Royal Thames Yacht Club. But before they were ready, the Royal Sydney Yacht Squadron challenged.

The man behind this was Sir Frank Packer, a rough, tough Australian newspaper tycoon and father of Kerry Packer of floodlit cricket fame. Packer was eventually to bedevil his own challenge with his interfering management style but he was certainly a go-getter and made some very shrewd moves.

The first was to secure a four-year charter of *Vim* and have her shipped to Sydney. The second was to hire a brilliant young designer-engineer named Alan Payne who went straight to the Stevens Institute in Hoboken and started work on the first ever Australian 12-metre. There was then nothing to prevent a challenger (other than pride) from using US sailcloth, and Packer ordered a supply for his sailmakers, Pearce and Cole.

Payne was a first-class mechanical engineer and he devised a new primary winch system which allowed the power of four brawny Aussies to be devoted to winding in the genoa sheets. This, he felt, could be a crucial advantage in a tacking duel.

The New York Yacht Club did not appear to take the Packer challenge too seriously and only one new 12-metre was built: *Nefertiti*, designed by sailmaker Ted Hood. He made her beamier than normal to create a wider sheeting base for the sails and she was powerful and fast in strong winds and spinnaker reaches. The helmsman was Don McNamara, aggressive and tactless.

Weatherly had been remodelled by A.E. Luders and 'Bus' Mosbacher, who had put up such a fight with *Vim* in the previous defence trials, was given her helm. *Easterner* was back but once again was only given a good helmsman and crew when it was too late while *Columbia* had a new owner and crew who fell short of what was required. The selection was narrowed down to *Nefertiti* versus *Weatherly* with the latter finally gaining the nod from the NYYC Committee.

From trials between their new boat, named *Gretel*, and *Vim*, the Australians already knew that *Gretel* was fast but, even after arrival in Newport, Payne had no hesitation in making major alterations. She had a vast wardrobe of 85 sails while winches seemed to come and go daily.

While Payne had a fairly free hand with the technical side, the crew did not. Under Packer's autocratic management no-one knew who was going to be helmsman from day to day. The challenge helmsman, Jock Sturrock, was not named until the day before the first race and the navigator was changed on the morning of the first race.

Mosbacher was not going to stand any nonsense from these noisy Aussies and at the start of the first race managed to get under *Gretel*'s bow and push her over the line early. *Gretel* had the wrong main up and broke a backstay, in spite of which she was beaten by just four minutes.

The second race, held in a good breeze, was a very different affair. Mosbacher again got the better of the start but after a short while Sturrock began making repeated quick tacks which the yacht ahead had to follow in order to maintain a close covering position. It was immediately apparent that the powerful Aussie crew was gaining ground on every tack and Mosbacher was obliged to break away and head straight for the next mark, desperately hoping there would not be a wind shift.

Weatherly stayed just ahead at the windward mark but as she set her spinnaker there was trouble with the pole end, and as her crew fought with it *Gretel* picked up an extra-big swell and went surfing past. Mosbacher luffed sharply, attempting to bar their way but *Weatherly*'s spinnaker guy parted and the pole folded round the forestay; they were beaten!

The Australians then mistakenly requested a lay-day and so missed a further day of good wind. Two days later the yachts met in light conditions under which *Weatherly* was faster and Mosbacher the better tactician. The Americans were the winners by over eight minutes.

The fourth race was notable for the fact that Mosbacher held off the overtaking Australians with a Hoyt-like trick that got *Gretel* off her fastest point of sailing. After getting well off the direct course to the finish *Weatherly* rehoisted her spinnaker and just made it to the line by 26 seconds.

Better tactics and pointing ability gave *Weatherly* the final race by a generous three minutes 40 seconds and to the relief of the Americans the America's Cup was safe for the time being. Although slightly chaotic, this first Australian challenge had technical merit and was a real red-blooded effort. Never again would a challenge by the Australians be taken so lightly.

1964: Sovereign *v* Constellation

The *Gretel* challenge had given the Americans a real fright. Although the Deed of Gift requires the challenger to be built in the challenging country, with modern 12-metres the actual hull-construction is a relatively minor matter compared to research, testing, rigging, deck hardware and sails, all of which the Australians had bought from the USA.

Alarmed that they could in future be beaten by their own technology, the New York Yacht Club made some new 'interpretations'. In future not only hulls but design research, sails, sailcloth and all other equipment had to originate in the challenging country. As usual, there was a good deal of grumbling about conflict of interest, the NYCC being able to act as legislator in a competition in which it was also the defender, but in fact they were doing other countries a favour.

Cut off from US sources of supply, countries such as Britain, Australia and France were forced to develop their own industries. In masts, hardware, instrumentation and testing, other countries gradually became the equals or superiors to the USA although it took a very long time to catch up in sailcloth technology.

Back in Britain, David Boyd had already been selected by Tony Boyden to design a new 12-metre and testing at the Stevens tank was completed before the new ban took effect. Unfortunately, the delay caused by the fact that the *Gretel* challenge had slipped in ahead of an expected British one resulted in a lot of steam going out of the Royal Thames Yacht Club initiative. After a promising research-based start the Red Duster syndicate headed by Lord Craigmyle dropped out and efforts by John Illingworth to get Boyden into 6-metre racing also flopped.

Initially, Illingworth, the one British yachtsman who was really successful on the international scene, held a brief as technical adviser but was dropped after Boyd was confirmed as designer. With the benefit of tank-testing at Stevens Institute, Boyd had gone right away from his *Sceptre* tadpole shape and come up with a straightforward 12-metre that looked pretty much like current US designs.

This could have been worked up into a reasonable boat but once again the follow-through was lacking. The mast and sails were terrible and Boyden chose Rugby-players instead of experienced sailors as crew. Most surprising of all, he chose as helmsman the ornithologist and painter Peter Scott. Though Scott had been an outstanding all-round sportsman before the war, he had not been active in sailing for some time and was completely out of his depth in match-racing. And once again, there was no credible trial-horse other than the improved *Sceptre*. To fill this glaring omission the Australian brothers Frank and John Livingston came over for Cowes Week 1963 and asked Illingworth to build a 12-metre for them but it was too late. No yard would commit itself to delivery for early spring 1964. The only solution was to build a 'twin' *Sovereign* at the same Scottish yard using existing moulds.

When *Kurrewa V* appeared, she was given to Owen Aisher to campaign. He put in a good, ocean-racing crew and, as she was not expected to be the challenger, she used imported Hood sails. She turned out to be the faster yacht.

On the other side of the Atlantic two new boats were built: *American Eagle*, designed by A.E. Luders for a syndicate headed by Pierre S. Dupont, and *Constellation*, the latest from Sparkman and Stephens, for Walter Gublemann and Eric Ridder.

***Above:** The 1964 series was preceded by a tremendously hard-fought defender elimination series between* American Eagle *and* Constellation *(seen here), sailed by Bob Bavier. Afterwards,* Constellation *beat the latest British challenger* Sovereign *with embarrassing ease.*

In designing *Constellation* Stephens had not only done tank-testing but had had *Weatherly* fitted-out as a floating laboratory with strain-gauges to measure dynamic loadings at various points. This made it possible to refine the engineering of the new boat. Considerable use was made of titanium (since banned) in the mast, boom and winch drums. The mast and boom were designed to bend so that fuller sails could be set initially and flattened off as the wind increased. Another feature since disallowed was her big, open cockpit with slatted floor; lightweight and nice to work in but not watertight.

American Eagle was a striking-looking boat with low freeboard and a wide, flat counter. She was very fast and in early trials soon got the upper hand over *Constellation*. The latter's problem was helmsmanship. She was originally steered by Eric Ridder who was one of her owners and a good 6-metre sailor. But he realized that he was not getting the best out of the boat and handed over to his relief helmsman Bob Bavier.

Bavier was a long-time sailing opponent of Bill Cox, the skipper of *American Eagle*, and these two set about each other as if their lives depended on it. In the second race of the final defender trials, with *American Eagle* just in front at the beginning of a 4½-mile beat to the finish, Bavier initiated the fiercest and most protracted tacking duel yet seen, with *Constellation* tacking 40 times and *American Eagle* 42 times. This exhausting process ended with *Constellation* breaking through into the lead and, as Bavier described in his book *A View from the Cockpit*, 'the Eagle's heart was broken'.

In the actual challenge series, *Constellation* won every race without the slightest difficulty, once by the humiliating margin of 20 minutes 24 seconds. Afterwards Olin Stephens commented, 'It's too bad for all of us who have put so much into it — we've put in so much that there isn't a contest left.'

1967: Dame Pattie *v* Intrepid

Right after the *Gretel* challenge in 1962, both Sir Frank Packer and another Australian businessman, Emil Christensen, indicated their wish to challenge again, but first they had to wait for the lamentable *Sovereign* affair to run its course. Meanwhile, they developed their own sailcloth from a locally-made yarn named Kadron. Packer tried to capitalize on the 'grandfather' clause which made it possible for existing boats to go on using the US-made equipment that they still had in stock.

Instead of building a new boat he had *Gretel* 'remodelled', jacking up the deck and sliding a new hull underneath but in trials the Christensen boat, designed by Alan Payne's former assistant Warwick Hood and named *Dame Pattie*, proved superior. But her misfortune was to come up against a real breakthrough boat, *Intrepid*. Curiously Olin Stephens did not believe in the breakthrough theory of design because in his opinion intense effort on a number of fronts would bring sufficient tiny improvements to give an overall superiority. But *Intrepid* was different.

The syndicate, under the leadership of William Strawbridge, gave Stephens plenty of time and took every distraction off his shoulders. The problem with 12-metre design is to pack in as much displacement as possible without resulting in a bulbous lumpy keel. Stephens felt he could reduce the wetted surface of the keel by placing the rudder on a bulge above and behind the keel proper. This brought a dramatic drop in resistance by smoothing and lengthening the quarter-wave. He also fitted a trim-tab or 'kicker' whose effect was to improve the lift characteristics of the keel and, when used in conjunction with the rudder, improved turning ability.

The best possible crew was lined up with 'Bus' Mosbacher as skipper and Vic Romagna in charge of spinnaker handling. Halsey Herreshof's aerodynamic experiments showed a considerable benefit from lowering the boom almost to the deck. This made it impossible to sail with the usual pedestal winches on deck so these were mounted upside down *beneath* the deck. This in turn created a 'black gang' of up to seven people working out of sight below deck, while the yacht appeared to be sailing with a skeleton crew of helmsman, navigator and three tailers.

Intrepid was the easy winner of the selection trials and also of the America's Cup, which she won in four straight races.

1970: Gretel II *v* Intrepid

By the end of the 1960s, there was so much world-wide interest in the America's Cup that more countries were interested in getting in on the act. Following the *Sceptre* challenge, when both Britain and Australia had tried to shoulder each other out of the queue, the New York Yacht Club announced that it would regard all challenges received within 30 days of the previous match to be simultaneous. Clearly, they would have to fight it out for the right to be the eventual challenger.

Right after the *Dame Pattie* match, challenges were received from Australia, Britain, France and Greece, but Britain and Greece dropped out. The French challenge came from Marcel Bich who made an immense fortune from the humble Bic ball-point pen.

'Baron' Bich had bought *Kurrewa V* as a plaything for his nine children and became entranced by 12-metre sailing. He bought two more 12-metres, *Constellation* and *Sovereign*, and ordered a new design from Britton Chance Jr. This up-to-date boat, very much in the *Intrepid* style, was built in France by a Swiss and named *Chancegger*, but even this was just one more step on the road for the Baron, who now ordered designer André Mauric to produce an all-French design.

For once the Americans, whose technology had proved so superior in the post-war period, were led up the garden path by their own research. The rule allows a longer boat if it is also heavier and has less sail and results at the Stevens Institute tank indicated that it was worth paring away at the keel area even further, pushing more and more displacement into the body of the hull and the fattened 'bustle'. *Valiant*, the boat that Sparkman and Stephens designed for the 1970 series was the heaviest 12-metre ever at over 70,000lb (31,780kg) and *Intrepid* was remodelled by Chance to bring her up to a similar weight. Both boats proved to be lumbering lead-mines. In light airs they were desperately under-powered and in heavy conditions they were so wet and clumsy that they were in danger of filling up and sinking.

In Australia, Alan Payne had a shrewd idea that the Americans were going for jumbo 12-metres and designed a much livelier boat of around 61,000lb (27,694kg) displacement.

The American trials narrowed down to a battle between *Valiant* and *Intrepid* with the latter coming out on top — but as she had been extensively altered it was hard to realize that they were both pretty slow.

In the first-ever challenger elimination races, *Gretel II*, skippered mostly by Jim Hardy, did not have too much difficulty in disposing of Baron Bich's *France*. Without doubt, *Gretel II* was a faster boat than the remodelled *Intrepid* but the Australians threw away the series by poor crewing and not knowing the rules.

The only real secret weapon that the Americans had up their sleeve was helmsman Bill Ficker who sailed the dead lump of a boat that was *Intrepid '70* with extreme skill and care, virtually never making a tactical mistake. *Gretel II* finished ahead twice, losing one result on protest and the series by four races to two.

ENTER ALAN BOND

When the flurry of challenges dropped through the letterbox of the New York Yacht Club in West 44th Street, they boiled down to just two: Baron Bich of France and Alan Bond of Western Australia. Bich engaged the most successful Olympic sailor of all time, Paul Elvström, to manage the whole affair. This was wildly unpopular in France and also came at a time when Elvström was under great personal and business stress. *France* sank in the North Sea while under tow and finally Elvström suffered a breakdown. The Bich contract was cancelled and the Baron decided on a low-profile challenge using the salvaged *France*, to keep his hand in.

Alan Bond, who emigrated to Australia from Britain as a teenager, was the classic self-made man. Starting as a sign-writer he had rapidly worked his way in building, property, real-estate, minerals exploration and other things with ever-increasing success. Bouncy, gregarious, aggressive and shrewd he was in some ways a modern Tommy Lipton — entering into the America's Cup game partly because of the sheer challenge and partly because he thought he could do himself a great deal of good in the process.

And he was right. Who outside Western Australia had heard of Alan Bond in 1970, and who in the entire world *hasn't* heard of him and the mighty Bond Corporation now?

1974: Southern Cross *v* Courageous

Although fond of boats, Bond never deluded himself that he should be at the helm of his challengers, but he has always been closely involved in their management. From the outset he adopted the highest possible profile and has never backed away from a good fight. When he made his challenge for 1974, Bond commented that he would be bringing his own lawyer plus a video team, just to make sure the club did not try to get up to any of its old tricks.

***Below:** The yellow* Southern Cross *was the first challenger backed by Alan Bond and the first 12-metre designed by Ben Lexcen. Their initial assault was brushed aside with little difficulty by the best of all the Sparkman and Stephens 12-metres,* Courageous, *sailed on this occasion by Ted Hood and Dennis Conner.*

Below: Courageous *sailing in a light wind. This great yacht was the successful defender in 1974 and 1977 and continued to be a triallist right up to 1986. In 1977, her skipper was the extrovert Ted Turner who brought a fresh breath of enthusiasm to the event that it was beginning to lack.*

Actually the poor old NYYC was taking quite a verbal battering and not all from overseas. Yachtsmen from other parts of the United States resented having to go cap in hand to the NYYC for permission to get in on the act.

Bond put in charge of his design effort Bob Miller, the immensely talented but eccentric designer who later changed his name to Ben Lexcen. Ben-Bob's designs tend to have clean, fair, straightforward lines without the bumps, lumps or angles that other designers use in an effort to squeeze an advantage from the rules.

A new character upon the America's Cup scene at this time was Ted Turner, the 'Mouth of the South'. Loud, irreverent, bursting with energy, he seemed more like an American from the John Cox Stevens era than the 1970s, but he was also a terrific sailor who had raced successfully in everything from dinghies to ocean racers and had won the SORC series in Florida. Turner first appears as helmsman of *Mariner*, the revolutionary Britton Chance design planned for the 1974 defence.

Another example of the test tank misleading the designer, *Mariner* had an exceptionally big 'bustle' that ended in a cut-off underwater transom or 'fast-back'. This was supposed to fool the water into believing the hull was longer than it was, but although it seemed to work in the tank, at full size the water refused to be fooled. *Mariner* was a failure except insofar as it got Ted Turner involved.

The big success was *Courageous*, the best-ever 12-metre from Sparkman and Stephens. Drawing back from the excessive weight of *Valiant*, she weighed 56,000lb (25,424kg) on a waterline length of 44ft 6in (13.56m) and was built of aluminium. The underwater shape was an improvement on *Intrepid* but with a more salient keel and rudder and she was in every way a refined, able boat with virtually no weak points.

Courageous had a very complicated afterguard. Bob Bavier was skipper but midway through the trials Ted Hood was brought in as tactician. The only good thing about *Mariner* had been her excellent starts so after she was dropped from trials, her starting helmsman, Dennis Conner, joined the crew of *Courageous*. Part way through the final trials Bavier was 'excused', leaving Hood and Conner, and they just managed to beat *Intrepid*, sailed by San Diego boatbuilder Jerry Driscoll.

Among other things the US trials were a battle between sailmakers. The science of sailmaking was beginning to change very rapidly thanks to new materials and the use of computers in design. It was also the first occasion on which real computers, rather than just instruments, were carried on yachts, opening a new front in the technology war that has become more important with each subsequent match.

In the challenger trials, *Southern Cross* brushed aside *France* without any difficulty but then went down 4-nil to *Courageous* in the match proper.

1977: Australia *v* Courageous

Because so many had tried and failed, the America's Cup had acquired the status of an Everest. Eventually, someone was certain to conquer it if only they kept on trying hard enough and for long enough.

Alan Bond, by no means satisfied by his first foray to Newport, Rhode Island,

promptly filed a new challenge. Lexcen was again named as designer and he teamed up with a draughtsman named Johan Valentijn. The latter was well-informed about *Courageous*, and *Australia* came out as a refinement of that boat. In fact, virtually all the yachts in the 1977 campaign were *Courageous* clones except for *Sverige*, the first-ever Swedish challenger, which was designed by Pelle Petterson.

Sverige was small, light and nimble and was steered by a tiller, something that had not been seen on an America's Cup challenger in a hundred years.

All the yachts were made more sea-worthy thanks to changes in the International 12-metre Class rules. Cockpits had to be above the waterline and watertight, like on an offshore boat, and the primary winches had to be above-deck.

There were two Australian challengers in 1977, but *Gretel II* was eliminated after a tough fight with *Sverige*. *Australia*, the new Bond boat, which was being steered by Noel Robins, easily defeated Baron Bich's *France I* and then went on to beat *Sverige*.

The defender trials looked like being almost exclusively a battle between the two major US sailmakers, North and Hood. Lowell North was the skipper of *Enterprise* while Ted Hood designed his own 12-metre *Independence*.

What stopped this rather unattractive contest from actually getting on to the starting blocks was the appearance of Ted Turner. Many thought that Turner, who had twice been turned down for membership of the New York Yacht Club, would never be chosen as defender because of his irreverent attitude and uninhibited behaviour but the committee included Bob Bavier, Briggs Cunningham and Bus Mosbacher, each of whom had defended the cup, and knew that it was performance that mattered in the end. When Turner narrowly beat both *Independence* and *Enterprise* in the trials, he was selected.

Once again, the actual match was something of an anticlimax, for not only was *Courageous* marginally faster than *Australia*, Turner and his tactician Gary Jobson sailed a better series and won in four straight races.

Above: Australia *made two challenges and performed much better on the second occasion, in 1980. Borrowing the newly-developed 'walking-stick' mast from the British* Lionheart, Australia *took one race off the defending* Freedom *but superior tactics by her skipper Dennis Conner were a crucial factor in favour of the American yacht.*

12
12
KA·5
KA·5
US·3
US·30

At the post-race press conference, 'Captain Outrageous' Turner was so drunk that he fell under the table insensible. The public just loved every moment of it.

1980: Australia *v* Freedom

There was a generally accepted opinion that the design of 12-metres had reached a plateau and that there were no real opportunities left for a major breakthrough. Practically all the boats were cautious efforts to improve on *Courageous* and Alan Bond did not even bother to order a new boat but came back with a fresh challenge using the existing *Australia*.

Sweden's Pelle Petterson also planned a second campaign with an existing boat while the irrepressible Baron Bich had a new one, designed by Dutchman Johan Valentijn, that had no revolutionary features. The only boat that offered anything new was the British *Lionheart*, designed by Ian Howlett. She was a big, heavy 12-metre built for speed in a straight line, and not greatly different from the *Courageous* model but her rig, for which her skipper John Oakeley took a lot of the responsibility, was most certainly different.

Oakeley revived the pre-war idea of a 'walking stick' mast with a sharply bent-back tip. The main idea of this was that because the mainsail was wider at the top there was more area within the same overall dimensions but it proved more efficient aerodynamically as well. Unfortunately, the 1980 British challenge failed for lack of sufficient money and poor management.

But 1980 was the year when Dennis Conner got his first chance to skipper a yacht in the America's Cup. A top helmsman with an Olympic silver medal, Star World Championship, Congressional Cup, SORC and many other championships behind him, Conner is the world's greatest 'percentage yachtsman'.

He never expects or looks for startling new departures in design or daring game-plans. He works on the basis that if he spends more time and effort in perfecting every aspect of a boat's performance, then he will be successful. A full two years was spent working up *Freedom* for the 1980 Cup.

Not only does the Conner style demand complete dedication over a very long period, it also requires enormously increased funding in order to keep a complete 12-metre team in action. This step up in the level of activity finally took 12-metre racing out of the hands of private individuals and brought in corporate sponsors.

When the other challengers fell by the wayside, *Australia* became the challenger — and a formidable one — but superior starting, tactics, sail-trimming and overall strategy by Conner won the day. Nevertheless, it is noteworthy that *Australia* won one race and *Freedom*'s winning margins in the others were small so the Americans had no grounds for complacency.

Left: Freedom *and* Australia *in the light winds and misty atmosphere so typical of Newport in September. The uneasy swell, poor visibility and fickle winds have always been factors that make it hard to beat a defending American yacht in this arena.*

NEMESIS

Yachting is an international game, especially at the top level. Owners, designers, builders, sailmakers, skippers and crew all mill around the world taking part in the major events so it is almost impossible to pin down one particular yacht and crew within national boundaries. After 1980, the New York Yacht Club acknowledged this by removing the previous requirement for a challenger to get all its technology and equipment in its country of origin.

This change enabled Ben Lexcen to undertake extensive design analysis at the Netherlands Ship Model Basin. The Dutch testing station had a very good computer-aided design system. Trying out new design ideas using the traditional methods of drafting, model-making and tank testing is so slow that it is really hard for a designer to come up with radical solutions. The Dutch system allowed Lexcen to throw idea after idea into the melting pot and get rapid answers on whether they were worth proceeding with.

Exactly who came up with the ideas for *Australia II*'s now famous winged keel will always be obscure as Dr Peter Van Oosanen at first protested that he had only put tools into the hands of Lexcen but later agreed that his team had already made tests on winglets for keels. But so had Lexcen. Probably, the truth is that there was an input from both sides.

Below: Australia II*'s famous and much-disputed winged keel that was a vital factor in the 1983 match. The wings themselves are made from solid lead and the resulting keel has a considerably lower centre of gravity than a conventional fin. The downward slope of the wings, which increased draught as the yacht heeled, was one of the features which most annoyed the defenders.*

The final design for the revolutionary keel showed a fin that was very short where it joined the hull and became both longer and fatter towards the bottom. The bulbous nose of the keel blended into thick, stubby wings which were angled downwards from the horizontal. This had the added advantage that when the yacht heeled, its draught increased, something that caused great annoyance to the Americans in 1983.

Testing of the winged keel indicated fairly spectacular performance gains and Lexcen then persuaded Alan Bond to build the boat.

1983: Australia II *v* Liberty

In addition to Bond and *Australia II*, there were two other Australian efforts, plus one contender each from France, Italy, Canada and Great Britain.

The international businessman Peter de Savary ran a high-profile *Victory* campaign.

The first *Victory* was poorly constructed and a disappointing performer but the second boat, *Victory '83*, designed by Ian Howlett was a lot better and, in the view of many, perhaps the fastest of all the 'pre-wing' 12-metres. But although *Victory '83* was good enough to reach the finals of the challenger trials, she was well beaten by *Australia II*.

Only two US syndicates came forward to defend the cup: Conner headed one and his arch rival in the Star Class, Tom Blackaller, the other.

Conner had commissioned two new designs; one from Sparkman and Stephens and the other from Johan Valentijn. Both had their problems and Conner therefore commissioned a third boat, *Liberty*, from Valentijn; almost inevitably she was something of a compromise.

Blackaller requested a 'conventional' 12-metre from Dave Pedrick and got exactly that: one that had the greatest difficulty in beating the old reliable *Courageous*. Conner won the defender trials but he was never under any illusion that he was sailing a superlative boat.

Alan Bond chose the talented and highly-qualified John Bertrand to skipper *Australia II* and both Bertrand and Conner have published books about their America's Cup experiences. Both are ghosted and need to be taken with a pinch of salt but what is clear is that while Conner always believed that *Australia II* was a faster boat than *Liberty*, Bertrand never really did, and in spite of the Australian yacht's better turning circle Bertrand never once gained a decisive advantage on the start line.

When the two boats met on 14 September 1983 it was clear that an upset was on the cards after *Australia II* took an early lead, was overtaken by *Liberty* and was attacking again when her steering mechanism failed, in spite of which she lost by a scant 70 seconds.

Gear failure hit the Australians in the second race too, when the mainsail headboard collapsed, but again it was a close race

***Left:** 'The red boat'* Liberty, *from the air. She also had some hidden tricks, including three sets of measurement marks that enabled Dennis Conner to use three different rating certificates for different weather conditions. In spite of this, she was never as fast as* Australia II.

Above: Duel in the sun between Liberty *and* Australia II. *The historic 1983 match finally freed the America's Cup from the iron grip of the New York Yacht Club and began a new era of rapid change in which the whole concept of the competition was called into question for the first time since 1958.*

with *Liberty* winning by a modest one minute 33 seconds. With no technical problems and a light wind, *Australia II* showed her true potential in the third race, winning by a massive three minutes 14 seconds, but the next time Conner made a brilliant start, and held on grimly to win by 43 seconds.

With *Liberty* in the lead by three races to one and only needing one more to win, it seemed as if the Australians were facing an impossible task once again, but this time things really were different. *Australia II* had lost a race through gear failure and now it was *Liberty*'s turn as the hydraulics that controlled her jumper-struts (the small stays that stiffen the upper part of the mast) failed and she was powerless to prevent the Australians from winning.

Fate smiled on the Australians again in race six when a big wind-shift allowed Bertrand to take the lead, after which *Australia II* proved she really was the faster yacht by just sailing away into the distance and winning by a remarkable three minutes 25 seconds, the greatest-ever winning margin by a challenging yacht.

With the score at three all and the series for the first time being decided by the final race, the whole world sat up and took notice. Practically the entire population of Australia sat up all night glued to their television sets, hoping for victory. After 132 years the America's Cup had become a global event.

And what a cliff-hanger it was! Brilliant sailing by Conner and his crew kept *Liberty* ahead for most of the race, but on the last-but-one leg *Australia II* found a little extra wind and pulled ahead. On the final beat, the Americans attacked desperately, tacking no less than 47 times, but the Australians held them off and crossed the finish line just 41 seconds ahead. The New York Yacht Club had finally lost the America's Cup.

THE GREAT COMEBACK

Dennis Conner almost immediately began planning and working to get the America's Cup back. The most important first step was to create a completely new computer-aided design facility that was master-minded by Science Applications International Corporation and went far beyond what the Dutch and Lexcen had used in 1983, involving use of the Cray supercomputer. The design team consisted of Britton Chance, Dave Pedrick and Bruce Nelson.

Conner then established a training base in Hawaii where he could sail nearly all the year round in windy conditions — it was generally agreed that there would be plenty of wind in

Fremantle where the new holder of the cup, the Royal Perth Yacht Club was going to mount the defence. Then began the most rigorous, most exhaustive, most thorough testing and training programme in the history of yacht design.

For the 1987 series there were no fewer than 13 challengers but only four potential defenders. Six syndicates came from the United States, two each from Italy and France and one each from Britain, Canada and New Zealand.

Suddenly it seemed as if everyone had gone 12-metre crazy and a type of yacht that was supposed to be the most expensive and esoteric in the world was becoming almost common. After 1983 there was a lot of rather wild talk about 'radical' design solutions but most designers were not able to produce anything much more radical than bigger, heavier versions of *Australia II*, re-optimized for the stronger winds and the bigger seas of the Indian Ocean.

However, *USA*, designed by Gary Mull for Tom Blackaller's 'Golden Gate' syndicate, was radical. She had two rudders, one at each end of the yacht and no keel in the accepted sense but instead a torpedo-like lump of ballast on the end of streamlined struts. Under-funded and under-developed she was only beginning to reach her potential by the end of the challenger trials.

Probably the most impressive of the European yachts was *French Kiss*, the cheekily-named 12-metre sponsored by Serge Krasnianski's 'Kis' group. The very first 12-metre design by Philippe Briand proved to be an outstanding heavy-air boat and her high bow — a feature not seen on these boats for many years, was widely copied by others.

The other really major surprise of the 1987 series was New Zealand's *Kiwi Magic* built in glass reinforced plastics — never before used for a 12-metre.

As the challenger trials proceeded, and the weaker syndicates gradually fell by the wayside, the four remaining were *French Kiss* versus *Kiwi Magic* and *Stars and Stripes* versus the revolutionary *USA*. Both semi-finals were tremendously hard-fought and resulted in *Kiwi Magic* meeting *Stars and Stripes* in the challenger final. This set of races, sailed in very strong winds, was undoubtedly the most exciting of the whole campaign, with the New Zealand yacht proving the more agile but the American one slightly faster in a straight line.

The defender trials were both less interesting and less productive. Alan Bond gave Ben Lexcen complete charge of design but this time he seemed to run out of originality. *Australia III* was a dog and *Australia IV* not all that much better.

Kevin Parry's *Kookaburra* syndicate had more steam behind it from the word go: more technical know-how, a better integrated design team and a better selection of helmsmen. Toward the end of the defender trials an improved *Australia IV* was still not quite as fast as Parry's *Kookaburra III*.

At times, the Australian defender trials seemed more like a ritual dance than a real battle in which two boats from the same camp were competing against each other. The challenger trials were more like the real thing.

1987: Stars and Stripes *v* Kookaburra III

By the time *Stars and Stripes* finally met *Kookaburra III*, the American boat was 'on a roll' to such an extent that very little could beat her. Dennis Conner was by far the most experienced 12-metre helmsman in the world and had the most impressive design team and exhaustive trials behind him. He also had a boat that was tremendously fast in a straight line at the expense of some agility. Conner believed that he could carry the slight disadvantage of a clumsy boat provided it could 'out-drag' the others in the fresh winds and high seas of Gage Roads.

Below: *One of the toughest fights in the long series of trials leading up to the 1987 series was that between* Stars and Stripes, *sailed by Dennis Conner, and the very radical and interesting* USA, *with Tom Blackaller in command. Many felt that if only Blackaller had had more time for development,* USA *might have proved the faster yacht.*

US-55
12
S1
USA

Far left: Stars and Stripes *leads the defending* Kookaburra III. *This striking aerial picture shows just why yacht racing in Western Australia is a lot more interesting to watch than in Newport, Rhode Island. Strong winds, clean air and hot sunshine transformed the event into something truly photogenic.*

Left: *The Australian attitude to Dennis Conner's 1987 victory was one of grudging admiration. It was unfortunate that this turned to exasperation when the San Diego Yacht Club appeared to be incapable of making its mind up about how to organize the next match.*

Everyone thought that *Stars and Stripes* had been optimized for strong winds to such an extent that she would be a dead duck if the wind fell light but in the first race, with lightish winds, she won by one minute 41 seconds. On following days, with more wind, the Americans were never in trouble, and won in four straight races.

Dennis Conner thus became the first man to lose the America's Cup and the first to regain it. He has been criticized for being relentless. His arch rival Tom Blackaller once said, 'I wish to hell he had not turned the sport into something where it costs you 20 million bucks to compete.' It is true that he raised the level of the game to an unprecedented height and made it impossible for amateurs to compete, but it seems hard to criticize a man for aiming towards perfection.

1988: New Zealand *v* Stars and Stripes II

If 1987 represented the America's Cup's zenith then 1988 was surely its nadir with months of non-stop disputes culminating in a pointless mis-match between two totally different types of yacht.

Conner's 1987 campaign had been mounted by the 'Sail America Foundation', a purpose-built charity with San Diego Yacht Club as the titular challenger only. Having won the Cup, Sail America claimed the right to organize the next defence by which they hoped to profit sufficiently to at least pay off their 1987 debts. But before they had completed their planning, or even announced the venue, Michael Fay of New Zealand launched a 'pre-emptive' challenge in August 1987 in which he claimed the right to be the sole challenger using an entirely new type of yacht of 90ft waterline length, which was already under construction.

Arguments about whether this was legal started immediately and show little signs of dying down. Basically, use of the 12-metre

Below: *A sweet moment for Dennis Conner, repaying the many months of hard work in preparing for the 1987 challenge, as he finally regains the coveted trophy.*

K
KZ-1
US-1

class in all post-war matches had been a matter of 'mutual consent' between the parties, as permitted by the Deed of Gift, which also states that if consent is absent a match should be in yachts not exceeding 90ft WL. Invoking this clause, Fay claimed the right to sail an 1887-style match within ten months.

Stunned by this approach, Sail America refused to accept the challenge but the New York Supreme Court, guardians of the Deed of Gift, vindicated Fay. This left Conner's team in the unenviable position of having neither the time nor the money to respond in a similar yacht to *New Zealand* yet unable to refuse a match. It also left all other potential challengers in the wilderness and although Britain's *Blue Arrow* group, led by the ebullient Peter de Savary, made vigorous efforts to get in on the action including building an extraordinary hydrofoil boat, they never even reached the starting line.

Smarting from what they perceived as a 'sneak attack' from New Zealand, the Americans hit on the plan of responding with a 60ft catamaran, in effect a double-sized 'C' Class, which offered the prospect of much more speed while remaining well within the overall dimensions set by Fay.

Though Fay protested furiously that this was not a valid 'match', Judge Carmen Ciparick of the New York Supreme Court ruled that they should sail first and argue later. Hence in September 1988 the 130 monohull sloop *New Zealand* was trounced in two races off San Diego by the 60ft catamaran *Stars and Stripes*, in an unpleasant atmosphere of bitterness and mutual recrimination.

Following this damaging episode, there was a general willingness to take stock and try to rebuild the event. The most likely scenario is for a further defence, preceded by an international elimination series, at San Diego in 1991, with either versions of the 12-metre or a new 85-ft-long class.

THE 12-METRE

Under the International Rule, the rating in metres is found by the formula:

$$\frac{L+2d-F+\sqrt{S}}{2.37}$$

where L = Length in metres
D = Girth difference in metres
F = Freeboard in metres
S = Sail area in square metres

In the International 12-metre class, the product of this formula must not exceed 12. This simple formula is made complex by the way in which the various terms are arrived at. For instance the length, L, is not the actual length overall of the yacht but 'rated length' between two girth stations about 7in (180mm) above the waterline, at bow and stern. The intention of this is to include the ends of the hull in the measurement of length in order to prevent exaggerated overhangs. The L figure can be manipulated to a degree depending on how steeply the ends rise out of the water and various tricks are used to make the hull longer than it appears to the rule.

Girth difference is that between a taut line from the deck edge to a point 4ft 11in (1500mm) below the waterline and the length of a line drawn on the hull surface between those two points. Its effect is to place a heavy penalty on a 'wine-glass' section and helps to make the hull heavy and deep-bodied.

Freeboard, the height of the boat above the water, is a minus factor in the rule. You get 'paid' for having a high-freeboard, seaworthy boat but this adds to the structural weight and reduces stability.

Sail area is measured as if the mainsail were a triangle. To it is added the area of the 'fore-triangle', the area bounded by the mast, the forestay and the deck. That part of the jib which overlaps the mainsail is not measured, which is why the yachts have such large overlapping headsails.

All 12-metres have to be built under the survey of Lloyds Register whose rules control the structural dimensions. This ensures that all boats comply with a minimum structural weight. All the yachts were built of wood until aluminium construction was permitted in 1970. More recently, glass reinforced plastics construction has been permitted but the structural weight is supposed to be as nearly as possible exactly the same as aluminium construction.

The basic type of yacht produced by the 12-metre rule is heavy, narrow and deep compared to modern offshore yachts. However, the former are built with great sophistication and their gear and equipment is the most advanced available.

Only manual power can be used to control the sails so very efficient winching systems are used to harness man-power to the best advantage. Extensive use is also made of hydraulics to control the operation of the rig. The sails, the 'engine' of any sailing boat, receive enormous attention on a 12-metre which is a very sensitive machine that responds to extremely subtle changes in the shape or set of a sail. Advanced materials, particularly Kevlar and Mylar, are used in addition to conventional Dacron or its equivalents.

Very extensive electronics are essential and these have three basic functions: navigation, performance measurement and performance recording. Everything that is happening on board needs to be recorded for analysis and with modern systems this can be done in real time via telemetry. Great effort is, therefore, put into both the design of on-board computers and the software that makes them useful. The modern 12-metre can hardly go sailing at all without a functioning computer.

Opposite: *A striking study of the American catamaran* Stars and Stripes II *and the monohull* New Zealand *in the 1988 America's Cup off San Diego.*

The Great Sailors

To find the great names in sailing means spreading a very wide net and some will inevitably slip through for, unlike other sports, many have not been competing but simply doing their own thing . . . like Joshua Slocum who, after the death of his first wife and the failure of his business, set off in a small boat in search of his soul and became the first man in history to circle the globe alone.

The sea has always presented man with his greatest challenge and some remarkable men and women have risen to it. Gold medallists and glory seekers, loners and drop-outs are all represented here. Some were great helmsmen, others hardly knew one end of a boat from the other but learned as they went along. All experienced hardship and loneliness, a few found fame and fortune but most just discovered a way of life that they could not tear themselves away from.

Left: *Robin Knox-Johnston grins from the cockpit of* Suhaili, *the yacht in which he sailed alone around the world. Notice how very basic the yacht appears compared to a modern racing yacht,* Suhaili *having a planked deck and few but sturdy fittings.*

Sir Owen AISHER

b 1900

One of the greatest British supporters and encouragers of sailing, which he took up in the 1930s and in which he was still active in the 1980s, Aisher's main interest has been in offshore racing and he has competed in virtually every event in European waters, in a long series of yachts all named *Yeoman*.

The first was a cruising ketch and the second a 6-metre, while the Nicholson-designed *Yeoman III* was his first ocean racer. In her he won the 1951 Fastnet Race and later, with typical generosity, he and subsequent owners gave this yacht to the Royal Ocean Racing Club so that they could have an up-to-date club boat. Always a great encourager of clubs, especially those designed to cater for the general public rather than some privileged group, he was instrumental in the founding of both the Island Sailing Club and the Little Ship Club.

He was closely involved in the first two post-war challenges for the America's Cup, in both cases fitting out yachts which were used as trial horses. More recently, he has built several yachts for the Admiral's Cup competition.

Robin AISHER

b 1933

Son of Sir Owen, Robin Aisher has been as deeply involved in sailing as his father. He captained the British Admiral's Cup team on three occasions and was voted Yachtsman of the Year in 1975, after captaining the winning team. He was also an Olympic bronze medallist in the 5.5 metre class at Acapulco in 1968 and has been a long-serving chairman of the Royal Yachting Association's Olympic Committee. He is highly involved in the committee-work side of yachting, has been Commodore of the Royal Ocean Racing Club and represents Great Britain on the International Yacht Racing Union.

John BERTRAND

b 1947

In 1983, Australian John Bertrand became the first man to win the America's Cup from the New York Yacht Club. Australia had long made efforts to win the America's Cup but finally, in 1983, Alan Bond managed to bring together a world-beating yacht, *Australia II*, and a skipper, Bertrand, with sufficient confidence and ability to make good use of it.

Bertrand believed that lack of confidence rather than ability was behind the previous Australian failures and during the long training build-up to 1983 he emphasized to his crew that if they truly believed that they were as good as the Americans, then they would win.

Bertrand himself was an all-round sailor of proven ability who had sailed in the Olympics in the Finn class and had spent a number of years working in the United States as a sailmaker, giving him a unique insight into the strengths and weaknesses of his opponents.

The most remarkable feature of the 1983 match was that *Australia II* came back to win from 3-1 down, which showed just how important Bertrand's psychological training had been. Up to then, the America's Cup was like an un-climbed Everest of sport — a seemingly impossible goal.

After his historic win in 1983, Bertrand pulled out of America's Cup sailing. However, it would be very surprising indeed if he did not return to the fray in the future.

Right: *A joyous victory salute from John Bertrand, following* Australia II*'s historic 1983 victory in the America's Cup. Bertrand, who had worked in the USA and sailed against Dennis Conner on a number of occasions, always felt that winning the cup was as much a psychological barrier as a technical one.*

Chay BLYTH

b 1940

To paratrooper Chay Blyth, the idea of doing things the hard way was so ingrained that one wonders if he could possibly have imagined taking the easy route in life. He was still in the Army when, in 1966, Captain John Ridgway asked for a volunteer to row across the

Atlantic with him. Blyth stepped forward and together they completed the crossing under oars in 92 days.

The following year Chay left the Army and decided to sail around the world. As he then knew next to nothing about sailing and his 30ft (9.14m) stock glass fibre cruiser *Dytiscus* was not really up to it, a single-handed non-stop round the world trip was a pretty bold opening shot. Nevertheless, he reached the Cape of Good Hope before the cruiser performed a backwards somersault and he retired to Port Elizabeth.

This only increased his desire to achieve something tremendous but the question was, what? The oceans of the world had been crossed and re-crossed by everything from a 12ft (3.65m) yacht to an amphibious jeep. Chichester had beaten the record of the clippers and Knox-Johnston had gone around non-stop. It was a chance remark made by his wife Maureen that set Blyth thinking: 'Why not sail around the world the other way?' she said.

With the help of a publicity agent, Blyth sold to the British Steel Corporation the idea of sailing non-stop around the world against the prevailing winds, that is heading west-bound round Cape Horn and continuing south of the three great capes until he got back to the Atlantic. The corporation under-wrote the building of the 59ft (17.98m) steel ketch *British Steel* to a design by Robert Clark — one of his best — tremendously strong, quite fast and not excessively heavy.

In October 1969 Blyth set off from the Hamble on the voyage which many experts felt would prove impossible. They were very nearly right: attempting to round Cape Horn he was driven right down to the ice limits by gales that smashed his self-steering. Off New Zealand, *British Steel* was rolled over backwards by tremendous seas and the mast bent as it smashed into the water. But Blyth fought his way back into the Atlantic and in August 1970, in the middle of Cowes Week, *British Steel* sailed back into the Solent to complete a 292 day non-stop circumnavigation, 21 days faster than Knox-Johnston in spite of having sailed 'the wrong way'.

After this, Blyth began a long and fruitful collaboration with the expatriate millionaire 'Union Jack' Hayward, who underwrote the building of the 77ft (23.5m) foam-sandwich ketch *Great Britain II* so that Blyth could enter the first Whitbread Round the World Race in 1973. This boat, designed by Alan Gurney, started the race as a ketch and finished it as a sloop after the mizzen had fallen down.

Blyth shipped a squad of paras as crew and fed them on dehydrated curry, an ordeal almost as great as the race itself. Three men died during the event, one from *Great Britain II*. After Blyth's main rival Eric Tabarly had been dismasted (twice) *Great Britain* took the lead, was easily the first to finish and won nine of the 12 major trophies but was not the handicap winner. The redoubtable *GB II* has sailed in every Whitbread race since.

Blyth decided that an 80ft (24.38m) trimaran would be the right boat for an ocean criss-cross race proposed by Whitbread. But the race was cancelled, leaving Blyth with a bigger boat than he wanted for the 1976 Observer Single-handed Transatlantic Race. On his 500 mile qualifying trip *GB III* collided with a ship, lost one of her outriggers and capsized. It was the end of his hopes of competing in this race.

Blyth's next boat, the 54ft (16.4m) trimaran *Great Britain IV* won the 1978 Round Britain Race but was then sold in favour of the 65ft (19.81m) trimaran *Brittany Ferries GB*, which turned out to be one of his most successful boats. He teamed up with Rob James to sail her in the 1981 Two-handed Transatlantic Race. They won, also creating

Above: *Chay Blyth with his wife Maureen and daughter Samantha aboard* British Steel, *the yacht in which he sailed around the world against the prevailing winds in 1969. It was Maureen who suggested this feat, which many had felt would prove impossible.*

a new record for crossing the Atlantic from east to west with an astonishing time of just 14 days, 14 hours.

Later the same year he was re-united with his old yacht *GB II*, renamed *United Friendly* for the 1981/2 Whitbread Race. She was no longer the latest thing in design but she was the first British yacht to finish. Then it was back to the trimaran for the 1982 Round Britain Race, sharing the work with Peter Bateman; but this time they had to be content with second place.

Chay has made two assaults on the record held by the clipper ship *Flying Cloud*, which sailed from New York to San Francisco in 89 days 21 hours, but has suffered extraordinary ill-luck in this venture. On the first occasion his trimaran capsized off Cape Horn. At the second attempt, while the yacht was being delivered across the Atlantic without Chay aboard, it capsized and was lost. Another, less suitable trimaran was bought but this venture also ended at Cape Horn, with the boat upside down.

He has had more luck with Richard Branson, who he assisted on both of his *Virgin Atlantic Challenger* adventures. The first of the two giant speedboats sank almost in sight of the Scilly Isles but on the second attempt, in 1986, Branson and Blyth set a new record for crossing the Atlantic under power.

Blyth has now 'retired' from ocean racing but it is hard to believe that he will not be tempted into further exploits in the future.

Tony BULLIMORE

b 1940

Bullimore has been one of the most successful British skippers of offshore multihulls, particularly in short-handed racing. He was elected joint Yachtsman of the Year in 1985 with Nigel Irens who designed and built the 60ft (18.28m) trimaran *Apricot*.

From 1966 to 1974 he sailed the 42ft (12.80m) trimaran *Toria*, including competing in the Observer Single-handed Transatlantic Race. In 1981 he commissioned a 40ft (12.19m) trimaran which has had various names such as *City of Birmingham* and *IT '82* and had a number of racing successes including first in class in the Round Britain Race and the Quebec-St Malo Race.

In 1985 he commissioned *Apricot* from Irens and together they won the Round the Island, Round Britain and Round Europe races. The following year he was first in class in the Carlsberg Double-handed Transatlantic Race but in the disastrous Route du Rhum race of 1986 *Apricot* was wrecked while attempting to enter Brest harbour in a gale.

During 1988, Bullimore began to campaign a new *Apricot*, which was designed this time by Martyn Smith.

Sir Francis CHICHESTER

b 1901–d 1972

When asked, after returning from his famous single-handed circumnavigation, why he did it, Chichester replied 'Because it intensifies life.' In his book about the voyage he is much more specific, listing seven unique achievements, the most important being: fastest voyage around the world by any small vessel (226 days) and the longest passage by a yacht without a port of call (15,500 miles). He was also the only 66-year-old to attempt such a feat — and he succeeded.

Chichester was a perpetual loner who constantly needed to do extraordinary things. At the age of 18 he emigrated to New Zealand, vowing not to return until he had amassed savings of £20,000 which he finally managed after taking on practically every job from gold prospector to car salesman. In the interim, he had learned to fly and on his return to England he bought a De Havilland Gipsy Moth, in which he flew first to Australia, then crossed the Tasman to New Zealand. Converting the Moth to a seaplane he attempted a round the world journey but flew into overhead cables in Japan, very nearly killing himself.

Back in England, he married the tough-minded Sheila Craven who became his mainstay. When the Second World War broke out he tried to join the Royal Air Force. He was turned down because of poor eyesight but eventually became a navigation instructor.

After the war, he opened a small shop in St James's, publishing and selling charts and maps. By coincidence, this was just round the corner from the Royal Ocean Racing Club. Invited on some sailing trips, he decided to take up the sport, buying an old boat which he renamed *Gipsy Moth II*. After a few seasons he yearned for something better and commissioned a 39ft (11.88m) cruiser-racer.

Gipsy Moth III was a very successful yacht, fast, comfortable, well-balanced and easy to sail. In 1960, Chichester entered her for the first Observer Single-handed Transatlantic Race. There were just five competitors and *Gipsy Moth* was the largest and fastest by a considerable margin. Surviving some extremely bad weather, Chichester reached the Ambrose Light in 40 days, winning the race by 8 days.

Chichester had been ill and dispirited before the race but it proved just what he needed to give him a new start in life at the age of 58. He enjoyed public attention and began to think in terms of epic yachting achievements. The first goal was to cross the Atlantic in 30 days. He nearly managed this in 1962 and finally cracked it with three minutes to spare during the second OSTAR race. However, France's Eric Tabarly beat him by nearly three days in *Pen Duick II*.

Having crossed the Atlantic six times in *Gipsy Moth III*, Chichester planned bigger achievements in a faster boat. He did a lot of research into the clipper-ship passages to Australia and published a book entitled *Along the Clipper Way*. By now a famous man, he had no great difficulty in raising money to build a new super-yacht.

Illingworth and Primrose, then the leading designers of racing yachts in England, were chosen to prepare the plans but Chichester had very clear ideas about what he wanted. In his book, he blames John Illingworth for letting the project get out of control but the truth is that he constantly interfered with the design process, resulting in a series of unsuccessful compromises. For instance, he blames Illingworth for the fact that the displacement was higher than he wanted. In fact, Chichester insisted that the original plan for a deep fin keel and separate skeg rudder be changed to one with a continuous keel with attached rudder. This increased the displacement, raised the centre of buoyancy and adversely affected the steering.

Gipsy Moth IV was finally ready in spring 1966, and at the end of August Chichester sailed on a non-stop single-handed passage to Sydney which he completed in the fast time of 104 days. After refitting and some alterations to the boat, he set off on the return journey which nearly ended prematurely in the Tasman when *Gipsy Moth IV* suffered a severe knockdown which fortunately did not result in dismasting.

Due to advances in radio technology, Chichester was able to keep in touch with the world and the British public could follow his battles with the ocean on a day-to-day basis. When he reached Cape Horn photographers zoomed over in an aircraft to record the scene and the pictures of *Gipsy Moth IV* scudding along before enormous seas under storm jib alone became one of the most enduring images of the 1960s.

When he returned to Plymouth at the end of May 1967, Chichester received an astonishing public welcome — and went almost straight to hospital with a duodenal ulcer. Recovering, he sailed *Gipsy Moth IV* to

***Below:** Sir Francis Chichester waves from* Gipsy Moth IV *as he nears the end of his 1966/7 round the world voyage. He never liked the yacht, which he disposed of by donating it to the National Maritime Museum, but it did enable him to successfully complete his greatest feat — his single-handed circumnavigation.*

Above: *Dennis Conner, the first man to lose the America's Cup and the first to regain it, at the 1987 series in Australia. His technique of steamrolling the opposition with superior resources and an exhaustive development campaign has not always won him friends, though there can be no doubting his ability.*

Greenwich where she can still be seen, and was knighted by Queen Elizabeth II who used Drake's sword to perform the ceremony.

Having neatly disposed of the hated *Gipsy Moth IV* by giving it to the National Maritime Museum, Chichester ordered a new and even larger yacht from the veteran designer Robert Clark, the attractive and fast 60ft (18.28m) *Gipsy Moth V.* In this new yacht he planned an ocean speed record of 4,000 miles in 20 days and very nearly managed it until calms lost him two days.

Recurring illness was plaguing Chichester but, at the age of 70 and very clearly unwell, he entered for the 1972 OSTAR, perhaps believing that the challenge would help him to snap out of it. A few days after the start a French weather ship went alongside to investigate the apparently untended *Gipsy Moth V.* Giles Chichester and two others were then put aboard from a Royal Navy vessel to sail the yacht back to Plymouth. In the confusion, the weather ship rammed and sank an American yacht that was offering assistance, with the loss of seven on board.

Chichester died shortly afterwards but his achievements as a yachtsman and navigator were enormous, especially as they were all performed in late middle age.

Dennis CONNER

b 1943

Dennis Conner was the first man in history to lose the America's Cup, in 1983, when *Liberty* was beaten by four races to three by *Australia II* off Newport, Rhode Island and the first to regain it, in 1987, when *Stars and Stripes* beat *Kookaburra III* four-nil off Fremantle.

The America's Cup competition overshadows everything else he has ever done, but Conner was one of the top racing helmsmen in the world before he ever got involved in 12-metre racing.

Born in 1943, in San Diego, California he learned to sail as a teenager by joining the San Diego Yacht Club junior programme. He has a tremendous urge to win — a degree of drive and commitment that can be almost frightening at times.

One of his earliest and strongest influences was Malin Burham who won the Star World Championship when he was only 17. Conner's ambition was to sail this tricky and very demanding two-man keelboat and in 1968 he made his first serious crack at the sport by entering for the US Olympic trials. An incredible $50,000 was spent on the Star in an effort to have the very best boat, equipment and sails but, in the final trials, although Conner and his partner Alan Raffee were fastest they hit a mark in a vital race.

The Star World Championship is one of the hardest events in yachting to win and Conner achieved this for the first time in 1971. In 1977 he won it in five straight races. (In between, he learned to sail a quite different type of keelboat, the planing *Tempest* and won a bronze medal at the 1976 Olympics in Canada.) The thing about Star racing is that all the boats tend to sail at about the same speed so that tactical mistakes, however small, make all the difference. Conner became the world's greatest 'percentage yachtsman', never missing an opportunity to grab some tiny advantage.

The other west coast event that has moulded Conner's sailing is the Congressional Cup. Other than the America's Cup, the Congressional Cup is the top match-racing competition and Conner has succeeded in winning it twice.

He has also twice been skipper of the winning yacht of the SORC, the top US offshore circuit, and twice skipper of American Admiral's Cup yachts.

His first appearance on the America's Cup scene was in 1974, when he sailed as tactician to Ted Turner aboard *Mariner.* Turner became exasperated and walked off, leaving Conner the helmsman and although the yacht was slow, he was much the most successful starting helmsman. When *Courageous* was chosen to defend the cup, Conner was therefore brought in as tactician and starting helmsman with Ted Hood as skipper. They beat the challenger, *Southern Cross*, four-nil.

This won him command of *Freedom* for the 1980 defence and his meticulous three-year preparation changed the rules of the game. As Halsey Herreshof put it, the days when a New York stockbroker could take three months away from his business to defend the America's Cup were over. *Australia*, the 1980 challenger sailed by Sir Jim Hardy, was a fast boat and *Freedom* won thanks to the better tactics of Conner rather than by speed.

In 1983 Conner found himself competing against a challenger that was so much faster that the real upset would have been if *Australia II* had *not* won. For years the joke had been that if the New York Yacht Club ever lost the America's Cup, they would replace it with the head of the man that had lost it but what really upset Conner in 1983 was that, when the unthinkable finally happened, the club simply abandoned him. Many commentators concluded that regaining the America's Cup would be a 'holy war' for Conner although he plays this down. There was very little doubt that he would make a comeback, and do it in the name of San Diego Yacht Club, so finally breaking the long dominance of the US East Coast in yachting. His preparations for the 1987 series were the most lengthy, thorough, exhaustive and ultimately the most successful. He did not so much beat the Australians as roll over them.

Conner was once accused by Ted Turner of being a professional, of taking the fun out of the game. This he resents as in his opinion it should not be considered a crime to try harder than anyone else.

Harold CUDMORE

b 1945

Ireland's best-known yachtsman, Harold Cudmore is one of the world's foremost match-racing helmsmen and was the overall skipper of *White Crusader*, the 1987 British Challenger for the America's Cup.

After cutting his teeth in dinghy sailing, Cudmore entered for the 1976 Half Ton Cup with a hotted-up production boat named *Silver Shamrock* and won in a light-weather series in Trieste. He came within an ace of doing the same thing again the following year, in Sydney, but his mast fell down just a short way from the finish of the offshore race.

In 1979, Cudmore sailed on Graham Walker's one-tonner *Indulgence*, the beginning of a fruitful co-operation for both men. In 1981 they were rivals, however, when Cudmore sailed the Castro-designed *Justine III* with unprecedented success, winning all five events in that year's One Ton Cup. Subsequently, Cudmore has skippered both of Walker's Admiral's Cup campaigns, including the notable 1985 series when their first boat sank, only to be replaced in remarkably short order by *Phoenix*.

However, it is in match-racing that Cudmore excels. He has won the prestigious Lymington Cup series more than anyone else — five times — and has also won the Australian equivalent. He was deeply involved in the *Victory '83* America's Cup challenge but left when he was unable to get Peter de Savary to hand over full control of the sailing programme.

***Above:** Harold Cudmore, the mercurial Irish helmsman, who is one of the world's greatest experts in match-racing. He was skipper of the British challenge for the America's Cup in 1987, which came remarkably close to success in view of its lack of funding. Cudmore is at his best in starting and is also well-known for skill in the protest-room.*

After this he became skipper for two years of the top American maxi-racer, *Kialoa*, enhancing his reputation as one of the World's top professional skippers.

As 'Sailing Director' from the outset of the *White Horse* challenge, Cudmore got the full control he wanted but, once again, this British effort was another example of 'too little and too late'. Nevertheless, most agree that it was a fine campaign which came close to success and there is little doubt that Cudmore will try again.

Ann DAVISON

b 1922

The first woman to sail single-handed across the Atlantic, in the 23ft (7.01m) sloop, *Felicity Ann*, in 1952. With her husband Bill, Ann planned a cruise to the Pacific but no sooner had they left than their yacht foundered, near Portland Bill on the south coast of England. Bill and Ann were in the water for nearly 14 hours and after they finally managed to struggle ashore, Bill died of exposure.

Ann was shattered both physically and mentally but, somehow, found the courage to rebuild her life and plan a solo voyage. She could not bear the thought of another sailing companion. In May 1952, she left Plymouth in the little *Felicity Ann* and finally reached Miami in August the following year, after a number of stops along the way.

Her main barriers were the psychological ones of being the first woman to cross the Atlantic alone and, in recent years, many have followed the same route without difficulty. After reaching America, Ann was able to put the past behind her and remarried.

Chris DICKSON

b 1961

At 25, New Zealander Dickson was the youngest helmsman taking part in the 1987 America's Cup series, and one of the most talented. The first-time effort by New Zealand was startlingly successful and, with Dickson at the helm, *Kiwi Magic* beat all the foreign challengers except Dennis Conner. With his piercing blue eyes, Dickson was described as looking like a Second World War U-boat commander and it is certain that he aims to fire some more torpedoes in the same direction in future.

Dickson's relationship with backer Michael Fay was stormy and at one stage Fay threatened to send Dickson home for psychiatric treatment but this was mostly a clash between two highly motivated personalities.

Vito DUMAS

b 1900

The Argentine yachtsman Vito Dumas was the first to sail around the world single-handed, south of the three great capes. He did so in the 32ft (9.75m) double-ender *Legh II* which he had owned since she was built in 1933. Remarkably, he made his great voyage in war-time, leaving in June 1942 when his business had failed and he had few resources.

On the first leg of the voyage, from Montevideo to Cape Town, he nearly died from a seriously-infected wound in his arm and had to cope with a major leak in the hull of *Legh II*. The next leg, which was an epic of endurance sailed in constant storms and with very little food and water, was the 104-day passage to New Zealand. After recuperating there for just a month he sailed 5,000 miles to Valparaiso, in Chile before undertaking the short but very dangerous rounding of Cape Horn. He arrived back in the River Plate in July 1943.

After the war, Dumas made two more notable cruises, one in the faithful *Legh II* and another in *Sirio* during which he sailed non-stop to New York; 7,000 miles in 117 days. Dumas wrote an influential book *Alone through the Roaring Forties*. He was one of the first to suggest that a small yacht could be kept running at full speed before the great waves of the Southern Ocean rather than heaving-to or dragging warps to slow down. By practising what he preached, he averaged better than 100 miles per day in *Legh II*.

Paul ELVSTRÖM

b 1930

The Dane Paul Elvström is the most successful racing yachtsman of all time, with a total of four Olympic gold medals plus innumerable championship wins in a remarkable variety of classes. His first Gold Medal was won in the 1948 Olympics at Torquay when the single-handed class was the Firefly. Elvström was just 18 at the time and took physical fitness much more seriously than other sailors, with the result that he was able to sail harder for longer.

After 1948, the Finn dinghy became the Olympic single-hander and Elvström won Gold Medals in the three subsequent games. He was not only stronger and more skilful than others but also knew the rules better. In fact, his *Paul Elvström explains the Racing Rules* book is used by yachtsmen throughout the world.

Elvström also became one of the top sailmakers and designed a number of small racing yachts, as well as sailing other types of boat such as the Soling keelboat, the 5-0-5 dinghy and many others.

In the early 1970s he had a short, disastrous experience with the America's Cup when he was contracted to manage the 1974 challenge on behalf of Baron Bich of France. His decision to use his own rather than a French crew made him extremely unpopular in France and his contract was cancelled after one of the 12-metres sank on a delivery trip. Elvström also got into business difficulties during the 1970s, losing control of the company to one of his former employees. But after surviving a nervous breakdown, he made a successful comeback and is still one of the world's best helmsmen.

In the 1984 Olympics, Elvström sailed a Tornado catamaran, taking along his daughter Trine as crew and they represented Denmark yet again in 1988.

Uffa *FOX*

b 1898–d 1972

Combining to an unique degree the talents of designer, boatbuilder, helmsman, seaman, writer and raconteur, Uffa Fox lived life to the full and his pleasure in doing so gave enormous satisfaction to others.

Born at Cowes, in the Isle of Wight, he was apprenticed to S. E. Saunders, the builder of many advanced, experimental fast powerboats and record-breakers, and later of flying boats. Here he learned the secret of lightweight construction and the shapes needed for fast planing hulls, which he later applied to sailing dinghies.

Uffa became a boat-builder in his own right at the age of 21, setting up home and

Below: *Uffa Fox, seen here sailing with Prince Philip aboard one of his favourite designs, the Flying 15 keelboat, was a great pioneer of small-boat racing and was largely responsible for development of the planing dinghy. His books have the rare quality of being both informative and amusing.*

shop aboard a superannuated chain-ferry or 'floating bridge'. His employees had to learn to carry on without him during lengthy absences while he went off to sail in great races such as the Transatlantic.

One of his best-known and most influential designs was the International 14ft dinghy *Avenger*, built in 1928, which ushered in the era of planing dinghies. She hit the dinghy world like a bombshell, winning 52 out of 57 races in her first season. Virtually all modern dinghies are developments of *Avenger* and Uffa himself used her as the basis of a number of successful one-designs.

His especial pleasure was the sliding seat sailing canoe, one of the fastest of all small boats, then and now. He designed a pair of them named *Valiant* and *East Anglian* which he and Roger de Quincey took across the Atlantic to challenge American canoe-sailors in 1933. They won the International Canoe Trophy and as a result the American and European canoe rules were combined to create the International 10sq Metre Canoe.

Although he designed a number of larger yachts, they were not so successful as his small boats. During the Second World War he designed the Airborne Lifeboat which fitted beneath the belly of a bomber and could be dropped by parachute to ditched aircrew.

During the 1930s Uffa wrote a series of books in which the designs of famous yachts were shown together with his well-informed and highly-coloured comments. Now classics, they are jealously guarded by those lucky enough to own copies.

In the post-war era, Uffa designed a number of successful small boats, including the very well-known Flying 15 keelboat which was actually one of a series from 10 to 50ft (3 to 15m) waterline length. He also became a friend of the Royal Family, introducing Prince Charles to sailing and keeping him and his father, the Duke of Edinburgh, amused with his endless stories and salty songs.

Fittingly, his final books were called *The Joys of Life* and *More Joys of Life*.

Clare FRANCIS

b 1946

The outstanding British woman sailor who was trained as a dancer but later turned to sailing, Clare Francis learnt to sail as a child with her parents. Her first major exploit was the 1974 Round Britain Race in which she

Below: Clare Francis aboard Robertson's Golly, *the yacht that she sailed in the stormy 1976 Single-handed Transatlantic Race. In addition to handling the yacht, she sent back newspaper reports by radio and made a film for TV at the same time!*

Left: *Today, Clare Francis is less active in the sailing world because she has turned her skills to writing best sellers, but her earlier experiences at sea are not wasted. Her long-distance ocean racing gives a special feeling of authenticity to her novels.*

shared a Nicholson 32 with Eve Bonham. With this experience behind her, Clare entered for the 1976 Observer Single-handed Transatlantic Race, sailing the Ohlson 38 *Robertson's Golly*. In what turned out to be a very windy race, Clare put up a remarkable performance, crossing the Atlantic in 29 days — better than Francis Chichester's best time.

While sailing *Robertson's Golly*, Clare sent daily newspaper reports and prepared a documentary for the BBC that made her a public figure because she was able to show, perhaps better than anyone before, just what it is like to be in a small yacht in very bad weather. Her unassuming naturalness, charm and spirit won her a permanent place in the hearts of the public.

The following year, Clare was skipper of the Swan 65 *ADC Accutrac* for the second Whitbread Round the World Race. Others got around the world a little faster but *ADC Accutrac* was the only competitor to keep the same crew throughout and complete this supreme test with remarkably little trouble.

Subsequently, Clare Francis has become an extremely successful writer and maintains a fine cruising yacht.

Alain GERBAULT

b 1893 – d 1941

Alain Gerbault was a hero in France even before he sailed around the world. Born in 1893, into a well-to-do family, he served with distinction as a fighter pilot in the First World War. Afterwards he became a leading tennis player, winning major tournaments. While playing in England in 1921 he visited Ralph Stock who, after the war, had sailed to the Pacific in a yacht named *Dream Ship* and written a book about his experiences. Gerbault told Stock how empty and false his life seemed and how hollow his victories on the tennis court. He envied Stock who had sailed into the sunset and turned his dreams into reality!

While talking thus, Gerbault espied the *Firecrest*, moored near Stock's *Dream Ship II*, and impulsively decided to buy her. She was most unsuitable for a long voyage, being a long, narrow, heavy racing yacht, rigged as a gaff cutter. Gerbault bought her anyway.

Firecrest was taken to the Mediterranean where Gerbault acted out the role of intrepid yachtsman preparing for a great voyage while actually spending most of his time socializing and playing tennis. Eventually, however, in June 1923, he sailed from Gibraltar on what turned out to be a horrific non-stop passage to New York. This was the first single-handed east-west crossing of the North Atlantic and practically everything that could go wrong did. It took 101 days, by the end of which he had practically no food left and a small supply of tainted water. He could easily have stopped at Bermuda but what he lacked in skill as a sailor he more than made up for in pride and determination. On his arrival in the United States he became an instant celebrity and returned to France to receive the Legion d'honneur and a prize of 10,000 francs.

Extensive repairs and alterations were made to *Firecrest*, including conversion from gaff to Bermudan rig, and Gerbault sailed again in September 1924. During a further delay for repairs at Bermuda he took on a boy as cook but the youngster was severely burned in a galley fire and died from his injuries. Gerbault was extremely shocked and never again sailed with a crew.

Sailing from Bermuda to Panama he was again treated as a celebrity — invited to parties, played exhibition tennis matches and so on — but eventually began the long Pacific passage to Tahiti, mecca of most world-wandering yachtsmen. There he spent an extended period cruising in the islands and writing about the people.

The long-suffering *Firecrest* was nearly lost when driven ashore on Uvea in the Wallis Islands but the French navy brought new keelbolts and other needy supplies in the warship *Cassiopée*.

Gerbault continued via the Coral Sea and Arafura Sea to the Indian Ocean, where he called at Keeling Cocos Island on his way to Durban. From here, he made his way back into the Atlantic and eventually regained France after a circumnavigation which had taken six years and during which he had spent 700 days at sea.

In France he was lionized — a super-celebrity. He gave *Firecrest* to the nation as a training ship but she sank on her first voyage in this new role. He then ordered a new and much more sensible yacht of 34ft (10.36m) overall which, with characteristic modesty, was named the *Alain Gerbault*.

The man whose previous half-hearted attempt to leave civilization behind had been conducted in a blaze of publicity now really did disappear. In his new yacht, he left France quietly and sailed back to the Pacific where, for several years, he cruised from island to island, getting to know the people and writing about them. Interned by the Japanese, he died of fever in Timor in 1941, a fact that went unreported for a further three years.

Bob & Nancy GRIFFITHS

b 1917–d 1984/b 1920

The Griffiths of New Zealand circumnavigated the world three times, and their third rounding was the most remarkable in that it was carried out in latitude 60° South, among the ice-fields of the Antarctic. They did this in their yacht *Awahnee II*.

They first began cruising and made their first circumnavigation with *Awahnee*, a 53ft (16.1m) yacht designed by Uffa Fox, but this yacht was wrecked on a reef in the Pacific. Their next boat, based on the same design, used the then unfamiliar material of ferro-cement. In this, the Griffiths set off on a cruise that lasted for eight years, 150,000 miles and included a further complete circumnavigation. Their son Reid virtually grew up aboard the yacht.

In 1970, the Griffiths decided to make the shortest possible circumnavigation. The circumference of the earth at latitude 60° is half that at the equator and the distance, starting and finishing from New Zealand, approximately 12,000 miles. They had to endure extreme cold and ferocious storms even though it was the southern summer. The complete circumnavigation took 111 days, including 27 spent in port.

After having safely regained New Zealand, *Awahnee II* was struck by lightning and dismasted only 60 miles from her home port. This epic voyage was the last of the Griffiths' really spectacular exploits.

John GUZZWELL

b 1927

John Guzzwell was the 'third man' in the drama of the *Tzu Hang* capsize (see page 190); he bore the brunt of making the yacht seaworthy again since he was a skilled cabinet-maker and boatbuilder. But this episode was just an interruption in his own circumnavigation aboard 21ft (6.4m) *Trekka*.

Guzzwell came from a sea-faring family and had sailed from Jersey to South Africa as a boy. Then he emigrated to Canada, where he decided he would like to sail around the world in the smallest practicable boat. Jack Laurent Giles designed *Trekka* for him and Guzzwell laminated the keel in the basement of the YMCA in Victoria, British Columbia and assembled the yacht in the back of a fish and chip shop.

Leaving Victoria in 1955, he sailed to Hawaii — where he met and became friendly with the Smeetons. Meeting him again in New Zealand, the Smeetons persuaded Guzzwell to help them sail round Cape Horn. After sharing their terrible ordeals, he went back to New Zealand, dusted off *Trekka* and continued on his way, returning to Victoria after four years, having sailed around the world without mishap.

Later he married, built a superb 45ft (13.71m) ketch named *Treasure* to a Laurent Giles design and, in this, he and his wife and two young sons sailed to New Zealand, where they settled.

Col. H. G. 'Blondie' HASLER

b 1914–d 1987

The man who led and was one of only two to survive the war-time 'Cockle-shell heroes' canoe attack on Bordeaux, Blondie Hasler was a highly innovative yachtsman who made major contributions to the sport.

After the war, he won the RORC Class III points championship in the 30-square metre keelboat *Tre-Sang*. This light-displacement coastal racer would not even be allowed to enter today's races.

He wanted to make sailing easier by developing new ideas for self-steering and rigs that could be controlled without a large, trained crew. He felt that a single-handed race across the Atlantic would help to produce practical sea-worthy yachts and easily-handled rigs, and proposed to the Royal Western Yacht Club that they organize a race from Plymouth to Newport, Rhode Island. The first was sailed in 1960 and won by Francis Chichester, sailing the conventional 39ft (11.88m) *Gipsy Moth III*. But the boat that epitomized Hasler's ideas was his own *Jester*, a modified Scandinavian Folkboat of 25ft (7.62m) overall to which he had added a self-steering gear of his own design and a Chinese junk rig.

Although not as efficient as the modern Bermudan rig, the fully-battened junk sail has two major advantages. It is semi-balanced, having area both ahead of and abaft the mast and therefore requires no boom and only light mainsheet forces; and reefing is very simple as the sail folds up on to itself like a Venetian blind. Hasler made it possible to sail *Jester* without going on deck.

Left: *'Blondie' Hasler, seen here with his son Thomas, for whom he designed a special dinghy named the Peanut, was one of the most innovative of yachtsmen. He developed self-steering for yachts and a modern form of Chinese junk rig. He suggested both the Single-handed Transatlantic Race and the Round Britain Race and competed in both in* Jester, *the yacht that embodied many of his ideas.*

Eventually, his self-steering system was put into production by the Gibb company and used by many long-distance yachtsmen.

Although not fast, *Jester* is remarkably seaworthy and competed in every Single-handed Transatlantic Race until 1988 when she was abandoned by owner M. Richey.

Hasler lost interest in the Single-handed Transatlantic Race and sold *Jester* when large, specially developed keelboats and big multi-hulls began to compete as these conflicted with his idea of a seaworthy yacht.

Eric & Susan HISCOCK

b 1908–d 1986/b 1914

This famous cruising couple have had an enormous influence on yachtsmen through their books, particularly *Voyaging under Sail* and *Cruising under Sail* which are the accepted handbooks of ocean cruising. They circumnavigated the world twice and were indefatigable writers, photographers and lecturers, their theme being that ocean voyaging can be safe and pleasant provided proper preparations are made.

Their best-known and most successful yacht was the 30ft (9.14m) overall *Wanderer III*. In her, they cruised the oceans of the world for 17 years, from 1952. When they returned from their first voyage, in 1955, *Wanderer III* was put on show at the London Boat Show where her two owners stood patiently for hour after hour answering questions from would-be sea-tramps. The great thing about the Hiscocks was that they seemed a perfectly normal middle-aged couple and this inspired hundreds of others to believe that crossing oceans was within the ability of ordinary people.

The Hiscocks were 'drop-outs' before the term was invented but never lost sight of the middle-class values of thrift and careful planning. As a result they were able to live by writing as they sailed.

Following their second circumnavigation they decided that they deserved the comfort of a larger ship and exchanged *Wanderer III* for the 49ft (14.93m) Dutch-built steel ketch *Wanderer IV* but although the new boat provided many more comforts she proved a clumsy sailer and the Hiscocks never really liked her. Even so, they sailed to New Zealand where they eventually changed to a slightly smaller, wooden yacht, the fifth and final boat to be named *Wanderer*.

John ILLINGWORTH

b 1903–d 1985

Captain John Illingworth, RN was the most important influence in post-war offshore racing in Europe. He was at the same time the leading designer, skipper, clubman and general inspirer and initiator of the sport during its greatest period of growth. He won his first offshore race in 1929 and sailed his last full racing season in 1969.

Yorkshire-born Illingworth was an engineering officer in the Navy who reached the rank of Captain having had responsibility for submarine and coastal forces designs. His first yacht was *Maid of Malham* in which he won the 1938 RORC Championship. Immediately after the war, he was stationed in Australia and when a group of Sydney yachtsmen suggested a cruise to Hobart during the Christmas holidays he countered by proposing a race. This was the origin of the Sydney–Hobart Race, one of the classic offshore events. To compete, he bought a light-displacement 34ft 9in (10.59m) sloop named *Rani*. In a windy race, many of the yachts hove-to or retired but *Rani* kept sailing at full speed and won by 17 hours.

Returning to Britain he commissioned his most famous yacht *Myth of Malham* from designer Jack Laurent Giles; 37ft 9in (11.5m) long she embodied all his ideas for a completely dedicated offshore racing boat, in which all traditional ideas of aesthetics and suitability for cruising were ruthlessly discarded. Other designers dismissed her as an 'ugly machine' but could not deny her success. In her, Illingworth won the Fastnet Races in 1947 and 1951 and many other principal events.

Retiring from the Navy, Illingworth became a full-time yacht designer and was soon producing a string of successful yachts. Many were quite advanced and controversial in design, especially the ultra-light displacement ones such as the *Blue Charm* series and their larger versions, *Midnight* and *Outlaw.* They pioneered ultra-light offshore racing, were fast to windward, wild and difficult downwind and frightfully uncomfortable. He clashed with Sir Francis Chichester over the design of *Gipsy Moth IV*, each man blaming the other for creating a yacht that neither felt was what they had wanted.

Although a tough and strict skipper, Illingworth was particularly good at encouraging young men to take up offshore sailing and gave many their first opening into the sport. As well as being Commodore of the RORC, he helped to create the Junior Offshore Group and played a major part in the creation of the Sail Training Association, whose schooners have given so many young people their first taste of life afloat.

He spoke French rather well and did much to encourage offshore racing enthusiasts in that country. As a result, he received many design commissions from France and eventually set up a production-line system at Cherbourg to build the Maica class of small offshore yacht. During the 1950s and 1960s Illingworth dominated the sport and his commitment has left a lasting legacy.

Naomi JAMES

b 1948

New Zealander Naomi James (née Power) was the first woman to sail singlehanded around the world, in 1977/8. The 54ft (16.45m) cutter *Spirit of Cutty Sark*, lent to her by Chay Blyth, was temporarily renamed *Express Crusader.* This yacht is virtually the same size as Chichester's *Gipsy Moth IV* but heavier and more powerful and with more sail on a single mast. The fact that Naomi James was able to handle such a big boat alone says a lot both for her strength and for modern equipment such as powerful self-tailing winches.

Naomi had intended to sail non-stop but damage to the self-steering gear made her put

in to Cape Town. South of New Zealand the lower shrouds failed at the mast tangs and eventually Naomi continued under jury rig, making a further stop for repairs at the Falklands. The complete circumnavigation took 272 days, of which 266 were sailing days. Initially she had been as fast as Chichester but was much slower on the return journey.

Together with her husband Rob, Naomi competed in and won the 1982 Round Britain Race, sailing the 60ft (18.28m) trimaran *Colt Cars GB.*

Irving & Electra JOHNSON

b 1905/b 1911

The Johnsons circumnavigated the world under sail seven times, and this is believed to be an unbroken record. They did so on two sizeable yachts, each named *Yankee* and each a former North Sea pilot vessel.

Even before acquiring the first *Yankee*, Irving Johnson had more sailing experience than almost anyone in the world. As a young man he sailed on the German four-masted barque *Peking* and took some of the best movie-film ever of a big sailing ship in heavy weather. He then sailed as mate to another American sailor of legendary skill, Warwick Tompkins, on a lengthy cruise that took them to Europe and back.

After marrying Electra, herself a sailor of great experience and ability, Johnson conceived the idea of running long-distance cruises with paying guests as crew. They bought a 92ft (28m) Dutch pilot schooner, refitted her and, in 1933, set off on their first 18-month circumnavigation with a crew of 15 young people, many of whom had no sailing experience. The Johnsons were assisted by two experienced mates, however, and this proved to be a successful formula. Two more round trips were made before the Second World War.

Irving Johnson served with distinction in the US Navy during the war, the first *Yankee* meanwhile having been given to a naval academy. In 1946, the Johnsons were lucky to find and buy the last sailing pilot schooner built in Germany, a 96ft (29.26m) overall steel schooner that became the second *Yankee.* In this vessel they continued the pre-war formula, their crew now including their two sons, who had both been born on the first *Yankee.*

The Johnsons' voyages were carefully-conceived and efficiently carried out and *Yankee* was always kept in an excellent state of

***Left:** Naomi James at the chart-table of* Express Crusader, *in which she was the first woman to sail alone around the world. She also won the Round Britain Race in partnership with her husbar d Rob prior to his tragic deatl by drowning when he fell overboard from the trimarar* Colt Cars GB.

maintenance. As a result, parents were ready to entrust their offspring to a cruise with the Johnsons and there was also a plentiful supply of adults wishing to break away from a routine life. Between 1947 and 1958 the second *Yankee* made an astonishing four complete circumnavigations, all with paying guests as crew and all without serious accident. Thanks to the Johnsons, hundreds of people enjoyed the unique experience of a long voyage under sail while also learning the skills of seamanship.

After their seventh circumnavigation, the Johnsons 'retired' to a 50ft (15.24m) centreboard ketch which they could handle without crew and which was able to travel on European inland waterways.

Robin KNOX-JOHNSTON

b 1939

During the past 20 years, Robin Knox-Johnston has done just about everything possible in the way of sailing on the high seas but he earned a permanent place in history for his single-handed non-stop voyage round the world aboard *Suhaili* in 1968/9.

This made him the first to sail single-handed non-stop around the globe while two other competitors in *The Sunday Times* Golden Globe competition dropped out. The French ocean voyager Bernard Moitessier was chasing *Suhaili* in this race but after rounding Cape Horn, instead of 'turning left' to head back towards France, he went straight on and sailed around the world a second time. Commander Nigel Tetley was also well astern of *Suhaili*, and only about 1,000 miles from home, when his trimaran began to break up and he was forced to take to the life-raft. This left Knox-Johnston as the sole competitor and after 313 days at sea his battered little ketch *Suhaili* sailed safely into Falmouth.

Robin had not intended to make it in *Suhaili*. This dumpy little cruising yacht had been built in Bombay for a group including Robin when he was serving as a merchant seaman in the Far East. They wanted a nice, fast, modern cruising ketch, but what they finally got, built very heavily in 1¼in (30mm) teak, was *Suhaili*.

During 1965, Robin sailed *Suhaili* home to England together with his brother Chris and a friend. The previous year, the Observer Single-handed Transatlantic Race had been won by Eric Tabarly, and a headline in *Paris Match* read, 'Frenchman supreme on Anglo-Saxon ocean'. This, said Robin, 'made my blood boil' and it gave him the impetus he needed to sail alone around the world in *The Sunday Times* race.

In this post-Chichester era, Knox-Johnston needed a big, light, easily-handled modern yacht but was unable to raise the funds and he reluctantly entered the race in *Suhaili*, suitably modified for single-handed sailing. Even then he had to scrimp, save and borrow to have her overhauled and stocked up with a year's supplies.

Of the seven competitors, nearly everyone rated Knox-Johnston the least likely to win but it turned out to be a tortoise-and-hare contest. One by one the faster boats pulled out with damage of one kind or another while leaky, overloaded *Suhaili* plodded gamely on.

Wishing to hand over films and diaries, he approached the New Zealand port of Otago during a severe storm and had just managed to reach shelter in a river when the yacht went aground. Though help was at hand he refused it and continued after refloating the yacht (the self-steering gear had been wrecked in a previous gale). And eventually, of course, *Suhaili* did sail triumphantly home to Falmouth.

Knox-Johnston had the great advantage of being a professional seaman before embarking on small-boat adventures and thus possessed both the technical skills and the mental discipline needed to endure the loneliness and the hardship. And his love of boats and the sea is a life-time affair.

He teamed up with the ex-naval yachtsman Leslie Williams for the 1970 Round Britain Race, sailing the 60ft (18.28m) *Ocean Spirit*. The pundits thought that such a big boat would be too much of a handful for two men but in spite of various misfortunes she

Below: Robin Knox-Johnston, whose first and greatest achievement was his non-stop single-handed circumnavigaton in Suhaili, *in 1968/9. Since then, he has taken part in virtually every type of sailing competition, specializing in long-distance ocean racing, often single-handed. He was one of the pioneers of offshore multihull racing and has won the Round Britain Race twice — once in a monohull and once in a catamaran.*

was the first to finish — the only time a monohull has achieved this in the history of the race. He was again co-skipper with Williams of the 79ft (24.08m) *Heath's Condor* for the second Whitbread Round the World Race in 1977. The revolutionary carbon fibre mast collapsed during the first leg but, remasted, she was the first yacht home.

For the 1974 Round Britain Race, Robin wanted a big catamaran. *British Oxygen*, shared with Jerry Boxall, was the largest pure racing catamaran built at that time — having an overall length of 70ft (21.33m). She was a boat of tremendous potential, never fully realized as the gear, sails and general know-how for a multihull of this size did not exist in 1974. However, she just managed to beat the much lighter, simpler 50ft (15.24m) trimaran *Three Cheers* to the finish, after repeatedly breaking halyards and other gear.

Robin's faith in the basic design remained firm, and he had an up-dated version built from the same moulds. *Sea Falcon* was a fast and successful yacht which performed with credit in several major races until being written off in a collision with a ship.

Robin has always preferred the catamaran form and stuck to it for his most recent yacht, the 60ft (18.28m) *British Airways*. Built on a very tight budget, she is something of a compromise being a little heavy for the major events such as the Single-handed Transatlantic or Route du Rhum but ideal for a tough, long-distance marathon. With her, Knox-Johnston has performed with credit in the Monaco–New York Race, the Round Britain (1986) and several others. The boat also holds the British record for crossing the Atlantic, west to east.

Knox-Johnston also sailed in the victorious Admiral's Cup teams of 1973 and 1975 and won the RORC Class I championship of 1976.

Highly conscious of the need to give as well as receive from the world of sailing, he is Chairman of the Organizing Committee of the BOC Single-handed Around the World Race and serves on many committees, charities and the like. Having lavished knighthoods on Francis Chichester and Alex Rose, the Honours Committee obviously decided that they could not go on bestowing this title on every Briton who sailed around the world, so Robin received the lesser honour of CBE for a greater achievement.

Chris LAW

b 1952

During 1988 the co-ordinator of the still-born Blue Arrow America's Cup challenge, Chris Law is one of Britain's most successful helmsmen. Winner of a rugby scholarship to Millfield School he was a member of the English Schools rugby team in 1971 and could have reached the top in this sport if he had not instead turned his attention to sailing.

His size and strength gave him great advantages in sailing the single-handed Finn dinghy and he won the National, European and World Championships in the period leading up to the 1976 Olympics but unfortunately had to sail a second-choice boat during the British trials and failed to gain selection. Apart from that his domination of the class was complete — for instance, he won the hotly-contested Kiel Week with a perfect score of six wins.

For the following Olympics he turned his attention to the Soling 3-man keelboat and proved the master of that too. He was the British representative at the 1984 games but finished a slightly disappointing 4th. Meanwhile, he was gaining experience of bigger boats, having sailed on *Moonshine*, which was a member of the winning Admiral's Cup team in 1977.

During 1982, he got his first experience of sailing a 12-metre and in the following year was briefly tried out as a helmsman on *Victory '83*.

Above: *Chris Law was the best Finn sailor of his generation even though he failed to gain Olympic selection. More recently he has proved himself one of the most successful British helmsmen in a wide range of competitions. He was chief helmsman of the 12-metre* White Crusader *in 1987.*

When he went out to join the *White Crusader* challenge in Australia, he was very much No. 3 after Harold Cudmore and Edward Warden-Owen but by sheer grit and ability worked his way through to the position of principal helmsman under Cudmore's overall command. Although this challenge also failed, Law emerged with a lot of credit and was snapped up by Peter de Savary for the Blue Arrow challenge. A strong, steady and very level-headed helmsman, he may yet prove to be the best that Britain has to offer.

David LEWIS

b 1927

New Zealand-born Dr Lewis was a medical practitioner in London before taking part in the first Single-handed Transatlantic Race, sailing the sturdy little Laurent Giles-designed 25ft (7.62m) *Cardinal Vertue*. He came third, after Chichester and Hasler.

He sold *Cardinal Vertue* and had a 40ft (12.19m) catamaran designed by Colin Mudie and built by Prouts of Canvey Island. *Rehu Moana* (Ocean Spray) was very innovative and generally successful except for the rig which consisted of a Hasler-style junk sail set beneath an arched, goal-post mast. This collapsed and was replaced by a conventional rig.

Lewis seemed drawn to cold places and his first cruise in her was to the Arctic, where his idea of hauling the yacht out on to the ice proved impractical but he did succeed in sending photographs by radio, the first time this had been done from a small boat.

***Below:** David Lewis (right of picture) seen with his family aboard* Isbjorn, *the yacht in which he spent two years researching Polynesian methods of navigation. He had already sailed around the world in the catamaran* Rehu Moana *and later made an ill-fated attempt to circumnavigate Antarctica in a small yacht.*

He next entered in the 1964 OSTAR — crossing the Atlantic in 38 days — considerably slower than the 30 days of the winner, Francis Chichester. Afterwards he set off on a world cruise with his wife and two daughters, stopping in Patagonia to study the local population.

On the way across the Pacific, Lewis began a study of the traditional Polynesian methods of navigation and later wrote a fascinating book, *We the Navigators*. The Lewis family completed a three-year circumnavigation in *Rehu Moana* in 1967 — the first to be safely completed in a catamaran. It is described in his book *Daughters of the Wind*.

Lewis received a research fellowship from the Australian National University to continue research into Pacific navigation, and exchanged *Rehu Moana* for a motor-sailer, *Isbjorn*. After completing his research, he again felt the call of the ice. In 1972 he set off in the 32ft (9.75m) steel yacht *Ice Bird* in an attempt to sail single-handed around Antarctica, capsizing twice and surviving incredible hardships. (This venture is also described in a book, *Ice Bird*.)

Bernard MOITESSIER

b 1925

Most world-girdling yachtsmen are drop-outs of a kind but none dropped further than Bernard Moitessier. He achieved notoriety in 1969 when he appeared to be heading for fastest time in *The Sunday Times* Golden Globe Race. Starting from France, he had already sailed non-stop around the world south of the three great capes and, after doubling Cape Horn, faced only the relatively straightforward passage back to Europe. Instead he went straight on, continuing round the world a second time without stopping until he finally came to rest in Tahiti.

Most people felt that he must have gone mad, but Moitessier, on the contrary, had found a kind of serenity. He was truly at home on the ocean to a degree probably never achieved by any other man and he simply could not bear the idea of returning to civilization.

In the 1950s, Moitessier had already become an accomplished sea-tramp, wandering the oceans of the world on his 28ft (8.53m) double-ender *Marie-Terese II* until she was wrecked on a reef. His book *Un Vagabond des Mers du Sud* made him enough money to buy a new boat. This was the 39ft (11.88m) steel ketch *Joshua*, which he planned in conjunction with naval architect Jean Knocker; this was an immensely sensible and practical yacht, completely devoid of frills and fancy fittings because Moitessier had learned the hard way that simple things quite often turn out to be the best.

In her, Moitessier and his wife Francoise made a circumnavigation that included the longest non-stop passage then made by a yacht: 15,000 miles from Tahiti to Gibraltar. During this very long passage, mostly in high latitudes, he rediscovered the 'secret' of Vito Dumas: in storms, do not heave-to or drag warps but keep sailing at full speed so that the waves do not sweep violently over the yacht.

George MUHLHAUSER

b 1876–d 1923

Lieutenant George H.P. Muhlhauser RN (ret'd) was the second British yachtsman to circumnavigate the world and his 62ft (18.89m) gaff yawl *Amaryllis* was the third small yacht of any nationality to do so. In fact, since the first Briton to sail around the world was Lord Brassey whose 565-ton schooner *Sunbeam* had a full professional crew, Muhlhauser was the first to sail himself around. He left England in September 1920 and returned in July 1923.

Muhlhauser was an aloof man of almost frightening competence; before the war he had owned a small yacht named *Wilful*, and his idea of a fun cruise had been to sail to Norway and, after making a landfall, to turn round and sail back without entering port. During the war he served with considerable distinction as navigator or commanding officer of a variety of patrol boats, minesweepers and Q-ships; warships disguised as merchant vessels. He had a successful business, wrote a book on navigation and was a member of the Royal Cruising Club.

Amaryllis was a big heavy cruising yacht with a gaff yawl rig and must have been a brute to handle. Initially, Muhlhauser had three amateur 'guests' as crew but they left for various reasons when they reached America. For the rest of the time he handled this big boat with the help of a variety of unreliable paid hands.

Muhlhauser tried to sell the heavy old *Amaryllis* in New Zealand, but without success, so he continued his cruise sailing north of Australia and through the archipelago to Singapore. After crossing the Indian Ocean, he beat up the Red Sea, a notoriously difficult and dangerous passage, in just 30 days. This was a remarkable feat of navigation in an unhandy vessel with a very small crew of which he was the only competent navigator.

After this epic voyage, Muhlhauser wrote in his journal that he was delighted to find that no-one took the slightest notice. However, his business was in trouble and he was also seriously ill with cancer; he died within months of his return. At his funeral, the coffin was covered by both the white and the blue ensigns.

Conor O'BRIEN

b 1882–d 1945

Conor O'Brien was the first yachtsman to make a circumnavigation south of the three 'Great Capes' (Cape of Good Hope, Cape Leeuwin and Cape Horn). During the First World War he had been involved in gun-running with Erskine Childers, author of *Riddle of the Sands*. After the war, he designed the 42ft (12.80m) *Saoirse* along the lines of an Arklow fishing boat.

The majority of yachtsmen, before and since, circumnavigate in the west-bound direction, using the Panama Canal to avoid the need to beat to windward round Cape Horn or through the dangerous Straits of Magellan. O'Brien wanted to see how a yacht could cope with the clipper-ship route east-bound, in high southerly latitudes.

His circumnavigation was relatively fast, taking only 280 sailing days to cover 31,000 miles; he stopped only 12 times. Like Muhlhauser, O'Brien suffered from a succession of unsatisfactory crews and had no constant companion. *Saoirse* did not have a coppered bottom and suffered badly from worms in the tropics and from corrosion of her iron fastenings. He tried to sell her in New Zealand, but without success.

After his return, O'Brien wrote *Across Three Oceans*, one of the best cruising logs of the period, and other technical books. He was one of the first yachtsmen to have a strong technical grasp of yacht construction and rigging and his books were very influential.

Marc PAJOT

b 1946

Together with his brother Yves, Marc Pajot was one of France's top dinghy helmsmen, first in the 5-0-5 class and later the Flying Dutchman, in which they won a silver medal in the 1972 Olympics. He then turned to big boats and became one of the new breed of high-profile professional skippers.

Drawn like a moth to the big multihull racing scene, he became skipper of the 65ft (20m) catamaran *Elf Aquitaine* and achieved lasting fame by winning the 1982 Route du Rhum race, in spite of incredible difficulties which included the boat almost breaking in two beneath him.

He has appeared in virtually every arena of sailing and was the skipper of *French Kiss*, the challenger for the 1987 America's Cup.

Pajot has been largely responsible for raising the standing of sailing in the eyes of the French to new levels and is one of their highest-paid sportsmen.

Below: *Frenchman Marc Pajot is one of the country's best-known and highest-paid sportsmen. An Olympic competitor in the Flying Dutchman class with his brother Yves, he later moved into the new sport of multihull ocean-racing. He was skipper of the America's Cup challenger* French Kiss, *which proved a much better boat than most people expected.*

Rodney PATTISSON

b 1941

Rodney Pattisson is Britain's most successful Olympic sailor. Sailing in the Flying Dutchman, two-man dinghy class, he won gold medals at Acapulco in 1968 and Kiel in 1972, and in 1976 he won a silver medal at Kingston, Ontario.

The Flying Dutchman is a very technical class and Pattisson always took enormous pains over the setting up and tuning of his boats. Since retiring from the Flying Dutchman, he has competed in the America's Cup and offshore events such as the Admiral's Cup. He was also co-skipper with Lawrie Smith of *Victory '83*, beaten by *Australia II* in the challenger elimination series.

In 1985 he steered *Jade*, which won the One Ton Cup, and was a member of the British Admiral's Cup team. In 1987 he was co-skipper, with Lawrie Smith, of the Admiral's Cupper *Jamarella*.

Harry PIGEON

b 1872–d 1955

The Iowa-born farmer's son, Harry Pigeon, was the first yachtsman to circumnavigate the world twice: in 1921/5 and 1932/7. He did this in *Islander*, a 34ft (10.36m) yawl which he built himself in 1917 and lived aboard for many years. Thomas Fleming Day, the editor of *Rudder* magazine had published a booklet entitled *How to Build a Cruising Yawl* which contained plans for three different boats with simple lines suitable for amateur construction. Pigeon combined what he felt were the best features of all three designs in building *Islander*, which turned out to be a thoroughly practicable cruising yacht.

It cost Pigeon $1,000 to build his dream yacht, which he lived aboard in Los Angeles during the First World War while learning seamanship and navigation. After the war, he and a friend sailed to Hawaii and back which gave him the confidence to set off on his own a year later.

He was not trying to prove or win anything but just quietly meandered across the oceans of the world, stopping whenever the fancy took him. Five years later, he returned to the Pacific via the Panama Canal. At Balboa he met Alain Gerbault, still in the early stages of his circumnavigation with *Firecrest* (see page 177).

Pigeon then spent nearly four years writing a book and living aboard *Islander* before setting off on his second circumnavigation, as quietly and competently executed as the first. During the Second World War he married and in 1947, in his seventies, set off on a honeymoon cruise, but was caught in a typhoon in the New Hebrides during which the faithful *Islander* was driven on to the rocks and smashed.

He was engaged in building a replacement when he died. Pigeon's two fine voyages set the pattern for the numerous unsung heroes and heroines who have since made great journeys across the oceans.

William Albert ROBINSON

b 1903

One of the greatest of American ocean sailors, designers and builders, Robinson is also one of the best sea writers. His solo circumnavigation, begun in 1928, was in the smallest yacht to complete the voyage at that time, the 32ft (9.75m) *Svaap*.

During his circumnavigation, Robinson fell in love with life in the Pacific islands and returned to settle in Tahiti. But in 1937, he returned to the United States to found a shipyard in Connecticut where he planned to build old-time vessels such as Baltimore clippers and wooden fishing boats. He remained to manage the yard during the Second World War, during which it turned out an astonishing 200 small naval vessels, and he made a great deal of money.

Just before war broke out, Robinson had built his 'perfect cruising yacht', the 62ft (18.89m) brigantine, *Varua*. He lived aboard *Varua* during the war and afterwards sailed her to Tahiti. During the 1950s he made a complete circuit of the Pacific, during which he encountered and managed to survive 'the ultimate storm'.

His books include *Deep Water and Shoal*, *10,000 Leagues over the Sea* and *To the Great Southern Sea*.

Sir Alec ROSE

b 1908

It is usual to characterize Alec Rose as a jolly old grocer who for some inexplicable reason decided to sail around the world on his own. The reality is more complex; he was a man of great energy and ability who suffered a number of frustrating or even humiliating setbacks in life and reached middle age with a feeling of restless unfulfilment.

Born in Canterbury, in 1908, he worked on farms in Canada as a young man before returning to England to work for his father's trucking firm. When the Second World War broke out he volunteered for the Royal Navy and served for three years as an engineer

Left: *Rodney Pattisson at the helm of a Flying Dutchman, the class in which he won two gold and one silver Olympic medals. A reserved and retiring man, Pattisson has never sought to make capital from his success and the fact that he is Britain's most successful Olympic competitor is easily overlooked. In recent years he has sailed a number of successful offshore yachts in competitions such as the Admiral's Cup.*

aboard the small escort ship *HMS Leith*. In 1944 he received a commission and was appointed engineer in charge of a squadron of landing-craft being prepared for the invasion of Europe. Eventually, he collapsed from accumulated stress and was invalided out of the Navy.

After the war, he settled down to running his flower growing business but got into financial difficulties and had to sell up. During this period he had been converting a ship's boat into a yacht and when his marriage also failed he 'dropped out' and lived aboard the boat for a time.

On one of his cruises, he met and married his second wife Dorothy and took over a fruit and flower shop in Southsea. A couple of years later, he was bitten by the sailing bug once more and bought the very well-built 36ft (10.97m) cutter *Lively Lady* from the man who built her. She was an old-fashioned pre-war design by Fred Shepherd but very strongly built in teak on paduak frames.

With *Lively Lady* Rose conceived the idea of entering for the second Observer Single-handed Transatlantic Race. *Lively Lady* was given a modern rig (which caused incessant trouble) and not only entered but came a very creditable fourth in the 1964 OSTAR.

A year later, Chichester (who was five years older than Rose) more or less announced his intention of sailing single-handed around the world. Privately, and without any fanfare, Rose decided to do the same. Although he never courted publicity, his plans were known by the members of his sailing club at Eastney and the people of Southsea came to regard him as an unofficial mascot of the town. He never accepted any form of sponsorship but they gave him unstinting support and practical help.

Rose could have sailed the same year as Chichester, even making a race of it, but while he was preparing *Lively Lady* at Mashford's yard in Plympton she fell over at low tide and Rose had to postpone his departure for a year. Finally sailing from Plymouth on 6 July 1967, he sailed non-stop to Melbourne, arriving on 19 December, to a tremendous welcome.

After rest and repairs lasting a month he set off again but problems with his rigging caused him to put into Bluff, New Zealand for further repairs. From here he sailed non-stop back to Portsmouth, arriving on 4 July 1968, after a circumnavigation lasting just two days less than a year.

The public took to their hearts this quiet, decent 60-year-old who seemed like most people's idea of an ideal grandfather and he was given a hero's welcome. Soon afterwards he received a knighthood and promptly returned to his former life as a shopkeeper, no longer needing to feel that, somehow, he had missed out on life.

Joshua SLOCUM

b 1844–d 1909

Captain Joshua Slocum was the first to sail around the world alone. Sailing from Boston in April 1895, he took three years and two months to complete the circumnavigation and he did it in a boat which had been given away as a wreck, setting off with exactly $1.80 in cash. Whatever anyone else does hereafter, Slocum's achievement can never be surpassed.

Although at his lowest ebb in life at the outset of his great endeavour, with no assets and no prospects, Slocum was a professional seaman of immense experience who had spent nearly all his adult life at sea. Born in Nova Scotia he left home at 16 when his mother died and worked his way up from deck-hand to master by the time he was 25.

Having achieved command, at a time when shipping was enjoying one of its greatest booms, Slocum enjoyed a period of happiness and success. He married an Australian named Virginia Walker and they lived and raised a family aboard the various ships that he commanded. He went into fishing, ship-building, and ship-owning at various times, and was both master and part-owner of the 1,800-ton clipper-ship *Northern Light*. His happiest period came when he was the owner/master of the barque *Aquidneck*, 'which of all man's handiwork seemed to me the nearest to perfection of beauty', he wrote.

Things began to go horribly wrong for Slocum when Virginia died of a fever during a voyage to Buenos Aires. Mainly to provide a mother for his children, Slocum married his cousin Henrietta, but then had an even more disastrous trip to South America, with two of the children aboard the *Aquidneck*. A cholera epidemic made it impossible to unload the cargo and Slocum, not able to obtain compensation, was heavily out of pocket. There was also a mutiny on board. Finally, while loading a cargo of timber, the *Aquidneck* was caught by a sudden change of wind and wrecked.

Slocum had now lost everything but his self-respect. He could have applied to the nearest US consul for repatriation but instead he built an extraordinary 35ft (10.67m) dory, the *Liberdade*, with a Chinese junk-style rig and an extremely basic cabin covered with tarpaulin. In this primitive but very cleverly conceived craft, with his wife and two young sons as crew, Slocum sailed 5,000 miles from Brazil to Washington DC, one of the greatest small-boat voyages in history.

Regaining his native land, Slocum then undertook to deliver the ironclad monitor *Destroyer* to Brazil during the depths of winter, in an effort to recoup his finances. Using every reserve of strength and seamanship he succeeded in delivering the frightful vessel only to have the Brazilians renege on the contract.

In an unforgiving age, Slocum was now a washed-up, middle-aged failure. He could not find employment as master and a book about the voyage of the *Liberdade*, which he wrote and had printed at his own expense, was not exactly a best-seller.

In the winter of 1892, an old friend, Captain Eben Pierce, jokingly gave Slocum the wreck of an old oyster boat. Having nothing better to do, Slocum decided he would rebuild her.

The work took 13 months and Slocum raised the necessary funds for this by doing odd jobs on whaling ships. The rebuilt *Spray* was extremely wide and shallow with a broad, square transom and measured 37ft (11.28m). Surprisingly, she sailed very well, putting up good average speeds on passage. furthermore, she was well balanced and could sail for extended periods without steering.

Slocum does not say in his book exactly what drove him, merely recording, 'I had resolved on a voyage round the world' and, in April 1895, he set off. His equipment was extremely basic but he had a great knack for making the best of things. For instance, he found a castaway fishing dory and sawed it in half to make a combined dinghy, wash tub and bath. He had all his old navigation instruments but could not afford to have his chronometer cleaned and rated, so his only timepiece was a cheap clock — and even that had broken hands.

His very first ocean passage in the *Spray* was quite remarkable: 18 days from Cape Sable to Fayal in the Azores. There he re-supplied and was given a quantity of ripe plums and a white cheese which he unfortunately ate together, shortly after sailing. Seized by violent stomach cramps just as the *Spray* was heading into a severe storm, he reefed the sails and lashed the helm before collapsing. He awoke to find the *Spray* was being steered through the storm by 'the pilot of the *Pinta*', a

Left, top: *Sir Alec Rose returns to Portsmouth in July 1968, aboard* Lively Lady, *after his solo round the world voyage. The modest, middle-aged grocer from Southsea was a man of much greater skill and determination than he appeared but it was his unassuming manner that endeared him to the public.*

Left, below: *Sir Alec Rose with his mascot 'Algy' before setting off on his round the world trip.*

Right: The first and greatest of the French sailing super-stars, Eric Tabarly made his mark in the Single-handed Transatlantic Race, which he won in 1964 and 1976. A man of few words but enormous strength of will, he has been the role-model for a whole generation of tough, competent French professional yachtsmen.

friendly phantom who has since become more-or-less the patron saint of single-handed sailors. The *Spray* had sailed 90 miles through a rough sea while he lay unconscious, and she was dead on course. With typically puckish humour Slocum wrote, 'I felt grateful to the old pilot, but I marvelled some that he had not taken in the jib.'

From Gibraltar, Slocum and the *Spray* re-crossed the Atlantic to Brazil, then worked their way down the coast of South America to the Straits of Magellan, gateway to the Pacific. Here, the famous carpet-tack incident occurred when the murderous Fuegians boarded the *Spray* while Slocum slept. Forewarned, he had spread tacks on deck and was woken by the agonized yells of the bare-footed invaders.

Finally breaking out into the Pacific Slocum made a fine, 73-day passage to Samoa. From there he sailed to Australia, then north into the Coral Sea and thence into the Indian Ocean. From Christmas Island he sailed in 23 days to Keeling Cocos without once touching the helm. Durban and Capetown were his South African stopping points after which he made his third crossing of the Atlantic via St Helena and Ascension Island. After making further stops in the Caribbean, the *Spray* finally returned to Boston in June 1898, having sailed 46,000 miles in just three years.

In the months following his return, Slocum wrote *Sailing Alone Around the World*, in a charming, simple style that seemed so appropriate to the man and his ship. It was one of the greatest publishing successes in history. First printed in monthly instalments, the complete book was reprinted 16 times by the original publisher and has been translated into practically every language. At last, relatively wealthy, he was able to buy a farm for his wife.

Fame did not stop him from sailing and he made several cruises to the Caribbean but, in 1909, when he was 65, he and the *Spray* disappeared. The greatest memorial to this remarkable man is that he inspired so many to imitate him. As he wrote at the end of *Sailing Alone Around the World*, 'To young men contemplating a voyage I would say, go.'

Miles & Beryl SMEETON

b 1906–d 1988/b 1910–d 1979

The Smeetons are chiefly remembered for the two attempts to round Cape Horn made in their yacht *Tzu Hang* and described in their book *Once is Enough*.

In 1956, the Smeetons — who had already completed some very lengthy passages with *Tzu Hang* — sailed from Australia eastbound around Cape Horn. This had only been done by three yachts, one of which had capsized. As extra crew they shipped aboard John Guzzwell, a tough and competent Yorkshireman who had been engaged in his own circumnavigation aboard the self-built *Trekka*.

West of Cape Horn they were struck by a ferocious storm. Eventually *Tzu Hang* was pitch-poled, thrown end over end, the yacht was dismasted and the cabin-top smashed in. Beryl Smeeton was hurled violently overboard and seriously injured. Almost miraculously, they managed to get her back aboard and save the yacht from sinking. Under jury rig, they limped to safety in a Chilean port, where they recovered and rebuilt *Tzu Hang* with the help of Guzzwell.

Guzzwell then left to pursue his own plans and the Smeetons set off just before Christmas 1957 on their second attempt to round the Horn. This should have been the ideal time of year, at the height of the southern summer, but once again they were caught in a severe storm and once again *Tzu Hang* was rolled over by enormous waves, in nearly the same area as before. This time, after reaching safety, they had the yacht hoisted aboard ship and carried round Cape Horn.

Despite these experiences they continued to cruise the world for several years aboard the same yacht. In 1968, they broke their own rule that 'Once is enough and twice is too much' and this time successfully sailed round Cape Horn from east to west, assisted by relatively easy weather.

Eric TABARLY

b 1931

France's greatest sailor, Eric Tabarly symbolizes the beginning of an era in which complete competence and professionalism added to natural strength and determination would be the key factors in winning major, long-distance sailing events.

Tabarly was born into a family of sailors in the Britanny port of Lorient and was an experienced sailor before he joined the French navy. In the early 1960s he and his father bought and restored a lovely old Clyde pilot cutter designed by Will Fife and renamed her *Pen Duick*.

In 1964, Tabarly obtained leave of absence from the Navy to compete in the second Observer Single-handed Transatlantic Race. His *Pen Duick II* was a 44ft (13.4m) overall plywood ketch with a fairly radical fin and spade underwater profile and very light displacement, specially built for the race.

The yacht was built at the very last minute using borrowed money and reached the starting line in a scarcely-prepared condition. Her self-steering gear failed, forcing Tabarly to steer by hand, in spite of which he won the race by superior skill, endurance, and by having the fastest boat. Unlike the race

favourite Francis Chichester, Tabarly did not carry a ship-to-shore radio and was surprised to discover that he had won the race by more than two days from Chichester.

Tabarly was aged 33 at the time and a serving officer. He immediately became a sports hero in France (a role in which he found little pleasure, being reserved and rather taciturn) and was awarded the Legion d'honneur. He was also given a sinecure job at the Ministry of Sport which allowed him to concentrate on sailing full-time.

Tabarly has always been very forward-looking in his attitude to design and practically all his boats have been innovative. After his first OSTAR win, he commissioned a 57ft (17.37m) schooner, *Pen Duick III*, which proved devastatingly successful in the 1967 offshore racing season. But even then, he was planning a far more radical boat, the 67ft (20.42m) trimaran *Pen Duick IV*. Designed by Andre Allegre, this aluminium monster was a fantastically advanced concept with not the slightest concession to comfort or appearance. Eventually one of the most influential boats of the decade, it was a flop at its first appearance.

On the very first night of the OSTAR race, *Pen Duick IV* collided with an anchored merchant ship. Tabarly also found insurmountable problems with his self-steering gear and was forced to give up.

Tabarly then sorted out the trimaran properly and with Olivier de Kersauson and Alain Colas as crew made a record crossing of the Atlantic as part of a passage to the American West Coast. Here, they unofficially entered the Transpacific Race, beating the fastest monohull, *Windward Passage*, by a noteworthy 20 hours.

Tabarly switched his attention to the first Whitbread Round the World Race, scheduled for 1973, for which André Mauric designed the massively powerful 73ft (22.25m) ketch *Pen Duick VI*. Her most controversial feature was the depleted uranium metal keel, used in known defiance of the rules and specifically outlawed even as the race was taking place. It proved irrelevant as the mighty *Pen Duick VI* was dismasted twice and forced to retire.

To prove its potential, the latest *Pen Duick* had to wait for a subsequent occasion: the 1976 OSTAR for which *Pen Duick VI* was hardly suitable, having been designed for a crew of 18. But in an exceptionally tough race, during which the fleet was struck by no fewer than five gales, Tabarly was triumphant, bringing his ketch home in 23 days 20 hours. This extraordinary achievement was probably the high point of Tabarly's career.

Since 1976, he has continued to take part in many of the world's great races but not with the same degree of success. He has himself been responsible for a 'new wave' of tough young professional sailors keen to take over his mantle. Furthermore, his recent boats, although radical have not always been completely successful. His hydrofoil-stabilized trimaran *Paul Ricard* has never quite got into its stride and *Cote d'Or*, the yacht he sailed in the 1985 Whitbread Race, suffered from serious structural problems.

Perhaps his most permanent achievement has been to raise the status of yachting in France, and with it the self-esteem of French yachtsmen, to an unprecedented level.

Ted TURNER

b 1937

Known to the world as the pioneering entrepreneur of cable TV, Ted Turner is a reformed playboy who once complained that he had only managed to sail on 358 days in the year. Coming from a wealthy family he was able to indulge his whim for sailing to the full and grew to be a legend not only for his sailing skills but also for his big mouth, deep pocket and totally uninhibited behaviour.

Starting as a dinghy sailor, he graduated to racing keelboats such as the Star and 5.5 metre but really came to the attention of the sailing world when he bought a Cal 40 offshore racing boat, named *Vamp X*. His first shot at the Southern Ocean Racing Circuit was a disaster as he had no idea of navigation, so the following year he recruited Buddy Friedrichs to be the wizard of the chart table and won the circuit outright. He did it by applying small-boat techniques offshore — constant trimming of the sails, constant high adrenalin excitement and constant effort.

His next boat was the former America's Cup trialist, *American Eagle*. Turner sailed his scarlet 'Big Bird' all over the world, winning many races — including the 1970 SORC.

In 1974 he got involved in the America's Cup, but his mount was the experimental *Mariner*, which featured a cut-off 'fast-back' under water. 'Dammit,' said Turner to the designer Briton Chance, 'Dammit, Brit; even a turd is tapered at both ends.' Remarks like this led many to suppose that the New York Yacht Club would never choose him to skipper a defender. But in 1977 he won the trials so convincingly sailing *Courageous* that the NYYC had no choice. Revelling in his 'Captain Outrageous' role, Turner trounced the Australian challenger and then, in a final act of defiance, appeared at the victory press conference dead drunk.

Two years later he was a member of the 1979 US Admiral's Cup team, sailing his fine Sparkman and Stephens design *Tenacious*. This was the year of the disastrous Fastnet storm and in the aftermath of tragedy it went almost unnoticed that *Tenacious* won the Fastnet Trophy. He himself said that it was the toughest race ever.

Noisy, brusque, larger-than-life, Ted Turner can appear overpowering ashore but

Left: Ted Turner is a man who throws himself into business or sport with the same complete enthusiasm and dedication. Noisy, brusque and inconoclastic, Turner made many enemies in the yachting establishment but proved himself to be an inspirational skipper, particularly in defending the America's Cup in 1977 and winning the Fastnet Race in 1979.

changes to a really skilled enthusiast afloat. The fact that he is now too busy in business to take part in top racing events is sailing's loss but the world's gain.

John Claus VOSS

b 1858–d 1922

In his book *The Venturesome Voyages of Captain Voss*, the author says that the impetus for his around the world venture was provided by a Canadian journalist named Norman Kenny Luxton, who asked whether he thought he could accomplish such a voyage in a smaller vessel than Slocum's *Spray* (see page 189). In actual fact, he failed because he terminated his voyage in England but it was remarkable enough, even so.

Voss was another professional seaman of long experience, having been master of several vessels in addition to being a sealer, smuggler, gold prospector and treasure hunter. Prior to meeting Luxton, however, he was a successful hotel owner in Victoria, British Columbia.

Luxton's question had been mere bar talk, but Voss was an adventurer and accepted the challenge. The extraordinary vessel he chose was basically an Indian red cedar, dug-out canoe. He reinforced this with a keelson and frames, adding extra strakes to raise the freeboard. Three very short masts made the *Tilikum* a stumpy-looking schooner, rather like an enlarged Cape Cod dory in shape, but with an Indian figurehead.

Luxton, hoping to get a good story, signed on as crew and the ill-assorted pair set off in July 1901. Luxton turned out to be no sailor and hated the whole business; he called Voss a dangerous drunk and got off in Suva. Voss recruited a man named Louis Begent, but when *Tilikum* arrived in Australia, Begent was not aboard. Voss said he had fallen overboard but Luxton, who had followed by ship, asserted Voss had murdered the missing man when drunk.

In Australia, and some of the other places he visited, Voss made money by exhibiting *Tilikum*. Being quite small and flat-bottomed, the boat could be loaded on to a railway wagon and moved around from town to town. Parting company with Luxton, Voss recruited a new companion named MacMillan and continued his voyage, following Slocum's course (see page 190) as far as Durban.

From South Africa, Voss and yet another mate crossed the Atlantic to Brazil and then re-crossed it to England via the Azores. He reached Margate in September 1904 after a voyage lasting three years and three months, then abandoned his circumnavigation and went to Japan. The *Tilikum* lay forgotten on the bank of the Thames until 1928 when it was returned to Canada, restored, and put on display at the Maritime Museum in Victoria.

Voss's book is much more coherent than might be expected from the wild man that Luxton portrayed but his views on how to survive in severe conditions were long considered controversial. But, whatever his faults, Voss must have been a seaman of great skill and determination to have sailed so far in such an odd boat as the *Tilikum*.

362
SIGMA

Cruising

Cruising is sailing's gentler side, in which travelling is more important than the destination. The newcomer will find that there is plenty to learn but that learning can be fun. Seamanship is an especially broad subject that covers everything concerned with the safe and sensible management of yachts. Here we look briefly at navigation equipment, safety, the rules of the road, health at sea and many other points. The essence of cruising is learning to live aboard a yacht and manage her properly. A chance to get away from 'civilization' and let wind and tide dictate your timetable for a while.

***Left:** The Sigma 362 is a typical modern, multi-purpose yacht which can be used for competitive racing or family cruising equally well. The crew of* Beyond Belief *have permitted themselves the luxury of sailing without wearing either life-jackets or harnesses, something that can only be condoned in such obviously agreeable weather.*

Opposite: *Negotiating a lock on the Crinan Canal in Scotland. A good crew knows in advance what to do, so there is no need for any shouting or running about with the attendant risk of something going wrong.*

Cruising can mean many different things to different people. Some like to travel as widely as possible, others to meander; some to head for the bright lights, some want to get as far away from civilization as possible, even prefer solitude, while others like company; some love every detail of owning and looking after a boat, others see it simply as a means of getting to interesting places.

For all, however, there are some common attractions. To be master of your own small ship — completely in command of your own fate — is a rare opportunity in today's crowded, regulated world. To be close to nature and feel the wind and spray on your face. To see dawn break over a restless ocean and the sun sink in glory from a quiet anchorage. To face storm and calm with equal confidence. To experience the thrill of making a landfall after a hard passage. All these things and many others add up to the potent, universal appeal of cruising.

HOW TO START

It used to be difficult to try cruising unless you knew someone who owned a boat. Now, there are plenty of ways to get started without needing to make a large investment which you might later regret.

Charter

It is possible to charter a yacht in several ways which provide an easy introduction to cruising. Chartering a yacht with a crew is expensive but very safe if you have no previous experience. And while price-lists for chartering with crew can look extremely alarming, if two or three families take an eight to 12 berth yacht with a skipper and cook, the price generally works out about the same as staying in a four star hotel. Not cheap but not outrageous. Yachts chartered with a

Below: *The appeal of cruising is not easy to define as it can take so many different forms but the feeling of being independent and self-sufficient has a potent attraction for most people.*

crew have to be fairly big and are usually based in attractive holiday areas — the Mediterranean, Caribbean etc., so travel to these places needs to be included in the cost of your cruising holiday. Many agencies offer cruising as an inclusive tour deal, which certainly makes it easier to work out the cost accurately.

Bare-boat charter

Many people find that what they really want is one good sailing holiday each year and that boat ownership, with all its associated costs and work, is a very expensive way of getting it. For them, paying £1,000 to charter a cruising yacht for two weeks works out a lot cheaper than paying £35,000 to buy one.

To charter and take away a yacht on your own responsibility obviously calls for experience and many charter firms expect the person in charge to hold the 'Yachtmaster' qualification or its equivalent. But this is not a chicken-or-egg situation; it is easily possible to get the necessary knowledge and experience via a sailing school.

Even so, taking away a yacht completely without supervision calls for both competence *and* confidence. A family crew in which one parent is the only proficient sailor can lead to a certain amount of tension or even real problems should the yacht run into bad weather. Therefore, it is wise not to undertake a bare-boat charter unless the majority of the people involved know what they are taking on. There are easier ways to start, and one is described below.

Flotilla sailing

This fairly recent development aims to give people the fun of sailing while taking some of the weight of responsibility off their shoulders. The idea is that you sail in a group of boats with a group leader who knows the area and can cope with any problems that may crop up with the boats.

Less experience is called for than with a bare-boat charter and many thousands of people whose previous experience was of day-sailing have made this their introduction to cruising. It is easy to be snobbish about flotilla sailing and imagine that it will be a kind of marine holiday-camp in which the customers are chivvied along like a flock of sheep. The reality, in a well run flotilla, is that the leader will give each crew as much freedom as they seem to deserve. Some crews find being in charge of a yacht quite nerve-wracking and are glad to stay within sight of the leader. For others, it is sufficient to say 'Let's meet up in another couple of days at such-and-such a place.'

The key to making flotillas work is really the VHF radio, which enables the leader to check that none of his fleet has strayed too far and that everyone is happy. Rafting up with the other yachts at a picturesque harbour or joining in a beach barbecue can be a lot of fun but you are not obliged to do so.

Above: A group of flotilla yachts raft-up at an overnight anchorage. Many small-boat sailors have found this to be an easy introduction to cruising, as a lot of the responsibility can be left to the flotilla leader.

People going on a flotilla holiday for the first time, however, should do so with their eyes open. Some firms may be optimistic about the number of people that can fit on to their yachts; six on a 30 footer is an awful squeeze unless you are close friends. The boats also get very heavy use and you should be assured that they are reasonably new, in good condition and well looked-after. Some areas are overcrowded with flotillas, especially parts of Greece and Yugoslavia. If you almost have to wait for one group to leave harbour in order to get in, it is difficult to feel that you are visiting an 'unspoilt' cruising-ground. The qualities of the team leader are all-important. His or her knowledge and personality can make all the difference between a good and a bad experience.

SAILING SCHOOLS

The teaching of sailing used to be confined mainly to dinghy sailing but in recent years there has been a big increase in the number of cruising schools. The emergence of specialized cruising schools has been paralleled by the rapid development in self-education programmes for yachtsmen. Every winter, thousands of people attend evening classes in navigation and other cruising subjects, with a view to taking the exam for a qualification such as 'Yachtmaster', organized in Britain by the Royal Yachting Association, or similar qualifications in other countries.

The Yachtmaster scheme is graded. One can begin as a 'competent crew' and then work up to coastal skipper and finally offshore yachtmaster. Although a lot of the work can be done in the classroom, practical experience is required and most beginners would find that a season of evening classes followed by a week at a cruising school would be a sensible course of action.

The great benefit of going to a cruising school, even if you already own a boat, is that the instructor can take you through all sorts of tricky tasks that you need to be able to handle but that might not crop up in months or even years of sailing. Examples might be fog, in which you have to navigate without going on deck, and all sorts of minor emergencies such as going aground, losing the ends of halyards, dropping things over the side and so on. In this manner, trainees are given a thorough workout on a whole range of tasks and problems in a relatively short time.

It is also thoroughly worthwhile to be able to go through some of the major emergency situations, such as 'man overboard', with someone of greater experience than yourself at hand. The 'man overboard' situation can be thoroughly frightening, even when the 'man' is a dummy, and it is something that every yachtsman who aspires to sail offshore should rehearse. Many yachtsmen of long experience have gone back to school in order to prepare themselves for taking the Yachtmaster exam and have been very surprised to find how challenging it actually is.

Above: Nowadays, the majority of newcomers to sailing take advantage of a sailing school to get over the early stages. Here a group watches a demonstration of reefing on a Wayfarer dinghy, one of the most popular dinghies for teaching.

NAVIGATION

This book is not a navigation primer, there are plenty of these available, but what follows is a quick run through the main aspects. For obvious reasons, whenever a yacht goes offshore, there must be someone competent in navigation aboard. Modern navigational aids have made life very much easier but one cannot assume that these will be available at all times. Electrical systems have a way of breaking down on yachts and there are many other reasons why a 'navaid' may go out of service temporarily.

Quite apart from the safety aspect, many people find navigation an interesting and satisfying subject in its own right. Those who have never studied navigation often believe that it involves advanced maths whereas, in fact, only simple arithmetic is required, even in astro-navigation (see page 201). When a yacht makes a passage in which there are several changes of course, tidal streams to be allowed for, perhaps not very good visibility or rough weather and at the end of it all, the chosen landfall appears right ahead and just at the time planned, it is a moment of intense satisfaction to the navigator — a complex task has been carried through successfully and with a result that is not just academic.

Chartwork

Navigation covers a number of areas of study but the basic one is chartwork — the drawing out and calculation of courses. Here we learn, for instance, about the form of the earth and how it is represented on charts. How all the features are shown on charts; the heights, depths, shoals and dangers, marks, lights and beacons. How charts are corrected and kept up to date and which ones you need. Next, the basic geometry of ruling off courses is considered and this leads immediately to magnetic variation and deviation, which make it necessary to convert a true bearing first to a magnetic one and then to a compass bearing before it can be useful on board.

The compass itself has to be understood, and particularly the way it is adjusted and the things that can cause it to give an incorrect reading — such as the presence of metals nearby. In the days when the Yachtmaster qualification was a real 'ticket', issued by the

Above: *The navigator at her chart table. Although many electronic instruments are available to help the modern yacht navigator, it is still vital to possess the basic skills of chartwork.*

Board of Trade, one had to sit a two-hour written examination on magnetism and the mariner's compass. Thankfully, the modern exams emphasize the practical rather than the theoretical but the compass is still the most important instrument on board ship and it is still essential to know how it works. Next, comes use of the hand-bearing compass, an essential tool of the coastal navigator, enabling him to produce a 'fix' from bearings of the shore or seamarks.

Tide

It is not possible to set a course until tidal streams have been calculated and, similarly, it is not possible to enter a harbour or cross a sand-bank until the tidal height has been worked out. Incidentally, this is one area of navigation where the navigator still cannot get much help from clever instruments, unless prepared to carry around a full-sized personal computer. Tidal heights just have to be worked out from the tables and one can be certain that the Yachtmaster examiner will want to know the tidal height at a non-standard port, at mid-tide, part-way between springs and neaps.

Some people are lucky enough to sail in areas such as the Baltic or the Mediterranean, where the tidal rise and fall is so slight that it can be ignored. If the chart shows sufficient depth for your yacht, then you can sail there. For the rest of us, tides have to be taken seriously and if you sail in an area such as the Channel Islands — extremely seriously. It is first necessary to really understand what the chart is telling you.

After the hydrographic survey ship has done its vital work of measuring the depth of water at thousands of different points, these measurements are reduced to 'chart datum' before being printed. Charts are drawn as if the sea everywhere were at a fixed level, and on modern charts this corresponds closely to Lowest Astronomical Tide (LAT), which is the lowest level that the tide is predicted to fall to, leaving aside unpredictable influences such as barometric pressure or prolonged strong winds. The opposite end of the scale is Highest Astronomical Tide or HAT, and mid-way between the two is the half-tide line or Mean Sea Level.

Spring tides rise higher and sink lower in relation to the Mean Sea Level than neap tides, when the tidal oscillation is at its least. The tide tables give daily predictions for standard ports, followed by a long list of the differences which make it possible to convert the predictions so that they apply to any selected spot and time.

What the navigator wants to know is: when will there be sufficient water to cross a certain shoal? To find this, he must find the day's range for that particular place and the times of high and low water at that place for the day in question. He can then work out a table showing the height of tide above chart datum for each hour of the day, and this will give him the information that he needs for a safe passage.

It is not just the depth of water that is important to the navigator. He must equally be informed about the direction and strength of the tidal stream. Many people without navigational training get muddled by the terminology here. Tidal streams are the semi-diurnal movements of the sea caused by the rising and falling tides. Currents are water movements that are not caused by the tide and go on running in the same direction for long periods of time. The exception that proves the rule is the Gulf Stream, which is a *current*!

We must know about tidal streams in order to set a course, because it will influence the time taken to cover a certain distance and the heading that must be steered. The sea is like a moving carpet: if a yacht sets course directly for its destination it will end up off track by the amount the carpet has moved during the time taken for the passage. The navigator must calculate the angle at which to head off in order to counteract the tide and correct the estimate of the time that will be taken. He does this with what is called a 'vector diagram' on the chart though, nowadays, a calculator will do the same job without the need for putting pencil to paper.

The information comes from the chart itself, where details of the set and drift (angle and rate) of the tidal stream can be found, or from the tidal stream atlas which shows the same information in a graphic fashion. For yachting enthusiasts, the 'pocket' tidal stream atlas is one of the most vital tools of the trade. The slower the yacht, the more important the influence of the tidal stream.

Position finding

The navigator's most fundamental duty is to know the ship's position at any time. Nowadays, he has all sorts of gadgets to help him but the fundamental method is the gloomy-sounding 'Dead reckoning'. This would be better termed 'DED' reckoning, as the origin is thought to be 'deduced reckoning', and provided the navigator does his job no-one will end up dead. The DR position is derived purely from a record of the courses and distances sailed — simple geometry. To the DR position, the external influences such as tidal stream, current (if any) and leeway (the amount the yacht slips sideways through the water) are applied to find 'Estimated Position', which represents the navigator's best estimate of position.

The estimated position gradually loses accuracy as time passes, because the information that goes to make it up is not precise. Therefore, as often as possible, the navigator aims to obtain a 'fix'; that is, a definite indication of position. He obtains this from a number of sources: the only fix which can be regarded as totally reliable is one derived from bearings of three or more fixed objects — points of land or seamarks. One bearing gives a line of position, a second changes it into a point of position and a third, if it crosses at or near the intersection of the other two, confirms the accuracy of the fix.

Single lines of position can be obtained from: the distant flash of a light-house or buoy, a radio bearing or perhaps a change in the depth of water. The imaginative navigator draws in information from every available source and uses all of it to establish and confirm the accuracy of his position.

Astro-navigation

For the ocean navigator, there is no friendly beam from the lighthouse or flash from a channel buoy, and even the coastal radio beacons are soon out of range. Although, once again, modern electronics will come to his aid, the basic and still vital method of

***Below:** A 'Cardinal' navigation buoy. The colour and the two cones pointing upwards indicate that it lies to the north of the danger-point while the quick flashing light tells the same story in darkness.*

Above: Searching for a gap in the clouds in order to get a sextant altitude of the sun. Although old-fashioned, astro-navigation has the advantage of not relying on any external sources of information. Many people also find it very satisfying to be able to find the yacht's position using this traditional method.

navigating out of sight of land is 'astro'. Even many yachtsmen regard astro-navigation as a black art while those who have developed the skill know that it is not particularly difficult and enormously satisfying to master.

The basis of astro-navigation is that the position of the sun, planets and stars is known and can be found for any moment of time from the Nautical Almanac. The navigator 'observes' a selection of celestial bodies with a sextant and from this can derive the ship's position. The very ingenious way in which this is done was devised by the French, 19th-century navigator and scientist Marc St Hilaire.

Known as the 'Intercept method', it consists of first assuming a position for the ship (based on dead reckoning) and then working out what the altitude of the chosen celestial bodies would be if the ship were in that position at a particular moment in time. This is purely a paper calculation from the almanac and tables. The navigator then compares this theoretical result with his actual observations taken by sextant and the differences can be converted into distances towards or away from the estimated position. Two or, preferably, three observations will give lines of position that cross to give a fix.

The working out of sight results — 'sight reduction' as it is termed — used to be an arduous business involving a whole series of tables and calculation using log tables. Now, the paperwork has been made much easier by better laid-out almanacs and 'short method' tables. Most text-books suggest simple formats for the different types of sight which guide the navigator through a series of easy steps. Easiest of all, is sight reduction by calculator. It is now possible to obtain programmed calculators which contain all the almanac information (or which work it out from first principles) and only require the raw data in order to come up with an answer. The prudent navigator will, of course, be able to do the job with pencil and paper as well.

There are two special cases of astro-navigation which are so useful and simple that even the coastal navigator can make regular use of them. An observation of the Pole Star (Polaris) gives the ship's latitude without any calculation. An observation of the sun as it passes through its zenith also gives latitude, after only one small sum. There is also the easy and popular running fix produced by taking an altitude of the sun during the morning, a zenith distance at noon and a further altitude during the afternoon. The morning position line is moved forward by the distance the ships sailed between the time of observation and noon, and the afternoon one backwards correspondingly, so that all three lines cross to give a noon position. There's just one snag — you must have a clear sky.

Electronic aids

Although some yachtsmen take a traditional view and distrust anything that depends on 'trickery', modern electronic systems are so numerous and so useful that it is foolish to ignore them.

Depth Echo sounders were one of the first electronic aids and are still one of the most useful. Even the smallest boat can have a simple battery-powered sounder at very reasonable cost. Many additional features, such as sounders which make a paper trace of the bottom or present the information as a diagram on a display screen, or set off alarms when a certain depth is reached, are available but not strictly essential.

Radio Direction Finding D/F has also been around for many years and the equipment is reasonably priced. Beacons at various points on the coast (usually at lighthouses) or on lightships or buoys, emit radio signals including an identifying morse signature. By using a rotating 'loop' aerial, a bearing of the transmitting station can be found. The older type of D/F set, in which you waved a hand-held aerial around and attempted to read the bearing off a small compass, was only moderately accurate but sets which measure the bearing automatically give a better result. A relatively new development is the VHF radio lighthouse which makes it possible to find the bearing of the transmitter with just a basic receiving set and no directional aerial.

Hyperbolic Radio Position Fixing Systems The systems known as Decca in Europe and LORAN in the United States have really transformed the situation for the coastal navigator. In a highly ingenious way, the phase difference between signals from synchronized radio signals is measured by the receiver and used to give lines of position. Both systems have been available for many years but what has changed is the size and convenience of the receiving set — and the price. One used to need special charts overprinted with coloured lines radiating from the transmitting stations. Lane information from the receiver was then plotted on the chart to give a fix. Nowadays, all this is done internally by the set, which displays a latitude and longitude position directly. The accuracy is remarkable: better than 1/10th of a nautical mile under average conditions.

Just as useful as the position given by this type of navaid, is the ability to select and store a number of 'waypoints'. Selected by the navigator, these are points which might correspond to the position of buoys he wishes to round or points he wishes to reach. Once these are stored, the set can be asked to provide, at any time, the course and distance to any of the waypoints. In effect, the set 'knows' where it is and constantly recalculates the distance and bearing of the waypoint. A further very useful feature is the provision of a 'panic button', to be pressed in the event of having a man overboard. This creates a new waypoint the instant the button is pressed so that the yacht can be turned around and return to exactly the same spot.

Unfortunately, Decca and LORAN are different systems, although they do a similar job, so it is not possible to use the same set for both. The drawback that applies to either is that they are essentially coastal systems. Decca has a range of 300 to 400 miles by day and 200 to 300 at night. LORAN, which operates at a lower frequency, has a range of up to 1000 miles — after which accuracy becomes suspect. Both suffer from some forms of interference and corrections have to be applied for certain areas and times. The chains of stations are land-based so they do not help the ocean navigator.

SATNAV For the ocean yachtsman, satellite position fixing systems provide an answer, though not such a convenient one as Decca or LORAN. A bigger aerial, more power and a more expensive set are required to hook into the SATNAV system and for the time being, the accuracy is not so great. The satellites of the Transit series, the ones currently in use, are not constantly in view but pass overhead at intervals from 35 to 100 minutes, depending on latitude. Most sets go into DR mode between fixes but for this they have to be receiving information from a log and compass. Some sets are capable of combining the inputs from Decca and LORAN in addition to SATNAV but they are very expensive for the average yachtsman.

The present SATNAV system is due to be replaced by a new and much improved one named NAVSTAR GPS, which will provide a position accurate to within 100 metres at all times, anywhere on the earth's surface. Its introduction has been delayed by the space shuttle disaster, which caused a serious backlog of satellite launchings. When available, it is expected to be the complete answer to ocean navigation.

Satellites are being used increasingly by shipping for communication as well as position fixing and these facilities gradually filter down to the yachtsman. For instance, if you pick up your telephone at home you can ask for a call to a ship at sea anywhere in the world and your conversation will go via the INMARSAT system. The same is true of Telex messages and these facilities are theoretically available to anyone prepared to pay for them.

Other devices

Many yachtsmen are already using the NAVTEX system, which works like a one-way telex. Weather forecasts, navigational warnings, and other useful information is received on board and either printed on a paper tape or displayed on a small screen. The great value of the system is that it cuts out the

__Below:__ An up-to-date navigation table on an ocean racing yacht showing some of the enormous variety of electronic instruments that are nowadays considered essential. The strip of paper is emerging from the NAVTEX set, which receives broadcast information in a printed form.

risk of missing important messages, particularly weather forecasts. The set can be programmed to select the information you want to receive; for instance, if you are sailing in the English Channel, you do not need to know about icebergs.

A system which larger racing yachts find especially useful is Weatherfax. Weather maps are broadcast by the meteorological offices of various countries in a form that can be picked up by a special receiver and printed back into its original map form. A fully-detailed synoptic chart contains so much more information than can be dictated using the traditional type of broadcast weather forecast, that the high cost of the equipment is considered well worth while for long-distance races.

Distress beacons

Many yachts which cross oceans now carry Emergency Position Indicating Beacons (EPIRB). These small, battery operated automatic sets send out a distress signal that can be overheard by aircraft or by satellites, using the international aircraft distress frequencies of 121.5 and 243 MHz. Because of their altitude, aircraft can receive these signals at a much greater range than a station at sea-level. The COSPAS-SARSAT satellites monitor 121.5 and 400.025 Mhz distress frequencies but because of their position there can be a delay of up to 3 hours before the message gets to the ground.

Some major races have used the ARGOS satellite transponder system, which not only gives the position of each yacht fitted with a beacon several times per day but has an emergency signal as well. Unfortunately, this is a very expensive system which is not really within the means of the average yachtsman.

Radar

Because of the heavy power requirement, radar used to be restricted to motor yachts or large sailing yachts with generators. Recent developments have reduced the power requirement so much that radar is now practical for virtually any craft with an engine and an electrical system. The limiting factor is more in the aerial which has to be at a reasonable height above the water, because the signal is limited by the horizon in the same way as human vision. Sailing yachts heel over and motor yachts roll so that the radar beam may be pointing up into the sky or down into the sea. To overcome this, the radar engineers have to use a broad-beam transmitting aerial and this has neither the range nor the discrimination of the narrow-beam type used on ships.

Even so, radar is a marvellous aid and is especially reassuring when sailing in crowded waters. Sailing in fog is never a pleasant experience but a lot of risk is taken away by radar. Modern, software-based radars have many additional features such as clutter-suppression, small-echo enhancement, collision prediction and superimposition of charts on the radar 'picture' to keep yachtsmen well informed.

Radio

By far the commonest type of radio equipment carried by yachts is the VHF radio telephone. It is cheap, easy to install, simple to use and tremendously useful. It enables the yachtsman to speak to other yachts, ships, harbourmasters and marinas, yacht clubs, coastguards and coast radio stations. Via the latter, the yacht can be linked to the normal telephone system. Although often cluttered and frequently abused by thoughtless chatterboxes, the VHF system is a tremendous safety aid. Because of the enormous number of VHF sets in use, there is now a virtually unbroken chain of coast radio stations sited all around Europe, the USA and much of the Far East.

The drawback of VHF is its short range — around 25 miles for a sailing yacht with a masthead aerial. Nevertheless, this is quite sufficient to keep most yachtsmen in contact with the outside world for most of their sailing time. The relatively new cellular radio-telephone systems also work perfectly well aboard yachts, although many people go sailing to get away from the telephone. As the aerial is normally fitted to the set in the case of portables, its range is even less than marine VHF. Some yachtsmen dabble with Citizens Band radio but this cannot be taken seriously as a safety or communications system.

For longer range, up to 400 miles, the Medium Frequency service is available but not much used by yachtsmen since the changeover to Single Side-band propagation made the sets a lot more expensive. Most yachtsmen are either content to make do with VHF or go the whole hog with High Frequency (HF) equipment which offers world-wide telephony and telegraphy by using the skywave effect, which means that the signal is bounced off the ionosphere in order to reach beyond the visible horizon and ranges of around 6000 miles can be achieved. Although modern sets are very efficient they are quite bulky and require a hefty power supply in order to achieve the standard 400 watts PEP signal, so this type of radio is effectively limited to larger, world-girdling yachts.

Instruments

A great variety of performance instruments have been developed for sailing yachts — many of which are really only of interest to the racing yachtsman. Speed and distance run logs are of interest to all, however, as are wind-speed and direction. These can be linked up to micro-processors to form an automatic dead-reckoning computer.

The future for electronics aboard yachts seems to be limitless, with every kind of information from stock-market prices to bed-time stories being available via satellite link.

RULES OF THE WAVES

Right of way

Sandwiched between navigation and seamanship are the right of way rules which, in turn, embrace lights, shapes and sounds. The International Regulations for Preventing Collisions at Sea (IRPCAS) are essential knowledge for all offshore yachtsmen, even if they do not have to learn them by heart as ship's officers must. The sailing and steering rules, which say which vessel gives way whenever there is a risk of collision, are only one part of these rules.

The other vital section deals with the navigation lights that every vessel has to show at night and the shapes that are shown by day. These are best demonstrated by the diagrams on pages 206/7; suffice to say here that the purpose of a ship's navigation lights are twofold: to show what kind of vessel it is and to indicate in which direction it is heading. The whole essence of the rule is that whether by day or by night, the competent mariner must be able to say immediately what his obligations are in regard to any other vessel in sight: whether to stand on, give way or take some other action. All the rules are quite specific and there can never be any ambiguity.

Many newcomers to sailing have vaguely formed ideas about the right of way rules, including oversimplifications such as 'power gives way to sail'. They should realize, however, that there are many exceptions and that it is *dangerous* to sail around without a proper knowledge of the rules.

Lights and buoys

Lighthouses date back to antiquity, and are the oldest of all aids to mariners. The simple burning beacon does not provide sufficient information, however, for it begs the question 'Which beacon is it?' In the 19th century, rotating lights were invented which send out an identifying signal. These were followed by buoys with flashing lights which also signal their identity. Until very recently, these visible marks were the most important source of pilotage information, but currently there is pressure from lighthouse authorities to reduce the coverage because maintaining lights and buoys is so expensive. The idea is that electronic navigation is so accurate and universal that it is possible to reduce the reliance on visible signals. This development is viewed with some concern both by professional mariners and yachtsmen and it looks as if it could form the basis of a long-running battle in the future.

Various countries used to have different buoyage systems — the most glaring example being totally different conventions on the English and French coasts. In recent years, the IALA System 'A' has been adopted by almost all maritime nations except those in the Far East. The basis of this is that cardinal buoys have double cone topmarks that indicate in which direction the danger lies. A buoy surmounted by two cones pointing upwards indicate that the danger lies to the south of it. Two cones pointing downwards indicate that the danger lies to the north.

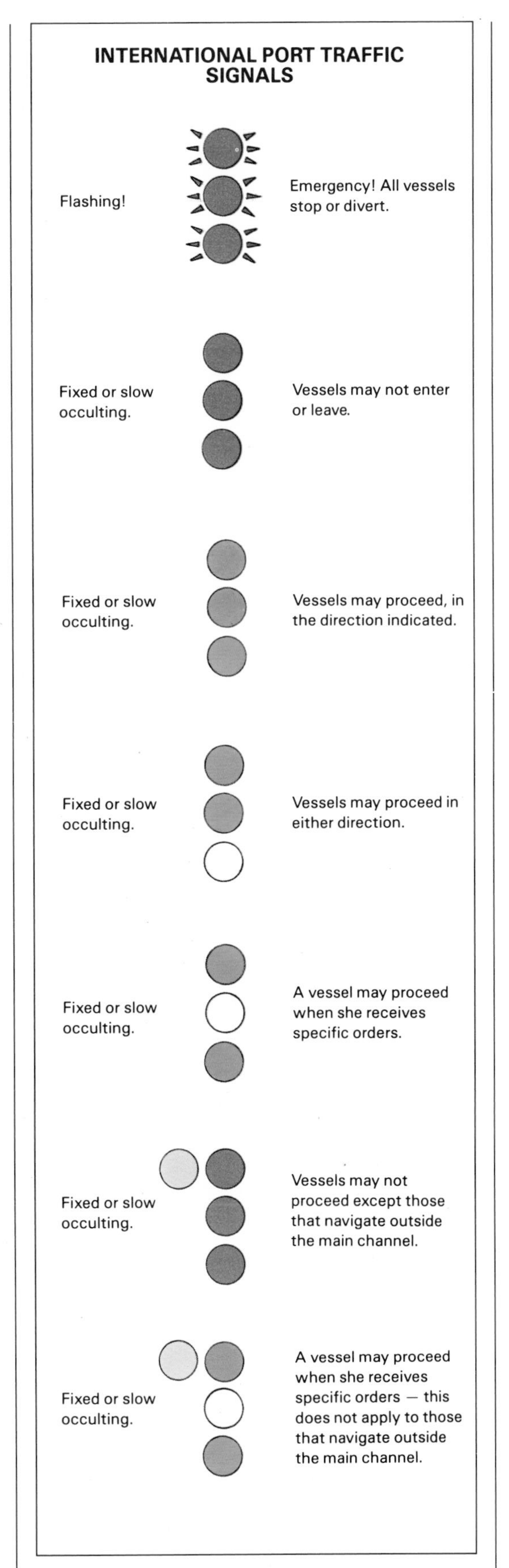

ARCS AND RANGES FOR NAVIGATION LIGHTS ON YACHTS

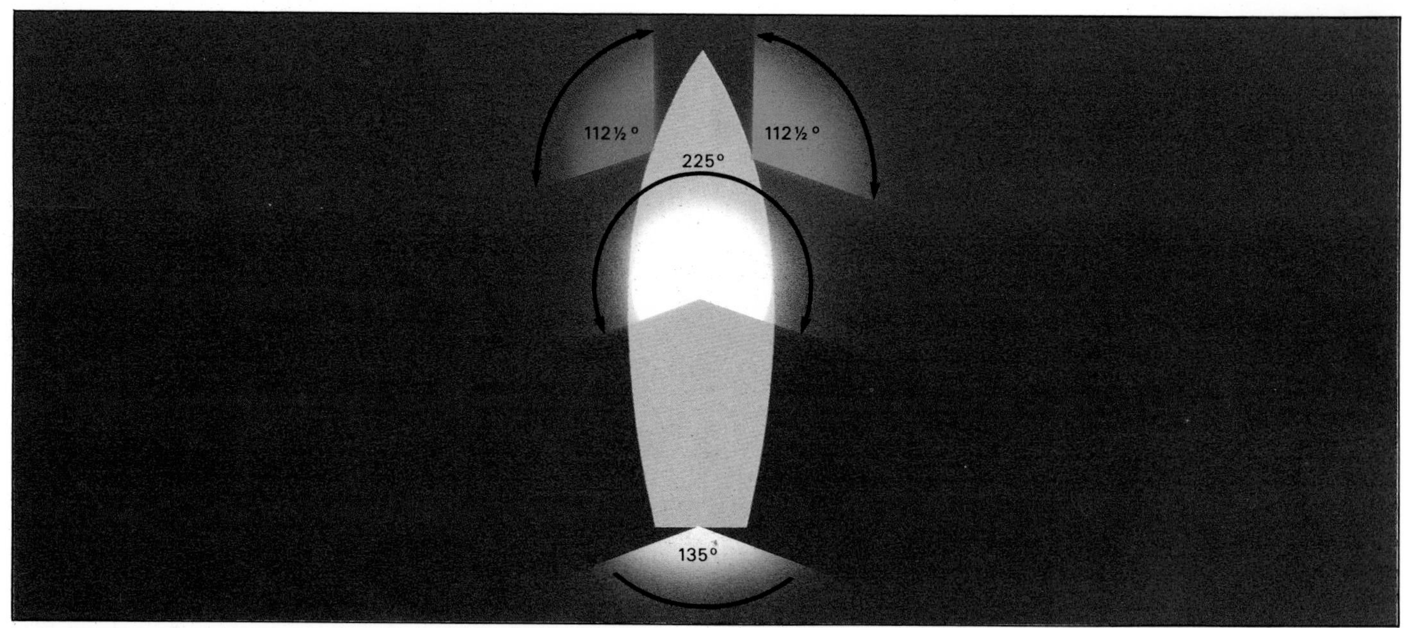

Yachts 12–50m overall, range 2 miles; under 12m, 1 mile. Port and starboard sidelights can be combined in a single bi-coloured lantern in yachts under 20m. Masthead light and sternlight may be combined in a single all-round white light in yachts under 12m overall. White masthead light (vessel under power): yachts 20–50m overall, 5 miles; 12–20m, 3 miles; under 12m, 2 miles.

LIGHTS FOR POWER-DRIVEN VESSELS UNDER WAY OR SAILING YACHTS, USING THEIR ENGINE

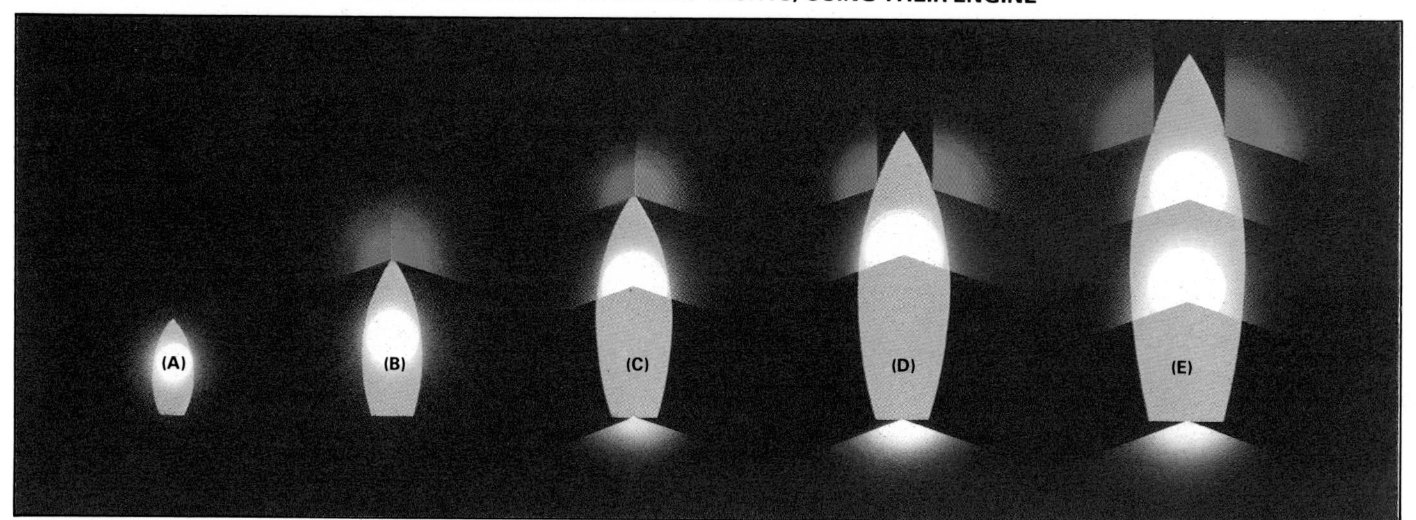

(A) Small boat of less than 7m and less than 7 knots.

(B) Yacht of less than 12m (using all-round white masthead light).

(C) Yacht of under 20m (using combined sidelights).

(D) Yacht over 20m.

(E) Yacht over 50m (aft masthead light higher).

LIGHTS FOR SAILING YACHTS UNDER WAY (NOT USING ENGINE)

If *not* using tri-colour masthead light, a sailing yacht *may* use two all-round lights near masthead: red over green, in addition to other lights.

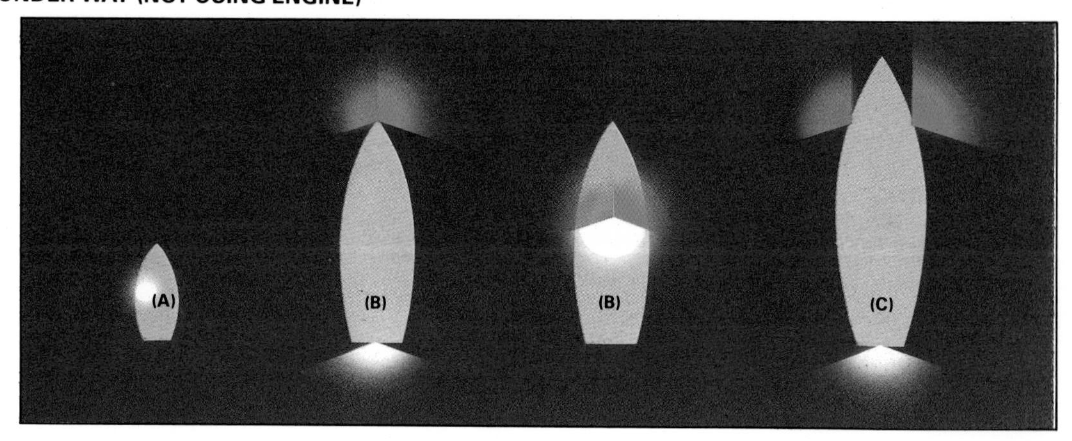

(A) Dinghy under 7m overall (should show sidelights if possible).

(B) Under 20m. *Either* combined sidelights plus sternlight *or* all-round tri-colour.

(C) Over 20m. Separate sidelights and sternlight.

IMPORTANT LIGHTS AND SHAPES

Vessel at anchor: an all-round white light. If over 50m, another white light aft and lower.

At anchor by day: a black ball forward.

Not under command: 2 all-round red lights plus normal lights if under way.

Not under command by day: 2 black balls forward.

Sailing vessel using engine by day: a cone, point down, forward.

'I have divers down': International code flag 'A'.

Vessel aground: not under command lights plus anchor light.

Aground by day: 3 black balls in a vertical line.

Tug and tow: tug shows normal steaming lights plus 2 white all-round lights if tow is less than 200m or 3 if more. Tow shows sidelights plus sternlight.

Tug and tow over 200m, by day: black diamonds on both vessels.

Vessel fishing: all-round red over white plus steaming lights.

Fishing or trawling by day: 2 cones, points together or basket if vessel is under 20m.

Trawling: all-round green over white plus all-round white aft, plus normal steaming lights.

Pilot boat: all-round white over red plus normal lights for the vessel.

Vessel restricted in manoeuvring ability: all-round red, white, red plus normal lights.

Vessel restricted in manoeuvring ability by day: ball, diamond, ball in vertical line.

Dredger: all-round red, white, red plus two reds on obstructed side and two greens on clear side.

Vessel constrained by draught: 3 all-round red lights by night, plus normal lights, a cylinder by day.

NAVIGATION MARKS AND LIGHTS

LATERAL MARKS
Used to mark the limits of a channel or river.

If lit, red, any rhythm.

If lit, green, any rhythm.

Direction of buoyage.

CARDINAL MARKS
Used to show in which direction a danger lies. Buoys, always spars or pillars; lights, always quick flashing white.

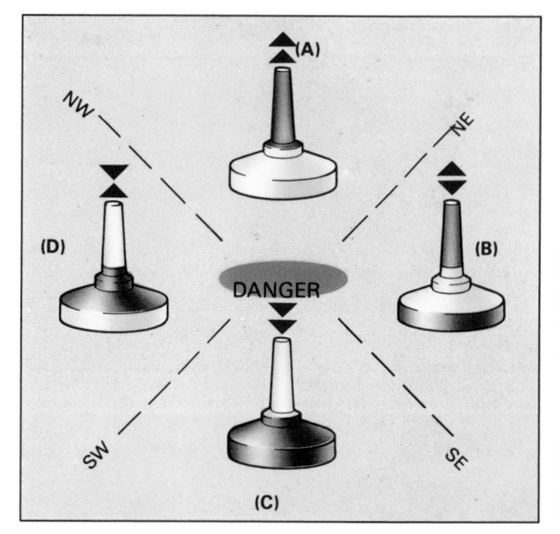

(A) V Qk Fl or Qk Fl.
(B) V Qk Fl (3) every 5 sec or Qk Fl (3) every 10 sec.
(C) V Qk Fl (6) every 10 sec or Qk Fl (6)+LF every 15 sec.
(D) V Qk Fl (9) every 10 sec or Qk Fl (9) every 15 sec.

ISOLATED DANGER
SAFE WATER
SPECIAL MARKS

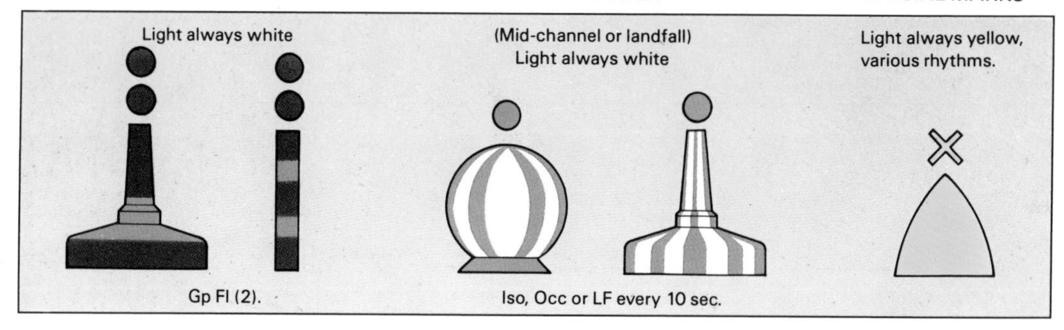

These cardinal buoys have specific colours and coded flashing lights which tell the same story. This type of buoyage is used mainly for shoals or sand-banks which have navigable water all round them. Isolated dangers, such as a single rock, are shown by a pillar buoy with two balls on top.

The sides of a channel are shown by lateral marks which are red cans or spars to port and green cones or spars to starboard. In rivers, the sense is always upstream but in large channels, such as the English Channel, the direction of buoyage is taken as being clockwise around the whole of Europe. There are also safe water and special marks with particular shapes and topmarks.

Books and charts

Every seagoing vessel needs a small library. The charts are the most important feature and as they are so expensive, need to be kept up to date from *Notices to Mariners*. Tide tables, a tidal stream atlas, lists of lights and pilotage information can be obtained separately but most yachtsmen rely on one of the nautical almanacs which contain all this and much other information.

Chandlery shops sell some very fancy log-books but a school exercise book is just as useful, especially the kind that has graph paper on one side of each page. This can be called a deck log and is used for noting courses, distances, times, tides and all the other hour-by-hour information. You can copy the relevant parts out into a smart book when you are not bucking into a force six, with spray dribbling on to the chart table.

Nearly everyone likes to have on board one or two guide books or 'pilots' giving details of the areas that they might visit. These can, of course, be extremely valuable sources of general information but should not be used for navigational purposes as things such as lights and sandbanks do change. This is why up-to-date charts and specialist annual publications are essential; guide books cannot be expected to — and indeed do not — provide this sort of service.

SEAMANSHIP

This wonderfully broad title covers everything from fancy ropework to first aid and it is not the intention to do more than summarize the essentials here. The essence of seamanship is the safe and efficient handling of a ship at sea.

Ropework

Ropes and lines, though made of plastics rather than natural fibres, are just as important today as ever. No sail can be hoisted without correct use of a halyard on a winch and neither can it be belayed without correct use of a cleat or rope clamp. The competent crew must know the appropriate bends and hitches for each use of a line.

Anchor warps need to be stretchy and nylon rope is often used for this reason. Many yachts manage without a full-length anchor chain, which is both heavy and expensive, but rely on a short length of chain plus a nylon warp. This answers for most situations although considerably greater scope is needed than with chain alone.

Nylon warp chafes easily and needs to be joined to the chain with a hard eye and shackle. It may also need protection at the point where it comes through the bow fairlead.

Sheets and halyards are almost always of the braided rope variety and chemically pre-stretched so that they do not stretch in use. Racing yachts may use special low-stretch lines made of Kevlar or wire to cut down stretch. It is very important for newcomers to sailing to be shown the correct way to put a line on to a winch, with at least three turns, as there is a real risk of getting hurt if it is not done properly. The strain in sheets and halyards can be very great and potentially dangerous. A line must always be put on to a winch in such a way that it can be safely eased or 'surged' under strain, by holding on to the free end with one hand and helping the turns to slip round the drum of the winch with the other.

A line must never be cleated unless it can be safely eased under full strain. With a traditional cleat this means bringing the line to the 'open' side of the cleat and taking a full turn before beginning any locking turns. Many modern yachts, especially racing yachts, use rope clamps or clutches rather than cleats. These tend to wear out lines at one particular point and need to be watched carefully. There is also a risk of letting a line go abruptly if the operation of the clutch is not fully understood.

Strong, abrasion-resistant lines are needed for warps, and the traditional three-stranded construction is often preferred for the ease of splicing. The majority of yachts these days are kept at marina berths where the warps may be in use for months at a time. In this case, it is wise to make up special lines which are protected with short lengths of plastic hose or water-piping at the points where chafe may occur.

Every yacht must carry sufficient warp to lie alongside a quayside where she will rise and fall with the tide. This is correctly done with three pairs of lines. The bow and stern lines, which stop the boat moving away from the wall must be taken well beyond the length of the yacht and, if she is to be left unattended for any length of time, be about three times the tidal range in length. Springs are the lines which stop the boat moving ahead or astern and are taken from the bow of the boat to a point ashore roughly opposite the stern and vice-versa. They do not need to be quite as long as the bow and stern lines but may need adjustment as the boat rises and falls with the tide. If lying alongside a floating pontoon, short 'breast' lines from bow and stern are used to keep the boat close alongside, while the springs stop it moving ahead or astern.

__Below:__ '. . . Round the tree and down the rabbit-hole'. The versatile bowline is one of the most useful knots aboard a yacht. Here, the sheets are being bent to the clew of a headsail with bowlines.

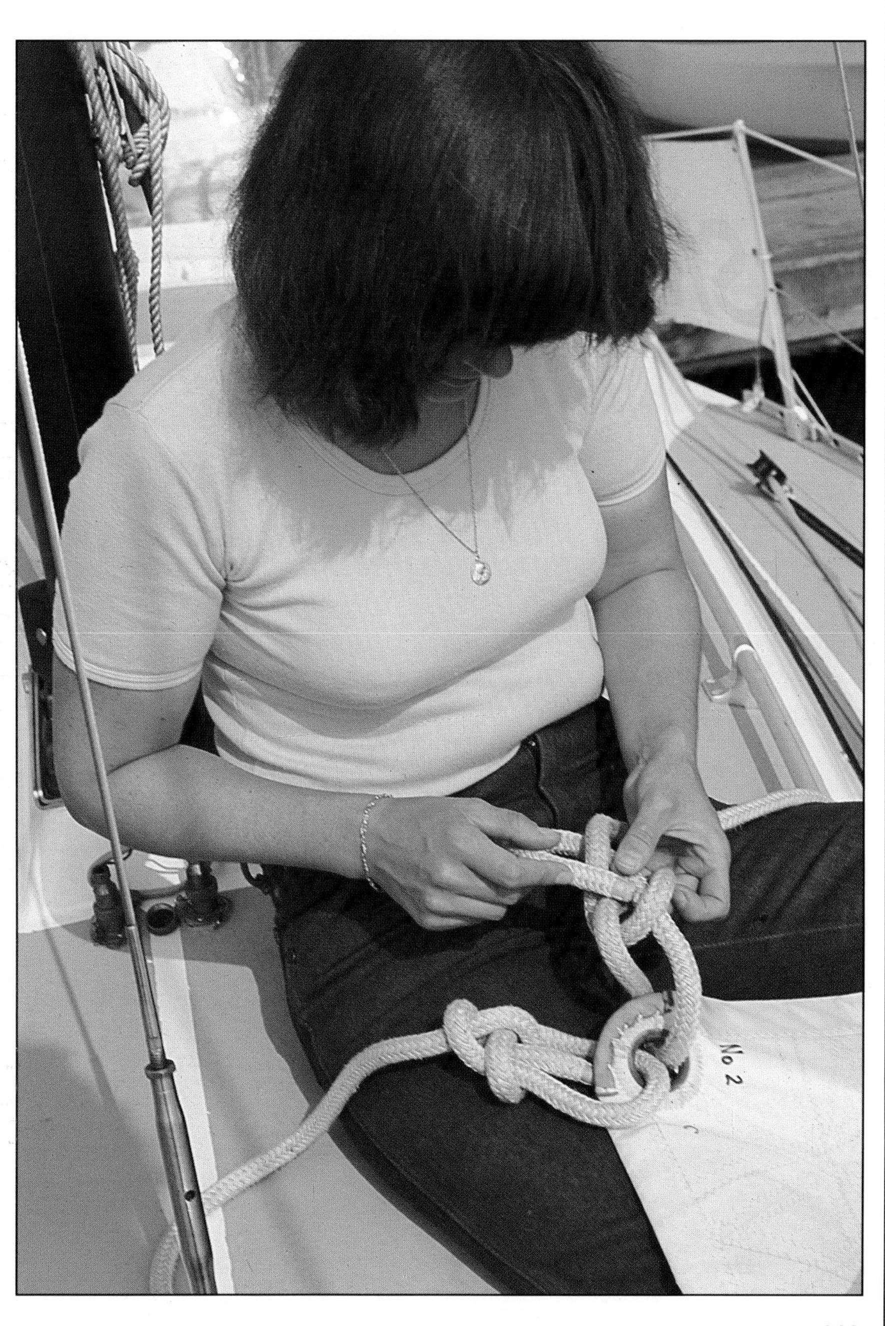

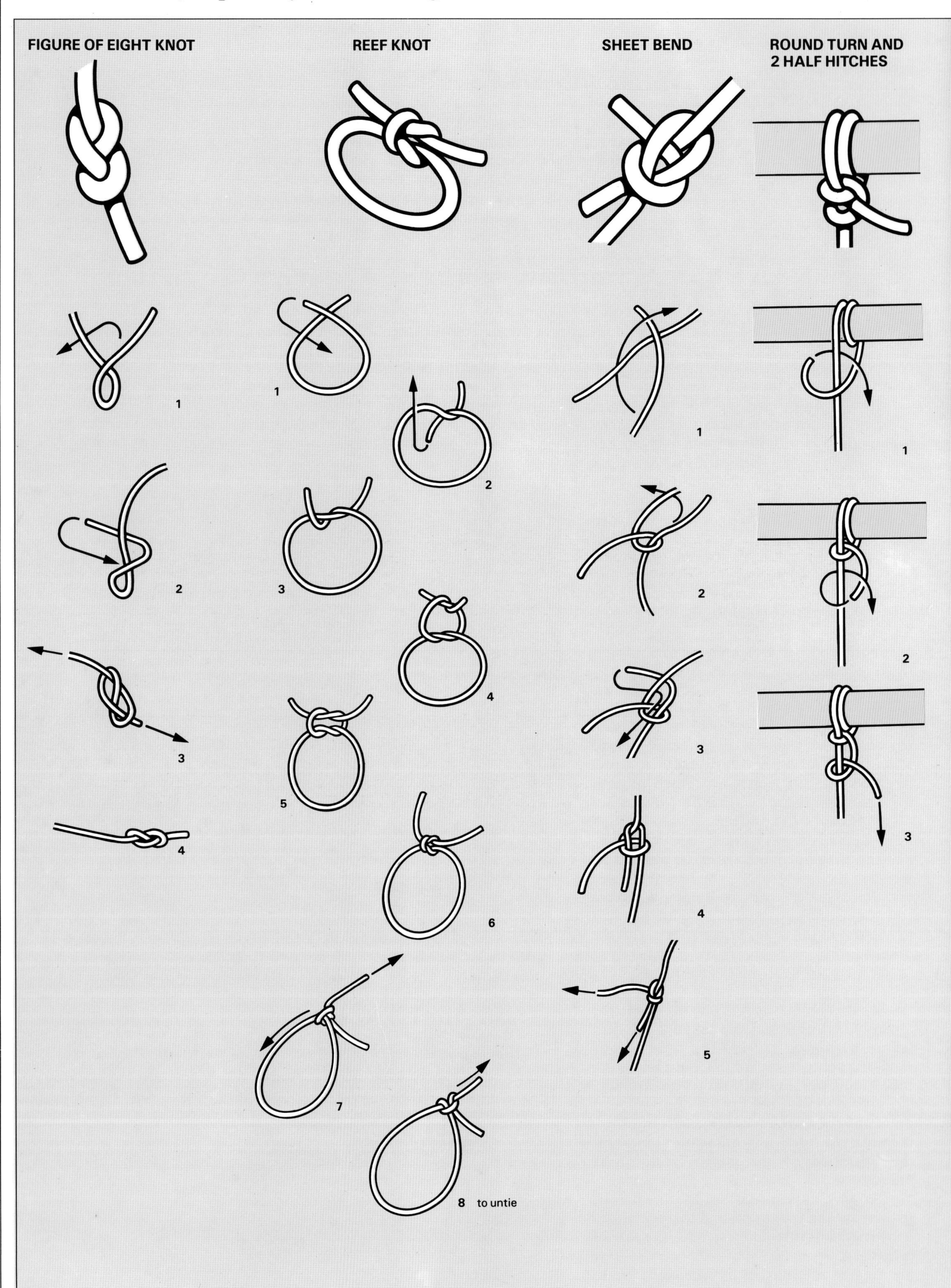
FIGURE OF EIGHT KNOT
REEF KNOT
SHEET BEND
ROUND TURN AND
2 HALF HITCHES
1
2
3
4
5
6
7
8 to untie

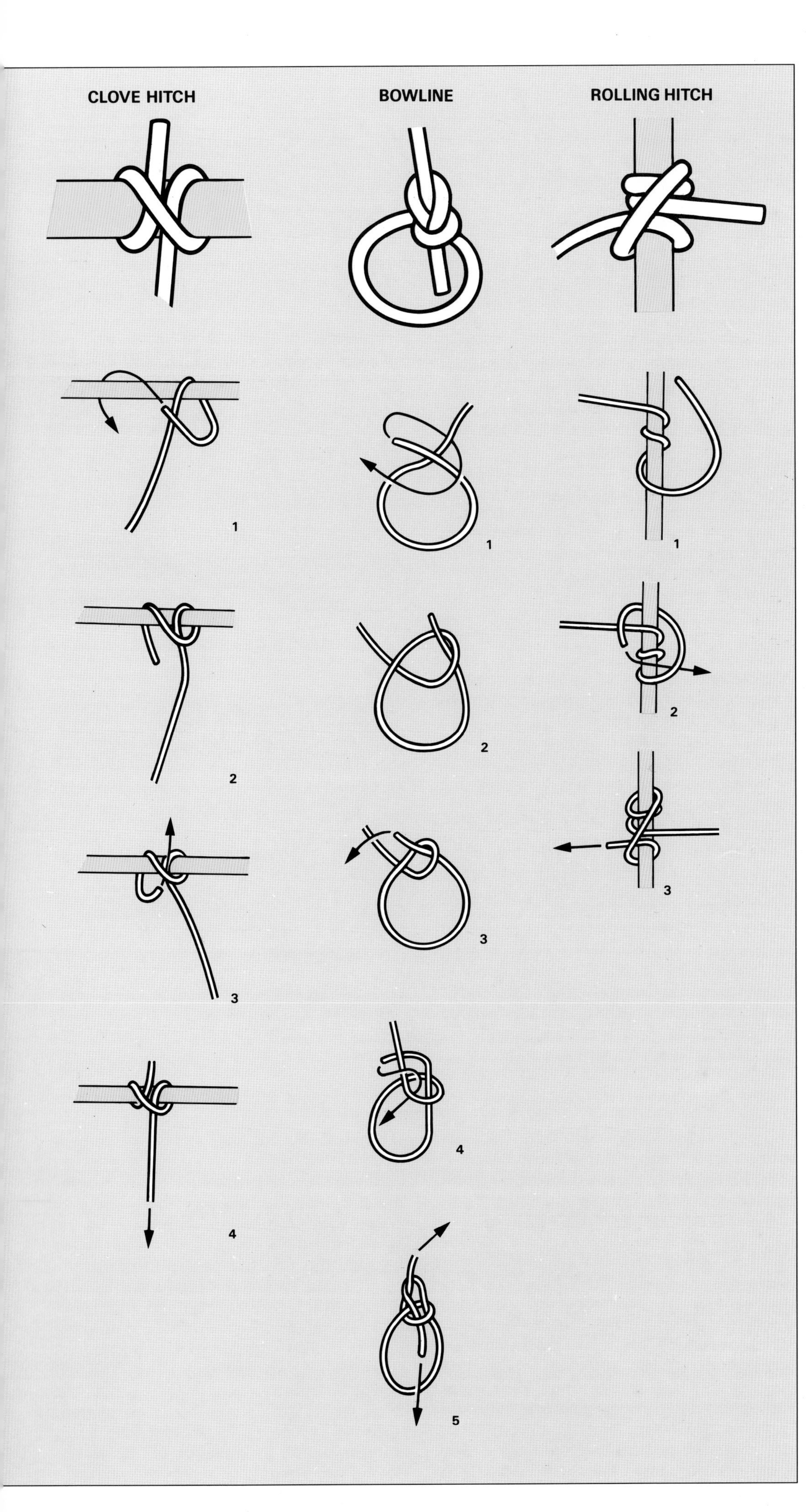

Figure of eight: *Used to stop a rope, particularly a sheet, from running away through a block or fairlead. Unlike a simple thumb-knot, the figure of eight does not jam solid after it has been under pressure. Leave a short 'tail'; otherwise the knot tends to undo itself.*

Reef knot: *One of the most useful knots, with dozens of uses where two ends of the same size line are used. Steps 6–8 show how it can be undone by pulling one end firmly towards the knot.*

Sheet bend: *Used to join two lines and safe to use even if they are of different thicknesses. Pull firmly into place (step 5) to secure from slipping under load.*

Round turn and two half hitches: *Often used to secure fenders to the rail, a painter to a ring or nearly any kind of line to a solid fitting. Do not use on a line that has to be eased under load, as the inner turn will tend to jam tightly until the strain is eased.*

Clove hitch: *A quick and easy way of making a loop that tightens. Not a secure hitch if the thing it is tied to is free to rotate.*

Bowline: *A strong, secure way of making a loop in the end of a rope. Used for mooring lines, attaching sheets to sails and many other applications. Loosen by bending the knot in half.*

Rolling hitch: *A knot which, if tied correctly, will not slide along the thing it is tied to; the* only *way of attaching a line to another that is already under strain.*

When casting off or coming alongside, members of the crew should be given their orders and places in advance and the helmsman should have a clear idea what he is going to do. Nothing is worse than a yacht coming alongside in a disorderly panic with a lot of shouting and running about. A well-drilled crew should do it in silence.

Sailors of old knew dozens of knots but the modern yachtsmen needs about eight, with some variations.

The figure of eight is a stopper-knot to avoid losing the end of a line through a fairlead.

The reef knot has many uses and is formed from two half-hitches made in opposite directions. If the second hitch is formed the wrong way it makes a granny-knot which slips.

A sheet-bend is normally used to join two lines of different thickness.

The bowline is one of the most useful knots on board and forms a secure loop in the end of a line. Among its many uses is attaching sheets to a headsail. Like all properly-tied knots, it is completely secure but can be readily untied once the strain is taken off.

A rolling hitch is particularly useful for attaching a line to a vertical object such as a mast, a shroud or another tight line. If tied correctly it will not slide down.

A clove hitch is the correct way to attach a burgee to its halyard and it can also be used to attach a mooring line to a bollard, though an extra locking hitch is needed to make it permanent.

A round turn and two half hitches is the correct way to fix a line to a solid object such as a rail or spar. A variation of it is the **fisherman's bend**, which is used for attaching a line to an anchor. The first half hitch is tucked under the round turn to stop the knot from seizing up tightly under strain.

A becket hitch, similar to a sheet bend, is used to fix a line to an eye or becket.

In addition to these, the knotsman should be able to make a neat whipping on the end of a rope to stop it unravelling, instead of relying on burning it — which is only suitable for very small lines. An eye-splice in three-stranded rope is both easy and essential though end-splices are not much used today. Plaited and sheathed ropes can also be spliced and the various rope manufacturers issue instruction cards appropriate to each type of rope. In the case of sheathed rope it is helpful to have a special tool like a giant needle to pull pieces of the core along inside the sheath.

Sea clothing

When you see what awful clothing mariners of a century ago had to put up with, one wonders how they could ever bear to go to sea in bad weather. Today we are spoiled by manufacturers who produce ranges of clothing suitable for everything from windsurfing to sailing around the world. The aim is to be dry, warm and comfortable but this is amazingly difficult to achieve. For windsurfing or dinghy sailing, it is possible to wear a wet-suit which keeps you warm even though wet, or a dry-suit which is completely waterproof, but neither of these solutions is practical for cruising.

If you dress up in a completely waterproof 'diving suit' you will eventually become soaked with perspiration condensing on the inside. The body gives off perspiration all the time and this needs to pass out through the clothing and evaporate. This is particularly difficult to achieve with seagoing clothing but for cruising the most satisfactory arrangement is to have separate jacket and trousers with a big overlap between the two. This will keep all but the most determined wave out but permits a certain amount of air circulation, especially when movement of the arms 'pumps' the air in and out of the jacket. Having two separate garments also makes it

EYE-SPLICE IN THREE-STRANDED ROPE

1 Unravel strands, then tie to stop unravelling further. Tuck any two adjacent strands under 2 strands of standing part.

2 Turn over. Tuck remaining strand.

3 Turn over again. Tuck first 2 strands a second time.

4 Turn over. Tuck remaining strand a second time, repeat as 3, 4 for third tuck.

5 Trim ends of strands. Roll and pull the splice to make it settle down.

easier to go to the toilet — an activity which can be quite difficult enough on a small yacht in rough weather.

Sea clothing must be very tough to resist the inevitable bumps and bangs from gear, and abrasion from the non-slip deck surface. For this reason, extra patches on the seat and knees are essential. All seams must be covered with waterproof tape and glue on the inside so that water cannot get in through the stitching holes. A lining is very important to reduce condensation. The problem with sea clothing is that the air may be very warm and steamy on the inside but ice-cold on the outside, and this encourages condensation. Therefore, a lining to keep out the cold, plus warm but absorbent underlayers are required.

A prime piece of safety equipment that should be worn whenever on deck, except in very gentle conditions, is the safety harness. As these are tricky to put on correctly over oilskins, many manufacturers make jackets with built-in lifelines. This is ideal, as it is virtually impossible to forget to put the harness on. Some clothing has a built-in life-jacket as well but this makes for a complicated, heavy and over-hot garment some of the time. It is better to regard a life-jacket as a separate garment.

Feet need to be kept warm and dry and must not slip on wet decks. This is where the yachtsman's famous 'yellow wellies' come in! A full set of offshore oilskins and boots is an expensive investment but it is a wonderful feeling to be able to get kitted up and go on deck knowing that you can take whatever the sea can throw at you and remain quite happy and comfortable.

Living on board

This is something that takes time to master and is really the essence of cruising. Day trips lead to weekend trips which, in turn, prepare one for more ambitious cruises, with a great deal of learning in between. Every aspect of life needs fresh attention. Simple acts such as

__Below:__ Modern waterproof clothing can be colourful and stylish as well as practical. The garments shown here are made from water-proofed nylon with taped and doped seams to stop water creeping in through the stitching. A lining is virtually essential on waterproofs that are going to be used for any length of time, in order to prevent condensation forming on the inside.

cooking, washing, changing, eating and drinking all need extra care. The key is an almost obsessive neatness and a great deal of consideration for others. It is depressing to come off watch after an arduous four hours only to find the cabin full of other people's gear strewn around, wet oilskins underfoot and unwashed washing-up swilling around in the sink.

The only solution to living at close quarters on board a small yacht is to leave everything as you would wish to find it — always. Keep yourself and your gear tidy. Never leave chores hoping that someone else will do them. Be ready on time to take over a watch, or better still a few minutes early, so you can get used to the feel of the yacht before taking the helm. Be cheerful, calm and supportive to other members of the crew.

This chapter so far should give the idea that cruising takes time to get into and a lot of knowledge needs to be absorbed. But beginners should take comfort in the fact that the learning can be fun too, and the rewards are unsurpassed. Picture yourself at the helm of a yacht broad-reaching easily over a gentle swell with a nice force 4 on the quarter. It is quiet on board, with the swish of the bow-wave the only sound as the dawn lightens the eastern horizon. Away to the west, the friendly flash of a distant lighthouse fades in the growing light. The yacht feels alive under your hand and as you turn to scan the horizon the first glowing sliver of sun appears. You feel completely at one with the world around you and at the same time humbled, knowing that your boat is no more than a dot on the wide ocean. Money cannot buy such moments! But before you set sail, there are two more vitally important matters to consider — your health and safety.

Above: *The interior of a small yacht has to combine many functions, such as sleeping, cooking and navigating, in the same small space. The temptation in modern production yachts is to cram in too many bunks at the expense of proper stowage for all the stores and personal gear needed for cruising.*

Right: *Sleeping aboard is a wonderful adventure for children but a forward vee-berth such as this one can really only be used in harbour. Under way in a choppy sea, the children would be thrown around like peas in a whistle while berths further aft would be relatively comfortable.*

HEALTH AT SEA

Health is a subject that must always be taken seriously when cruising, if only because help may not be readily at hand. In fact, the sea is a healthy place because the everyday bugs and germs that can make our lives a misery ashore are not found on the ocean. To balance this, there is an above-average risk of injury on board a yacht, if the crew are not vigilant.

Anyone taking up cruising seriously would be well advised to take a first-aid course and it goes without saying that every yacht should carry a first-aid kit, including a good manual. And the latter should be read through and be familiar to you before any accident can happen. Don't wait for an emergency before opening it up. Many people, especially motorists, seem to regard the possession of a first-aid kit as an amulet that will somehow ward off danger. Most don't even know what is in the neat little plastic box that they carry in the car. What do they think they are going to do at the scene of a major road accident with sticking plaster and a bottle of antiseptic? The answer in most cases is that they will run around like headless chickens waiting for an ambulance to arrive.

This will not do if you are faced with a serious accident when you are at sea. Bleeding will have to be stopped, broken limbs immobilized, burns dressed. Naturally, you would seek help as soon as possible following an accident but the immediate emergency has to be dealt with on board, by the crew. This is why there is no substitute for first-aid training. Ask yourself what you would do if faced with serious bleeding. Do you know the pressure-points for the various parts of the body? You can find these in your first-aid book, but having them demonstrated by a qualified instructor is very much better.

The type of first-aid kit that you can buy in a chemist's shop is adequate for minor accidents but does not contain any prescription items. This might be considered adequate for coastal and short-hop cruising but if you plan to be on board for any length of time you will have to enlist the aid of your friendly general practitioner in order to obtain prescription items. If you belong to a sailing club, a doctor member who may well have made up his own list of items might be prepared to sign one for you.

Prescribed drugs are not the only thing that you will need to buy in addition to the standard first-aid kit. You must be sure to have sufficient large dressings to cope with a serious wound and large, sterile burn dressings. In the case of a bad accident on board, the advice you receive is likely to be 'Get the patient into a bunk, keep him warm, give pain-killers and head for harbour.' This might require you to give an injection (though only a doctor is allowed to give morphine). So ask your doctor what injections you are allowed to give (not the same in every country) and, if necessary, get instruction in how they are given.

If you are on a long voyage where it is simply not possible to wait for medical attention and you get something like a jagged splinter or fish-hook stuck into your flesh, it will have to be cut out, so one or two disposable scalpels are required. A wound may need to be stitched and for this, packets of sutures already threaded on to needles is the answer. Steri-strips can be used to close a small wound but not a major one, where copious bleeding or sweating will prevent them from sticking.

When faced by a medical emergency — if your yacht is equipped with a radio-telephone — call the nearest Coast Radio Station using the 'Pan Medico' procedure. A doctor will offer advice, assess the situation and decide whether to call the emergency services. However, even in coastal waters this may take some time, especially if the weather is bad or the yacht's position is not known with complete accuracy. On an ocean passage, prompt assistance *cannot* be relied upon, so a high degree of self-reliance is essential.

DANGERS ON BOARD

The purpose of this section is not to act as a first-aid manual but to point out some of the dangers that are particularly prevalent afloat, so that you are forewarned and can prepare yourself sensibly for any conceivable emergency.

Falls and injuries

The deck of a yacht is liberally provided with items that seem destined to trip you over and propel you into other hard, projecting fittings, so here are some do's and don'ts for your protection. Although it may seem romantic, it is *not* a good idea to walk on deck in bare feet, except in the calmest weather. Cruising yachts should be built with plenty of hand-holds (not all are) and you should train yourself to walk on deck either constantly touching a holding-point or ready to grab one. Never step on sails. They are slippery, they may hide a sharp fitting and anyway it is bad for them! Ropes roll when you step on them. Some have to be on deck but it helps enormously to make it a rule to always coil off and tidy any line that is not actually in use.

Be aware which lines are under load — or may be at any minute. Very nasty accidents have been caused by stepping on a loose line that turns out to be the sheet of a spinnaker that has temporarily collapsed. When the sail suddenly fills, the line flies up and becomes bar taught in an instant. Never stand or sit in a bight of rope under load — the classic example is the vee formed in a genoa sheet between its turning block and the winch.

Opposite: *Two crewmen working at the mast of the round-the-world yacht* Drum *show just how dangerous an environment a yacht can be in bad weather. The violent motion, angle of heel, constant spray and low temperatures all increase the risk of accident and make it more difficult to cope with, when one occurs.*

Left: *Mike Birch, one of the world's leading single-handed yachtsmen, shows the safe way to use a bosun's chair. Notice the pockets on either side of the seat to hold small items and the fact that the heavy spanner is secured by its own line so that it cannot fall on to someone on deck.*

When something goes wrong on board such as a slipping halyard, a runaway anchor chain or a sheet slipping on a winch, never try to stop it with your hand. The result is liable to be rope-burnt hands or worse. It is preferable to lose the anchor chain than your fingers. Wires need particular care because they so often conceal broken strands that will lacerate your hands. So don't let wire run through your hands ever and make it a rule to wear appropriate leather gloves available from chandlery shops.

Falls are always a risk because of the boat's motion. People fall down hatches and companionways, across cockpits and out of bunks. Apart from the obvious solution of keeping a good hand-hold and minding your step, it helps a lot to be properly dressed. The fall across the cockpit that would be extremely painful to someone wearing light clothing would hardly bother the same person wearing pile underclothes, waterproofs and a life-jacket.

The swinging boom is such an obvious danger you would think everyone would be aware of it yet every year people get hit on the head by booms, mostly because they were not given warning. This is why it is absolutely mandatory for the helmsman to give the warning 'Ready about' before tacking and 'Stand by to gybe' before gybeing. The real danger is the inadvertent gybe, and to prevent this a foreguy should always be used when running dead downwind in a seaway. Better still, don't run dead downwind — a series of broad reaches is both faster and more comfortable anyway.

When a yacht is coming alongside, never try to stop it with hand or foot. If it looks as if there is going to be a crash — hold a fender in the gap but not part of your anatomy. When coming alongside a yacht or quay in a dinghy, do not hold on to the side, because if you do you will get your fingers crushed.

Going aloft is a particular danger. There comes a time on every yacht when a trip up the mast is called for, if only to check that all is well, but it is amazing how casual many yachtsmen are about using a bosun's chair. Note that no professional rigger will go aloft on a snap-shackle of the kind usually used for headsail or spinnaker halyards. These can open, so a screw-in shackle should be used. When a man goes aloft, another should be on deck constantly watching him, not only to make sure no-one helpfully casts off the halyard that is holding the man aloft but also to ensure others do not stand directly below, where they may be on the receiving end of falling tools.

Above: The galley is a danger-point on any yacht because of the obvious risks of working with hot things on an unsteady platform. Good design and the careful siting of items such as a fire-extinguisher or fire-blanket can cut down the risks considerably.

Burns and scalds

Cooking on board is inherently risky and extra care is always needed. On short coastal passages or even cross-channel ones, most yachtsmen contrive not to do any 'real' cooking because of the obvious difficulties but even on short trips there are dangers which can be minimized by forethought. It should go without saying that the cooker on a yacht should be gimballed and should have a fiddle rail around it to stop pans from falling off. Just as important, is a really strong 'crash bar' around the galley area to stop the cook lurching on to a hot cooker. Many authorities recommend a broad belt which the cook can lean on when the galley is on the high side, but others feel this prevents them from dodging out of the way when things start to fly around, as they can do.

Hot water is the greatest danger and as you cannot use an electric kettle on a yacht, water has to be heated in a kettle on the cooker. Life can be made much easier by the provision of a large vacuum flask, preferably the type with a tap on it; this can be filled with boiling water before the night watches begin so that hot drinks can be made up without the need to boil a kettle.

Never cook while wearing shorts — the risk from an overturned pan or kettle is too great. At the very least, a substantial apron should be worn and preferably oilskin trousers. Pans should always have tops, although it is difficult to find ones with lids that fasten down, and the kettle should be the kind with a whistle but no lid. A pressure cooker is a favourite item in the galley not only because it saves water and energy but because the lid is fastened very securely and hot foods or liquids cannot spill over.

Nearly everyone thinks about fire in the galley but many act in an illogical way, by fitting a fire-extinguisher right next to the cooker. When there is a flare-up on the cooker, you then cannot get to the extinguisher. Instead, fit it a little distance away and as near as possible to the hatch so that in the event of a serious fire it can be grabbed from on deck. Setting off a fire-extinguisher to put out a burning chip-pan (assuming you are crazy enough to fry chips on board) is a messy and inefficient way of going about things. A fire-blanket is quick, effective and can be used again.

If someone does get burnt, the first thing to do — as quickly as possible — is to cool them down and you cannot do wrong by applying copious cold water or, where practicable, placing the injured part in the water. Only when it is clear that there is no longer any heat in the affected area should you think about further treatment. For minor burns, the spray-on analgesics work wonders but for more serious ones an all-over dressing of sterile, non-stick gauze is required. Dehydration and shock often follow a burn and have to be treated by keeping the victim warm and still, and giving plenty to drink (NOT alcohol). It is for just such serious situations that a First-aid course is *essential preparation*. Unfortunately, it is all too easy to do more harm than good if you don't know how to handle the situation properly.

Blows to the head

Following a hard blow to the head, there is a risk of concussion — only cowboys get straight up off the floor and carry on punching. Apart from the physical damage, watch carefully for nausea, drowsiness, dilated or unequal pupils in a person who has been hit on the head. If these signs are present the victim should be kept quiet, warm and still but not allowed to go to sleep, and should be treated by a doctor as soon as possible.

Dislocation or fracture

If someone dislocates a limb, *do not* try to put it back unless you have medical training — you may make matters worse. In the case of a fracture or break, immobilize the limb. With a finger, the best way is to tape it to the adjoining one and then splint the back of the hand. An arm or leg needs splinting to prevent movement and yachts are generally well-provided with suitable sail-battens, broom-sticks etc to do this. See your first-aid book for full instructions.

Drowning

If someone has been in the water and is recovered not breathing, you have to start mouth-to-mouth resuscitation right away and keep it up for a long time — at least 30 minutes before assuming all is lost. The great advantage of the method is that it can be done anywhere — in a life-raft for instance or even in the water. A person who has been in the water will almost certainly be suffering from hypothermia as well (see below) so you have to start with the warming-up procedures just as quickly as possible. Again, know your first-aid manual and use it conscientiously.

Hypothermia

Chilling of the body core is always dangerous because its first effect is that the sufferer loses the will to do anything about it. People who become icy cold, grey and seem dopey in their reactions have to be treated as an emergency.

Prevention is better than cure however, and will always come from wearing proper clothing — adequate warm layers covered by waterproofs. People suffering from sea-sickness can be quite irresponsible and will try to stay on deck in soaking clothes because they cannot face going below. They have to be firmly ordered to do so, either to lie down and stay there, or to change into dry clothes and come back on deck fully kitted up. If it means that they are sick on the floor as a result, well, bad luck; much worse things can happen at sea, such as collapsing from hypothermia.

If someone really is suffering from hypothermia, they have to be got out of wet clothes and into a sleeping bag as soon as possible. An insulating 'space blanket' is a great help but even plastic sacks help in dire emergency. Hot drinks will help but hot water-bottles are a bit difficult to arrange on a boat. A close embrace from another person is said to be very helpful. But by far the most important thing to remember is not to let anyone drift into that state of listlessness that heralds hypothermia.

'Personal freshness'

Failure to keep clean is not only offensive to others but unhealthy, as it can quickly lead to skin problems, so it is appropriate that we consider it here. On a passage, especially if rough, one tends to work and sleep in the same clothes and, clearly, things will get smelly after a while. On a small yacht where a shower is not possible, one must be self-disciplined about washing and have a really thorough flannel wash whenever possible. Moistened travel wipes or 'baby wipes' can be a great help, especially to get salt off the face and neck or for use on the private parts. Underclothes should always be cotton or wool rather than synthetics, which seem to get smelly much more quickly.

Sea-sickness

The dreaded *mal de mer* can spoil anyone's enjoyment of sailing and many never try sailing on the sea for fear of it. This is too craven a reaction. Although some people really are martyrs to sea-sickness, most get over it after a while. The trick is to take drugs at the outset — swallow your pride and a pill — so that the dreaded queasiness and lassitude can never get a grip. In time, most people find that the tendency to feel ill passes and they can stop taking drugs.

Several things help. Before a trip, eat simple, healthy food to settle the stomach and particularly avoid heavy, greasy meals. Avoid alcohol; most people cannot even think of drinking if they feel sea-sick but it helps a lot to give it up a day or two before. Be rested and relaxed if possible. Remember that although it can be extremely unpleasant, very few people die of sea-sickness even though many have wished they could at the time.

Modern drugs are a great help because they work without making you feel so dry and drowsy as older preparations used to do. Some swear by little elastic bracelets which place an 'acupuncture' pressure on the wrist.

Stomach problems

English yachtsmen drink the water from the ship's tanks while French ones know better and only drink bottled water. If you do not mind your tea tasting of glass fibre it is wise to drop sterilizing tablets in the water-tank, especially after topping up from a hose-pipe. Wash salads with salt or permanganate in the water, and peel vegetables. Have two chopping-boards and knives, one pair for raw things, one for cooked. Wage an unceasing battle against flies!

Sunburn

One may be on deck from dawn till dusk while cruising and must give the skin time to acclimatize to the sun. The answer is to wear a hat, a long-sleeved shirt and long trousers (on a boat, one is generally seated, so the knees are particularly vulnerable if they are exposed). To protect your lips from chapping, use a lip salve if necessary.

Below: *Sailing away to the sunshine is a dream that many people have had and an ever-increasing number manage to realize. The fact that so many are making prolonged cruises in safety is largely due to the practical, seaworthy design of modern cruising yachts.*

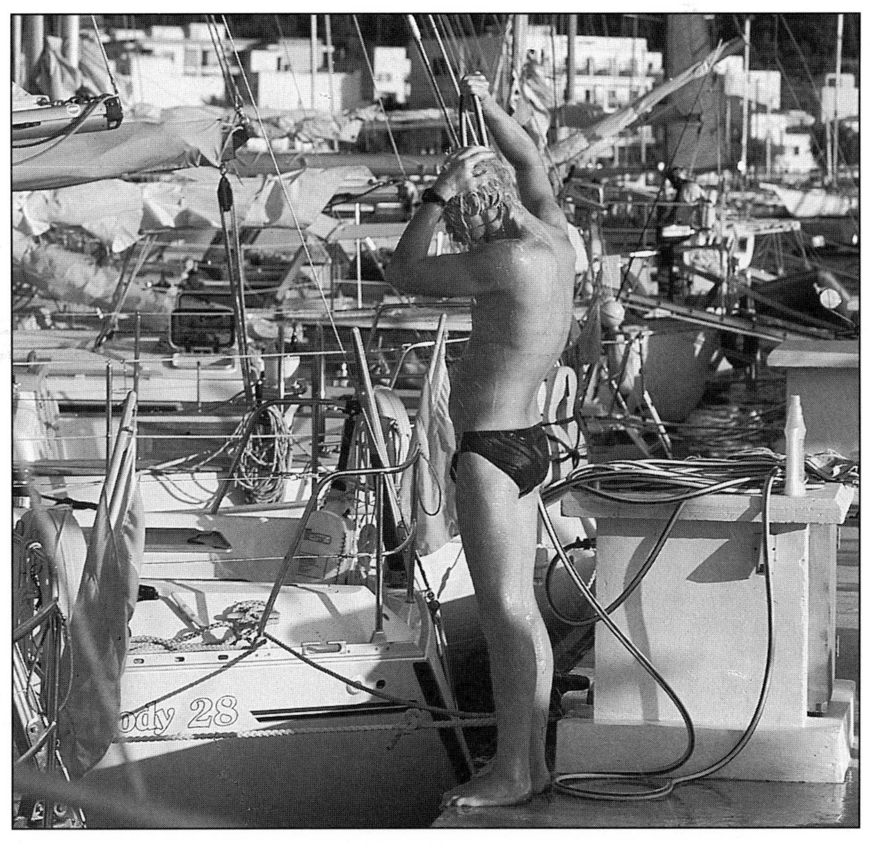

G-1909

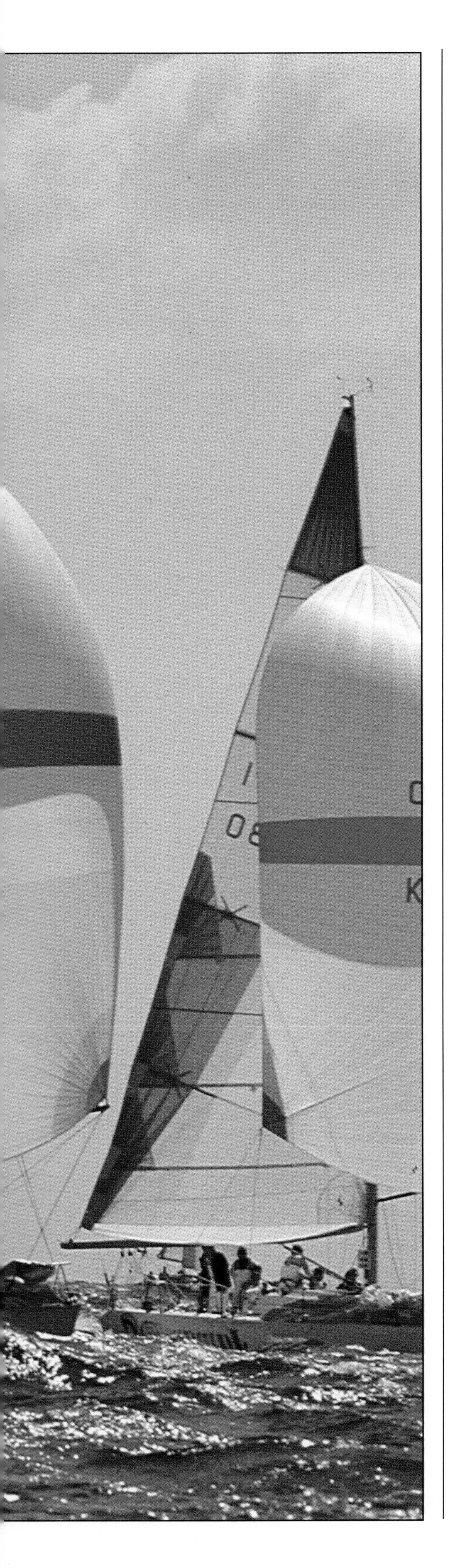

The Major Records

In this reference section we give the results of some of the most important of the classic yacht races, from their inception up to the present day. What is the fastest sailing boat in the world and who has sailed across the Atlantic fastest? Find out here!

Left: *Close-quarters action under spinnaker during the third inshore race of the 1987 Admiral's Cup series. If the weather were always like this, sailing would be the most delightful of sports!*

Country abbreviations used in these records are as follows (the capital letters denote the abbreviation): ARGentina, AUStralia, BELgium, BRAzil, BULgaria, CZechoslovakia, DENmark, FRAnce, GERmany, Great Britain, GREece, HOLland, Hong Kong, HUNgary, INDia, IREland, ITAly, JaPaN, MEXico, NETHerlands, New Zealand, South Africa, SPAin, SWEden, SWItzerland, United States, USSR, W. GERmany, YUGoslavia.

National codes used by the International Yacht Racing Union are as follows: Argentina A, Australia KA, Austria OE, Belgium B, Bermuda KB, Brazil BL, Bulgaria BU, Canada KC, Czechoslovakia CZ, Denmark D, Finland L, France F, Germany G, German Democratic Republic DDR, Greece GR, Holland H, Hong Kong KH, Hungary M, India IND, Ireland IR, Italy I, Japan J, Mexico MX, New Zealand KZ, Norway N, South Africa SA, Spain E, Sweden S, Switzerland Z, United Kingdom K, USA US, USSR SR, Yugoslavia Y.

BERMUDA RACE

YEAR	DIV	WINNER
1906		*Tamerlane* F. Maier
1907		*Dervish* H. Morss
1908		(No records)
1909		(No records)
1910		*Vagrant* H. Vanderbilt
		(No more races until 1923)
1923		*Malabar IV* J. Alden
1924		*Memory* R. Bavier
1926		*Malabar VII* J. Alden
1928		*Rugosa II* R. Grinnell
1930		*Malay* R. Ferris
1932		*Malabar X* J. Alden
1934		*Edlu* R. Schaefer
1936		*Kirawan* R. Baruch
1938		*Baruna* H. Taylor
1946		*Gesture* A. Fuller
1948		*Baruna* H. Taylor
1950		*Argyll* W. Moore
1952		*Carina* R. Nye
1954		*Malay* D. Strohmeier
1956		*Finisterre* C. Mitchell
1958		*Finisterre* C. Mitchell
1960		*Finisterre* C. Mitchell
1962		*Nina* De Coursey Fales
1964		*Burgoo* M. Ernstof
1966		*Thunderbird* V. Learson
1968		*Robin* E. Hood
1970		*Carina II* R. Nye
1972		*Noryema VIII* R. Amey (GB)
1974		*Scaramouche* C. Kirsch
1976		*Running Tide* A. Van Metre
1978		*Babe* A. Gay
1980		*Holger Danske* R. Wilson
1982		*Brigadoon III* R. Morton
1984	IOR Div	*Pamir* F.H. Curren Jr.
	MHS Div	*Merrythought* J. King
1986	IOR Div	*Silver Star* D. Clarke
	IMS Div	*Puritan* D. Robinson

All US unless otherwise recorded.
Div results were introduced in 1984.

FASTNET TROPHY

YEAR	WINNER
1925	*Jolie Brise* E.G. Martin (GB)
1926	*Ilex* R. Engineers YC (GB)
1927	*Tally Ho* Lord Stalbridge (GB)
1928	*Nina* P. Hammond (US)
1929	*Jolie Brise* R. Somerset (GB)
1930	*Jolie Brise* R. Somerset (GB)
1931	*Dorade* R. Stephens (US)
1933	*Dorade* R. Stephens (US)
1935	*Stormy Weather* P. Le Boutillier (US)
1937	*Zeearend* C. Bruynzeel (NETH)
1939	*Bloodhound* I. Bell (GB)
1947	*Myth of Malham* J. Illingworth (GB)
1949	*Myth of Malham* J. Illingworth (GB)
1951	*Yeoman III* O. Aisher (GB)
1953	*Favona* Sir M. Newton (GB)
1955	*Carina II* R. Nye (US)
1957	*Carina II* R. Nye (US)
1959	*Anitra* S. Hansen (SWE)
1961	*Zwerver* W. Van der Vorm (NETH)
1963	*Clarion of Wight* D. Boyer & D. Miller (GB)
1965	*Rabbit* R. Carter (US)
1967	*Pen Duick III* E. Tabarly (FRA)
1969	*Red Rooster* R. Carter (US)
1971	*Ragamuffin* S. Fischer (AUS)
1973	*Saga* E. Lorentzen (BRA)
1975	*Golden Delicious* P. Nicholson (GB)
1977	*Imp* D. Allen (US)
1979	*Tenacious* R. Turner (US)
1981	*Nordicus* G. Taylor & C. Volters (BEL)
1983	*Condor* R. Bell (GB)
1985	*Panda* P. Whipp (GB)
1987	*Juno* M. Peacock (GB)
	(*Irish Independent Full Pelt* (T. Power & S. Fein) Ireland, had a better corrected time but was entered in the Open Division and thus not eligible for the Fastnet Trophy.)

ADMIRAL'S CUP

YEAR	WINNER	TEAM
1957	Great Britain	*Myth of Malham* J. Illingworth & P. Green
		Uomie S. Slater
		Jocasta G. Pattinson
1959	Great Britain	*Griffin II* RORC, Major G. Potter
		Ramrod S. Slater & R. McLoughlin
		Myth of Malham J. Illingworth & P. Green
1961	US	*Windrose* J. Isbrantsen
		Figaro W. Snaith
		Cyane H. du Pont
1963	Great Britain	*Clarion of Wight* D. Boyer & D. Miller
		Outlaw Hon M. Aitken & R. Lowein
		Noryema III R. Amey
1965	Great Britain	*Quiver IV* S. Clarke
		Noryema IV R. Amey
		Firebrand D. Miller
1967	Australia	*Mercedes III* H. Kaufman
		Balandra R. Crichton-Brown
		Caprice of Huon G. Reynolds
1969	US	*Red Rooster* R. Carter
		Carina II R. Nye
		Palawan T. Watson
1971	Great Britain	*Prospect of Whitby* A. Slater
		Morning Cloud Rt Hon E. Heath
		Cervantes IV R. Watson
1973	Germany	*Saudade* A. Buell
		Rubin H-O. Schumann
		Carina III D. Monheim
1975	Great Britain	*Noryema* R. Amey
		Yeoman XX R. Aisher
		Battlecry J. Prentice
1977	Great Britain	*Moonshine* J. Rogers & W. Green
		Yeoman XX R. Aisher
		Marionette C. Dunning
1979	Australia	*Ragamuffin* S. Fischer
		Impetuous G. Lambert & J. Crisp
		Police Car P. Cantwell
1981	Great Britain	*Victory of Burnham* P. de Savary
		Dragon Mr & Mrs P. Saffery Cooper
		Yeoman XXIII R. Aisher
1983	Germany	*Sabina* H. Noak
		Outsider T. Hansen
		Pinta W. Illbruck
1985	Germany	*Diva* D. Langloh
		Outsider T. Hansen
		Rubin H-O. Schumann
1987	New Zealand	*Goldcorp* R. Dodson & M. Canning
		Propaganda B. Wooley & A. Burr
		Kiwi P. Walker

SYDNEY–HOBART RACE

YEAR	WINNER
1945	*Rani* Captain J. Illingworth, RN (GB)
1946	*Christina* J.R. Bull (AUS)
1947	*Westward* G.D. Gibson (AUS)
1948	*Westward* G.D. Gibson (AUS)
1949	*Trade Winds* M.E. Davey (AUS)
1950	*Nerida* C.P. Hazelgrove (AUS)
1951	*Struen Marie* T. Williamson (AUS)
1952	*Ingrid* J.S. Taylor (AUS)
1953	*Ripple* R.C. Hobson (AUS)
1954	*Solveig* T. & M. Halvorsen (AUS)
1955	*Moonbi* H.S. Evans (AUS)
1956	*Solo* V. Meyer (AUS)
1957	*Anitra* M. & T. Halvorsen (AUS)
1958	*Siandra* G. Newlands (AUS)
1959	*Cherana* R. Williams (AUS)
1960	*Siandra* G. Newlands (AUS)
1961	*Rival* A. Burgin and N. Rundle (AUS)
1962	*Solo* V. Meyer (AUS)
1963	*Freya* M. & T. Halvorsen (AUS)
1964	*Freya* M. & T. Halvorsen (AUS)
1965	*Freya* M. & T. Halvorsen (AUS)
1966	*Cadence* H.S. Mason (AUS)
1967	*Rainbow* C. Bouzaid (NZ)
1968	*Koomooloo* D. O'Neil (AUS)
1969	*Morning Cloud* E. Heath (GB)
1970	*Pacha* R. Crichton-Brown (AUS)
1971	*Pathfinder* B. Wilson (NZ)
1972	*American Eagle* R.E. Turner (US)
1973	*Ceil III* W. Turnbull (HK)
1974	*Love and War* P. Kurts (AUS)
1975	*Rampage* P. Packer (AUS)
1976	*Piccolo* J. Pickles (AUS)
1977	*Kialoa* J.B. Kilroy (US)
1978	*Love and War* P. Kurts (AUS)
1979	*Screw Loose* R.J. Cumming (AUS)
1980	*(Ceramco) New Zealand* P. Blake (NZ)
1981	*Zeus II* J.R. Dunstan (AUS)
1982	*Scallywag* R. Johnston (AUS)
1983	*Challenge* L. Abrahams (AUS)
1984	*Indian Pacific* J. Eyles and G. Hauchmeyer (AUS)
1985	*Sagacious* G. Appleby (AUS)
1986	*Extension* A. Dunn (AUS)
1987	*Sovereign* B. Lewis (AUS)

SOUTHERN CROSS CUP

YEAR	WINNER	TEAM
1967	New South Wales	*Mercedes III* E. Kaufman
		Moonbird N. Brooker
		Calliope C. Middleton
1969	New South Wales	*Ragamuffin* S. Fischer
		Mercedes III E. Kaufman
		Boambillee V. Walsh
1971	New Zealand	*Pathfinder* B. Wilson
		Runaway J. Lidgard
		Wai-Aniwa R.H. Walker
1973	Great Britain	*Prospect of Whitby* A. Slater
		Superstar E.A. Graham
		Quailo III D. Parr
1975	New Zealand	*Prospect of Ponsonby* N.R. Angus
		Tempo C. Johnson
		Quicksilver R. Wilson
1977	New Zealand	*Swuzzlebubble* I. Gibbs
		Jenny H Jenny H Syndicate
		Smir Noff Agen R.H. Walker
1979	New South Wales	*Deception* J.H. Bleakley
		Relentless P. Hankin
		Diamond Cutter A. Sweeney
1981	New South Wales	*Beach Inspector* G. Jones & R. Hudson
		Smuggler T. Simpson
		Szechwan J.S. Whitty
1983	New Zealand	*Pacific Sundance* D.G. Hogg & O.C. Morris
		Geronimo O. Championship
		Exador T. & K. McCall
1985	Great Britain	*Highland Fling* I. Laidlaw
		Cifraline III C. Griffiths
		Panda P. Whipp
1987	Australia	*Joint Venture* R. Elliott
		Madeline's Daughter P. Kurts
		Sagacious V G.J. Appleby

TWO TON CUP

28ft RATING RORC

YEAR	VENUE	WINNER
1967		*Airela* (ITA)
1968		*La Meloria* (ITA)

33ft RATING IOR

YEAR	VENUE	WINNER
1971		*Villanella* (ITA)
1972		*Locura* (US)

32ft RATING IOR

YEAR	VENUE	WINNER
1974	San Remo	*Aggressive* (US)
1975	Detroit	*Ricochet* (US)
1976	Kiel	*Williwaw* (GER)
1977	No series	
1978	Rio de Janeiro	*Iorana* (US)
1979	Poole	*Gitana VII* (FRA)
1980	No series	
1981	Porto Cervo	*Hitchhiker* (AUS)

ONE TON CUP (MODERN)

22ft RATING RORC

YEAR	VENUE	WINNER
1965	Le Havre	*Diana II* (DEN)
1966	Copenhagen	*Tina* (US)
1967	Le Havre	*Optimist* (W.GER)
1968	Heligoland	*Optimist* (W.GER)
1969	Heligoland	*Rainbow* (NZ)

27.5ft RATING IOR

YEAR	VENUE	WINNER
1971	Auckland	*Stormy Petrel* (AUS)
1972	Sydney	*Wai-Aniwa* (NZ)
1973	Porto Cervo	*Ydra* (ITA)
1974	Torquay	*Gumboots* (GB)
1975	Rhode Island	*Pied Piper* (US)
1976	Marseille	*Resolute Salmon* (US)
1977	Auckland	*The Red Lion* (NZ)
1978	Flensburg	*Tilsalg* (W.GER)
1979	Newport, R.I.	*Pendragon* (US)
1980	Naples	*Filo da Torcere* (ITA)
1981	Cork	*Justine III* (IRE)
1982	No series	
1983	Rio de Janeiro	*Linda* (ITA)

30.5ft RATING IOR

YEAR	VENUE	WINNER
1984	La Trinite	*Passion II* (FRA)
1985	Poole	*Jade* (GB)
1986	Palma, Majorca	*Andelstanken* (DEN)
1987	Kiel	*Fram X* (NOR)
1988	San Francisco	*Propaganda* (NZ)

THREE-QUARTER TON CUP

24.5ft RATING IOR

YEAR	VENUE	WINNER
1974	Miami	*Swampfire* (US)
1975	Hanko	*Solent Saracen* (GB)
1976	Plymouth	*Finn Fire II* (FIN)
1977	La Rochelle	*Joe Louis* (FRA)
1978	Victoria BC	*Pendragon* (US)
1979	Hundested	*Regnbagen* (SWE)
1980	La Trinite	*Maligawa* (FRA)
1981	Helsinki	*Soldier Blue* (DEN)
1982	Denia	*Lille Du* (DEN)
1983	Trieste	*Botta Dritta III* (ITA)
1984	Kiel	*Positron* (W.GER)
1985	Marstrand	*Green Piece 85* (DEN)
1986	Torquay	*Indulgence* (GB)
1987	Nieuwpoort	*Jelfi-X* (HOL)
1988	Elba	*Okyalos IV* (GRE)

HALF TON CUP

18ft RATING IOR

YEAR	VENUE	WINNER
1966	La Rochelle	*Raki* (FRA)
1967	La Rochelle	*Safari* (FRA)
1968	La Rochelle	*Dame d'Iroise* (FRA)
1969	Sandhamn	*Scampi* (SWE)
1970	Sandhamn	*Scampi II* (SWE)

21.8ft RATING IOR

YEAR	VENUE	WINNER
1971	Portsmouth	*Scampi III* (SWE)
1972	Marstrand	*Bes* (DEN)
1973	Hundested	*Impensable* (FRA)
1974	La Rochelle	*North Star* (W.GER)
1975	Chicago	*Foxy Lady* (AUS)
1976	Trieste	*Silver Shamrock* (IRE)
1977	Sydney	*Gunboat Rangiriri* (NZ)
1978	Poole	*Waverider* (NZ)

22ft RATING IOR

YEAR	VENUE	WINNER
1979	Scheveningen	*Waverider* (NZ)
1980	Sandhamn	*Ar Bigouden* (FRA)
1981	Poole	*King One* (FRA)
1982	Piraeus	*Atalanti II* (GRE)
1983	Hanko	*Freelance* (FRA)
1984	Troon	*C* (FRA)
1985	Porto Ercole	*Antheor* (FRA)
1986	Helsinki	*C* (FRA)
1987	La Rochelle	*R Chateau Video* (FRA)
1988	Poole	*Skipper Elf Aquitaine* (FRA)

QUARTER TON CUP

15ft RATING RORC

YEAR	VENUE	WINNER
1967	La Rochelle	*Defender* (BEL)
1968	Breskens	*Piranha* (NETH)
1969	Breskens	*Listang* (W.GER)
1970	Travemunde	*Fleur d'Ecume* (FRA)

18ft RATING IOR

YEAR	VENUE	WINNER
1971	La Rochelle	*Tequila* (FRA)
1972	La Rochelle	*Petite Fleur* (FRA)
1973	Weymouth	*Eygthene* (USA)
1974	Malmo	*Accent* (SWE)
1975	Deauville	*45° South* (NZ)
1976	Corpus Christi	*Magic Bus* (NZ)
1977	Helsinki	*Manzanita* (SPA)
1978	Sajima	*Magician V* (JPN)

18.5ft RATING IOR

YEAR	VENUE	WINNER
1979	San Remo	*Bullit* (FRA)
1980	Panmure	*Bullit* (FRA)
1981	Marseille	*Lacydon Protis* (FRA)
1982	Melbourne	*Quartermaster* (AUS)
1983	No series	
1984	Nieuwpoort	*Comte de Flandres* (FRA)
1985	Ajaccio	*Royal Flush* (SA)
1986	Copenhagen	*Comte de Flandres* (AUS)
1987	Crosshaven	*McDonalds* (DEN)
1988	Travemunde	*McDonalds* (SWE)

MINI TON CUP

15ft RATING IOR

YEAR	VENUE	WINNER
1978	Cala Galera	*Wahoo* (AUS)

16.5ft RATING IOR

YEAR	VENUE	WINNER
1979	Estartit	*Wahoo* (ITA)
1980	Edinburgh	*Mr. Bill's Dog* (US)
1981	Bodensee	*Gullisara* (ITA)
1982	Marstrand	*Gullisara* (ITA)
1983	St. Raphael	*Kminispri* (W.GER)
1984	Corfu	*Ligule'* (ITA)
1985	Hanko	*Creola* (ITA)
1986	Lake Garda	*Witchie* (NOR)
1987	Medemblik	*Mannaggia* (ITA)
1988	Varseberg	*For Sale* (NOR)

AMERICA'S CUP

YEAR	DEFENDER	CHALLENGER	SCORE
1870	*Magic* (New York Yacht Club)	*Cambria* (Royal Thames YC)	1-0
1871	*Columbia* and *Sappho* (NYYC)	*Livonia* (Royal Harwich YC)	4-1
1876	*Madeleine* (NYYC)	*Countess of Dufferin* (Royal Canadian YC)	2-0
1881	*Mischief* (NYYC)	*Atalanta* (Bay of Quinte YC)	2-0
1885	*Puritan* (NYYC)	*Genesta* (Royal Yacht Squadron)	2-0
1886	*Mayflower* (NYYC)	*Galatea* (Royal Northern YC)	2-0
1887	*Volunteer* (NYYC)	*Thistle* (Royal Clyde YC)	2-0
1893	*Vigilant* (NYYC)	*Valkyrie II* (Royal Yacht Squadron)	3-0
1895	*Defender* (NYYC)	*Valkyrie III* (Royal Yacht Squadron)	3-0
1899	*Columbia* (NYYC)	*Shamrock* (Royal Ulster YC)	3-0
1901	*Columbia* (NYYC)	*Shamrock II* (Royal Ulster YC)	3-0
1903	*Reliance* (NYYC)	*Shamrock III* (Royal Ulster YC)	3-0
1920	*Resolute* (NYYC)	*Shamrock IV* (Royal Ulster YC)	3-2
1930	*Enterprise* (NYYC)	*Shamrock V* (Royal Ulster YC)	4-0
1934	*Rainbow* (NYYC)	*Endeavour* (Royal Yacht Squadron)	4-2
1937	*Ranger* (NYYC)	*Endeavour II* (Royal Yacht Squadron)	4-0
1958	*Columbia* (NYYC)	*Sceptre* (Royal Yacht Squadron)	4-0
1962	*Weatherly* (NYYC)	*Gretel* (Royal Sydney Yacht Squadron)	4-1
1964	*Constellation* (NYYC)	*Sovereign* (Royal Thames YC)	4-0
1967	*Intrepid* (NYYC)	*Dame Pattie* (Royal Sydney Yacht Squadron)	4-0
1970	*Intrepid* (NYYC)	*Gretel II* (Royal Sydney Yacht Squadron)	4-1
1974	*Courageous* (NYYC)	*Southern Cross* (Royal Perth YC)	4-0
1977	*Courageous* (NYYC)	*Australia* (Sun City YC)	4-0
1980	*Freedom* (NYYC)	*Australia* (Royal Perth YC)	4-1
1983	*Liberty* (NYYC)	*Australia II* (Royal Perth YC)	3-4
1987	*Kookaburra III* (Royal Perth YC)	*Stars and Stripes* (San Diego YC)	0-4
1988	*Stars and Stripes II* (San Diego YC)	*New Zealand* (Mercury Bay Boating Club)	2-0

Number of matches so far: 27

SINGLE-HANDED TRANSATLANTIC RACE

YEAR	CLASS	RESULT	TIME D H M*
1960		1 *Gipsy Moth III* F. Chichester (GB)	40/12/30
		2 *Jester* Lt Col H.G. Hasler (GB)	48/12/02
		3 *Cardinal Vertue* D. Lewis (NZ)	55/00/50
1964		1 *Pen Duick II* E. Tabarly (FRA)	27/03/56
		2 *Gipsy Moth III* F. Chichester (GB)	29/23/57
		3 *Akka* V. Howells (GB)	32/18/08
1968		1 *Sir Thomas Lipton* G. Williams (GB)	25/20/33
		2 *Voortrekker* B. Dalling (SA)	26/13/42
		3 *Cheers* T. Follett (US)	27/00/13
1972		1 *Pen Duick IV* A. Colas (FRA)	20/13/15
		2 *Vendredi 13* J-Y. Terlain (FRA)	21/05/14
		3 *Cap 33* J-M. Vidal (FRA)	24/05/40
1976		1 *Pen Duick VI* E. Tabarly (FRA)	23/20/12
		2 *Club Mediterranee* A. Colas (FRA)	26/13/36
		3 *Third Turtle* M. Birch (CAN)	24/20/39
1980		1 *Moxie* P. Weld (US)	17/23/12
		2 *Three Legs of Mann III* N. Keig (GB)	18/06/12
		3 *Foster Jeans* P. Steggall (US)	18/06/52
1984	Class I	*Umopro Jardin* Y. Fauconnier (FRA)	16/22/25
		Fleury Michon P. Poupon (FRA)	16/11/55
	Class II	*Region Centre* M. Pajot (FRA)	16/12/18
	Class III	*Destination St Croix* J. Petith (US)	18/09/09
	Class IV	*City of Slidell* L. Tonizzo (US)	20/23/40
	Class V	*Swansea Bay* C. Butler (GB)	30/14/48
1988	Class I	*Fleury Michon* P. Poupon (FRA)	10/09/15
	Class II	*Dogwatch A* N. Burgess (Monaco)	21/05/46
	Class III	*Damiana* M. Reppy (US)	19/08/28
	Class IV	*MTC* N. Bailey (GB)	16/17/03
	Class V	*Curtana* R. Wilson (US)	21/17/17
	Class VI	*Caledonia* R. Stuart (GB)	21/06/16

The Single-handed Transatlantic Race, organized by the Royal Western Yacht Club, was known as the Observer Single-handed Transatlantic Race (OSTAR) from 1960 to 1980 inclusive. From 1984, it became the Carlsberg Single-handed Transatlantic Race.

*D H M in 'Time' column indicates Days, Hours, Minutes.
Class results were introduced in 1984.

Left: Stars and Stripes, *sailed by Dennis Conner, squeezes up on to the lee bow of* Kookaburra III *during the 1987 match for the America's Cup. The sparkling weather conditions of Western Australia transformed the event into a superb spectacle of a kind not seen during all the years that the event was held off Newport, Rhode Island.*

ROUND BRITAIN RACE

YEAR	WINNER	TIME D H M*
1966	*Toria* D. Kelsall & M. Minter-Kemp	19
1970	*Ocean Spirit* L. Williams & R. Knox-Johnston	20
1974	*British Oxygen* R. Knox-Johnston & J. Boxall	18
1978	*Great Britain IV* C. Blyth & R. James	21
1982	*Colt Cars GB* R. & N. James	8/16/03
1985	*Apricot* T. Bullimore & N. Irens	9/07/33

* D H M in 'Time' column indicates Days, Hours, Minutes.

BOC CHALLENGE — AROUND ALONE (Single-handed round the world race)

YEAR	CLASS	WINNER	TIME D H M*
1982/3	Class 1	*Credit Agricole* P. Jeantot (FRA)	159/02/26
	Class 2	*Koden Okera V* Y. Tada (JPN)	207/13/55
1986/7	Class 1	*Credit Agricole III* P. Jeantot (FRA)	134/05/23
	Class 2	*Airco Distributor* M. Plant (US)	157/11/44

*D H M in 'Time' column indicates Days, Hours, Minutes.

WHITBREAD ROUND THE WORLD RACE

YEAR	YACHT	D H M Elapsed time	D H M* Corrected time
1973/4	1 *Sayula II*	152/09/11	133/12/32
	2 *Adventure*	162/19/06	135/08/03
	3 *Grand Louis*	162/01/19	138/14/52
	4 *Kriter*	156/14/10	141/01/53
	5 *Guia*	177/19/23	142/19/20
	6 *Great Britain II*	144/10/43	144/10/43
	(14 finishers)		
1977/8	1 *Flyer*	136/05/28	119/01/00
	2 *King's Legend*	138/15/47	121/11/17
	3 *Traite de Rome*	154/20/58	121/18/50
	4 *Disque d'Or*	142/00/37	122/10/56
	5 *ADC Accutrac*	145/15/28	126/20/18
	6 *Gauloises II*	156/23/00	127/07/54
	(15 finishers)		
1981/2	1 *Flyer II*	120/06/34	119/01/12
	2 *Charles Heidsieck*	131/21/34	120/07/55
	3 *Kriter IX*	134/07/37	120/10/50
	4 *Disque d'Or*	143/13/00	123/11/45
	5 *Outward Bound*	151/15/19	124/11/55
	6 *Xargo III*	147/15/10	124/19/02
	(20 finishers)		
1985/6	1 *L'Esprit d'Equipe*	132/00/15	111/23/09
	2 *Philips Innovator*	127/03/00	112/21/31
	3 *Fazer Finland*	128/05/25	115/00/49
	4 *UBS Switzerland*	117/14/31	117/04/47
	5 *Rucanor Tristar*	139/10/26	118/09/29
	6 *Fortuna Lights*	137/21/22	121/00/06
	(15 finishers)		

* D H M in 'Time' column indicates Days, Hours, Minutes.

OLYMPIC GOLD MEDALLISTS

YEAR	CLASS	WINNER
1900	½ ton	J. Texier (FRA)
	½–1 ton	L. Currie (GB)
	1–2 ton	M. Wiesner (GER)
	2–3 ton	E. Shaw (GB)
	3–10 ton	H. Taylor (US)
	10–20 ton	E. Billard (FRA)
	Open class	L. Currie (GB)
1904	No yachting events	
1908	6-metre	G. Laws (GB)
	7-metre	C. Rivett-Carnac (GB)
	8-metre	B. Cochrane (GB)
	12-metre	T. Glen-Coats (GB)
1912	6-metre	A. Thube (FRA)
	8-metre	T. Glad (NOR)
	10-metre	C. Hellstrom (SWE)
	12-metre	J. Anker (NOR)
1920	12ft dinghy	J. Joseph (NETH)
	18ft dinghy	F. Richards (GB)
	6-metre (old)	E. Cornellie (BEL)
	6-metre (new)	A. Brecke (NOR)
	6.5-metre	J. Carp (NETH)
	7-metre	C. Macey (GB)
	8-metre (old)	A. Ringvold (NOR)
	8-metre (new)	M. Konow (NOR)
	10-metre (old)	E. Herseth (NOR)
	10-metre (new)	A. Arentz (NOR)
	12-metre (old)	H. Ostervold (NOR)
	12-metre (new)	J. Friele (NOR)
	30 sq metre	G. Lundquist (SWE)
	40 sq metre	T. Holm (SWE)
1924	Single-handed	L. Huybrechts (BEL)
	6-metre	E. Lunde (NOR)
	8-metre	A. Peingvold (NOR)
1928	Single-handed	S. Thorell (SWE)
	6-metre	Crown Prince Olav (NOR)
	8-metre	D. Bouche (FRA)
1932	Single-handed	J. Lebrun (FRA)
	Star	G. Gray (US)
	6-metre	T. Holm (SWE)
	8-metre	O. Churchill (US)
1936	Single-handed	D. Kagchelland (NETH)
	Star	P. Bischoff (GER)
	6-metre	M. Konow (NOR)
	8-metre	G. Reggio (ITA)
1948	Firefly (single-handed)	P. Elvström (DEN)
	Swallow	S. Morris (GB)
	Star	H. Smart (US)
	Dragon	T. Thorvaldsen (NOR)
	6-metre	H. Whiton (US)
1952	Finn	P. Elvström (DEN)
	Star	A. Straulino (ITA)
	Dragon	T. Thorvaldsen (NOR)
	5.5-metre	B. Chance (US)
	6-metre	H. Whiton (US)
1956	Finn	P. Elvström (DEN)
	12 sq metre Sharpie	P. Mander (NZ)
	Star	H. Williams (US)
	Dragon	F. Bohlin (SWE)
	5.5-metre	L. Thorn (SWE)
1960	Finn	P. Elvström (DEN)
	Flying Dutchman	P. Lunde (NOR)
	Star	T. Pinegin (USSR)
	Dragon	King Constantine (GRE)
	5.5-metre	G. O'Day (US)
1964	Finn	W. Kuhweide (W.GER)
	Flying Dutchman	H. Pedersen (NZ)
	Star	D. Knowles (US)
	Dragon	O. Berntsen (DEN)
	5.5-metre	W. Northam (AUS)
1968	Finn	V. Mankin (USSR)
	Flying Dutchman	R. Pattisson (GB)
	Star	L. North (US)
	Dragon	G. Friedrichs (US)
	5.5-metre	U. Sundelin (SWE)
1972	Finn	S. Maury (FRA)
	Flying Dutchman	R. Pattisson (GB)
	Tempest	V. Mankin (USSR)
	Star	D. Forbes (AUS)
	Dragon	J. Cuneo (AUS)
	Soling	H. Melges (US)
1976	Finn	J. Schumann (E.GER)
	470	F. Hubner (W.GER)
	Flying Dutchman	J. Diesch (W.GER)
	Tornado	R. White (GB)
	Tempest	J. Albrechtson (SWE)
	Soling	P. Hoj-Jensen (DEN)
1980	Finn	E. Rechardt (FIN)
	470	M. Soares (BRA)
	Flying Dutchman	A. Abascal (SPA)
	Tornado	A. Welter (BRA)
	Star	V. Mankin (USSR)
	Soling	P. Hoj-Jensen (DEN)
1984	Sailboard	S. Van den Berg (NETH)
	Finn	R. Coutts (NZ)
	470	L. Doreste (SPA)
	Flying Dutchman	J. McKee (US)
	Tornado	R. Sellers (NZ)
	Star	W. Buchan (US)
	Soling	R. Haines (US)
1988	Sailboard	B. Kendall (NZ)
	Finn	J. Doreste (SPA)
	470 (men)	T. Peponnet (FRA)
	470 (women)	A. Jolly (US)
	Flying Dutchman	J. Bojsen-Moller (DEN)
	Tornado	J-Y. Le Deroff (FRA)
	Star	M. McIntyre (GB)
	Soling	J. Schumann (E.GER)

CROSSBOW II

SPEED RECORDS

The idea of sailing for speed records is relatively new. During the 1950s, some attempts were made to establish speeds over a measured mile in the Solent, without much success. But in 1972, partly in response to a number of wild and unsubstantiated claims for record speeds under sail, the World Sailing Speed Record Committee was established in Britain and set down requirements for speed records and ratifying claims. Since 1972, the Royal Yachting Association has organized an annual Speed Week at Portland Harbour, in Dorset (where conditions for speed sailing are particularly good). Speed record competitions have also been organized elsewhere in the world, particularly France but also in the USA, Australia, New Zealand, Sweden and other countries.

The most important record is the outright world sailing speed record, for which there are no restrictions whatever on type of boat, sail area, size, number of crew or anything else other than the fact that the craft must sail on water and be propelled by the wind. In addition, there are a series of classes based on maximum sail area. The record is for the fastest one-way run over a course of 500 metres, as this is a convenient distance that can be accurately measured by transits on the shore.

In the early days of the competition, the outright record was held for several years (see table) by the 60ft (18.28m) proa *Crossbow*, specially designed for the event by Roderick Macalpine-Downie and owned by Timothy Colman of Norwich. Later, these two produced a second craft — the 60ft (18.28m) catamaran *Crossbow II* — which had two rigs, one on each hull. With this, in 1980, the record was raised to 36 knots.

In recent years, however, this competition has been increasingly dominated by sailboards and in 1986 Pascal Maka of France set a new outright world record of 38.86 knots on a sailboard. For these extremely fast speeds, a very small sailboard with insufficient buoyancy to support a person unless moving — and a very efficient fully-battened sail — is used.

Only two classes have escaped the clutches of the sailboards. 'B' Class (up to 21.84 sq m sail area) has been held since 1976 by the hydrofoil catamaran *Icarus*, owned by a syndicate headed by James Grogono and including the author of this book.

'C' Class is currently held by the kite-propelled catamaran *Jacob's Ladder*, sailed by Ian Day and Martin Rayment. The great appeal of the world record competition is that it encourages completely experimental craft such as *Icarus* and *Jacob's Ladder* which would otherwise have no reason to exist.

Claims are made regularly for new records for various races and trans-ocean passages

***Left:** The 60ft (18.29m) biplane rigged catamaran* Crossbow II *which, in 1980, set a World Sailing Speed Record of 36 knots that went unchallenged for a further 6 years. A unique feature of* Crossbow II *was that the hulls were 'slewed', the leeward one running several feet ahead of the windward one in order to reduce aerodynamic interference between the two rigs.*

and some are given in the table. These records are collected by Sir Peter Johnson on behalf of the Offshore Racing Council and the World Sailing Speed Record Committee.

The record for the transatlantic passage West to East, from Sandy Hook, near New York to Lizard Point, has been broken repeatedly in recent years.

HISTORY OF THE WORLD SAILING SPEED RECORDS

(In 1974, which was the first year of 'class' records, the best speeds achieved at Portland do not appear to have been formally ratified as records, but they are included here nevertheless. From 1983 the best speed by a woman was made an official record for the first time. Originally it applied to the 10 m² Class and was transferred to the 8 m² Class when that was introduced in 1986. All the sailboards which held 10 m² records prior to 1986 actually used sails smaller than 8 m² but they have been left in the class in which they were competing at the time. Since 1986 some single-handed sailboards have established records using sails between 8–10 m² and in one instance, in 'A' Class.)

UNLIMITED CLASS (OUTRIGHT WORLD SAILING SPEED RECORD)

BOAT	OWNER/HELMSMAN	COUNTRY	PLACE	DATE	SPEED: knots (km/hr)
Crossbow	T. Colman	GB	Portland	October 1972	26.3
Crossbow	T. Colman	GB	Portland	October 1973	29.3
Crossbow	T. Colman	GB	Portland	October 1975	31.1
Crossbow II	T. Colman	GB	Portland	October 1976	31.8
Crossbow II	T. Colman	GB	Portland	October 1977	33.8
Crossbow II	T. Colman	GB	Portland	17 November 1980	36.0
Sailboard	P. Maka	FRA	Sotovento	23 July 1986	38.86 (72.05)

'C' CLASS (from 21.84 up to 27.88 m² sail area)

BOAT	OWNER/HELMSMAN	COUNTRY	PLACE	DATE	SPEED: knots (km/hr)
Clifton Flasher	Flasher Synd./N. Irens	GB	Portland	October 1974	22.1
(NF)2	W.S. Bradfield/D. White	US	Port Jefferson, NY	18 November 1978	24.4
Jacob's Ladder	I. Day/M. Rayment	GB	Portland	13 October 1982	25.03

'B' CLASS (from 13.94 up to 21.84 m² sail area)

BOAT	OWNER/HELMSMAN	COUNTRY	PLACE	DATE	SPEED: knots (km/hr)
Orlando	G.E. Ward	GB	Portland	October 1974	16.31
(NF)2	W.S. Bradfield	US	Port Jefferson, NY	October 1975	17.2
Hobie 16	H. Pauloo	US	Portland	October 1975	19.9
Icarus	Icarus Syndicate	GB	Portland	October 1976	20.7
Icarus	Icarus Syndicate	GB	Portland	October 1977	22.2
(NF)2	W.S. Bradfield/D. White	US	Port Jefferson, NY	17 October 1978	23.0
Icarus	Icarus Syndicate	GB	Portland	8 October 1980	23.8
Icarus	Icarus Syndicate	GB	Portland	1 October 1981	24.47
Icarus	Icarus Syndicate	GB	Portland	14 October 1983	26.59 (49.2)
Icarus	Icarus Syndicate	GB	Portland	8 October 1985	28.15 (52.17)

'A' CLASS (from 10 up to 13.94 m² sail area)

BOAT	OWNER/HELMSMAN	COUNTRY	PLACE	DATE	SPEED: knots (km/hr)
Mayfly	P. Hansford	GB	Portland	October 1974	19.38
Mayfly	B. Wynne	GB	Portland	October 1976	21.1
Mayfly	B. Wynne	GB	Portland	3 October 1977	23.0
Black & White II	G. McKinlay/Gordon Way	GB	Portland	15 October 1983	25.39 (47.0)
Board	F. Haywood	US	Jervoise Bay, WA	12 December 1984	27.29 (50.5)
Tandem board	S. Griessman/Manu Bertin	FRA	Port St Louis	12 April 1986	29.95 (55.47)
Tandem board	S. Griessman/Manu Bertin	FRA	Sotovento	21 July 1986	35.06 (65.00)

10 m² CLASS

BOAT	OWNER/HELMSMAN	COUNTRY	PLACE	DATE	SPEED: knots (km/hr)
Boreas	R. Bratt	GB	Portland	October 1974	15.04
Windglider	D. Thijs	HOL	Portland	October 1977	19.1
Ten Cate Special	J. Van der Rest	HOL	Portland	21 October 1979	22.3
Olympic Gold	C. Colenso	GB	Portland	22 October 1979	22.95
Ten Cate Special	J. Van der Rest	HOL	Maalea Bay, Maui	18 July 1980	24.63
Ten Cate Special	J. Van der Rest	HOL	Veerse Meer	13 November 1981	25.11
Mistral Special	P. Pudenz	W. GER	Brest	28 September 1982	26.53
Ellesse Special	P. Maka	FRA	Portland	13 October 1982	27.82
Maui/Neil Pryde	F. Haywood	US	Portland	16 October 1983	30.83 (57.1)
Sailboard	M. Pucher	GER	Port St Louis	15 April 1985	32.35 (59.91)
Tandem board	S. Griessman/M. Bertin	FRA	Sotovento	21 July 1986	34.68 (64.29)

8–10 m² CLASS

BOAT	OWNER/HELMSMAN	COUNTRY	PLACE	DATE	SPEED: knots (km/hr)
Sailboard	F. Haywood	US	Fos-sur-Mer	4 April 1986	26.67 (52.17)
Sailboard	E. Beale	GB	Sotovento	13 July 1986	35.00 (64.89)
Sailboard	P. Maka	FRA	Sotovento	23 July 1986	38.86 (72.05)

WOMEN'S CLASS

BOAT	OWNER/HELMSMAN	COUNTRY	PLACE	DATE	SPEED: knots (km/hr)
Board	M-A. Maus	FRA	Portland	October 1983	24.47
Tiga (board	J. de Rosnay	US	Portland	18 October 1984	25.27 (46.81)
Tiga (board)	J. de Rosnay	US	Portland	22 October 1984	27.09 (50.22)
Sailboard	P. Whitcomb	US	Alberta, Canada	8 May 1986	28.06 (52.02)
Sailboard	B. Dunkerbeck	BEL/SPA	Sotovento	23 July 1986	33.77 (62.61)
Sailboard	E. Coquelle	FRA	St Marie	March 1988	34.72 (64.23)

RECORDS FOR VARIOUS PASSAGES

RACE OR PASSAGE	DISTANCE (naut. miles)	TIME D H M	YEAR	YACHT	LOA
Round the World, 3 stops (Whitbread Race)	27,430	117/14/32	1985/6	*UBS Switzerland*	80ft
Round the World, 3 stops Single-handed (BOC Race)	27,430	134/ 5/23	1986/7	*Credit Agricole III*	60ft
Round the World, non-stop Single-handed	25,500	150/ 6/ 1	1985/6	*American Promise*	60ft
Round the World, non-stop by a woman	25,100	189/ 4/ 0	1987/8	*First Lady*	38ft
Round the World, non-stop, 3 times	71,023	652/ 0/ 0	1986/8	*Parry Endeavour*	46ft
Transatlantic, Sandy Hook to Lizard Point	2,925	7/ 6/30	1988	*Jet Services V*	75ft
Transatlantic, Sandy Hook to Lizard Point, monohull	2,925	8/ 3/29	1988	*Phocea*	244ft
Transatlantic, Sandy Hook to Lizard, Single-handed	2,925	11/11/46	1987	*Ericsson*	65ft
Transatlantic, Plymouth to Newport, Single-handed	2,800	10/ 9/15	1988	*Fleury Michon IX*	60ft
Newport to Bermuda Race	635	2/14/29	1982	*Nirvana*	80ft
Fastnet Race	605	2/12/41	1985	*Nirvana*	80ft
Sydney–Hobart Race	630	2/14/36	1975	*Kialoa*	79ft
Transpacific Race (Multihulls)	2,225	7/ 7/30	1983	*Double Bullet*	65ft
Transpacific Race (Monohulls)	2,225	8/11/ 1	1977	*Merlin*	67ft
Quebec–St Malo Race	2,897	7/21/35	1988	*Jet Services V*	75ft

SKIPPER	COUNTRY	AVERAGE SPEED (knots)
Pierre Fehlmann	SWI	9.32
Philippe Jeantot	FRA	8.51
Dodge Morgan	US	7.07
Kay Cottee	AUS	5.53
Jon Sanders	AUS	4.53
Serge Madec	FRA	16.76
Bernard Tapie	FRA	14.96
Bruno Peyron	FRA	10.60
Philippe Poupon	FRA	11.23
Marvin Greene	US	10.16
Marvin Greene	US	9.97
John B. Kilroy	US	10.06
Bob Hanel	US	12.70
Bill Lee	US	11.0
Serge Madec	FRA	15.27

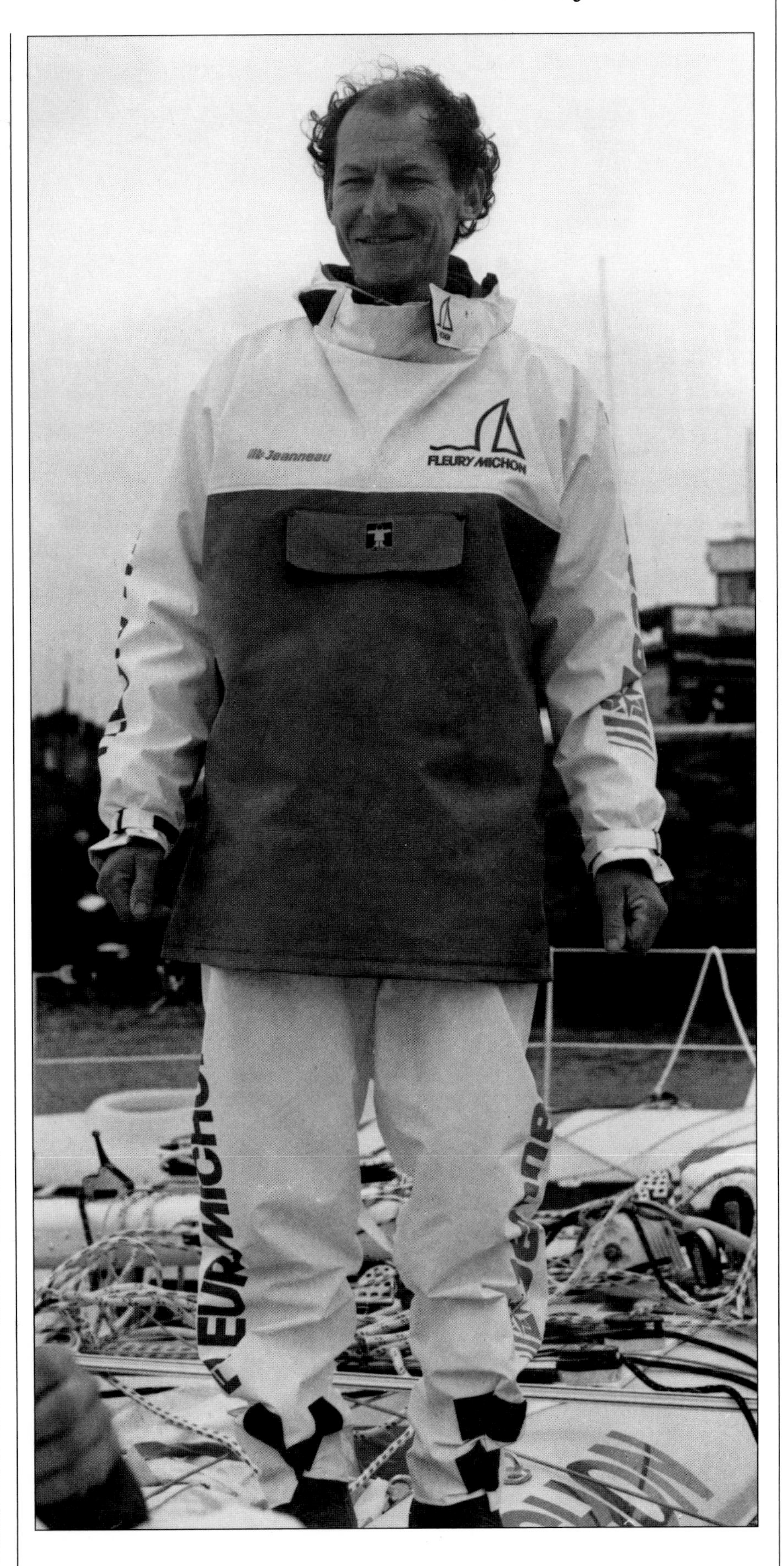

Above: *Philippe Poupon who, in 1988, set a new World Record for crossing the Atlantic from West to East, during the Carlsberg Single-handed Transatlantic Race. Sailing the 60ft (18.29m) trimaran* Fleury Michon, *he completed the crossing in 10 days, 9 hours and 15 minutes.*

INTERNATIONAL CODE FLAGS

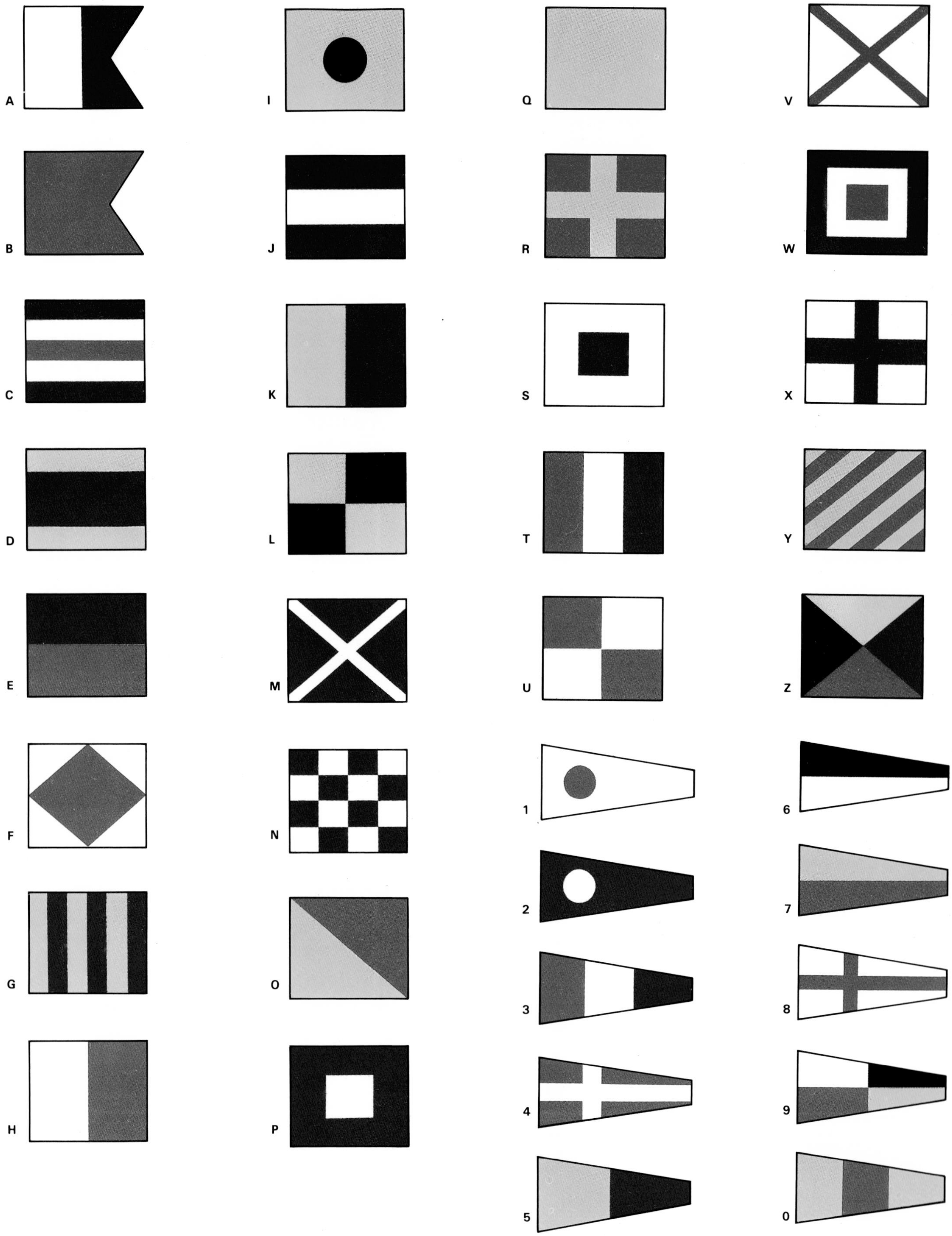

A I Q V

B J R W

C K S X

D L T Y

E M U Z

F N 1 6

G O 2 7

H P 3 8

4 9

5 0

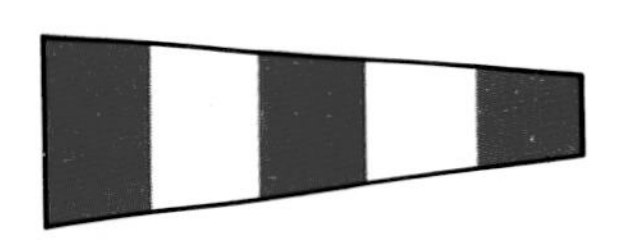

Code and answering pennant (AP)

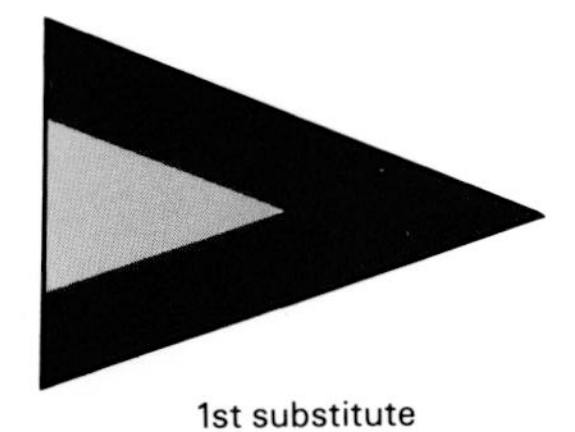

1st substitute

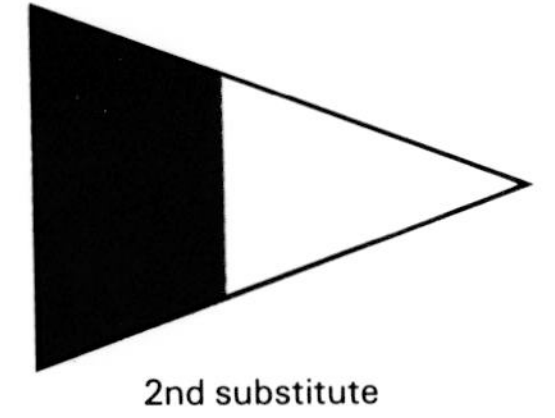

2nd substitute

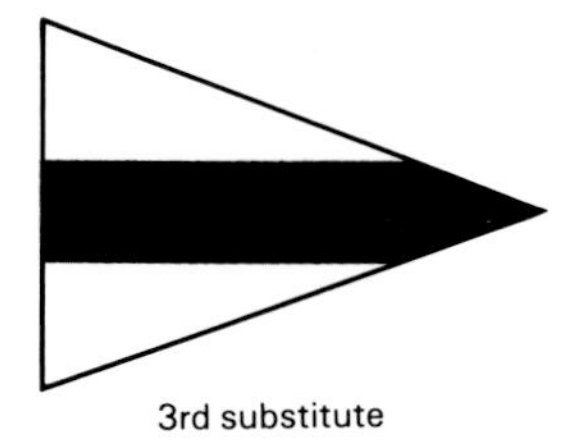

3rd substitute

Phonetic alphabet, and single-letter meanings for International Code Flags.

A Alpha: I have a diver down — keep clear at slow speed.
B Bravo: I am taking in, discharging or carrying dangerous goods.
C Charlie: Yes (or 'read the previous group in the affirmative').
D Delta: Keep clear, I am manoeuvring with difficulty.
E Echo: I am altering course to starboard.
F Foxtrot: I am disabled; communicate with me.
G Golf: I require a pilot (or by fishing vessels: 'I am hauling nets').
H Hotel: I have a pilot on board.
I India: I am altering course to port.
J Juliet: I am on fire and have a dangerous cargo — keep clear.
K Kilo: I wish to communicate with you.
L Lima: You should stop your vessel immediately.
M Mike: My vessel is stopped and not making way.
N November: No (or 'read the previous ground in the negative').
O Oscar: Man overboard.
P Papa: The vessel is about to proceed to sea (or by fishing vessels: 'my nets are stuck on an obstruction').
Q Quebec: My vessel is healthy and I request free pratique.
R Romeo: (no single-letter meaning).
S Sierra: I am operating astern propulsion.
T Tango: Keep clear, I am engaged in pair-trawling.
U Uniform: You are running into danger.
V Victor: I require assistance.
W Whisky: I require medical assistance.
X X-ray: Stop carrying out your intentions and watch for my signals.
Y Yankee: I am dragging my anchor.
Z Zulu: I require a tug (or by fishing vessels: 'I am shooting nets').

Glossary

Why do sailors say 'port' and 'starboard' rather than 'left' and 'right'? What makes the tide rise and fall? How do ships find their way at sea? Why doesn't a half tonner weigh half a ton? And why has tonnage got nothing to do with weight? Thousands of English words have a nautical origin and all of them have a precise and special meaning to the mariner. The modern yachtsman too, has his own special vocabulary, with jockey-poles and jumper struts helping to keep his composite-construction flyer on top line. If you haven't quite got the hang of it yet, this comprehensive glossary will make it all seem as plain as a pushpit.

***Left:** The flags of the International Code of Signals have single-letter meanings corresponding with various important and commonly used messages. Many more messages can be signalled using the flags in groups, and the great value of this system is that the messages are understood in any language. Many of the flags have further meanings when used to control yacht racing and these can be found in the Yacht Racing Rules.*

A

Aback The situation when the wind blows on the 'wrong' side of a sail. Square-rigged ships place some of their sails aback as a means of stopping or to assist going about but could be placed in danger if caught aback inadvertently. A yacht can back, i.e. hold against the wind, her headsail to help her to tack.
Abaft Towards the stern.
Abeam Bearing at right-angles to the fore-and-aft line of the vessel.
Aboard In or on board a vessel.
About A sailing boat 'comes about' when she tacks. 'Ready about' is the recognized warning hail when commencing to tack.
Accommodation The living quarters. Old yachts or very large modern ones, can have separate cabins for sleeping, eating, cooking and so on but in modern small yachts every space serves a number of functions. Day-time settees are night-time berths, the galley is part of the saloon and so on. The modern yacht designer makes absolutely maximum use of space available below deck.
Admiral's Cup Major racing series for offshore yachts organized biennially by the Royal Ocean Racing Club. It is contested by three-yacht teams from various nations and consists of three inshore races, the medium length Channel Race and the 600-mile Fastnet Race. (See *The Great Races.*)
Adrift Floating freely; not moored or anchored.
Advantage When a tackle is rove so that the final hauling part moves in the same direction as the moving block, it is said to be 'rove to advantage' and vice versa.
Aft At or towards the stern.
Afterguard The owner and his guests, as opposed to the crew.
Ahead, Astern Motion, in the direction of the bow or stern (e.g. 'going ahead') or in that direction, as in 'the buoy two miles ahead'.
A-hull A yacht is 'lying a-hull' when all sails have been lowered and she has been left to drift, normally with helm lashed down to minimize leeway.
Aldis lamp Electric signalling lamp with a moving mirror operated by a trigger.
Almanac A book giving predictions of all kinds of information needed by the navigator, such as the times, bearings, altitudes etc. of Sun, Moon, planets and stars. Most almanacs also include tide tables, lists of lights, radio beacons and a great variety of other valuable information.
All standing If a yacht goes aground with her sails still drawing or drops anchor or hits something in the same condition, she is said to have 'brought up all standing'.
Aloft Up above, or in the rigging. The opposite, now archaic word is 'alow'.
Alternating light The term, usually shortened to 'Alt'. on charts, meaning a navigational light which shows two colours alternately.
Altitude The angle between a celestial body and the plane of the rational horizon, as if measured from the centre of the earth. This key angle is calculated after measuring the altitude with a sextant and applying corrections. It enables the navigator to work out how far away he is from the terrestrial position of the observed body, the point on the earth's surface directly below it.
America's Cup The cup won in 1851 by the schooner-yacht *America* and the series of challenge matches named after it. (See *The America's Cup.*)
Amidships In the middle of the vessel.
Amplitude Angle between the bearing of the sun's rising and setting on a particular day and the true bearings east and west. The amplitude table makes it possible to check the compass by taking a bearing of either sunrise or sunset.
Anchor The means of attaching a vessel to the sea-bed. A heavy stone on the end of a rope was the first type of anchor but as this slides along the sea-bed easily, the pick-axe shape gradually evolved. A pick-shaped anchor will lie flat and fail to dig in unless it has a shank at right-angles to the fluke. The basic 'fisherman' or Admiralty pattern anchor is still a good one, but is awkward to stow on board a yacht. More holding-power for a given weight can be achieved by the Danforth anchor or its many derivatives, which have flat, tapered blades that dig into the bottom or 'burying' anchors such as the CQR or Meon types. The Bruce anchor is a scoop-shaped anchor especially effective in very large sizes for oil rigs and the like.
Anemometer Device for measuring wind speed.
Answering pennant Red-and-white striped flag which, in the International Code of Signals, indicates that a message has been received and understood. When displayed by a race committee it indicates a postponement of the start.
Antifouling Special paint applied to the underwater parts of the hull to prevent marine organisms and plants from attaching themselves. Various compounds of copper, tin and mercury form the basis of antifouling but in recent years there has been increasing restriction of the use of toxic metals because of the dangers of pollution.
Apparent wind The wind actually felt on board a yacht, being a combination of the true wind and the boat's own movement through the air.
Aspect ratio The ratio of the area to the chord of an aero- or hydro-foil. The higher the aspect ratio, the lower the drag caused by end vortex so a tall, narrow sail or deep, narrow keel is more efficient than a short, wide one.
Astern Behind the vessel. When moving backwards, a vessel is said to be 'going astern'.
Athwart Across the vessel. From side to side.
Auto-pilot Device for steering a yacht automatically. Normally electronic, as opposed to wind-powered devices which are referred to as 'self-steering'.
Auxiliary Engine that is fitted to a sailing yacht.
Awash A rock or shoal that is partly covered by water. A wreck or sunken vessel that is visible but with the sea washing over.
Aweigh With the anchor clear of the bottom, i.e. in the process of being 'weighed'.
Azimuth Term used to indicate the bearing of a celestial body.

B

Back When the wind changes direction in an anticlockwise sense it is said to 'back'. The opposite is 'veer'.
Back splice To prevent the end of a rope from unravelling, or to form a handle, the strands can be formed into a crown knot and then tucked back along the lay.
Backstay Stay that prevents the mast from falling over forwards. In a racing yacht, the backstay can have the additional function of increasing tension in the forestay or, in the case of fractional rig, of promoting mast bend and hence freeing the mainsail leech. Running backstays ('runners' for short) are ones which must be released on the lee side and set up on the windward side during each tack as the boom fouls them. They control headstay tension and limit mast bend.
Baggywrinkle Fluffed-out rope ends fixed to the rigging on cruising yachts to prevent chafe damage to the sails.
Ballast Weight, fitted below the centre of gravity to give a yacht stability. In a modern yacht the majority of the ballast is in the form of an external keel made from iron or lead. In addition, smaller amounts of ballast can be carried in the bilges as fine-adjustment of the ballasting.

Bar A shoal at the entrance of a river or harbour.
Bare-boat A yacht chartered without accompanying crew.
Bare poles A yacht that has no sail set at all is said to be 'under bare poles'.
Barge Flat-bottomed trading vessel.
Batten Thin, flexible strips of wood or plastics fitted into pockets in a sail to stiffen or extend the leech. A sail in which the battens reach right across from luff to leech is 'fully-battened'.
Beacon A navigational sign or signal set on the shore or on a danger-point to warn mariners of its presence. A beacon may have a special shape or colour to indicate its function; it may show a light or make a sound signal or broadcast radio signals to advertise its presence and function.
Beam The width of a yacht at its widest point is its overall beam but waterline beam is equally important in design terms while the various rating rules may call for beam measurement at specific levels in an effort to gauge the shape of the hull.
Bearing The direction of an object from the observer, as defined by compass notation.
Bear up, bear down In the past, confusion has resulted from the old terms 'helm up' or 'helm down' to indicate pulling the tiller towards you or pushing it away. Most sailors now accept 'up' as meaning towards the wind and vice versa. Hence, 'bear up', 'head up' and 'point up' mean to sail closer to the wind while 'bear away', 'bear down', 'head off' have the contrary meaning.
Beat, beating Sailing upwind by steering as close to the wind as the yacht is able, in a series of tacks.
Beaufort Scale Scale in which wind force is graded by the numbers 1 – 12 with corresponding descriptions of sea-state.
Becket Small circle or loop of rope.
Belay Make fast a rope to a cleat or pin.
Bend A knot used to join two ropes or a rope to an object.
Bermuda Race See *The Great Races*.
Bermudan rig Having a mainsail which is 'jib-headed', i.e. triangular and coming to a point at the top of the mast. The Bermudan rig is simpler and more efficient than gaff rig in which a spar supports the upper edge of the mainsail.
Berth Literally, a sleeping-place aboard ship but also a place where the ship can 'lie' while in harbour. Giving something a 'wide berth' means keeping well clear of it.
Bight Loop of rope or loop-shaped bay.
Bilge The lowest point of the inside of the hull, where any water will collect.
Bilge pump Means of removing water from the bilge. The most popular hand-pump is the diaphragm type which is able to remove debris as well as clean water.
Binnacle A housing or stand for the main compass which also contains its correctors and lamps.
Bitts, bitter end The strong-point to which the inboard end of a ship's anchor cable was attached was called the 'bitts'; hence, if you reached the 'bitter end' there was no more cable left. If a yachtsman forgets to fix the end of the anchor warp or chain to a strong-point he may well feel bitter as he watches the whole lot disappear to the bottom.
Block Device for changing the direction of pull in a line. Normally, a wheel, grooved to take the appropriate size of rope or wire, contained in a shell or casing which can be attached to a fixed point in various ways.
Blooper (or big boy) A large, light sail which is set flying (not attached to a stay) from the stem head. Normally used at the same time as a spinnaker and on the opposite side, the blooper increases sail area and improves balance of the sail-plan when running.
Board-sailing (windsurfing). Sailing on a surfboard-like craft having a mast which is attached to the board by a universal joint, enabling it to swivel in any direction. The rig has a curved, double boom or 'wish-bone' which the sailor holds by hand or is attached to by a body-harness.
Bobstay A stay from the stem to the bowsprit end to stop it from bending upwards.
Bollard Short, sturdy post on deck or quayside for attaching mooring lines.
Boltrope Rope sewn along the edges of a sail to give it strength.
Boom A spar along the lower edge of a sail to which the sheet is attached so that the sail can be trimmed for various wind-directions.
Boot-top A band of paint (usually in a contrasting colour) at the waterline marking the change from bottom to topside.
Bosun's chair Small seat or harness attached to a halyard and used to hoist crew aloft.
Bottlescrew (More correctly called a rigging-screw or turn-buckle.) A tubular fitting threaded in opposite senses at each end so that rotating the body pulls the ends together. Used for tensioning wire rigging such as the shrouds and stays of a yacht.
Bow or bows The forward part of a sailing vessel.
Bower The main anchor, usually carried forward.
Bowline Knot forming a loop that will not slip or jamb. One of the commonest knots used on a yacht, it has many uses.
Bowsprit Spar extending forward from the stem-head to enable extra headsails to be set.
Broach To round up into the wind uncontrollably. If a boat is running before a steep sea there is a tendency

Board-sailing takes many forms. This is a special 'sinker' made for speed competitions.

for the bow to bury into the wave ahead and for the stern to be swept round by the one astern and this can lead to loss of control. In sailing, the term normally refers to the situation when the helmsman loses control of a yacht that is being pressed hard on a spinnaker reach.
Bulkhead The internal divisions of a vessel. In a modern yacht bulkheads are normally athwartships and are an essential part of the strength of the hull. There may be a watertight bulkhead forward to guard against flooding following a collision.
Bulwark The part of the topside that extends above the deck.
Bump In measuring a yacht for IOR rating, various measurements are taken at specific points on the hull and the formula can be deceived by placing bumps on the hull to increase the measurement at that point. There are rules to limit the extent of bumping.
Bumpkin A short boom projecting over the stern, like a bowsprit in reverse, to provide a sheeting point for a mizzen.
Bunk Nautical bed.
Bunting Woollen cloth that is used to make flags.
Buoy An anchored floating mark placed for navigational purposes or as a turning mark in a race. The International Association of Lighthouse Authorities (IALA) controls the buoyage system used around the coasts of the world though many countries still have local systems, especially for rivers and inland waters. The shape and colour of buoys, the sounds they make and lights they display warn the mariner of various dangers. (See *Cruising*.)
Burgee Flag flown at the masthead. Normally pointed and with a design indicating the yacht club to which the vessel belongs.
By the head Trimmed bow-down. The converse is 'By the stern'.
By the lee With the wind blowing from the same side as the main boom, when a sailing vessel is running.

C

Cable Originally, the extra-strong rope used for the anchor was called cable and hence cable is used as the term for anchor line even when it is actually chain. Also used as a unit of distance at sea: a cable is 100 fathoms, or 200 yards or a tenth of a nautical mile.
Call-sign Every vessel licensed to use a radio transmitter is allocated a call-sign, a group of letters and numbers which must be given when contacting a coast radio station.
Canvas Strictly, a cloth woven from hemp but also a general word for sails.
Capsize When a boat heels beyond the point of no return and either turns right over or lies swamped on her side, she is said to be 'capsized'.
Capstan A vertically-mounted cylinder, turned by machinery, used for weighing anchor.
Carbon fibre Material with very high strength and low stretch characteristics used to reinforce high-stress areas of a yacht's structure.
Cardinal North, South, East and West are the Cardinal Points of the compass.
Careen To pull a vessel over on her side in order to clean the bottom of fouling or for repairs.
Carry way To go on moving through the water without propulsion.
Cartography The science of chart-making.
Carvel Planked hull construction in which the planks lie flush so that the outside of the hull presents a smooth surface.
Cascover Nylon and resin covering used to make wooden hulls more durable and waterproof.
Cast off To let go lines connecting a vessel to the shore, to a buoy or to another vessel.
Cat-boat In the USA, a small sailing boat with a single sail.
Catamaran Boat that has two parallel hulls.
Caulk, caulking To caulk is to drive a material such as cotton, oakum or old rope into the gap between the planks of a wooden vessel, to make the hull waterproof. The caulked seam is then sealed to keep the caulking dry.
Centre-board Retractable keel fitted on the centre-line of a dinghy or yacht, particularly used on small craft kept ashore. Centre-boards are normally pivoted at their forward end and fit into a watertight casing in the bottom of the boat whereas a dagger-board is a simple sliding keel which moves straight up and down.
Centre of buoyancy (CB) The point through which the total buoyancy of the hull can be considered to act.
Centre of effort (CE) The geometrical centre of the sail-plan. Since sails are aerofoils rather than flat plates, the real centre of effort is further forward than the geometrical one.
Centre of lateral resistance (CLR) The geometrical centre of a vessel's underwater profile. The relationship between CE and CLR is important in achieving balance in a sailing vessel.
Chafe Wear away by continual rubbing.
Chain-plates Fittings on the sides of a yacht to which the shrouds are attached.
Chart Map of a sea area, showing the depth of water, any land features, hazards, navigational marks, buoys etc. Charts invariably have a compass rose printed on them so that the navigator can rule off courses and this also shows the magnetic variation for the area covered. Chart datum is the water-level from which charted depths and heights are measured, usually the lowest level to which the tide is predicted to fall.
Chart-table Table or desk set aside for navigation.
Chine The angle between the bottom and topsides. Where this is a sharp angle, the boat is said to be 'hard-chined'.
Chinese gybe An unintentional gybe in which the main boom comes across but the upper part of the sail remains on the original side.
Chock-a-block When the blocks of a tackle come together so no further movement is possible. Also known as 'two blocks'.
Chronometer Accurate timepiece. Vital for finding longitude by astro-navigation. Not so important nowadays when correct time can be readily obtained by radio and there are other methods of ocean position-finding.
Class A collection of yachts to the same design or built to the same measurement or rule is called a 'class' and this implies some kind of club or organization to run the affairs of the class. In the case of small racing boats this generally consists of an owner's association, affiliated to a national sailing authority or in the case of International classes, to the International Yacht Racing Union.
Classification Both ships and yachts can be surveyed for seaworthiness by a classification society such as Lloyd's Register, American Bureau of Shipping or government departments. After survey, a vessel is given a classification lasting a certain number of years until a further survey is called for. The original purpose was an assurance of seaworthiness to shippers and underwriters of cargo. Certain types of yacht, such as the International 12-metre Class, can only be built under Lloyd's Special Survey, which means constant supervision by a surveyor during building, and according to scantlings rules which lay down the structural requirements. This is expensive but many cruising yachts are built under 'series production survey', which means that the classification society has approved the premises and working methods and makes regular visits. This acts as a guarantee to the purchaser that a yacht has been properly built.

Claw Partial ring used as a means of attaching vang or mainsheet to a boom which cannot have a fixed attachment point because it is to be used for roller-reefing.
Claw off To sail to windward away from a lee shore, especially when the weather is bad.
Cleat Fitting for belaying a line. A simple cleat consists of a bar fixed at its centre, around which the line is wound in a figure-of-eight pattern but there are many other forms of cleat designed to jamb, grip or squeeze a line.
Clipper Fast sailing ship designed to 'clip' the time required for a journey. First applied to Baltimore clippers, small despatch-boats, blockade-runners and slavers from the Baltimore area. In the 1840s and 1850s American shipping enjoyed a hectic boom which called for faster ships and resulted in the famous clipper-ships of McKay and others. British clippers built for the tea trade and the Australian wool trade came later.
Close-hauled Sailing as close to the wind as possible.
Clove-hitch Bend formed from two half-hitches. (See *Cruising*.)
Coachroof Part of the cabin roof which is raised above deck-level in order to give increased head-room.
Coaming Raised edge to hatches, cockpits or other deck-openings to stop water running in.
Coble Open fishing boat of the Yorkshire coast with a double keel aft to enable it to be beached stern first.
Cocked hat Small triangle formed on the chart where lines of position cross. A small cocked hat indicates an accurate position.
Cockpit Sunken area of the deck with seats for helmsman and crew. In a modern yacht, the tiller or wheel is in the cockpit and most of the control lines are brought back to this area to give a centralized control point.
Coil Way of stowing rope by arranging it in series of turns.
Coir Hairy, lightweight rope that floats and is made from coconut husk; it is not much used nowadays.
Companion Ladder between decks.
Compass Instrument showing the yacht's heading. Normally magnetic but others are possible — such as instruments that point to a particular radio transmitter. Gyros are not normally found on yachts. Magnetic compasses must be corrected or calibrated for deviation (caused by the vessel's residual magnetism) and its reading must also be corrected for variation, the difference between magnetic and true north in the area in which the vessel is sailing.
Composite Built using a mixture of materials, e.g. wooden planking on metal frames or in modern racing yachts, a mixture of different plastics and reinforcement fibres.
Con To give orders to the helmsman while manoeuvring.
Counter Overhanging part of the stern.
Course General term for direction at sea; needs to be used with care to avoid imprecision. 'Track' is the line across the sea-bed that the vessel follows and 'required track' the intended line. 'Heading' refers to the direction in which the vessel is pointing regardless of track which may be affected by tidal stream, leeway etc. 'Course to steer' is the heading required to make good a particular track. 'Wake course' is the line the vessel makes through the water. 'Compass course' is the heading to be steered by the helmsman after any corrections for variation and deviation.
Cove line Incised line along the topsides of a yacht below the sheer-strake. Traditionally gilded, nowadays it is painted.
Covering board Outermost plank of the deck, which covers the top of the topside planking.
Cowes Harbour on the Isle of Wight which is the home of the best-known traditional yachting regatta in Britain, Cowes Week. Run by a group of yacht clubs which together form the Cowes Combined Clubs, it provides racing for more than 30 classes of yacht.
CQR Type of patented stockless plough anchor. The name is a play on 'secure'.
Cradle A frame to support a vessel when it is ashore.
Cringle Reinforced hole in a sail for attaching things such as reefing lines.
Cross-trees Spreaders fixed across a mast with outer ends fixed to the shrouds, to give mid-panel support to the mast.
Crutch A supporting stanchion to hold the boom when not in use. Also, the semicircular fittings that hold the oars on a dinghy — often called rowlocks.
Cuddy Small cabin or shelter.
Cunningham hole or eye American helmsman Briggs Cunningham had a favourite cotton mainsail that stretched until it was too long on the luff. He therefore fitted an extra eyelet in the luff above the original tack and used this to tension the luff. Today, every racing mainsail is fitted with a Cunningham eye.
Current Continuous water-flow in the same direction. Not to be confused with tidal stream which changes direction with every turn of the tide.
Cutter Sailing boat with one mast and two headsails.

D

Dacron Dupont's polyester fibre, used for making sailcloth. In Britain, the equivalent is ICI's Terylene.
Dan buoy A small float with a flagstaff attached to it for marking position at sea. Offshore racing yachts must carry a dan buoy with a flag and light, attached to a lifebuoy which is thrown over to mark the position of a man overboard.
Danforth Popular type of anchor with two hinged blades which dig into the bottom. Very easy to stow as it folds away flat.
Davit Small crane or hoist for lifting small boat aboard.
Dead reckoning Position-finding purely by plotting course, distance and tidal set and drift without receiving any information from outside the yacht.
Deadwood Area of solid timbering between the bottom of the hull and the top of the ballast.
Decca Navigator A 'hyperbolic' radio position fixing system in which the signals from a 'master' and two 'slave' transmitters are resolved by the receiving set to give a latitude and longitude position. Originally, special charts overprinted with lines of position had to be used but the modern Decca set does all the 'working out' internally and gives a direct read-out of position. In addition, there are very useful features such as the ability to store a number of 'way-points' and to display course and distance to any one of them.
Deck Horizontal surfaces aboard ship. A yacht has just one deck but a ship may have several, at different levels.
Deckhead The underside of a deck and hence the cabin roof.
Departure The last point at which a definite fix can be obtained by bearings of the shore as a vessel sails away from the land. Hence the reference point from which dead reckoning calculations begin.
Depth sounder Often called 'echo-sounder' or, in USA, 'fathometer'. A relatively simple electronic device that sends out an impulse that bounces off the sea-bed and returns to the transducer. The time taken for the echo to return indicates the depth. A straightforward sounder without any special features is a reliable device found on virtually any sea-going yacht.
Deviation Error of the magnetic compass caused by vessel's own residual magnetism. In a yacht, large metal objects such as the engine create deviation which can seldom be completely corrected because the effect is different at various headings and

angles of heel. The compass adjuster places small correcting magnets alongside the compass to reduce deviation to acceptable limits and then prepares a deviation card showing the errors on various headings. Steel yachts normally need to be fitted with Kelvin spheres, iron balls which compensate for the fact that the vessel is longer than it is wide.
Diagonal and double-diagonal Method of wood construction in which thinner, narrower planks than normal are laid at 45 degrees to each other over a mould. With modern moulded wood construction, waterproof glue is applied between the layers to obtain a seamless wooden shell.
Diamonds Stays that stiffen the upper part of a fractionally-rigged mast.
Dinghy Small boat, normally kept ashore or carried aboard a seagoing yacht.
Dipping lug Rig in which the lugsail yard projects forward of the mast and in which the yard must be partly lowered and 'dipped' behind the mast on tacking.
Displacement The weight of any floating vessel which is exactly equivalent to the weight of water displaced.
Distress signals Signals made to indicate that a ship needs help. These can be flag, semaphore, smoke, hand or lamp signals but by far the most effective signals are by radio or by setting off pyrotechnics. Certain radio frequencies are set aside for distress working and there is supposed to be a silent period for three minutes past every hour and half hour when distress calls have a better chance of being heard. When a ship indicates she is in distress, any other ship in the vicinity has an absolute obligation under international law to render whatever assistance lies within her power.
Dodgers Canvas screens rigged along the lifelines alongside the cockpit to give protection from the weather.
Dogwatch So that watch-keepers should not have to keep the same watches each day, two half-watches of two hours each are kept between 1600 and 2000. Traditionally, this is also when the main meal of the day is served and is a social period because the whole crew is awake at the same time.
Dory Small open boat originally used by fishermen working from schooners on the Newfoundland Grand Banks. Nowadays, a small, open runabout, usually with a double-vee bottom and squarish plan-form.
Downhaul Tackle or other device to place a downward pull on a sail or spar.
Drag Resistance to motion.
Drag anchor, to Pull the anchor along the bottom when it fails to grip.
Draught The depth of water that a vessel needs to float. Not to be confused with 'draft', the sectional depth of a sail.
Drogue Device for producing drag in the water. Normally a strong, canvas cone with a metal ring to keep the mouth open and provide attachment points. Used as a sea-anchor or drag to slow a boat down in heavy weather.

E

Ease Relax the tension on sheets, or other running rigging.
Ebb The time during which the tide is falling, flowing back.
Eddy A circular swirl of water or airflow which does not follow the main direction of stream.
Ensign Flag, carried at the stern, to show the nationality of a vessel. Some countries use the same ensign for every type of vessel while others — Great Britain for instance — have different ensigns for merchant ships and naval vessels. A number of countries allow a special yacht ensign 'defaced' with the device of a particular yacht club.
Entry That part of the forebody that cuts the water.
Eye Loop in the end of a line, often formed round a metal thimble.
Eye-splice Loop formed in the end of a line by turning it back on itself and tucking the strands through the lay several times.

F

Fair Of a wind, one which will enable a sailing boat to reach its destination without tacking. Of a hull, one that has even, pleasing curves, free from bumps or discontinuities.
Fairlead Fitting, usually metal, to give a rope its correct line of pull and prevent it from chafing on sharp edges.
Fairway The main navigable channel. Usually the deepest part.
Fall The hauling end of a tackle or halyard.
Fastnet Race Biennial 600-mile race from Cowes to Plymouth via the Fastnet Rock, a lighthouse off the South Coast of Ireland. It was the first really serious offshore race in Europe, first sailed in 1925 and now forms the climax of the Admiral's Cup Series. In 1979 the Fastnet fleet was hit by exceptionally bad weather which resulted in the deaths of 15 people, the only really serious disaster in the history of the sport. (See *The Great Races*.)
Fathom Nautical measure of depth equal to 6ft or 1.83m. Charts in most countries use metres rather than fathoms nowadays.
Feather Of oars, to twist them to the horizontal on the backstroke to reduce their air-drag. Of propellers, to twist the blades into the line of the water-flow as a means of reducing drag when not required. Of a sailing boat, to sail closer to the wind than would normally be advantageous so as to get through a squall without reefing.
Fender Soft or padded bumper to prevent damage when a vessel is lying alongside.

Putting out the fenders.

Ferro-cement Material which can be used for building the hulls of yachts in which a specially formulated cement mortar is 'plastered' on to a framework of steel and wire mesh.
Fetch To arrive at or make up to a desired point. Also, the unsheltered distance to the nearest weather shore.
Fiddle Raised edges or divisions fitted to cabin furniture to stop things falling off.
Fitting out Preparing a boat for the sea by painting the hull, making good repairs, overhauling equipment, shipping supplies and so on.
Fix A reliable navigational position arrived at by good cross-bearings or astronomical observation.
Flare Outward slope of a boat's topsides. Also, a pyrotechnic signal.
Flashing Navigational light in which period of light is less than period of darkness. To identify a light, the flashes may be coloured, arranged into groups of a particular duration or indicate a Morse code signal.

Flood Inward flow of the rising tide.
Flotsam Floating wreckage.
Fluke The flattened blades or palms of an anchor that provide resistance to its being pulled through the ground.
Flush deck Continuous deck unbroken by a coachroof or doghouse.
Fog signals Coded signals that a vessel makes with her fog-horn to give information about herself, e.g. under way, stopped, towing, fishing, under sail, at anchor etc.
Foot The lower edge of a sail.
Fore and aft Lengthways in relation to the vessel.
Forecastle Pronounced *fo'c'sle*. Accommodation under the deck forward. Traditionally, where the seamen lived.
Foredeck The deck forward of the mast. On a racing yacht the foredeck hand is in charge of headsails and spinnakers.
Foreguy Line leading forward from main or spinnaker boom to prevent it from swinging aft.
Forestay The stay that prevents the mast from falling over backwards. In a yacht it is also the attachment for the main headsail.
Fore-triangle The area bounded by the forestay, the mast and the foredeck.
Forward Towards the bow.
Foul Obstructed or entangled; the opposite to clear.
Founder Sink, due to ingress of water.
Frames The transverse structural members of a hull. Often wrongly called 'ribs'.
Freeboard The vertical height between the waterline and the deck edge. An important factor in most rating rules.
Full and bye Close-hauled but with the sails pulling well.
Furl To gather in and secure sails.

G

Gaff The spar to which the upper edge of a sail is laced.
Gale Wind of Force 8 or 9 on the Beaufort scale (37–54 knots, 19–27 metres per second). Winds of Force 10 and 11 are called storms while Force 12 is a hurricane.
Galley Marine kitchen.
Gallows A goal-post shaped frame to support the main-boom when it is not in use.
Genoa Large jib that overlaps the mainsail.
Gimbals Pair of concentric rings fixed to each other with swivels so that a weighted object, such as a compass, can be mounted in the centre, allowing it to remain horizontal when the vessel heels.
Glass Reinforced Plastics (GRP) The proper name for what most people call glass-fibre. A structural laminate which is formed from thin glass fibres, arranged in strands, or random mat or woven into a cloth and fixed with a synthetic resin, usually polyester or epoxy. 'Fibreglass' is a registered trade mark.
Go about To tack.
Goose-neck Fitting that attaches a boom to the mast with a universal joint action.
Goose-winged Running with mainsail set on one side and headsail on the opposite side.
Great circle A circle on the surface of the earth with its centre at the centre of the earth, e.g. all meridians and the Equator are great circles. The shortest distance between two points on the earth's surface will always form part of a great circle so ships wish to sail along them to save fuel. However, a great circle forms a curve when drawn on a Mercator projection so in practice ships steer a series of straight courses called rhumb lines, which together form an approximate great circle.
Greenwich Mean Time The time at the Prime Meridian which runs through the Royal Observatory at Greenwich, London. It is used as the basis of all nautical almanacs and hence is the starting point for any astro-navigational calculation.
Ground, to Come in contact with the bottom.
Gunter Rig in which a gaff is hoisted until it is nearly parallel with the mast, so extending its effective height. The Mirror Dinghy is an example of a modern dinghy with gunter rig.
Gunwhale The rail or reinforcement that runs around the top outer edge of the deck.
Guy Wire or rope used to steady a spar etc. When setting a spinnaker, the line attached to the free clew is called the 'sheet' and the one attached at the spinnaker-boom end is called the 'guy'.
Gybe Alter course when running so that the stern swings through the eye of the wind and the main-boom is swung across from one side to the other.
Gypsy Serrated wheel fixed to the side of a windlass which grips the anchor chain. Normally attached to the windlass via a brake which can be released in order to let the anchor go.

H

Halyard Line for hoisting a sail or flag.
Hand-hold An essential feature of any sea-going craft; it should be possible to find a secure hand-hold wherever you are in the boat. Normally fitted along the sides of the cabin-top or coachroof and at strategic points inside the cabin.
'Handy-billy' a portable tackle used for a variety of tasks.
Hank A sliding clip for attaching a headsail to its stay.
Hard A ramp or piece of firm ground where small boats may be launched.
Harness (safety) A strong body-harness from which a line can be used to clip on to suitable strong-points on deck, to prevent falling overboard. Together with life-jacket, the most important safety aid on a sea-going yacht. Also, trapeze harness, a device to allow the body-weight to be carried on a wire to increase the stability of a small boat or sailboard.
Hasler gear Self-steering of the type designed by the late Col. 'Blondie' Hasler who was famous for introducing the Chinese junk rig to European cruising yachts and for developing one of the most effective wind-vane self-steering systems. The Hasler gear uses an additional servo rudder of very narrow chord which is turned by a wind-vane mounted above it. The servo-rudder is pivoted so that when the blade is turned it exerts a sideways force which is harnessed to operate the yacht's main rudder.
Hatch An aperture giving access through a deck. In yachts, hatches must be fitted with waterproof covers; these are often made from some kind of transparent plastic so that the hatch also serves as a skylight.
Hawse The hole through which the anchor cable enters the hull. A pipe leading the cable down to the cable-locker is called a 'hawse-pipe'.
Hawser Strong rope used for mooring, warping, towing etc.
Heads Sea toilet. So called because the ship's toilet used to be right forward at the 'beak-head'.
Headsail Any sail that is set forward of the mast.
Head-sea Waves coming from ahead.
Heave-to To bring a vessel to a stop.
Heaving line A light line with a heavy knot at one end which can be thrown effectively and used as a messenger for a heavier line.
Heel To lean over. Also, the lower end of a mast.
Helm The tiller or wheel.
Helmsman The person who is steering.
Highfield lever An over-centre lever used for setting up running backstays; not seen much nowadays.
High seas, the Those parts of the ocean not claimed as part of any state's territorial waters.
Hitch Knot used to attach a rope to spar or stay but not to another rope.

Hoist To haul up a sail etc. Also, the luff of a fore-and-aft sail and that part of a flag which lies next to the staff.
Holding The ground available for anchoring, which may provide good or bad holding.
Horse A bar athwartships along which the sheet can slide on tacking.
Hounds The point at which the lower shrouds meet the mast. A modern yacht may have a 'hounds band' at this point to which the shrouds are attached.
Hull The main body or shell of a vessel below the deck.
Hydraulics Means of applying force remotely by pumping fluid, usually oil, along pipes. Much used in modern racing yachts to apply tension selectively to various parts of the rig or to raise the whole rig to alter the general tension. The attraction of hydraulics on a yacht is that a force of many tons can be applied quickly and easily by one person using a hand-pump and can be accurately measured with a pressure gauge so that tuning settings are repeatable. Hydraulics can also be used for remote control of steering and for applications such as the powering of an anchor windlass by the main engine.

I

Ice-box Container for keeping food and drinks cool on board. A simple version is a heavily-insulated box into which ice or chilled blocks are put with the food. Many modern yachts have electric or compressor-driven chillers to make the ice-box a small deep-freeze.
Inboard Towards the centre of the vessel.
Injection moulding Method of making small fittings by injecting plastics into metal moulds under high pressure. Numerous small cleats, fairleads etc. are made this way.
Inshore Towards the shore.
'International' In sailing terms, normally refers to a class of boat adopted for international class racing by the International Yacht Racing Union. The exception is the International 10 sq metre Canoe which is administered by the Canoe Union. The classes selected for the Olympics must be drawn from the International classes which range in size from the International 12-metre down to the International Optimist.
International Code of Signals Set of coloured flags and pennants which represent the letters of the alphabet, the numbers 1–9 and some procedural points. By using single flags or groups of two or three, a whole volume of messages can be formed and these have the advantage of being intelligible in any language without translation.
International Offshore Rule (IOR) The rating rule under which most of the major offshore events are run. Created in 1971 as a fusion of the main European and American rules, it uses an intricate series of measurements of the yacht's hull and rig to produce a Rating in feet which is an evaluation of its potential speed. The Rating can be used in a number of ways to give a handicap figure.
International Yacht Racing Union The world governing body of yacht racing. Its members are national sailing authorities and it is responsible for the racing rules, administration of the International classes, organization of the Olympic regatta and other matters. In recent years there has been a degree of tension between the IYRU which claims control of all yachting and the ORC which actually controls offshore racing.
Irons, in When a sailing vessel is caught head to wind and unable to pay off on to either tack, she is said to be 'in irons'.
Isophase Light with equal periods of light and darkness.

J

J Class The Universal Rule of measurement, designed in the USA by Nathanael Herreshof, had a number of rating bands designated by letters of the Alphabet with 'J' the largest ever to be used. Yachts of 'J' Class rating were used for the America's Cup in the 1930s. Only ten were built and the last was *Ranger*, built for the 1937 defence; she far outclassed any racing yacht built up to that time.
Jackstaff Small flag-pole in the bows.
Jackstay Solid metal rod fixed to a spar or yard to bend sails to.
Jib On sailing vessels with a bowsprit, the jib or jibs are the headsails set from the bowsprit and the sail set on the main forestay is called a 'staysail'. On modern yachts, the majority of which are sloops, the sail set on the main forestay is called the 'jib' (or genoa) and another headsail, set abaft it either flying or on an inner forestay, is called a 'staysail'.
Jockey-pole A short spar rigged from the mast to the spinnaker guy. When a yacht is spinnaker reaching with its spinnaker boom right forward on the forestay, the guy meets it at a very shallow angle placing a heavy compression strain on the boom. The jockey pole alleviates this and keeps the guy from chafing on the shrouds.
Junior Offshore Group Club formed in the 1950s to cater for those who wished to race yachts too small to enter the events of the Royal Ocean Racing Club. The Midget Ocean Racing Club answered the same need in the USA.
Junk European name for the type of sailing vessel used in the Far East that has a fully-battened, balanced sail. The two great advantages of junk rig are the extreme simplicity of reefing — the sail just folds down on to itself like a Venetian blind — and the fact that being balanced, sheeting forces are low.

Chinese 'junk' rig has many practical advantages.

Jury-rig Any kind of makeshift arrangement rigged temporarily after damage, particularly dismasting.

K

Kedge Light anchor for temporary use.
Keel Originally, the lowest continuous fore-and-aft structural member — the ship's 'back-bone' — but in yachts, the downwards extension of the hull that provides resistance to sideways movement through the water. The 'centre-board' or 'dagger-board' of a dinghy is an unballasted keel but the majority of sea-going yachts carry iron or lead in their keels to give the hull stability. As yachts became lighter and faster, so keels have developed into pure foils sticking straight out from the underside of the canoe body, with the rudder being separate rather than a hinged extension to the keel. Developments aimed at lowering the centre of gravity and improving the lift/drag ratio have resulted in keels with the weight concentrated in a bulb at the bottom or in wings or in a combination of the two.
Keelson An internal keel to provide additional strength.
Ketch Two-masted vessel with the mizzen-mast stepped forward of the rudder-post. Originally used as a small coastal trading vessel.
Kevlar Dupont's aramid fibre which can be woven into a cloth having very high strength and low stretch characteristics. Very commonly used for the sails of offshore racing yachts where its great advantage is that a given sail can be used over a wider range of wind-speeds than one made of conventional materials. Disadvantages are high cost, tendency to tear unexpectedly, and difficulty of handling due to stiffness of the material.
Kicking-strap, or kicker Called a 'vang' in the USA. A tackle or adjustable strut used to produce a downward pull on the main-boom. Without a kicking-strap, the boom tends to rise as soon as the mainsheet is eased and it is no longer possible to control the shape of the sail.
King-plank The central plank in a laid deck.
King-spoke The spoke of the wheel that is upright when the helm is central, usually given a distinctive mark.
Kites Additional lightweight sails used by square-rigged ships to employ light following winds.
Knot General term for bends, hitches and tucks in ropes. Also, a speed of one nautical mile per hour.

L

LANBY Large Automatic Navigation Buoy. A large floating beacon which provides almost all the services of a light-ship but is unmanned and therefore cheaper.
Lanyard Short piece of rope with several uses such as a handle or lashing.
Lash, to; lashing To secure objects on board by tying them down; and the kind of light line used for this purpose.
Launch To place a vessel into the water. Also, a small motor-boat or tender.
Lay The direction the strands of a rope are twisted up is called the 'lay'.
Lazy A spare line of any kind which is rigged but is not currently in use.
Lead A line with a lead weight at its end used for measuring depth of water before echo-sounders came into general use. A series of knots and pieces of material at intervals enabled the leadsman to know how much line had run out.
Lee, leeward The down-wind side of anything; in the direction of the wind. If a yacht is 'in the lee' of something it means that she is sheltered from the wind by it.
Lee-board A flat-bottomed sailing barge cannot be fitted with a keel so, to prevent it from going sideways through the water, pivotted boards are lowered down on the lee side and these have to be changed over on tacking. Most commonly seen on Thames sailing barges and various Dutch round and flat-bottomed barges.
Lee-cloth Canvas sides to a bunk to prevent the occupant from falling out when the vessel heels. When not required they can be folded away under the mattress so that the bunk may be used as a settee.
Leeway The sideways drift of a vessel, relative to course.
Level rating The concept of racing in rated yachts but at a fixed rating level so that the races can take place without handicap — first home wins.
Life-jacket Garment providing buoyancy. A 'life-jacket' should be made to strict standards with the intention of supporting the wearer's head above the water even if unconscious. Garments designed for active watersports such as dinghy-racing, board-sailing etc. and which provide a lower level of safety are called 'buoyancy aids'.
Life-line Lines fixed around the deck to stop the crew from falling overboard. A yacht normally has rigid tubular rails at the bow and stern known as the 'pulpit' and 'pushpit' and the life-lines run from these through a series of stanchions mounted on the deck-edge.
Life-raft Inflatable rafts carried by ships, yachts and aircraft in case of emergency. They are normally made with a roof to give protection from the weather and carry basic supplies of water and dried food. One lesson of the 1979 Fastnet disaster was that a life-raft was not necessarily a safer place to be than a badly disabled yacht and the recommendation nowadays is to stay with a yacht unless it is definitely sinking.
Lightship Ship resembling a floating lighthouse, moored to warn of a shoal or other danger. Many lightships are now being replaced by unmanned LANBYs.
Line squall Violent and dangerous squall associated with an active cold front. Its presence is often advertised by a line of low cloud.
List Permanent heel due to unbalanced weights or loading.
'Little America's Cup' Popular name for the International Catamaran Challenge Trophy, run on similar lines to the America's Cup but using catamarans of the International 'C' Class. The trophy was given by the Seacliffe Yacht Club of Long Island, New York and the first challenge was in 1961.
Locker Cupboard or closed-off storage space aboard ship.
Log Instrument for measuring distance run through the water.
Log-book Book in which navigational observations and other details of ship's business are recorded.
Loom The glow of a light below the visible horizon, caused by reflection from clouds. Also, handle of an oar.
LORAN American hyperbolic radio navigation system. The initials stand for Long Range Navigation.
Lubber line The line on the forward edge of a compass bowl that indicates the position of ship's head.
Luff The forward edge of a sail. Also, 'to luff' means to turn a sailing yacht towards head-to-wind. This is a legitimate defensive move in racing to prevent another yacht from passing to windward.

M

Mainsail The sail set on the mainmast. Not necessarily the largest sail as the genoa of a sloop often has greater area than the mainsail, but the one which is kept set as long as the yacht is under way. For this reason, the mainsail has to be of robust construction and able to cope with different wind strengths.
Make, to Verb with a general sense of 'do', 'carry out' or 'attain', e.g. 'make

harbour', to reach it; 'make way', move through the water; 'make fast', secure the lines; 'make sail', set more sails etc.
Marina Term originating in the USA for a yacht harbour which may have a range of complementary facilities such as shops, repair-yards, restaurants, living accommodation etc.
Marline Two-stranded thin line, either tarred or untarred.
Marline spike Spike used for separating the strands of a rope in order to splice it.
Maroon Explosive rocket used as a signal of distress or for calling out lifeboat crew.
Mast The main, vertical spar that holds the sails up. Formerly, all masts were of wood but today aluminium is the commonest material while a few are made of composite plastics. On some yachts the mast is made strong enough to stand without rigging but most are supported by stays in the fore-and-aft line and shrouds athwartships. For a racing yacht, the mast must be as thin as possible to reduce the air drag but at the same time not excessively heavy. It must also bend in a controlled way so that the shape of the sails can be adjusted.
Maxi-yacht Ocean racing yacht built at or near the maximum permitted IOR rating of 70ft.
Mayday The word used to preface a distress call. From the French *M'aidez* — help me.
Messenger A light line which can be used to bring a heavier one into place, e.g. reefing-lines or spare halyards.
Mini-Ton Level rating competition for yachts of 16.5ft rating.
Miss stays, to Fail to complete a tack.
Mizzen The sail set on the after-mast of a ketch or yawl. In a ketch the mizzen mast is stepped ahead of the rudder post and in a yawl abaft it. Yawls are relatively unusual nowadays but the ketch rig is still popular for cruising yachts because the total sail area is divided up into several more easily-handled units.
Moor, to Properly speaking, to moor is to lie to two anchors but the term more usually means to lie alongside, secure with warps.
Mooring Heavy ground-tackle which is left permanently in place so that a yacht can come and go without laying anchors each time. A mooring in tidal waters normally consists of a heavy ground chain with weights or anchors at each end and a lighter riser surmounted by a buoy.
Motor sailer Cruising yacht in which performance under sail and under power are given more-or-less equal priority in the design.

A marina need not be simply a boat-park — it can be integrated with other development.

Multihull Boat with more than one hull. The principal attraction of a multihull is that it derives its stability from beam rather than ballast and is thus lighter. Other advantages, which do not neccessarily attach to every multihull, are high performance, low draught, freedom from heeling and rolling, and a greater deck area. The big disadvantage of any unballasted craft is that it lacks the ultimate safety factor of being capable of righting itself from any angle.
Mylar Non-woven plastics film used in sailmaking. Since it has poor tear-strength, it is usually laminated to a woven substrate for sailmaking.

N

Nautical mile The distance on the earth's surface subtended by one minute of latitude at the earth's centre. Because the earth is not a perfect sphere the nautical mile is standardized as 6,080ft (1,852m).
Navigation The science of position-finding and of planning a safe course to the required destination.
Navigation lights The lights shown by sea-going vessels have the double purpose of showing what kind of vessel it is and in which direction it is heading. The lights that each type of vessel should show are laid down in the International Regulations for Preventing Collisions at Sea (IRPCAS).
Neap tides When the rise and fall is small, while the moon and sun are in quatrature.
Neaped or be-neaped When a grounded vessel cannot be floated off at high tide because the tidal range is decreasing. She must wait until spring tides return.
Newport, Rhode Island Venue of the America's Cup matches from 1920 to 1983.

O

Oar Long-handled paddle used as a lever to propel a boat. A single oar can be used to scull over the stern by twisting the blade at the same time as swinging it from side to side.
Observer Single-Handed Transatlantic Race Initiated by Lt. Col H.G. 'Blondie' Hasler in 1960 the 'OSTAR' was the first major transocean race for single-handed yachts. No longer sponsored by *The Observer*, the race is still organized by the Royal Western Yacht Club every four years and is now limited to yachts of up to 60ft.
Occulting light A navigational light whose periods of light are longer than the periods of darkness, i.e. the 'message' is carried by the periods of dark.
Ocean Cruising Club A club whose major requirement is that members must have cruised at least one thousand miles under sail non-stop.
Ocean racing The sport of racing on the open sea. Also called offshore racing.

Offing Distance away from the shore. Also, 'in the offing' means, to seaward.
Offshore one-designs A number of attempts have been made to produce one-design yachts suitable for offshore racing, in an endeavour to control the cost of the sport. Generally, these are overtaken by the desire of owners to have the most up-to-date boat possible but there have been a number of very successful one-design cruiser-racers such as the Cal 40, Contessa 32 and Sigma 33.
Offshore Racing Council World governing body of offshore racing that controls the International Offshore Rule (IOR) and the Measurement Handicap System (MHS).
Olympic Games Yachting has been an event of steadily-growing importance in the Olympic Games since 1900. The influence of the Olympics on yacht racing is immense, both on the boats themselves and on matters such as the Racing Rules, the type of course used, the scoring system, the method of deciding on disputes and many other administrative matters which are used as the standard throughout the sport. The classes at present used in the Olympic regatta are: sailboard (of a type chosen for each Olympiad), Finn, 470 (men), 470 (women), Flying Dutchman, Tornado, Star and Soling.
One Ton Cup The first of the 'level rating' competitions, it was the idea of Jean Peytel and was initiated in 1965 when it was contested by yachts rating 22ft under the now defunct RORC rating rule. The first winner was the Danish yacht *Diana* in a series held at Le Havre. The name came from the trophy itself which was an old one belonging to the Cercle de la Voile de Paris which had originally been for a type of keelboat rated at one ton. The other level-rating competitions (Half ton, Quarter ton etc.) are a play on the name of the event that inspired them.
One-design Class of small boat or yacht in which all examples are built to the same design so as to give the possibility of racing without handicap.
Onion Patch Trophy Series of races, similar in concept to the Admiral's Cup, beginning in Newport, Rhode Island and culminating in the Bermuda Race. (See *The Great Races*.)

P

Palm Sailmaker's thimble, set in a piece of stout leather that protects the hand.
Pay out To ease away.
Peak The top corner of a sail that is gaff-headed.
Pendant or pennant Tapered code flag used to indicate numbers and some procedural signals. Also, the lines used for pulling down a reef.
Pins Belaying pins are short lengths of metal or wood dropped through holes in a rail so as to form a 'belay' or securing point for lines. Cleats fulfil this function on a modern yacht. Clevis pins are the strong, solid pins that form the link between a fork-end of a rigging-screw or rigging terminal and a chain-plate or blade-end of the next piece of rigging in line. Split or Cotter pins are used to prevent clevis pins from falling out.
Pintle The verticle axle on which the rudder turns.
Pipe-cot Metal-framed bunk which can be folded against the ship's side when not in use.
Pitching Up-and-down motion of the bow and stern.
Pitch-pole End-over-end capsize.
Plane When a hull has sufficient speed for buoyancy to be replaced by dynamic lift, it is said to be 'planing'. To achieve this the boat involved must have a suitable shape, including a positive angle of attack in the fore-body to create lift and a substantially straight run so that it cannot get into exaggerated nose-up trim. It also needs a sufficiently high power-weight ratio to overcome the high-drag transition from the displacement to the planing condition.
Pooped, to be When a wave breaks over the stern of a vessel.
Port On the left hand side when looking forward.
Port tack Sailing with the wind coming from the port side, forward of the beam.
Portsmouth Yardstick An empirical rating system for dinghies and other small racing craft devised by K. Zilwood Milledge and administered in Britain by the Royal Yachting Association. A class is given a Portsmouth Number based on the average performance of many boats over a number of races and a simple time-on-time handicap formula is used to produce results. As no measuring is necessary the system is the commonest for handicapping mixed fleets of small boats.
Pram Small dinghy with a cut-off bow.
Proa Multihull consisting of one main hull and one outrigger. A Pacific proa carries its ama (outrigger) to windward and an Atlantic proa carries it to leeward.
Propeller Screw for translating engine torque into thrust.
Protest The procedure by which a racing yacht makes a claim that the Racing Rules have been broken. Following an incident in a race, the yacht wishing to enter a protest displays Code Flag B in the rigging and later makes a written submission to the protest committee or jury. They must then establish the facts and decide what action if any, to take.
Pulpit A fixed, solid section of guardrail around the bow of a yacht. A similar arrangement at the stern is jocularly known as a 'pushpit'.
Purchase A method of gaining mechanical advantage by use of rope rove through blocks or pulleys. The effectiveness of a purchase depends on the velocity ratio between the fall and the standing part but is reduced by the friction of the block or pulleys.

Q

Quarter Ton Cup Level rating competition for yachts that are rated 18.5ft IOR.
Quartering When wind or sea are coming from approximately 45 degrees abaft the beam, they are said to be 'quartering'.

R

Radar A word derived from 'Radio Direction and Range' which is the general term for the electromagnetic device that provides a 'picture' of the surroundings that does not depend on visible light. Modern developments have made possible radar suitable for virtually any boat with an electrical system. However, radar, like the human eye, can only see to the horizon which, with a height-of-eye of 6ft 6in (2m) is a mere 2.9 miles so the height at which the radar scanner can be fixed is critical. A development of great value is the RACON a beacon that incorporates a transponder triggered by radar signals. This produces a distinctive flash on the radar screen which in some cases is coded to show the identity of the beacon.
Radar reflector A purpose-built reflector for use at night and in poor visibility. The familiar reflector made from interlocking metal plates has now been largely replaced by ones which are contained within a neat plastics housing which is far easier to rig up and works better.
Radio Direction Finder A radio capable of receiving the signals from marine or aeronautical radio beacons and giving a line of position using a 'loop' aerial. Finding the bearing was formerly done by hand — a tedious

and fairly inaccurate process — but the automatic D/F sets now used give much better results.
Radio telephone By far the commonest type of radio fitted to yachts is the VHF radio telephone which allows spoken contact with shore stations or other ships up to a maximum of about 50 miles. To communicate over longer distances calls for the much more expensive medium or high-frequency single side-band radio equipment so this is normally only found on yachts that travel the oceans.
Rake Inclination of a mast away from the vertical.
Rating The process by which a yacht is given a number corresponding to her expected performance. Rating can be arrived at either by measurement, as in IOR or by averaging past performances, as in Portsmouth Yardsticks. Rating can be used in various ways to arrive at a handicap for a particular race or series. Rating is always given in feet, so it is not shown converted into metric units in the text.
Ratlines Lengths of rope tied across the shrouds so as to provide steps for easier climbing.
Reach, reaching A yacht is said to be sailing on a reach when the wind is from the side. When the wind is from ahead of abeam the yacht is on a 'close reach', when at right-angles to the yacht, on a 'beam reach' and when abaft the beam, on a 'broad reach'.
Reefing Reducing the sail area. Traditionally, mainsails are pulled down on to the boom by pendants at the tack and clew and this is still the favoured system on racing yachts as it does not spoil the shape of the sail.
Reeve Pass a rope through blocks to form a tackle. In general, a rope is said to be 'rove' whenever it is passed through holes or fittings to perform some useful function.
Rhumb line A line which cuts all meridians at the same angle. The importance of the rhumb line is that it appears as a straight line on a Mercator projection chart and so is the one invariably used for ruling off courses.
Rig The mast, sails, standing and running rigging. Also used to describe various arrangements of rig such as sloop rig, ketch rig etc.
Right of way The rules of the road for all types of seagoing vessel are described by the *International Regulations for Preventing Collisions at Sea (IRPCAS)*. The Yacht Racing Rules describe in far greater detail the rights and obligations of sailing yachts when racing.

Ratlines make it possible to climb the shrouds.

Roach Convex curve on the foot or leech of a sail. Almost all mainsails have a degree of roach; that is to say, they extend beyond a straight line between headboard and clew. Battens are needed to stop the roach from folding over.
Roller reefing and furling Reefing the mainsail by rotating its boom has been a familiar method for many years although it tends to make the reefed sail too baggy unless the boom is specially shaped. Roller reefing of headsails had to wait until suitable gear was developed but is now very popular as it is so much easier than changing sails and because one headsail can serve for a wide range of wind strengths. The most recent development is reefing and furling of the mainsail by rolling it up either inside a specially-made mast or just behind a normal one.
Rope Strictly, rope describes both fibre and wire cordage. Natural fibre ropes made from hemp, sisal or coconut coir have been almost entirely replaced by synthetic fibre ropes. Nylon is used for applications such as anchor cable where stretch is an advantage, Dacron/Terylene for sheets and general use, Kevlar where high strength and low stretch are important and various types of polypropylene for warps, floating ropes and other special purposes. The second great revolution in rope-making has been the change from twisted construction to plaited rope and the sheath and core type. Fibres, either natural or synthetic, are stronger if not twisted but need to be protected and held together. Most yacht rope therefore, is made from a core of continuous straight fibres, covered by a sheath of woven material. A different technique is needed to splice this type of rope. Steel wire rope is broadly divided into flexible and non-flexible depending on whether it is required for standing or running rigging.
Route du Rhum French-organized single-handed race from St Malo to Guadeloupe.
Rowlock Crutch fixed to gunwale of rowing boat to hold the oars.
Royal Ocean Racing Club Both a private member's club and the organizing authority for offshore racing in Britain, the RORC is organizer of the biennial Admiral's Cup and a full programme of races each year.
Rudder Device for steering a boat by deflecting the waterflow to one side or

the other. A rudder can be a simple blade hinged from the flat transom of a sailing dinghy or a movable flap on the after edge of the keel of a yacht or something between the two, such as a blade set on a skeg near the aft end of the waterline.
Run That part of the hull where the water is returning towards the centreline having passed the points of maximum beam and depth.
Running Sailing with the wind aft.
Running rigging Rigging that performs a function by moving, as opposed to fixed or 'standing' rigging.

S

Sail An arrangement of surfaces designed to extract kinetic energy from movement of the air. Can be made of cloth, flexible but non-woven material, or solid materials. Sails of practically every shape have been tried but the basic idea is to form an aerofoil which will create a pressure difference as air flows over it.
Sailboard Surfboard-like craft with rig fixed to it by a universal joint. A curved double boom or wishbone extends the clew of the sail and the sailor either holds this by hand or is attached to it by a body harness.
Sailcloth The material from which sails are made. Originally flax canvas, then cotton duck and now usually woven polyester fibre. Racing sails are often made or reinforced with Kevlar while non-woven Mylar is used either on its own for lightweight sails or laminated to cloth for high-strength ones.
Saloon The main living space of a cabin yacht.
Salvage Proportion of the value of a ship and her cargo claimed by one who has saved her from danger. An Admiralty Court assesses the value of the assistance rendered and awards an appropriate proportion of the value. When a ship is in difficulties, her master will often negotiate with a potential salvor on the basis of Lloyd's Open Form, the essence of which is 'No cure, no pay'. In other words, though a tug may spend days trying to secure a drifting ship, if she fails she will get nothing but if she succeeds in her endeavours she will be able to make a salvage claim.
Sandwich construction System in which two structural layers are separated by a lightweight spacer. The filler might be foamed plastics, end-grain balsa or, for a racing yacht an ultra-lightweight cellular material such as Nomex. The aim is to produce a structure that is both stiff and light.
Sardinia Cup Series of races for IOR-rated yachts organized by the Yacht Club Costa Smeralda along the lines of the Admiral's Cup.
Scandicap A handicap system used in the Baltic area that takes some of the measurements from IOR and uses them in a way that favours older or non-race oriented designs.
Scantlings The structural dimensions of a vessel. Classification societies such as Lloyd's Register have scantlings rules which lay down the minimum structure for various classes of yachts, e.g. the International 12-metre class which can only be built to Lloyd's rules.
Scope The amount of anchor cable that has been veered. With chain cable, scope is normally three times the depth of water. If rope is used, up to five times the depth may be needed.
Scow Flat-bottomed boat that has blunt ends.
Scupper Drain holes through rail, coaming or bulwark.
Sea anchor A device for slowing a boat down in bad weather.
Sea cock Valve for shutting off a pipe which is open to the sea.
Seamanship The art of managing a seagoing vessel.
Seize To bind two things tightly together with thin line, especially two parts of a rope.
Self-steering Device to make a yacht steer itself, usually by reference to the wind direction. Electronic helmsmen are normally called 'autopilots' or 'autohelmsmen'. Self-steering normally consists of a wind vane the movements of which either operate the rudder directly or via an auxiliary or servo-rudder. The advantages of self-steering are that it does not depend on electrical power and that once a yacht has been trimmed to sail at its best for a particular wind angle, it will go on doing so in spite of small shifts in the wind direction. The big disadvantage is that in the event of a major wind change, the yacht will set off in a new direction.
Set The direction of the tidal stream or the current.
Sextant Optical instrument for measuring angles.
Shackle A U-shaped metal fitting with removable pin across the arms, used for joining parts of rigging. A snap-shackle is one with a spring-loaded latch and is used for applications such as spinnaker sheets which must be capable of being released quickly and under load.
Sheave The grooved wheel in a block.
Sheer The curvature of the deck from amidships towards the ends. A conventionally sheered yacht is higher at the bow and stern than amidships but it is also possible to have reverse sheer with the greatest height of deck amidships.
Sheet The line used for trimming a sail.
Shroud Standing rigging that supports the mast in the athwartships plane.
Sight An astronomical observation, usually an altitude taken with a sextant.
Sitting out Also called 'lying out' and 'hiking out'. Placing crew weight as far outboard as possible, to increase stability. In dinghies this is done by leaning over the side with the feet secured under toe-straps or, in classes where it is permitted, standing on the gunwhale with weight supported by a wire from the mast to a body-harness. Some classes, such as the International 10sq metre Canoe have a plank extending from the side instead of a trapeze harness. In offshore racing, the crew may not put their torso outside the lifelines and therefore sit on the rail facing outboard with legs dangling over the side.
Skeg A section of fixed keel which is fitted to support or protect a propeller or rudder.
Slack water The period during which the tidal stream is changing direction.
Sliding seat A plank-like seat that can be shifted across from one side of a dinghy to the other to assist sitting out.
Slipway Inclined ramp or railway for pulling boats out of the water.
Sloop Sailing vessel with one mast and one headsail.
Snatch block A block made with an opening on one side so that a bight of rope can be inserted. The value of a snatch-block is that it can be applied to a rope that is already in use, e.g. to a sheet to alter its lead.
Sound To find the depth of water by lead line or echo sounder. The depths shown on the chart are known as 'soundings' and when a yacht sails on to the open ocean where depths are no longer shown on the chart she is said to be 'off soundings'.
Southern Ocean Racing Conference Group of clubs which jointly organize a very popular series of races around the coasts of Florida during February.
Speedometer Accurate speed measurement on yachts is relatively recent. Formerly, it was considered sufficient to measure distance run using a trailing log, and from this calculate average speed but in modern yacht racing a speed difference of 100th of a knot is significant. The first tolerably accurate speedometers used spinners or paddles whose rate of rotation was measured mechanically or electronically, but they were very sensitive to fouling and debris in the

water. More recent speedometers have no moving parts and measure speed either by measurement of waterflow by a sonic beam or by Doppler effect.
Spinnaker Large, lightweight sail which is set flying (i.e. not attached to a stay) forward of the mast. It is believed that the name derived from a baggy foresail set by the yacht *Sphinx* in the 1870s. For a long time spinnakers were thought of purely as a running sail and became more and more parachute-like in the search for greater area. Modern materials made possible the development of flatter spinnakers that can be carried on a reach.
Splice Join two ropes or form a loop by unravelling the end and tucking the strands back against the lay. With modern plaited or sheathed ropes, different techniques of splicing are called for.
Spreaders Struts between mast and shrouds to give mid-panel support to the spar. Also called 'crosstrees'. The thinner and more flexible a mast, the more spreaders it needs to keep it straight. Spreaders on small boats are often adjustable in the fore-and-aft line as a means of controlling the forwards bend of the mast.
Springs Mooring lines led from aft on the yacht to forward on the quay and vice versa. Their purpose is to stop the yacht from moving ahead or astern.
Spring tides Those when the tidal range is greatest, caused by the sun and moon being in syzygy (conjunction or opposition).
Squall Sudden temporary increase of wind; usually follows a depression.
Stanchion An upright post or support, most commonly used on yachts for supporting the life-lines.
Stand on Maintain present course.
Starboard To the right when facing forward.
Starboard tack Sailing with the wind coming from the starboard side, forward of the beam. A sailing vessel on starboard tack has right of way under both the Racing Rules and IRPCAS.
Stays Standing rigging in the fore-and-aft line.
Staysail Literally, a sail set on a stay but in practice usually a secondary headsail. A cutter sets a jib forward and a staysail further aft. Paradoxically, a light headsail set flying at the same time as a spinnaker is called a staysail even though it is not set on a stay. The same applies to a mizzen staysail which is a light, reaching or running sail hoisted from the mizzen mast of a ketch or yawl and tacked down somewhere between the main and mizzen masts.
Stem The structural member where the planking from both bows comes together. In a modern yacht, the stem is that part of the bow that first cuts through the water.
Stern Rear end of a boat.
Stiff Having a strong resistance to heeling and a quick motion. The opposite to tender.
Storm sails Small, heavily-made sails for use in extreme weather or when other sails have been damaged. Offshore racing yachts whose headsails are normally set on grooved headstays have to carry a storm jib capable of being hanked or buttoned right round the headstay and a storm trysail capable of being set and sheeted independently of the boom.
Stringer Lengthways structural member of a hull.
Surge Extra-high tide caused by prolonged strong winds from one quarter. Also, to allow a line to slip on a capstan or winch.
Swell Regular, underlying waves in the sea. A swell can often result from far-away storms and be completely independent of local conditions.
Sydney-Hobart Race Australia's best-known offshore race, run annually during the Christmas holidays.

T

Tabernacle A structure for supporting the heel of a mast which is deck-stepped rather than keel-stepped. This is often the case in small cruising yachts where the mast would take up valuable cabin space if keel-stepped. A tabernacle also offers the possibility of having the mast hinged at deck level to facilitate raising and lowering.
Tack, to A yacht is said to tack when her bow passes through the wind, from being close-hauled with the wind from one side to close-hauled with it from the other side. When the wind comes from the starboard side she is on starboard tack and vice versa. Also, the forward, lower corner of a sail is known as the tack.
Tackle Ropes and blocks forming a purchase.
Tail The fall of a sheet. 'To tail a sheet' is to keep tension on the free end so that it continues to grip on the winch drum. Self-tailing winches perform this function automatically so that only one person is needed to winch in a sheet.
Tan Red-coloured preservative applied to canvas sailcloth.
Telltale Pieces of wool or other light material attached to sails to show the airflow. Racing sails often have a number of telltales at different heights to help the trimmer see if the whole of it is pulling.
Tender Small boat which brings aboard the crew of a larger one. A yacht's tender has to be capable of being carried on board or towed astern.
Three Quarter Ton Cup Level rating competition for yachts that are rated at 24.55ft IOR.
Throat Upper forward corner of a gaff sail.
Thwart Plank fixed across a small boat to provide seats.
Tide Rise and fall of the sea caused by attraction of the moon and sun. Approximately semidiurnal, the tides precess by an average of 40 minutes per day over the period of a lunar month. The amount of rise and fall depends on whether the sun, moon and earth lie in line (syzygy) or at right angles (quadrature) and also if the moon is near or far from the earth. Tide tables predict the times and heights of tides at various standard ports and give details interpolating these predictions to other places. A tidal atlas is a set of 12 charts showing the tidal stream and strength at each hour of the tide.
Tiller Long handle fixed to the rudder-head to enable the helmsman to steer. The length of the tiller controls the amount of leverage available to the helmsman.
Toe-straps Straps fitted to a racing boat to enable the crew to sit far out over the gunwhale without falling overboard.
Toggle A link between different sections of standing rigging, giving it flexibility.
Tonnage Measure of the size of a ship. There are a number of different formulas for tonnage but most are concerned with measuring a ship's cargo-carrying capacity, not its weight. Net Registered Tonnage is the cubic capacity of a ship less machinery, living and navigating spaces and this is the one normally used for calculating harbour and canal dues. Thames Measurement (TM) is a formula, now archaic, for giving yachts a tonnage purely from their length and breadth dimensions. The only measure which gives the actual weight of a ship is displacement.
Tonne Metric ton, 1,000kg (2,205lb).
Topsides Sides of a yacht above the waterline.
Trade winds Regular steady winds that blow in two bands, one on each side of the tropics.
Transat-en-double Two-man double-crossing of the Atlantic race. French-organized, it starts and finishes at Lorient and involves rounding a buoy at Bermuda.

Transatlantic There have been many races across the Atlantic. Races for fully-crewed offshore racing yachts are organized nearly every year, often as a 'feeder' to major events such as the Admiral's Cup. In addition, there are now a number of 'spectaculars' held at intervals. The principal ones are: Single-handed Transatlantic, Two-handed Transatlantic, Transat en Double, Route du Rhum and Mini-transat.
Transom The flat stern of a square-ended boat. Originally, the after end of the planking was fastened to it.
Transpacific Race Biennial race from San Pedro, California to Honolulu.
Trapeze System allowing crew of racing boat to stand outside the hull with feet on gunwhale and weight supported by a wire from the mast. Invented by Beecher Moore in 1934, when the crew of his Thames Rater found they could stand on the side holding a knotted rope from the mast. Peter Scott added the idea of a belt with an attachment for a wire. Nowadays, a body-harness is used and this is not only more effective but more comfortable than 'hiking' over the side.
Traveller Sliding ring, slider or car designed to carry a sheet, especially mainsheet from one side to the other on tacking.
Trick Period of time spent at the helm.
Trim The fore-and-aft balance of a boat. If carrying too much weight forward a boat is said to be 'trimmed by the head'. Prior to measurement for an IOR rating, a racing yacht must be put in 'Measurement trim' with specified equipment stowed in particular areas. Also, the action of trimming or adjusting the sails.
Truck Cap fitted to the top of a mast. Normally carries flag halyards.
Trysail Storm sail set in place of the mainsail. A trysail is hoisted part of the way up the mast and has its own sheets so that it can be set independently of the boom. Thus it can be set after the mainsail has been lowered and lashed down, or if the boom has been damaged.
Tumblehome Inward slope of the topsides above the waterline.
Tuning Setting up and adjusting a boat so that everything is working at its best.

U

Una rig Having a single sail only.
Under way Moving through the water.
Under weigh Not anchored or made fast but not necessarily moving.
Universal Rule Rating rule developed by Nathanael Herreshof.

V

Vane Wind-sensing part of a self-steering gear.
Vang Tackle or fitting that prevents a boom or gaff from lifting. Also called a 'kicking strap'.
Variation The local difference between true and magnetic north. It is always indicated on charts and changes slowly over a period of years.
Veer Clockwise change of wind direction. Also, to ease out cable, especially when anchoring.
Ventilators Ventilation is essential on a yacht if it is not to become unbearably damp below. Ventilators must admit air but not water and most work on variations of the 'Dorade vent' principle, in which the air follows an 'S' path through a box while the water runs out through drains.

W

Warp Heavy line, mainly used for making fast to the shore. Also, the lengthways threads in sailcloth. The crossways threads are called the 'weft' or 'fill'.
Watch Period of time spent on duty aboard ship.
Wear ship Turn a square-rigged ship round by bringing the stern through the wind. With fore-and-aft rig, this would be a gybe.
Weather side The side on which the wind is blowing.
Weather-going tide Tidal stream running against the wind direction.
Weigh Lift the anchor off the bottom.
WEST system The Wood Epoxy Saturation Technique developed by Gougeon Bros of Michigan gave new life to timber construction. Using it, light, strong wooden structures can be made that are impervious to water.
Whipping Binding the end of a rope with twine to stop it unravelling. There are several different types of whipping.
Whitbread Round the World Race Race organized by the Royal Naval Sailing Association for fully-crewed, IOR rated yachts. First sailed in 1972 and at four year intervals since. There are four stop-over points but these have been changed for political reasons so the results are not strictly comparable.
Winch Machine used for pulling home a line. Since only human power may be used on any racing yacht, enormous effort has gone into improving the design of winches so that the limited power of the human arm can be used to the best advantage. Modern yachts depend completely on winches to hoist, trim and reef the sails.
Wind rode Lying to the wind rather than the stream.
Wind speed and direction instruments Small wind vane and anemometer, usually mounted at the masthead, giving a remote reading of the apparent wind speed and direction. These are vital in order to extract maximum performance from a yacht, especially when sailing at night.
Wishbone Double spar with curved sides, made so that a sail can be set between the two parts. Named after the yacht *Wishbone*, designed by Uffa Fox — although the device had already been used on the American yacht *Vamarie* designed by Cox and Stevens.

Y

Yard Spar fixed across a mast, from which a sail may be set.
Yawl Two-masted vessel in which the mizzen is shorter than the mainmast and stepped abaft the rudder-head.

Index

Page numbers in *italics* refer to illustration captions.
Page numbers in **bold** refer to main entries.